A Christmas Carol
and Its Adaptations

A Christmas Carol and Its Adaptations

A Critical Examination of
Dickens's Story and Its Productions
on Screen and Television

by FRED GUIDA

WITH A FOREWORD BY
Edward Wagenknecht

McFarland & Company, Inc., Publishers
Jefferson, North Carolina, and London

Front cover: Scrooge meets the Ghost of Christmas Yet to Come. Image from *Marley's Ghost*, a magic lantern show using hand-colored glass slides produced by Briggs and Company, United States, from original artwork by Joseph Boggs Beale, ca. 1895. Courtesy the Beale Collection.

Library of Congress Cataloguing-in-Publication Data

Guida, Fred.
    A Christmas carol and its adaptations : a critical examination
of Dickens's story and its productions on screen and television /
by Fred Guida; with a foreword by Edward Wagenknecht.
        p.   cm.
    Includes bibliographical references and index.
    ISBN 0-7864-0738-7 (illustrated case binding : 50# alkaline paper) ∞
    1. Dickens, Charles, 1812–1870. Christmas carol.   2. Dickens,
Charles, 1812–1870— Film and video adaptations.   3. Christmas
stories, English — Film and video adaptations.   I. Title.
PR4572.C7G85   2000
823'.821— dc21   99-45415
                                                                      CIP

British Library Cataloguing-in-Publication data are available

Manufactured in the United States of America

McFarland & Company, Inc., Publishers
    Box 611, Jefferson, North Carolina 28640
        www.mcfarlandpub.com

For Lisa, Founder of the Feast;
and the two young Guidas, Joe and Bill...

Contents

Acknowledgments

The debt that this volume owes to the work and in many cases the personal generosity and assistance of others is such that only a chapter-length section of acknowledgments could truly do it justice. What follows is a sincere, but I fear inadequate, attempt to say thank you, and I hope that the passage of time or my own carelessness has not caused me to forget anyone.

I would first of all like to thank Professor Edward Wagenknecht for contributing a foreword to this book, and for the illuminating thoughts and kind words contained therein; he also offered many invaluable comments and suggestions on my manuscript. Professor Wagenknecht's credentials are far too numerous to be listed here, but a few points must be noted: He has written many authoritative books and articles on Dickens over the years and, in more general terms, is quite simply one of the most distinguished and prolific literary scholars of the twentieth century. He is also a distinguished film scholar and was, in fact, one of the very first to recognize film as a subject worthy of serious criticism and scholarship — and yet his work in this area, indeed all of his work, has always been as passionate and

unpretentious as it is knowledgeable and critically astute; in this regard, most of us writing about film today have much to learn from him. And, apropos of this book, it is also worth noting that he has edited *The Fireside Book of Christmas Stories* and *A Fireside Book of Yuletide Tales*, without question the two finest anthologies of Christmas literature ever published. The fact that he was willing to look at the work of an unknown entity like myself, let alone write a foreword for it, is almost more than I can comprehend. There is an old saying that goes something like this: "The bigger they are, the nicer they are"; anyone doubting its veracity can contact me in care of the publisher and I will be happy to tell you that it is true.

I am also indebted to Paul Davis, professor emeritus of English at the University of New Mexico, and author of *The Lives and Times of Ebenezer Scrooge*, a great book which examines the *Carol's* role in our popular culture over the past one hundred and fifty years; it has strongly influenced my work, and no one seriously interested in *A Christmas Carol* can possibly be without it. He is also the author of *Charles Dickens A to Z*, an invaluable guide to Dickens's life and works. Professor Davis was kind enough to read and offer a thoughtful critique of my manuscript, and to generously make his Dickensian expertise and resources available to me on numerous occasions.

Sincere thanks are also due to Alan Bradford, professor of English at Connecticut College, for his reading and critique of an early version of my manuscript. Professor Bradford is a specialist in areas other than Dickens and, as such, was able to offer a particularly objective sense of perspective that was most helpful. I am also indebted to him for his encouragement early on when I had serious doubts as to whether a film buff type like myself, with no formal credentials in literature, had any business undertaking a project such as this.

Special thanks are also due to all of those who have preceded me in the endless task of attempting to document the theatrical and audiovisual life of the works of Charles Dickens. In particular, I wish to salute the pioneering efforts of F. Dubrez Fawcett, Malcolm Morley and Anna Laura Zambrano, as well as the more recent work of H. Philip Bolton and Michael Pointer.

I am also indebted to the many Dickens scholars that I have never met, but whose work has provided great pleasure and enlightenment over the years. Whatever merit this volume might have in the area of Dickens scholarship is due in large part to what I have learned from them; any errors of commission or omission are entirely my own. Thanks to Peter Ackroyd, Philip Collins, R. J. Cruikshank, Ruth Glancy, Edgar Johnson, Fred Kaplan, Norman Page, David Paroissien, Robert L. Patten, Michael Slater, et al.

For countless favors large and small, for tiny tidbits and enormous chunks of time, expertise and information, and for all manner of help and encouragement, I thank the following individuals in the United States: Roy Albert; Richard Bann; Spencer Berger; Kirk Bauer; H. Philip Bolton; Q. David Bowers; Mary Bradford; Kate

Brown; Rusty Casselton; Margaret Cousins; Rick DeCroix; Robert G. Dickson; Dennis Doros; John Dunning; Rob Edelman; Tony Esposito; Ron Evans; William K. Everson; Carl Feather; J. David Goldin; Rick Goldschmidt; Gary Goleas; Bill Grego; William Hawes; Jay Hickerson; Roger Hovis; Tim Hume; Ronnie James; Lawrence Karr; John King; Audrey Kupferberg; Lawrence Landino; Ted Larson; Joel Marks; David Miller; Mike Mongillo; Thea Musgrave; Charles Musser; Philip Parker; James Robert Parish; Howard Prouty; Vera Roberts; Philip Reed Rulon; Elias Savada; Shan V. Sayles; Anthony Slide; Michelle Snitkin; Andrew Susskind; Charles Turner; Jim Von Schilling; Robert W. Weathersby II; George F. Will; Feenie Ziner.

Ditto the following domestic organizations, institutions and individuals. The American Film Institute: Lisa Brody. American Magic Lantern Journal: M. Bergh. The American Magic-Lantern Theater: Terry Borton. Anthology Film Archives: Robert Haller, John Mhiripiri. Bridgeport Public Library (Bridgeport, CT). CBS Television: Ray Faiola, Nancy Delaney. Cleveland Public Library. Connecticut College, Charles E. Shain Library: Beth Hansen, Steve Bustamante, Jim Macdonald, et al. Connecticut Public Television: Joanne Whitehead. Corona Publishing Company: David Bowen. Country Music Hall of Fame: Alan Stoker. Doodyville Historical Society: Jeff Judson, Walter Mitchell, Bob Reed. "The Dukes of Hazzard" Fan Club: Aneesh A. Sehgal. Samuel French, Inc.: Henry Wallengren. Ford's Theatre (Washington, DC). George Eastman House: Jan-Christopher Horak. James Blackstone Memorial Library (Branford, CT). Kent State University: Jeanne Somers. Library of American Broadcasting: Michael Henry. Library of Congress: Fred Bauman, Cooper Graham, Rosemary Hanes, Jerry Hatfield, Wynn Matthias, Madeline Matz. Museum of Broadcast Communications, Chicago: Mary Crisanti. Museum of Modern Art: Ron Magliozzi, Mary Corliss,

Terry Geesken. The Museum of Television & Radio, New York: Kevin Scott. NBC Television: Louise Gallup-Roholt, Kori Sonderland. New Haven Free Public Library (New Haven, CT). New Haven Register: Joe Amarante. The New York Public Library for the Performing Arts: Vivian Gonzalez. Quinnipiac College: Manuel Carreiro, Raymond Foery, John Gourlie, Sharon Magnarelli. G. Schirmer, Inc.: Peggy Monastra. Showcase Productions: Alexander Kogan. Smithsonian Institution: Mimi Minnick, Scott Schwartz. Southern Connecticut State University (thanks for the inspiration, so long ago): Ken Gatzke, Ira Leonard, Dan Ort, Tom Shalvey. UCLA Film & Television Archives: Dan Einstein. The Vitaphone Project: Ron Hutchinson. Wesleyan Cinema Archives: Jeanine Basinger. WETA Television (Washington, DC): Nancy Noll Kolinski. Wisconsin Center for Film & Theatre Research: Maxine Fleckner-Ducey. Yale Center for British Art: Kay de Sanctis, Scott Wilcox. Yale Film Study Center: Michael Kerbel. Yale Department of Historical Sound Recordings: Richard Warren. Yale University: Beinecke Rare Book & Manuscript Library, Seeley G. Mudd Library, Sterling Memorial Library. Yale University Press: Harry Haskell. Walt Disney Studios: Scott McQueen, Dave Smith. Whitney Museum of American Art: Matthew Yokobosky.

The same thanks also go out to the following foreign institutions and individuals. Argentina: Enrique J. Bouchard. Australia — National Film & Sound Archive, Canberra: Richard Keys. Canada — CFCN Television, Calgary: Gordon Enno; Canadian Film Institute, Ottawa: Tom McSorley; Inuit Broadcasting Corporation, Ottawa: Melanie Legault; National Archives of Canada, Ottawa: Rosemary Bergeron, Caroline Forcier, Sarah Montgomery; Blaine Allen; Warren Graves; Mary Jane Miller; Philippe Spurrell. Czech Republic — Narodni Filmovy Archiv, Prague: Vladimír Opěla; KF a.s., Prague: Michal Goryl. Denmark — Det Danske Filmmuseum, Copenhagen: Lars Ølgaard. England — BBC Written Archives, Reading: John Davis; British Film Institute, London: Pat Perilli, Jacqui Roberts, Simon Baker, Jane Hockings, Tessa Forbes, Sian Parry, Luke McKernan; Malcolm Billingsley; Dickens House Museum, London: Andrew Xavier; *The Dickensian*: Malcolm Andrews; Independent Television Commission; The Theatre Museum; Ann Hecht; Annetta Hoffnung; Michael Pointer. France — Yolande Powell (Merci beaucoup!); TF1 International: Sylvie Pardon; Centre National de la Cinématographie, Bois d'Arcy: Eric Le Roy; l'Institut National de l'Audiovisuel, Bry sur Marne: Géraldine Bonetti. Germany — Hans-Danklev Hansen. Hungary — Magyar Filmintezet, Budapest: Klára Barabás. Italy — Centro Sperimentale di Cinematografia, Rome: Angelo Libertini; Cineteca Italiana, Milan: Gianni Comencini; Aldo Bernardini. Portugal — Cinemateca Portuguesa, Lisbon: Teresa Barreto Borges. Spain — Televisión Española, Bilbao: José Miguel Sánchez; Juan B. Heinik; Jon Letamendi; Documentación de Programas de Radio-Televisión Española, Madrid; Filmoteca Española: Ana Cristina Iriarte; Juan José Mardones; Tarragona: Al Jacobs.

I would also like to thank the venerable *Films in Review*, where portions of Chapter Five's discussion of the 1910 Edison *Carol* appeared in "Merry Christmas from Charles Dickens ... and Thomas Edison" (November/December 1994). I have also drawn a few scattered thoughts from my "Charles Dickens' 'A Christmas Carol'" (November/December 1991) and "British Silent Films [: An American Perspective]" (June 1992).

Thanks also to the following local individuals and businesses for a variety of logistical support and miscellaneous services with a smile: Bruce Manke & Video Imagination (North Haven, CT); the amazing Best Video (Hamden, CT); and in Branford, CT: Curry Printing, The Office Alternative, and Mary Stone at the Short Beach Post Office.

A final nod to Bill Haffner whose help and enthusiasm made this a better book in many places; and to Kara M. Pekar for doing such a fine job with the difficult task of indexing.

And on a purely personal note: Thanks to my parents, Bart and Kay Guida, and my in-laws Ray and Jean Grinold, for all manner of help and encouragement over the years. And finally, thanks to my wife and children for managing to retain their Christmas spirit (while I became more Scrooge-like) through several years of intense *Carol* mania during which time a heavy toll was taken on family life and finances. A healthy dose of insanity is required to tackle this kind of book, and a special kind of grace is required to put up with it.

Foreword

by Edward Wagenknecht

The cinematic quality of Dickens's writing was noticed early, never more unerringly than by D. W. Griffith. When he was, almost single-handedly, creating the syntax of the motion picture, he was often criticized for his innovations, to which he is reported to have replied, "Why not? Doesn't Dickens write that way?"

I am too old to claim to belong to the audiovisual generation, yet I can claim to have made my first vital contact with Dickens the Saturday night in 1911 when I first encountered Vitagraph's three-reel production of *A Tale of Two Cities*, with Maurice Costello, then my favorite actor, as Sydney Carton and the lovely Florence Turner, who many years later became a valued friend, as Lucie Manette. The *Carol* did not come my way until later, when I read it in the eighth grade, along with *The Merchant of Venice*, *Treasure Island*, and *The Courtship of Miles Standish*, under an excellent, literary-minded teacher, Miss Alice L. Burns. In one of A. Edward Newton's delightful collections of bookish essays, *The Greatest Book in the World and Other Papers*, in which the title piece of course concerns the King James Bible, the penultimate entry, "The Greatest Little Book in the World," is devoted to *A Christmas Carol*.

I suppose it was inevitable that sooner or later somebody would devote a book to the various film and television versions of the *Carol* that have been made. What was far from inevitable, however, was that the job should have been done so superlatively well as Mr. Guida has done it. He has written a truly splendid book; if I were not afraid of injuring him by appearing to oversell it, I might even call it a magnificent book.

The qualifications he brings to his job are many. He has apparently seen every film ever made that is worth seeing, along with a great many that are not, and he has remembered, marked, and inwardly digested them all. He also has an excellent knowledge not only of the *Carol* but of Dickens's whole oeuvre, and like all devotees of that master, he knows

1

that there are secrets about him that reveal themselves to love alone. Finally, though his book is far more scholarly than he would dream of being immodest enough to claim, his style and method are leisurely, relaxed, and companionable; unlike many of his contemporaries, he has made no special effort to conceal the fact that his work has been produced by a human being rather than by some sort of electronic contrivance.

He subjects what he considers the finest productions of the *Carol*, like those in which Alastair Sim and George C. Scott were featured, to the kind of searching analysis seldom accorded to films. He is not ashamed to admire the production in which Albert Finney appeared because it is a "musical," nor even *Mister Magoo's Christmas Carol* nor the animated cartoon version produced by Richard Williams. When we get back to the silent period (he begins in 1901), there is of course a great deal of material that neither he nor anybody else now extant has a chance to review at first hand, but he has taken endless pains, in some cases even to the extent of corresponding with foreign observers, to gather as much information as is available about them. All in all, he has written a highly unusual book, far off the beaten track, which has been richly and intelligently illustrated, and for which one cannot but invoke the most favorable reception possible, in quiet confidence that it will richly deserve the best it can possibly encounter.

Introduction

Call someone "an old Scrooge" and it is doubtful that more than one person in ten thousand will not instantly and completely comprehend your meaning. Likewise, one would have to look long and hard to find someone unfamiliar with at least the basic framework and moral of Charles Dickens's *A Christmas Carol*. Simply put, this "Ghostly little book," as Dickens himself called it, hereafter commonly referred to as the *Carol*, is one of the most famous and popular pieces of fiction ever committed to paper in any language. Indeed, as many commentators have pointed out before me, the *Carol* is more than a book. It is an important point of convergence within our popular culture; and for well over a century now, it has dotted the horizon of our collective consciousness with images as familiar as those of Big Ben, the Statue of Liberty, and the Eiffel Tower. And, of course, there is more to the *Carol* than popular imagery. It is also a book of ideas — ideas that are as timely today as the day on which they were written.

However, the concern here is not with literary criticism, but rather an overview of the film and television adaptations of the *Carol* that have proliferated over the past one hundred years, a span of time which we may generally, and I think accurately, refer to as the audiovisual age. On one level, this book is intended to be nothing more than a conversation among friends who share a mutual interest in the *Carols* that we look forward to every December; and since I do not consider this to be a scholarly book, at least not in the generally accepted sense, the tone of this conversation will be both informal and opinionated.

Practically speaking, this conversation will take the form of an extended discussion of what I think most *Carol* aficionados would agree are the best or most significant film and television versions; these also tend to be the *Carols* that most people are familiar with. However, I also hope to shed a little light on some lesser known *Carols*, particularly those that appeared in the early days of film and television. And perhaps there will be a surprise or two along the way as well — such as the fact that the first audiovisual *Carol* predates the movies.

On another (and, I suppose, more ambitious) level, I also hope to address what might be called the downside of the audiovisual age, namely the sad fact that as a society, we seem to be doing a lot more watching these days, and a whole lot less reading. Of course this is not the place for any kind of serious discussion of this subject; educators, psychologists and sociologists have been tackling the issue elsewhere for quite some time now. But it is fascinating to note the extent to which more and more people are coming to know the *Carol* (and Dickens) primarily, or exclusively, through film and television.

Now this is not necessarily a bad thing, nor is it a new thing; as we shall see, audiences were finding alternative methods of accessing Dickens's works long before the advent of film and television. In my own case, I have a vague recollection that my introduction to Dickens came at age eight or nine through seeing MGM's 1935 version of *David Copperfield* on television; and just as vague impressions were forming that there were discernible differences between films made by, say, Warner Bros. and Universal, it soon became apparent that films based on books by Charles Dickens were something very special indeed. And it may be that I saw it over the Christmas holiday, or the fact that a medley of Christmas songs played as the opening credits rolled, but I am also fairly certain that this viewing of *David Copperfield* was where I first connected Dickens with Christmas. Not long afterward, though, I remember being both charmed and frightened by the Alastair Sim version of *A Christmas Carol*, and from that time on the *Carol* has been for me, as with most people, the primary purveyor of Dickensian Christmas cheer. And, of course, countless others have undoubtedly been introduced to Dickens in a similar manner; indeed, as we have just seen, the distinguished critic and scholar Edward Wagenknecht, who has written authoritatively on both Dickens and film over the course of a career that has spanned most of the audiovisual age, has revealed that his introduction to Dickens came, in 1911, via a screening of *A Tale of Two Cities*.[1]

It should be noted here that this book is also intended to serve as a reference book, albeit a very unusual one. While the requisite trappings of the conventional reference work — notes, filmography, bibliography — are here, readers will find the text peppered with quotes from a cross-section of both popular and scholarly sources. The intent is to suggest the wide range of interdisciplinary interest in the *Carol*, and to refer the general reader to authoritative sources for further study.

Part One of this book is a survey of the literary, historical, and personal forces that were brought to bear on Dickens as he sat down to write the *Carol* in the closing weeks of the year 1843. While I doubt that there can be anything new here for the professional literary specialist, or, for that matter, for the countless devoted amateur Dickensians who have contributed so much to the existing body of Dickensian knowledge, I hope that the film buff and the general reader will find it a useful compression of important background material.

Part Two is a survey of the audiovisual *Carols*, primarily film and television, that have proliferated over the years. And just as it assumes that there is considerable interest out there in the who, what, when, and wheres of *Carol* adaptations, it also assumes that those *Carol* aficionados who do not happen to be audiovisual professionals might also be interested in the roots of the various media that produced these adaptations. Most of the productions discussed at length in this section are what I like to call "major *Carols*"—i.e., productions that attempt to tell the story in a serious, faithful and reasonably complete manner. (Please note that Chapter Five, which deals with the silent film era, is something of an exception. Since this period is filled with so much mystery and misunderstanding, I have attempted to discuss *everything* in as much detail as possible.) These major *Carols* can in turn be looked at against the larger chronological picture contained in the filmography. Be warned, however, that not all major *Carols* are created equal, nor is the designation necessarily synonymous with quality. For example, MGM's 1938 film version with Reginald Owen is a major *Carol* in the sense that it is a feature-length treatment made during Hollywood's "Golden Age" by its most prestigious studio. However, it is also a major failure when compared to such significant (and diverse) *Carols* as the 1951 British version with Alastair Sim or the 1962 animated musical version with Mister Magoo.

Part Three reminds us that while the *Carol* will always be Dickens's greatest and most famous Christmas story, it is by no means his only one. It also attempts to make the case that the endless *Carol* variations that we take so much for granted these days,

largely through television, and which somehow seem to be so "modern," have roots that stretch back to Dickens's own time.

Finally, comprising most of the back matter that one usually finds in this type of book, there is an annotated filmography of film and television *Carols* that is the most complete published to date.

In short, this is a book that aspires to be many things to many people. However, I will be delighted if it simply manages to contribute to the conversation that has been ongoing for over a century and a half now — the focus of which has been our mutual friend Charles Dickens, and his "Ghostly little book."

PART ONE

Prologue

The fairies came to his christening. One said, "My gift is early hardship; as a child he shall know the ugliness of life." The second said, "My gift is his abandonment; he shall be a castaway." The third, "His school shall be the streets." The fourth, "I will give him a sensitive spirit, so that he may feel early pain sharply, and remember it vividly all his life." The last fairy said, "I will give him genius. Out of the hardship shall come the power to live a hundred lives. The castaway shall have the freedom of the whole world of men and women. The education of the streets shall provide him with boundless treasures of comic and tragic invention. The humiliations of the child shall fertilise the imagination of the poet."

R. J. Cruikshank[1]

Literary Roots

A true feast actually has nothing to do with what you eat...but with what you remember.

Jeff Smith, the Frugal Gourmet

"Dickens dead? Then will Father Christmas die too?"[1] This remark, reportedly overheard by the English writer and critic Theodore Watts-Dunton and attributed to a young female street vendor upon hearing of Dickens's death in 1870, tells us much about the unique position that Charles Dickens occupied on the Victorian landscape during his relatively short lifetime as a writer and public figure. His work touched everyone, including the desperate poor, many of whom could not read but nevertheless knew him well by listening to others read aloud.

Not many of us, sad to say, read aloud these days; and there is certainly sufficient evidence to suggest that far too many of us read far too little. Nevertheless, the printed word in general — i.e., a book that one takes off the shelf and actually reads — seems to be holding up rather nicely in this brave new electronic world of home computers and CD-ROMs. As for Dickens in particular, even the most cursory survey reveals that two magnificent biographies have been published in recent years, new editions of the major works continue to appear, and there is no end in sight to the amount of grist to be milled in the halls of academia. In short, it would appear that Dickens is one dead white male who is very much alive and well.

But for the general reader of today (and, more to the point perhaps, that portion of the general public who know Dickens primarily through audiovisual adaptations of his works), like Watts-Dunton's costermonger of yesterday, the name Charles Dickens immediately conjures up images and associations of Christmas. To be sure, some of Dickens's other works have made their mark on American thought and culture; in this respect, one certainly thinks of *Oliver Twist*, *David Copperfield*, *A Tale of Two Cities*, and perhaps *Great Expectations*. There is, however, nothing else in the Dickens canon quite like *A Christmas Carol*; nothing else can boast even a fraction of its powerful hold on the popular consciousness. It has been adopted and adapted by virtually every medium imaginable, and with a rate of frequency that makes it far and away the most popular (and most pillaged) Dickens story. In fact, as Paul Davis suggests in *The Lives and Times of Ebenezer Scrooge*, one can probably make a strong case that there is nothing else quite like it in all of literature:

> I cannot remember when I first knew the story of *A Christmas Carol*. I may have heard it read aloud before a Christmas Eve fire, or listened to one of Lionel Barrymore's annual radio performances, or seen a dramatic version at the town hall in Connecticut where I spent my childhood Christmases. I do know that my acquaintance with Scrooge feels preliterate, different from my sense of Dick and Jane, Dr. Dolittle, or Robinson Crusoe. I remember when I first met the Hardy Boys, but I feel as if I've always known Scrooge and Tiny Tim.[2]

Some have gone so far as to claim that Dickens invented or discovered Christmas. A more sober claim might be to credit him with "rediscovering" it; he did, in any event, do more than anyone else to define our modern celebration of the holiday. But how did this come about? Why has the name Charles Dickens become virtually synonymous with Christmas? The answers are complex and multifaceted, and the intent here is to do no more than erect a few guideposts. That said, one can begin looking for answers in Dickens's words themselves — and in the times in which they were written.

As for those words, there is no question that Dickens's reputation as the author most associated with Christmas rests primarily on *A Christmas Carol*. He did, however, address the subject both before and after the *Carol's* lightning bolt appearance in December of 1843, most notably in *The Pickwick Papers*

prior to the *Carol*, and in the four *Christmas Books* that followed it. (As we shall see, not all of his subsequent *Christmas Books* were directly concerned with Christmas in terms of their subjects or themes. However, they were specifically written, and their publication timed, with the Christmas season in mind. He also authored or co-authored numerous short stories and sketches for release at Christmas, in some of which the holiday is directly addressed.) In this regard, someone with enough time on his hands could undoubtedly come up with the exact number of words that Dickens devoted to Christmas throughout his writing career. For present purposes, suffice to say that the percentage of Christmas related work is quite small when measured against the rest of his total output. Nevertheless it is a formidable body of work, the bulk of which is, quite understandably, forever overshadowed by *A Christmas Carol*; and anyone wishing to come to terms with the immortal story of Scrooge should begin with the realization that while it is a singular work of singular genius, it was not created in a vacuum. It was informed by an intimate knowledge of the harsh realities of urban life in a decade known as the Hungry Forties, as well as by a fond remembrance of the rich Christmas celebrations of England's rural past. It also offered, and still offers, much hope for the future.

While it is an obvious oversimplification, one can indeed argue that the *Carol* was, as suggested above, forged by a combination of seemingly contradictory forces. Call them what you will — light and dark, good and evil, rosy nostalgia and grim reality — they are, in effect, the *Carol's* co-authors. Let's begin with the rosy nostalgia.

While popular mythology can lead us to assume that Charles Dickens singlehandedly invented the practice of writing about Christmas — significantly, Dickens once referred to himself as "...the inventor of this sort of story"[3] — it is important to note that England has a very substantial history of

Christmas literature, and that *A Christmas Carol* was part of a much larger revival of interest in the celebration of the holiday.

In the decades prior to the *Carol's* appearance, the observance of Christmas had become a comparatively quiet affair. It bore little resemblance to the traditional "Olde English Christmas" in which the Lord of Misrule reigned merrily over the Twelve Days (or longer) of Christmas and in which all classes of people came together to share in the largesse of a benevolent nobility. These were Christmases redolent of wassail and plum-porridge, of savory mincemeat pies and roast game, of pantomimes and Boar's Head processions. An account of these Christmas traditions, by someone who was in a position to witness many of their later incarnations in the late seventeenth and early eighteenth centuries, can be found in Joseph Addison's *Christmas with Sir Roger* published in 1712:

Charles Dickens in 1843. Detail from sketch by Daniel Maclise. Courtesy Dickens House Museum.

I have often thought, says Sir ROGER [Addison's fictional narrator, Sir Roger de Coverley], it happens very well that *Christmas* should fall out in the middle of Winter. It is the most dead, uncomfortable time of the Year, when the poor People would suffer very much from their Poverty and Cold, if they had not good Cheer, warm Fires, and *Christmas* Gambols to support them. I love to rejoyce their poor Hearts at this Season, and to see the whole Village merry in my great Hall. I allow a double quantity of Malt to my small Beer, and set it a running for twelve Days to every one that calls for it. I have always a Piece of cold Beef and a Mince-Pye upon the Table, and am wonderfully pleased to see my Tenants pass away a whole Evening in playing their innocent Tricks, and smutting one another. Our Friend *Will.*

Wimble is as merry as any of them, and shews a thousand Roguish Tricks upon these Occasions.[4]

And for a more vivid, and truly moving, description one can turn to the famous introduction to the sixth canto of Sir Walter Scott's *Marmion* published in 1808:

The fire, with well-dried logs supplied,
Went roaring up the chimney wide;
The huge hall-table's oaken face,
Scrubb'd till it shone, the day to grace,
Bore then upon its massive board
No mark to part the squire and lord.
Then was brought in the lusty brawn,
By old blue-coated serving-man;
Then the grim boar's head frown'd on high,
Crested with bays and rosemary.

Well can the green-garb'd ranger tell,
How, when, and where, the monster fell;
What dogs before his death he tore,
And all the baiting of the boar.
The wassel round, in good brown bowls,
Garnish'd with ribbons, blithely trowls.
There the huge sirloin reek'd; hard by
Plum-porridge stood, and Christmas pie;
Nor fail'd old Scotland to produce,
At such high tide, her savoury goose.
Then came the merry maskers in,
And carols roar'd with blithesome din;
If unmelodious was the song,
It was a hearty note, and strong.
Who lists may in their mumming see
Traces of ancient mystery;
White shirts supplied the masquerade,
And smutted cheeks the visors made;
But, O! what maskers, richly dight,
Can boast of bosoms half so light!
England was merry England, when
Old Christmas brought his sports again.
'Twas Christmas broach'd the mightiest ale;
'Twas Christmas told the merriest tale;
A Christmas gambol oft could cheer
The poor man's heart through half the year.[5]

However, the ultimate description of such a Christmas, as well as what may be the most direct influence on Dickens's Christmas writings, came from the pen of an American writer; it will be found in Washington Irving's *The Sketch Book of Geoffrey Crayon, Gent.* This 1819–1820 collection of essays and stories, which includes *The Legend of Sleepy Hollow* and *Rip Van Winkle*, contains five consecutive chapters (*Christmas, The Stagecoach, Christmas Eve, Christmas Day* and *The Christmas Dinner*) which delineate, in extraordinarily loving detail, the rich holiday traditions of an "old-fashioned" English Christmas. No single quotation, however lengthy, can do justice to the picture that Irving paints, but it is interesting to observe how, early in his first chapter, he sets the stage by echoing Addison and Scott's earlier sentiments:

> The English, from the great prevalence of rural habits throughout every class of society, have always been fond of those festivals and holydays which agreeably interrupt the stillness of country life; and they were, in former days, particularly observant of the religious and social rites of Christmas. It is inspiring to read even the dry details which some antiquaries have given of the quaint humours, the burlesque pageants, the complete abandonment to mirth and good fellowship, with which this festival was celebrated. It seemed to throw open every door, and unlock every heart. It brought the peasant and the peer together, and blended all ranks in one warm generous flow of joy and kindness. The old halls of castles and manor houses resounded with the harp and the Christmas carol, and their ample boards groaned under the weight of hospitality. Even the poorest cottage welcomed the festive season with green decorations of bay and holly — the cheerful fire glanced its rays through the lattice, inviting the passenger to raise the latch, and join the gossip knot huddled round the hearth, beguiling the long evening with legendary jokes, and oft told Christmas tales.[6]

It is also worth noting here that Irving, although a distinguished and enthusiastic Anglophile, contributed to the establishment of an American Christmas tradition before Dickens was born, and that this tradition was beginning to take shape long before Ebenezer Scrooge and Bob Cratchit made their first transatlantic voyage.[7]

Today these images of Christmas have long since passed into the popular imagination, an integral part of our fascination with a misty, and yet not all that distant, past; a past that many of us reach out for every December. And they were largely images from the past, albeit the relatively recent past, for the generation coming of age in early nineteenth century England. The nation was changing, becoming more industrialized, more urbanized. Country customs — including Christmas customs — changed too.

The decidedly dour presence of various

sectors of organized religion also contributed mightily to the stifling of Christmas merrymaking. The influence of Calvinism, as well as of various dissenting groups that had sprouted from the Puritan tradition, a tradition that was essentially Calvinist at its core, did much to discourage, suppress, punish or forbid the celebration of Christmas. As author and political commentator George F. Will observed in a December 1993 syndicated column:

> Christmas in merrie England had become a rollicking good time after the Norman Conquest imported French flair. By 1252 Henry III was slaying 600 oxen to go with the salmon pies and roasted peacocks. By the 1640s Cromwell was not amused.[8]

Indeed; the Civil War (1642–1649) and Oliver Cromwell's subsequent term as lord protector of England were not bright days for Old Christmas. The holiday became respectable again with the Restoration (of King Charles II) in 1660, but somehow its celebration was never quite the same. Many traditions ran the risk of dying out altogether, and there is considerable evidence to suggest that, by the early nineteenth century, the Christmases described by Addison, Scott and Irving had by and large passed into memory. As Paul Davis notes, the portion of Scott's *Marmion* quoted above is "a nostalgic lament in the past tense for the rites of the Christmas feast that enabled one to see 'traces of ancient mystery.'"[9]

But, to our everlasting good fortune, some old customs and traditions refuse to die. The Christmas that Irving described at Bracebridge Hall was enormously appealing, and by the time that Dickens began his writing career in the mid–1830s, the signs of a renewed interest in really *celebrating* Christmas were becoming very apparent.[10] The spirit of the old ways certainly informed such major compilations of English language carols as Davies Gilbert's *Some Ancient Christmas Carols* (1822) and William Sandys's

Christmas Carols, Ancient and Modern (1833).[11] That same spirit is also in evidence in Thomas Kibble Hervey's 1836 work entitled *The Book of Christmas*, a fascinating history of Christmas celebrations which was illustrated by Robert Seymour, an early Dickens collaborator; indeed, one cannot help thinking that there would be a sizeable market for it today should some enterprising publisher decide to produce a new facsimile edition.[12] It is also worth mentioning that Hervey's book undoubtedly influenced William Sandys's later work, *Christmastide: Its History, Festivities, and Carols*[13]; significantly, this was successfully published in 1852, by which time the classic "Dickens Christmas" was becoming a widely accepted matter of fact.[14]

While it is always dangerous, or at best inadequate, to make definitive claims with regard to historical "firsts," it is also worth noting here that the official introduction of the Christmas tree to England is generally believed to have taken place in 1841, and that the first Christmas card is believed to have been actually produced in England in 1843. While the facts in both cases are not quite so cut and dried — these are, in any event, the latest dates possible — let us, for present purposes, accept these traditional dates. This means that in the context of the history of English Christmas celebrations, the Christmas tree predates the *Carol*, and the Christmas card appears more or less concurrently. Without question, Dickens's mighty pen was not the only force working to put Christmas back on the map of England.

This burgeoning interest in Christmas was indeed part of the backdrop against which the young Charles Dickens's first manuscript was "dropped stealthily one evening at twilight, with fear and trembling, into a dark letter-box, in a dark office, up a dark court in Fleet Street."[15] His first published work would appear in the December 1833 issue of *The Monthly Magazine* under the title "A Dinner at Poplar Walk"; it would later be gathered into *Sketches by Boz* and retitled "Mr Minns and his Cousin." While it foretold the humor that would enliven so much of his work, it was not a Christmas story; nevertheless, Dickens did much in the latter half of the 1830s to help lay a solid foundation for *A Christmas Carol*.

His first Christmas writing was a brief sketch entitled *A Christmas Dinner*; it was originally published in late December of 1835 as "Scenes and Characters No. 10 Christmas Festivities" in the weekly journal *Bell's Life in London*. In warm and glowing terms Dickens describes the happy rituals and traditions associated with a family's annual holiday reunion. He also invites the reader to partake of a generous draught of holiday cheer: "Fill your glass again, with a merry face and contented heart. Our life on it, but your Christmas shall be merry, and your new year a happy one!"[16] While some have found it fashionable (or simply expedient) to dismiss the obvious sentimentality that is present here, it is nevertheless an accurately observed and reported account of what such large family gatherings are — or at least should be — like. It was followed up a week later with another sketch, which might loosely be regarded as a companion piece, entitled *The New Year*.

As long as one doesn't get too carried away, it is possible to make the case, as indeed many commentators have over the years, that *A Christmas Dinner* contains, in microcosm, much of what we will later encounter in *A Christmas Carol*. To be sure, the beneficent effects of hearth and home are omnipresent, as is the call for charity and mercy. In this case, however, the concern is with charity and mercy in one's personal relationships; the broader concerns of the poor or underprivileged as a class are not addressed. Nevertheless, through some almost subliminal references to poverty and class distinctions (a preview, perhaps, of the "poor relations" who are present at the famous Dingley Dell Christmas to which we will shortly turn our attention) we can see simmering the larger concerns that will

come to a full boil nearly a decade later in the *Carol*. In an oft-quoted passage, we are even given what can only be called a truly fascinating preview of Tiny Tim:

> One little seat may be empty; one slight form that gladdened the father's heart, and roused the mother's pride to look upon, may not be there. Dwell not upon the past; think not that one short year ago, the fair child now resolving into dust, sat before you, with the bloom of health upon its cheek and the gaiety of infancy in its joyous eye.[17]

But in spite of the advice proffered in this intriguing passage, Dickens most definitely does want us to dwell on the past. This is an important point, and one that has been made often, but never better than in American author and scholar Frederick Busch's illuminating introduction to the Signet Classic edition of *A Christmas Carol and Other Christmas Stories* in which he writes: "And of course the passage is designed to contradict its injunctions, and to *insist* that the past, so powerfully suggested, be dwelled upon."[18]

And from Dickens's "middle period" we find this passage from his 1851 work entitled *What Christmas Is as We Grow Older* :

> Lost friend, lost child, lost parent, sister, brother, husband, wife, we will not so discard you! You shall hold your cherished places in our Christmas hearts, and by our Christmas fires; and in the season of immortal hope, and on the birthday of immortal mercy, we will shut out Nothing![19]

Without question, we find that the past reverberates loudly throughout Dickens's Christmas writings, as indeed it does throughout all of his work. And it is worth noting here that Dickens is not just concerned with a past made visible by a supernatural deus ex machina. In his Christmas writings, Dickens is ultimately concerned with the kind of past that most of us are far more likely to come up against: our own past, sometimes joyous and sometimes painful, the past that haunts all our hearths and hearts.

Already an accomplished journalist, and quite popular in his own right from the short stories and sketches that had been appearing in various periodicals for the previous two years (most under the pseudonym "Boz"), Dickens would find his career gathering momentum in the months following the publication of *A Christmas Dinner*. The first half of the year 1836 witnessed the initial collection and publication in volume form of his early works, the aforementioned *Sketches by Boz*, as well as the serialization (publication of a story in weekly or monthly installments) of the work that would quickly become (along with its author) a bona fide international phenomenon, *The Pickwick Papers*. It is in *Pickwick* that Dickens made one of his greatest contributions to the Christmas genre — second only, in fact, to the *Carol*.

Owing much to the picaresque novels of the previous century, *Pickwick* is a sprawling, episodic account of the travels and misadventures of a group of English gentlemen. Their leader, the genial retired businessman Samuel Pickwick, stands out as one of Dickens's most endearing creations. While the book's tone changes somewhat in its latter stages, when Mr. Pickwick learns firsthand what life is like in an English prison, it remains, in the words of one observer, "one of the funniest books ever written."[20] And, as many Pickwickian observers have pointed out over the years, it is one of the most richly nostalgic as well. Writing at a time in which the face of the nation was being unalterably changed by the onslaught of railroads and industry, the book looks back fondly on an England that was quickly slipping away: a more rural England, still capable of being explored, and linked by rumbling coaches and the warm fires of inviting coaching-inns. (Apropos of this discussion, one is reminded of Dylan Thomas's "...engulfing mufflers of the old coach days."[21])

This feeling of genuinely warm nostalgia is particularly evident in *Pickwick's* famous Christmas interlude at Dingley Dell, where Mr. Pickwick and companions have traveled to spend the holiday with the family of their friend and kindred spirit, Mr. Wardle. It is here, under the spell of a "huge fire of blazing logs," a "substantial supper," and a "mighty bowl of wassail," that the most famous of the book's many interpolated tales, *The Story of the Goblins who Stole a Sexton*, is told. In many respects this is a traditional Christmas ghost story, meant to be told before a Christmas Eve fire.[22] It concerns one Gabriel Grub, a miserable, nasty, sexton whose Christmas Eve plans entail drinking and digging a grave. On the night in question, he even out–Scrooges Scrooge by hitting a young caroler over the head with a lantern. He is redeemed, however, by a band of goblins who show him visions of how good life is and of what he is missing. (They also, quite literally, kick some sense into him.) Interestingly, one of the visions shown to Gabriel Grub is that of a young couple with many children who, although poor, are very content and clearly united by love and devotion. Grub is shown glimpses of the family at various stages of their lives, and at one point he witnesses the death of one of their children, a boy, described by Dickens as "the fairest and youngest."[23]

On the surface, the stories of Gabriel Grub and Ebenezer Scrooge appear to have much in common, but one should be careful not to attribute too much in the way of direct influence to this early work. It is perhaps best viewed, as many critics and commentators have suggested, as a rough outline or "prototype" (or, if you prefer, the germ of an idea) for what was to come.[24] In any event, it is ultimately not the story of the "surly sexton" that makes the interlude at Dingley Dell a Christmas classic. It is, rather, the context, and the setting, and the prevailing mood in which the tale is told.

Dickens sets the stage in the opening paragraphs of the Christmas section:

Carol forerunners: Gabriel Grub and the Goblin by Phiz. From *The Pickwick Papers*. Courtesy Dickens House Museum.

And numerous indeed are the hearts to which Christmas brings a brief season of happiness and enjoyment.... How many old recollections, and how many dormant sympathies, does Christmas time awaken!...

Happy, happy Christmas, that can win us back to the delusions of our childish days; that can recall to the old man the pleasures of his youth; that can transport the sailor and the traveler, thousands of miles away, back to his own fire-side and his quiet home![25]

The Christmas that the Pickwickians enjoy is filled with warmth — in every sense of the word — and overflowing with good food (and drink), fun and fellowship; and in the end, one is inclined to agree with Mr. Pickwick that, "this [Christmas at Dingley Dell] is, indeed, comfort."[26] While the Manor Farm at Dingley Dell is not the kind of grand country estate where Addison and Irving's Christmas revelries took place (and those, in turn, were considerably less opulent than the surroundings in which a medieval king would have presided at Christmas), Wardle nevertheless succeeds at keeping the old ways alive, albeit on a more modest scale, and with the help of his bumbling visitors from the city. As suggested earlier, the influence of Irving's Christmas at Bracebridge Hall is keenly felt here. It would be felt too at a later Christmas dinner — one considerably more humble, but lacking nothing in warmth and good spirits — at the home of Bob Cratchit.

But before *A Christmas Carol* exploded onto the world stage in December of 1843, Dickens touched on the subject of Christmas in early 1840, within the pages of the seldom read (or at least seldom discussed) *Master Humphrey's Clock*. Briefly, this was a weekly periodical, intended as a kind of literary miscellany, the various issues of which would be linked by the commentary and narration of a continuing character named Master Humphrey, a kindly old gentleman not unlike the already legendary Samuel Pickwick. (Mr. Pickwick would, in fact,

reappear in these pages, as would Sam Weller and family.) However, as Dickens scholars have pointed out, when it soon became apparent that the public preferred a new novel from Dickens, he responded with *The Old Curiosity Shop*, which quickly supplanted all other subject matter in the *Clock*. With the conclusion of *The Old Curiosity Shop*, *Barnaby Rudge* appeared within the *Clock's* pages, after which the publication was disbanded.

In the second chapter of *Master Humphrey's Clock*, in which Master Humphrey introduces the group of continuing characters that form his circle of friends, he relates how he first met his companion known simply as "the deaf gentleman." He recalls a Christmas Day on which, after having an early (and apparently solitary) dinner, he "walked out to cheer myself with the happiness of others ... and was glad to believe that for a season half the world of poverty was gay."[27] Since the material that makes up the framework of *Master Humphrey's Clock* is not well known to general readers, I think it appropriate to quote from this section at length:

> As the day closed in, I still rambled through the streets, feeling a companionship in the bright fires that cast their warm reflection on the windows as I passed, and losing all sense of my own loneliness in imagining the sociality and kind-fellowship that everywhere prevailed. At length I happened to stop before a Tavern, and, encountering a Bill of Fare in the window, it all at once brought it into my head to wonder what kind of people dined alone in Taverns upon Christmas Day.
>
> Solitary men are accustomed, I suppose, unconsciously to look upon solitude as their own peculiar property. I had sat alone in my room upon many, many anniversaries of this great holiday, and had never regarded it but as one of universal assemblage and rejoicing. I had excepted, and with an aching heart, a crowd of prisoners and beggars; but *these* were not the men for whom the Tavern

Rosy nostalgia: Christmas Eve at Dingley Dell by Phiz. From *The Pickwick Papers*. **Courtesy Dickens House Museum.**

doors were open. Had they any customers, or was it a mere form?—a form, no doubt.

Trying to feel quite sure of this, I walked away; but before I had gone many paces, I stopped and looked back. There was a provoking air of business in the lamp above the door which I could not overcome. I began to be afraid there might be many customers — young men, perhaps, struggling with the world, utter strangers in this great place, whose friends lived at a long distance off, and whose means were too slender to enable them to make the journey. The supposition gave rise to so many distressing little pictures, that, in preference to carrying them home with me, I determined to encounter the realities. So I turned and walked in.[28]

Once inside, Master Humphrey discovers a lone patron, silently brooding over a half-eaten meal.

While there is no question that the framing material in *Master Humphrey's Clock* should be grouped among his minor writings (*The Old Curiosity Shop* and *Barnaby Rudge* are, of course, quite another matter), it is perilous indeed to underestimate anything written by Dickens. One can point to an almost countless number of instances in which even a word, a phrase, a brief description, a minor incident, or an apparently casual comment can offer a clue to a grander design or, in some cases, a subliminal glimpse of things to come. Of course, not all of these nuggets are made of gold; but golden or not, they frequently offer valuable insights into the life and mind of their creator. The "Christmas episode" in *Master Humphrey's Clock* is, I think, such a case.

Along with another hint of the simmering social concerns already referred to— many of which he had already confronted directly in both *Oliver Twist* and *Nicholas Nickleby*—that past that Dickens wants us to confront is certainly in evidence here as well. We know little of Master Humphrey's background, but we do know that, as indicated in the episode quoted above, he knows what it is to be alone on Christmas Day. This is not to suggest that Dickens's art or life was influenced by any unhappy memories specifically related to Christmas. In fact, as Peter Ackroyd observes in his mesmerizing biography of Dickens:

> There is no reason to doubt ... that the Dickens family took Christmas more seriously than many of their contemporaries. For the first nineteen years of his life, John Dickens [Charles's father] would have experienced that festival in the opulent setting of Crewe Hall [where his parents were employed as servants], and there is every reason to suppose that he would try to recreate such an atmosphere in his own home with conjurings, dances, recitations, charades, forfeits, blind-man's-buffs, and card games like Pope Joan or Speculation.[29]

However, the childhood traumas and deprivations that Dickens experienced — his sense of being neglected and abandoned by his parents, the stint at Warren's Blacking factory where he labored pasting labels on pots of foul shoe polish, the constant threat of looming poverty, the interruptions to his education, his father's stay in debtor's prison — had a profound effect on his life and art. He was never able to shake these memories; indeed they haunted every corner of his life and every page of his writings.

In this sense (and in many others) Dickens has much in common with Charlie Chaplin, and even if one chooses to think that Dickens exaggerated his sufferings or was guilty of self-pity as an adult (Dickens *would* lose a competition aimed at determining whether he or Chaplin had a worse childhood), one must still remember that these experiences would undoubtedly be very frightening to any child.[30]

Christmas is, of course, the most joyous time of year for Dickens, and he tells us so with great frequency. But in Master Humphrey's Christmas, Dickens again reminds us that, along with the grand and joyous traditions associated with the traditional English Christmas, there must also be room at the feast for the phantoms of our past; and that, like old Mrs. Wardle, matriarch of the Manor Farm at Dingley Dell, we would all probably benefit from the therapeutic effects of a "gush of silent tears"[31] at Christmas time. And can we not find some bridge here between Master Humphrey, a man of means yet a solitary outsider looking in at the Christmas joy of others, and the successful young writer who could not forget what it was like to feel isolated and alone? Along these lines, what one wouldn't give to be a fly on the wall at some of the Dickens family's early Christmas celebrations, say in the years *just after* young Charles's sojourn at Warren's Blacking. A fairly large and undoubtedly boisterous family would be present, and let us assume that John Dickens is a veritable modern Misrule. (On this latter point, film buffs might think of W. C. Fields's brilliant portrayal of Wilkins Micawber in MGM's *David Copperfield* [32]; Micawber is known to have been largely inspired by Dickens's vision of his father.) Amidst whatever gaiety is taking place might we not observe one young man — still smarting from his experience at the blacking factory and with at least a hint of a faraway look in his eyes — feeling, in a very real sense, alone in a crowd? Might this explain the lack of a joyous "Christmas Chapter" in *David Copperfield*?

There is also an important bridge here back to Irving's Christmas at Bracebridge Hall. As suggested earlier, it would be difficult to imagine a more heartfelt tribute to an old English Christmas, and indeed its probable influence on both *The Pickwick Papers* and *A Christmas Carol* is obvious. As S. A. Muresianu has observed in *The History of the Victorian Christmas Book*, "It was perhaps Irving's nostalgia, his reverence for a past in which holiday celebration seemed to unite society in a genial and compassionate way, that most appealed to Dickens." [33] This, undoubtedly, strikes at the heart of the matter; but it is worth noting that Irving's narrator, the fictional Geoffrey Crayon, like Dickens's Master Humphrey, is also an outsider looking in. Indeed he tells us so in no uncertain terms: "Stranger and sojourner as I am in the land — though for me no social hearth may blaze, no hospitable roof throw open its doors, nor the warm grasp of friendship welcome me at the threshold — yet I feel the influence of the season beaming into my soul from the happy looks of those around me." [34] We encounter him here on a particular Christmas Eve while in the midst of a solitary tour of the Yorkshire countryside. He plans to spend the night at an inn when, while observing the festive holiday preparations going on about him, he chances to meet an old friend, Frank Bracebridge, who invites him to spend Christmas with him at his family's nearby home. He accepts the invitation gladly for, as he tells us, "the preparation I had seen for universal festivity and social enjoyment had made me feel a little impatient of my loneliness" [35]; and, as promised, he does indeed receive "a hearty welcome in something of the old-fashioned style." [36]

There is often an implication (or an inference) of frivolousness connected with the use of the word nostalgia; but we see that the nostalgia at work within Dickens was a rather complex thing. Small wonder then that the heart and mind that could articulate so beautifully the need to touch all of the past, the sweet and the bittersweet, could also be so sensitive to, and inspired by, a very different kind of stimulus; and that this stimulus would culminate in the shattering images of two children named Ignorance and Want.

Political and Economic Roots

His [Dickens's] radicalism is of the vaguest kind, and yet one always knows that it is there.

George Orwell

When we talk about *A Christmas Carol* being "of its time," we are indeed talking about much more than the contemporary Christmas revival just discussed with its delightful nostalgia for the glories of an Olde English Christmas. The intoxicating aromas of plum pudding and roast goose *are there*, and the lively strains of Sir Roger de Coverley linger long after one returns the book to its place on the shelf. (And probably more than a few readers over the years have been inspired to seek out a recipe for negus and smoking bishop.[1]) But there are other voices, loud voices belonging to an increasingly large, and increasingly restless, subculture — one mired in the most abject poverty, filth and despair imaginable. The cries of children, their young lives despoiled by unrelenting labor, are there too; and one senses the presence of an increasingly ambitious yet essentially voiceless lower middle class, a group that Dickens, of course, knew partic-

ularly well. And to these voices one can add the kind of sensory stimuli that abounded in Dickens's London, then the greatest city in the world, but impossibly overcrowded and lacking even the most basic provisions for adequate housing and sanitation. Add, too, the stench — both literal and figurative — of a society rotting from within, and of streets, alleys and rivers teeming with human waste. Old Joe's rag-and-bottle shop, and Fagin's den of thieves before it, were not figments of a young writer's fertile imagination. They were exceedingly real, a fact that no one knew better than Charles Dickens. These too are the *Carol's* co-authors.

But just as the previous chapter does not claim to be anything like a comprehensive history of English Christmas customs, nor of the literary tradition associated with those customs, neither does this chapter claim to represent anything like a complete socioeconomic and political history of early nine-

Grim reality: Ignorance and Want by John Leech. From *A Christmas Carol*. Courtesy Dickens House Museum.

teenth-century England. That task would require several shelves of books just to bring the proverbial tip of the iceberg into sight. Nevertheless, by touching on a few key facts and events, we begin to get a sense of the big picture; and we can share, however imperfectly, some small portion of Dickens's immense and extraordinarily complex frame of reference.

While keeping a watchful eye out for icebergs, one can begin by noting that Charles Dickens was born, in 1812, into a world clamoring for change. Indeed the Industrial Revolution had been underway for about three-quarters of a century, and the recent political revolutions in America and France attested to the fact that considerable change had already taken place. Amidst a slow but growing movement toward democracy (or at least a desire to start moving in that direction), dangerous ideas were taking root in many places, and the flame of liberty burned in many hearts — including many English hearts — fanned by a bracing wind on which was borne the notion that "the people" were worthy of some measure of respect.

This is not to say, however, that the sailing was smooth. There was a bloated and generally repressive aristocracy (and bureaucracy) to contend with, and if, for example, one looks at the decade in which Dickens was born, many potential flashpoints stand out. R. J. Cruikshank makes this clear in his *Charles Dickens and Early Victorian England*, a book that will quickly change the mind of anyone who thinks English history must be dull:

> In the eighteen months after Waterloo, riots and civil disturbances took place in twenty cities and a dozen shires. The Corn Law of 1815 made bread dear at a time when wages were falling, and there was much misery and want in both the industrial and rural areas. The Luddites, taking their name from the crazy youth Ned Ludd, broke up the machines which were replacing the traditional handcrafts. In the year that Dickens was born, the newspapers reported machine-wrecking in the Midlands and North, and the meeting of alarmed magistrates to put down the frenzy. The men in power, the Jenkinsons, Sidmouths, Eldons and the like, were men of narrow and unillumined minds and they were easily thrown into a fright. Repression was their one remedy for discontent. The Six Acts of 1819 brought Britain as near to the Police State as she has ever been in modern history. These statutes forbidding freedom of assembly and speech stifled the voice of protest — who could now sing "Britons never shall be slaves"? In the same year the "Massacre of Peterloo" took place. A crowd had peacefully gathered in St. Peter's Fields, Manchester, for a demonstration in favour of Parliamentary Reform. They were broken up by a charge of cavalry and yeomanry, eleven persons were killed, and some six hundred injured.[2]

In the 1830s — the decade which, as Cruikshank points out, marks the beginning of the "Age of Dickens" as well as Victoria — social issues were still very much on the front burner. While far from perfect, the Reform Act of 1832 initiated some badly needed electoral reforms and helped extend a vigorous public debate on many related topics. There was also the Poor Law Amendment Act of 1834 which was in part intended to discourage dependence on government relief by making that relief both unpleasant and undesirable. Throughout the decade there was considerable protest, some of it violent, against the harsh conditions caused by its implementation — some of the most important and memorable protest can, of course, be found between the covers of *Oliver Twist*. The price of bread was still an issue, and the movement for aggressive political reform known as Chartism provided yet another source of agitation.

In short, the 1830s were marked by more unrest, more unhappiness, and more potential flashpoints. And as the time drew near for the *Carol* to do its work — we are now in the Hungry Forties — there were many, Dickens among them, who felt that a massive uprising of that ravenous subculture was not an impossibility. (This seems an appropriate place to underscore an important point made by Cruikshank and many others: It is well to remember that in spite of the enormous potential for catastrophe, a massive general uprising or revolution did not take place in Victorian England as it did, and subsequently has, in so many other places. There are no easy explanations here — again the problem of icebergs looms heavy—but it has been observed that the English demonstrated an amazing ability to adapt to changing times and to keep chipping away at their problems, however slowly, in a reasonably rational manner. The spirit of the age was essentially one of optimism, and the country seems never to have lost its ability to remain focused on positive, long-range goals.[3])

One reason why Dickens was so aware of the looming threat of revolution was that his sensibility, his frame of reference, his life's blood, was essentially urban in nature. In contemporary parlance, the streets of London were his beat; he took long walks on them at all hours of the night when he needed to think, and he grew restless when away from them for too long. They inspired, informed, energized; and no one knew them better than he.

And what did he notice on those streets, what did he see and hear and smell on those walks? The answers are, of course, to be found in his books. But the short of it is that he took in everything, no detail too small, no rhythm or nuance too fleeting to go unnoticed or unfelt. One imagines a motion picture camera tracking its way through the labyrinth that was London, occasionally panning across the horizon for a new reference point, or zooming in to capture some minute bit of business. Everything recorded for posterity; deep focus, sharp detail. But what set Dickens apart from so many of his fellow citizens was that he refused to cover the lens when he got to places like Whitechapel, St Giles, Southwark and Saffron Hill. It was here that he encountered that lurking subculture, the urban poor, the new industrial working class—many uprooted from their country homes and carried into the industrial cities and towns by the power of steam and machinery, factories and railroads. Separate little worlds, breeding grounds of crime and disease, positively thriving in the shadows of so much wealth and power. This was the downside of the Industrial Revolution, a picture that decent

Englishmen were not supposed to notice—and indeed so many did not.

Against this backdrop of unrest and growing demand for change, one can look for specific events in Dickens's early life that might have planted the seeds that would bear such strong fruit in his first Christmas book. There is no doubt that the childhood miseries alluded to in the previous chapter—the blacking factory and the rough company that he met there, the constant threat of poverty, and so forth—left indelible psychic scars on Dickens the individual. They also contributed to what can only be called a larger, and deeply felt, social consciousness. He was quite young when he learned that there was pain and hunger and injustice in the world, and he was remarkably adept at pinpointing their root causes. But, for present purposes, it is perhaps enough to say that nothing was ever wasted on him, no scrap of information, no seemingly random bit of observation or experience. As every commentator on Dickens has noted in one way or another, he simply filed everything away for future use.

If, however, we were able to step back in time, and with benefit of an omniscient (and highly cinematic) birds' eye view look down on Dickens's life in the two years prior to the *Carol's* publication, an interesting pattern might emerge through the clouds. To begin with, the first half of 1842 was spent on his initial tour of America. The timing here is significant because the *Carol* is rife with political and economic implications and, as many commentators have pointed out, it was during the period of this first American tour that Dickens's personal politics first came into some sort of focus.

We have already established that Dickens was born into an age of great sociological and political upheaval. In such a context, one frequently encounters the term *radical*. However, it must be noted that while Dickens was a sincere advocate of sweeping reforms, the scope of which can indeed only be called radical, he was not *a radical* in the sense in which that term is generally used today. He abhorred violence, and in particular any form of mob violence. He was, in fact, known to have both feared and detested "the mob" in any form; he did not, for example, support the trade union movement of his day in spite of the fact that his sympathies were clearly on the side of the working man. Thus Dickens should in no way be linked with any of the more aggressive or truly radical political movements of his day, however much he may have agreed with some of their goals. This is an important point because, in America at least, Dickens is often depicted as someone who managed to be both a shameless sentimentalist *and* a flaming political radical.[4]

Nevertheless, it was with a certain radical spirit that Dickens went off to America. He had an idealized and romanticized idea of what he would find there, and he was sure that it would point the way for England to follow. As Steven Marcus has observed, "Dickens came to America in much the same frame of mind in which sympathetic visitors went to the Soviet Union in the 1920s and 1930s."[5] Unfortunately, as noted in a letter just two months after his arrival, Dickens's mood soon changed: "This is not the Republic I came to see. This is not the Republic of my imagination. I infinitely prefer a liberal Monarchy ... to such a Government as this."[6]

The questions of what went wrong, and why, are complex and have been authoritatively addressed elsewhere.[7] In brief, though, he found the country and many of its inhabitants to be rough and ill-mannered (interestingly, similar objections were raised by some Americans toward him), and he disliked what has been termed a social-climbing national climate. He also disliked the American press, which he felt was manipulative and patently dishonest. He was particularly outraged by the virulent attacks on him in American newspapers when he publicly called for an international copyright agreement that would insure that foreign writers, like himself, would be compensated for their work. (On this matter of the press, he seems to have felt that there was a little too much freedom running amok in the republic of his imagination.) In his letters and writings, one also finds that a wide array of disparate subjects, ranging from slavery to spitting in public, became particular targets of his wrath.

Why is all of this important to the present discussion? This is, after all, not a biography of Dickens, nor is it a critical analysis of his life and work per se. It is important because, once again, the *Carol* is rife with political and economic implications; on second thought, it may be more accurate to say that politics and economics are at the very heart of the *Carol*. Trouble is, as his American experiences help us to understand, the author of the *Carol* was not a terribly political person in the generally accepted sense of the word. For Dickens, even though the problems being attacked in the *Carol* would ultimately have to be addressed within the context of an existing political infrastructure, the true solution was not political but moral. Many distinguished Dickensian commentators have made this point crystal clear over the years,[8] but it has often escaped the general public. For the vast majority of us the *Carol* is not just another famous book, it is an important part of popular culture; indeed, to this day, Dickens himself is still something of a pop icon. And yet that segment of the populace that knows Dickens primarily or exclusively through film and television, or through a general familiarity with only his most famous books (perhaps just through the *Carol*), hears very little to suggest that Dickens's brand of radicalism was ultimately grounded in some pretty old-fashioned moral and religious beliefs. If the subject does come up, it is too often "explained" (as film critics are often wont to do) with a condescending reference to his "sentimentality." This side of Dickens can be inconvenient to deal with in the "modern" world.

When Dickens returned from America in late June of 1842 he was, at least in a political sense, a somewhat changed man. (This situation is brilliantly summed up by the distinguished Dickens scholar Fred Kaplan in his recent biography of Dickens: "Having gone to America thinking himself a radical, he returned recognizing that he was a left-of-center Whig."[9]) He was overflowing with energy and ambition, but he was not favorably impressed with America, and much of this energy was channeled toward addressing his negative experiences and perceptions, his primary weapon being the pages of his first travel book *American Notes for General Circulation*, which appeared in October of 1842. (The American assault would soon be taken up again in portions of *Martin Chuzzlewit*.)

In the months after his return from America, Dickens also came out in support of legislation aimed at prohibiting labor by women and children in mines; he observed conditions in the mines firsthand and for a time considered incorporating this theme into *Martin Chuzzlewit*. He also continued his practice of exploring London's slums and took great interest in Edwin Chadwick's *Report on the Sanitary Condition of the Labouring Population* which, as its title suggests, offered a strong indictment of the deplorable conditions in which so many of his countrymen existed. At one point, in spite of the tremendous demands that his growing fame and influence were placing on his time, he is known to have expressed interest in editing a new radical (or at least liberal) journal.

There is also the story of his finding a deaf and dumb boy, presumably abandoned and in Dickens's words "half dead,"[10] on the beach at Broadstairs where he was vacationing. Apart from the fact that Dickens arranged for the boy to be cared for, little is known of this incident or of the boy's subsequent fate; on the vast canvas of Dickens's busy life it is a footnote, and a minor one at that. And yet one would not be wrong in viewing it as a microcosm of the world that Dickens refused to ignore. In words that could be Dickens's own, Peter Ackroyd eloquently describes this boy as "one of the thousands of homeless children, many of them in some way disabled from ordinary life, who seem to drift across the landscape of the nineteenth century, discarded and forgotten."[11]

In November of 1842, Dickens began work on his next novel, *Martin Chuzzlewit*. It began its serial appearance at the start of the new year and concluded its run in July of 1844. While no serious analysis of what some critics consider his first mature work, or indeed his first masterpiece, will be attempted here, a couple of points are worth noting in the context of the *Carol* and the events immediately leading up to its production. For example, one cannot overlook the fact that while *Martin Chuzzlewit* has often been described as one of Dickens's greatest comic novels, its comedy is intertwined with some of his most bitter and biting satire in an explicit examination of greed, selfishness and hypocrisy. Like the *Carol*, it is also widely known as a story of redemption and reformation. In this context, it is important to note that scholars have pointed to similarities between the characters of old Martin Chuzzlewit and Ebenezer Scrooge and, more importantly, between Scrooge and Dickens himself. The point is that he was thinking and writing about these things in the period immediately before, and concurrent with, his work on *A Christmas Carol*.

Early in 1843, with work underway on *Martin Chuzzlewit*, Dickens received a copy of *The Second Report (Trades and Manufactures) of the Children's Employment Commission* from the aggressive social reformer Dr. Thomas Southwood Smith. He was appalled and infuriated by its descriptions of the horrible conditions in which young children were being forced to work, and he responded to Smith saying that he would write "a very cheap pamphlet, called 'An appeal to the People of England, on behalf of the Poor

Man's Child.'"[12] But shortly afterwards, he wrote back to Smith explaining that he would forgo the pamphlet saying that there were "reasons ... for deferring the production of that pamphlet until the end of the year. I am not at liberty to explain them further, just now; but *rest assured* that when you know them, and see what I do, and where, and how, you will certainly feel that a Sledge hammer has come down with twenty times the force — twenty thousand times the force — I could exert by following out my first idea."[13]

Before proceeding, it must be noted that Dickens was not the only patch of fertile ground upon which this profoundly disturbing report fell. It is known to have inspired Elizabeth Barrett Browning's "The Cry of the Children":

"For oh," say the children, "we are weary,
    And we cannot run or leap;
If we cared for any meadows, it were merely
    to drop down in them and sleep.
Our knees tremble sorely in the stooping,
    We fall upon our faces, trying to go;
And, underneath our heavy eyelids drooping
    The reddest flower would look as pale as
        snow.
For, all day, we drag our burden tiring
    Through the coal-dark, underground;
Or, all day, we drive the wheels of iron
    In the factories, round and round."[14]

One can also look to Thomas Hood's "The Song of the Shirt":

"O, men, with sisters dear!
    O, men, with mothers and wives!
It is not linen you're wearing out,
    But human creatures' lives!
        Stitch — stitch — stitch,
    In poverty, hunger, and dirt,
Sewing at once, with a double thread,
    A shroud as well as a shirt."[15]

The report's influence, whether direct, indirect, or vaguely subliminal, was certainly not limited to poetry. Many socially conscious novels began appearing, and the works of Elizabeth Gaskell lay not far ahead; and as R. J. Cruikshank reminds us, "It is an odd circumstance, much to be remarked in the political history of this era, that some of its warmest Radical writing came from its most eminent Conservative [Benjamin Disraeli]. There is, in fact, as much high explosive in Disraeli, the novelist, as in Dickens."[16] If there is a general point to be made here, it is that in the overtly political side of his writings, as with their "Christmasy" side, Dickens was not working in a vacuum.

As for the *Carol* itself, it is impossible to cite its official starting point with absolute precision. Nevertheless, its birth is generally placed in mid–September of 1843 when Dickens visited the Field Lane ragged school in Saffron Hill, one of London's worst slums. The ragged schools were, as their name suggests, set up to help the children of the very poor. They were generally run by the Evangelicals, a group that was frequently the butt of some of Dickens's most savage satire but with whom he was often able to find much common ground; he disapproved of their missionary fervor in attempting to save the souls of these children, but he wholeheartedly agreed with any attempt to introduce them to even the most basic education, indeed to some semblance of civilization. They were the children of that ubiquitous subculture — ignorant, filthy, diseased, undoubtedly dangerous, and destined for lives of almost unimaginable misery and crime. Years later, in an evocatively titled journalistic piece called *A Sleep to Startle Us*, Dickens very aptly summed up such children by saying that they were "young in years but youthful in nothing else."[17] While this was not the first time that he had seen or described such things, he was angry as never before and determined to act.

The specific direction that the story would take came to him a few weeks later while on a trip to Manchester, where he made a speech to benefit the Manchester Athenaeum, which had been founded to make some modest means of recreation and education available to the working class population of that city. He was moved by what he felt was the basic goodness of the working people that he met there, and he wanted to do something to both address and help that large constituency. He was soon hard at work on the *Carol.* It is not known with absolute certainty whether this was the "Sledge hammer" that he promised earlier in the year. It has, for example, been suggested that in using the hammer metaphor he may have been referring to his initial intention to incorporate some sort of message into *Martin Chuzzlewit.* Nevertheless, there can be no doubt that his "Ghostly little book" delivered a mighty blow for the poor and downtrodden — indeed for all of those who would listen — when it appeared a few weeks later, just in time for Christmas.

This Ghostly Little Book

The mystery of Christmas is in a manner identical with the mystery of Dickens. If ever we adequately explain the one we may adequately explain the other.

G. K. Chesterton

In terms of its theme, as well as the nuts and bolts of its storyline, *A Christmas Carol* is simply too well known to warrant much discussion or elaboration here; in any event, these issues must inevitably be dealt with in Part Two. There are, however, a few points still worth making, and a loose end or two to be dealt with before moving on.

In tandem with the forces discussed thus far, Dickens also had a very practical reason for wanting to tackle another writing project at this time: He needed the money. Cynical critics, clearly lacking both Christmas spirit and a basic understanding of Dickens and his work, have occasionally pounced on this fact in the apparent hope of revealing some hypocrisy on his part, the mention of which would presumably lessen at least some of the *Carol's* impact. But to do so is to overlook the obvious fact that the man was a professional writer who, through a combination of

incredible genius and incredibly hard work, was capable of creating two masterful works of fiction simultaneously. (It is also worth noting that this was not the first time that he had done so.) Along with the ongoing process of self-examination that is at the heart of his fiction, he knew what it was to be poor and he was terrified of a return to that state. He therefore kept a very watchful eye on his financial affairs and was always open to exploring new sources of income.

The *Carol* was written in about six weeks, apparently gaining a kind of feverish momentum as the work progressed; Dickens's close friend and confidant John Forster in fact tells us that it gripped him with "a strange mastery."[1] Trying to picture Dickens at work on the *Carol*, one can imagine the delight he must have felt when, for the first time, he was able to work on a major piece of fiction, albeit a short one, without the

More rosy nostalgia: Fezziwig's Christmas party by John Leech. From *A Christmas Carol.* **Courtesy Dickens House Museum.**

pressure of serial publication. He was, nevertheless, working with a window of just a few weeks in which the story had to be finished if it was to be out in time for Christmas — a deadline which, even if self-imposed, must have created its own kind of pressure. One can thus readily understand

Dickens's oft-quoted comment that he "broke out like a Madman"[2] when it was finished, and, as we know, he enjoyed himself immensely that memorable Christmas of 1843. (A final thought here: For anyone who remembers the rapturous feeling of setting aside school books when Christmas vacation arrives and Christmas Eve and Christmas Day are finally near, Dickens's words here require no explanation. One wonders, though, if young Ebenezer Scrooge also "broke out like a Madman" that Christmas that little Fan came to rescue him from another lonely holiday at school. For Dickens's sake, it would be nice to think that he did.)

Unfortunately, Dickens's euphoria was short-lived. In addition to the intimate tone with which he addressed his readers, Dickens went to extraordinary lengths to insure that *A Christmas Carol* would be a very personal and personalized gift to his public. He arranged for the little book itself to be bound in red cloth, gilt on its cover and page edges, and complete with eight illustrations — four of them hand-colored. One does not have to be a collector of rare books, or possess any knowledge of the craft of book production, to know that it was a thing of great beauty; so much so, in fact, that many of its imitators appropriated the *Carol's* look as well as its contents. However, because of the high costs involved in producing such a volume and its comparatively low sale price of five shillings, it failed to bring in much of a profit despite excellent sales.

Further contributing to his woes (financial and otherwise), Dickens had engaged himself in a battle with *Parley's Illuminated Library*, which had brought out a pirated edition of the *Carol* shortly after its appearance. He won his suit, but because the defendants declared bankruptcy, he was forced to pay his own legal costs.

In spite of these ironic and infuriating financial complications, Dickens could take comfort in the fact that reaction to the *Carol* was one of almost universal euphoria. Its message was being heard and, in fellow-author William Makepeace Thackeray's famous description, it was received as "a national benefit."[3]

And how does one begin to calculate or quantify just what that benefit was? As we have seen, there was a general revival of Christmas celebration in the air when Dickens began his writing career, and it was accelerating in the early and mid-forties. But there is no doubt that the *Carol* more than any other single factor helped put Christmas back on the map of England. Nor can there be any doubt about the extent to which it has shaped and informed our modern conception of the holiday. To be sure, we reap a very tangible benefit every December when, for a few weeks at least, the world does seem a little brighter, maybe a bit more cheerful; these are hopeful days when children are allowed to be children and when even the most Scrooge-like among us can look at a child playing with a new toy, or perhaps at a memento from our own Christmas past, and see some rather personal "traces of ancient mystery."

But just what exactly Dickens gave us in the *Carol* is not an easy question to answer. One thing at any rate is certain: It is wrong to dismiss the story as some sort of vague and unrealistic quasi-utopian tract, the product of a Victorian do-gooder whose solutions to life's problems were to eat, drink and be merry. Such charges, nevertheless, have surfaced in one form or another over the years. Often the complaint is that Dickens offered no real solutions to the problems being addressed in the *Carol*, while at the same time presenting a vision of Christmas that emphasized various worldly pleasures at the expense of any explicit religious content or message.[4] When encountering such objections, one is tempted to ask if the objector has ever actually read the *Carol*—for in it doesn't Jacob Marley, in responding with heartrending hindsight to Scrooge's praise for his former partner's business acumen, tell us that "Mankind was my business. The common welfare was my business; charity, mercy, forbearance, and benevolence, were all my business. The dealings of my trade were but a drop of water in the comprehensive ocean of my business!"[5] And later, as Scrooge and the Ghost of Christmas Present watch the festivities at the Cratchit

Christmas bounty: Scrooge meeting the Ghost of Christmas Present by John Leech. From *A Christmas Carol.* **Courtesy Dickens House Museum.**

household, doesn't the Ghost turn Scrooge's famous crack about decreasing the surplus population against him with a savage rebuke: "Man," said the Ghost, "if man you be in heart, not adamant, forbear that wicked cant until you have discovered What the surplus is, and Where it is. Will you decide what men shall live, what men shall die? It may be, that in the sight of Heaven, you are more worthless and less fit to live than millions like this poor man's child. Oh God! to hear the Insect on the leaf pronouncing on the too much life among his hungry brothers in the dust!"[6]

Again, for someone whose popular image — at least in the popular American mind of today — is that of a political radical, Dickens's life was grounded in some very basic religious precepts which ring loud and clear throughout the *Carol*. Indeed one might say that they are the key ingredient in the mortar that binds the *Carol's* aforementioned rosy nostalgia and grim reality together. It is true that throughout his adult life Dickens's involvement with any form of conventional organized religion was minimal (and sometimes downright hostile). Nevertheless he is known to have believed in a benevolent and all-powerful God who expected His people to take care of each other, and to treat each other well. Therein lies his solution.

One is reminded here of George Orwell's brilliant essay on Dickens, toward the beginning of which he states that Dickens's "whole 'message' is one that at first glance looks like an enormous platitude: If men would behave decently the world would be decent."[7] It is, however, a matter of no small significance that a writer like Orwell — i.e., a writer not inclined to reach for convenient bromides — goes on to wrap up this section of his essay by concluding that "'If men would behave decently the world would be decent' is not such a platitude as it sounds."[8]

It is also important to note, with the experts in this area, that religion per se was as much a part of the public debate in Dick-

ens's day as were the social and political issues already referred to. Where Dickens differed with many of those engaged in the debate was that he is known to have seen an intrinsic relationship between religion, and those claiming to be religious, and the horrific conditions being endured by the poor and destitute all around him. His religion then, his Christianity, was a personal call for action, and a very practical blueprint for change.

To answer the objection that the "Dickens Christmas" placed too much emphasis on food, drink, and what might be called general merrymaking, Dickens, if one may presume to speak for him, would probably say: "What's the problem? If decent people cannot enjoy themselves at this time of year, then when can they? Hasn't Scott [whom Dickens greatly admired] told us that 'A Christmas gambol oft could cheer the poor man's heart through half the year'?" He would also put such things in perspective: Think of the vivid description of all the wonderful fruits and confections that Scrooge and the Ghost of Christmas Present observe when they walk the streets of London on Christmas morning. This passage has been rightly described as sensual, and even erotic, but are these not the bountiful gifts of a generous God? And are not the mouth-watering treats piled up on the floor of Scrooge's chambers when he first meets the Ghost gifts of that same God, and symbols of what He wants *everyone* to share and enjoy?

While it is certainly true that then, as today, the shopkeepers benefited from the "Dickens Christmas," this was not Dickens's motivation for writing the *Carol*.[9] He did not approve of any form of excess in his own day, nor would he approve of the two or three month orgy of commercialism that precedes the modern American Christmas — a phenomenon which, as anyone who has ever tried to find a Christmas carol on the radio on December 26th can attest, ends rather abruptly when Christmas Day is over.

Dickens enjoyed life, but nowhere in the *Carol* does he suggest that any form of greed or gluttony is part of his vision of Christmas. Indeed, in his original manuscript, he is barely four pages into the story (i.e., long before the party at Fezziwig's) when he tells us that Christmas is "a good time: a *kind, forgiving, charitable,* pleasant time [emphasis added]."[10] And as for the revelry, he tells us to take pleasure in some rather simple things — home, family, and fellowship foremost among them; the epigraph which began this discussion at the start of Chapter One might just as well mark its conclusion. In lamenting what he called the "commercial racket" and misdirected energy that has become so commonplace in our modern celebration of Christmas, C. S. Lewis tells us that "Mr. Pickwick took a cod with him to Dingley Dell; the reformed Scrooge ordered a turkey for his clerk."[11] While one might respectfully add that there were also six barrels of oysters on that immortal journey to the Manor Farm, the point is well taken.

And there is, finally, one more benefit that we derive from Dickens's "Ghostly little book." Amidst all the talk of social significance and historical context, it's easy to lose sight of the fact that the *Carol* is a great yarn; an enchanting tale, deliciously chilling and deliriously happy. In short, it is an ingenious and wonderfully entertaining piece of fiction, a fact which no doubt explains why those of us addicted to its various film and television adaptations can usually find some merit, however slight, in even the most dismal production. And it requires no special circumstances to be savored over and over and over again, although if one is able to curl up with it in front of a Christmas Eve fire, or better yet hear it read (fire optional), so much the better. Nor does it require the magnificent voice of a Richard Burton or a James Earl Jones to put the *Carol* across, Dickens's voice will do. "I am standing in the spirit at your elbow"[12] he tells us in Stave Two. And so he is; one of the greatest novelists ever is tugging at our sleeves, and with childlike urgency and simplicity, is saying, "I want to tell you a story."

PART TWO

Pre-Cinema

Dickens created the world of his novels not only in the mode of the theatre but also with a bold, dynamic style that foreshadowed the techniques of film.

Anna Laura Zambrano

As noted earlier, the printed word is more than holding its own these days in spite of enormous competition from sources that were undreamed of less than a generation ago. And yet there are many whose experience of literature, especially "the classics," comes primarily from film and television. It is delivered in glossy packages from Hollywood, and in very tasteful packages from the BBC, but it is not the same experience as reading the original — which, for any number of reasons, many people choose not to do. Undoubtedly this says much about our popular culture, but it is at least both interesting and fun to acknowledge and celebrate these adaptations. However, it is an unfortunate viewer who, for example, knows the *Carol* solely through MGM's rather uninspired adaptation. Nevertheless it is a tribute to Dickens's genius that the essence of his story usually manages to shine through

even the most dreadful adaptations, and for this we should be thankful indeed. The message, however, is that there are all kinds of *Carols* out there — so let the viewer beware.

In this age of electronic *Carols* it is also important, and in a way rather humbling, to remember that the *Carol* has always been more than just a book; it is an integral part of our collective consciousness and always has been. The alternate means of dissemination may have changed over the past one hundred and fifty years, but long before the appearance of the first roll of cellulose nitrate film, or the first cathode ray tube, the *Carol* was finding ways to reach a large segment of the population that could neither read nor afford to buy the book.

Just over two weeks after its initial publication, a pirated edition of the *Carol* was selling in London for just a penny, and songs were written — and sheet music was sold! —

in its honor. Needless to say, theatrical adaptations were not far behind. As noted in Chapter Three, Dickens won his battle against *Parley's Illuminated Library* and its "reoriginated" version of the *Carol*, an outrageous copy which adhered to his story while simultaneously robbing it of its style, humor and sheer quality. Unfortunately, he wound up paying a heavy financial price for his victory. He paid a heavy physical and psychological toll as well, experiencing all manner of harassment from the pirates (Richard Egan Lee and Henry Hewitt) as well as extreme frustration with a legal system that eventually let the "vagabonds," as Dickens called them, off the financial hook. Regarding the option of taking action against piracy of his work, he would later write, "I shall not easily forget the expense, and anxiety, and horrible injustice of the *Carol* case, wherein, in asserting the plainest right on earth, I was really treated as if I were the robber instead of the robbed."[1]

While it would be wrong to suggest that Parley's *A Christmas Ghost Story* be treated as the first *Carol* adaptation—perhaps that honor belongs to some anonymous purchaser of the book who first read the *Carol* to his or her family over the 1843 holiday—the chicanery of Messrs. Lee and Hewitt, and their brazen defense of it, nevertheless gave Dickens much to think about in this initial period of *Carol* adaptation. The gist of their argument was that they were actually benefiting Dickens by making both him and his work known to a broad, popular (and largely poor) audience that might otherwise be passed by.[2]

Scholars and historians have demonstrated beyond question that Hewitt and Lee were indeed the pirates and vagabonds that Dickens claimed them to be. Nevertheless there was an ironic morsel of truth in their assertion that they were really Dickens's benefactors and not his enemies. Dickens was justifiably proud of pointing out that he "earned his bread," and his great success, through his own honest hard work and talent; indeed, were he an American, it would be difficult to imagine a more perfect embodiment of the classic American Dream in action. But while he enjoyed his success, and was in fact not above maintaining a certain kind of distance between himself and the lower classes, he never lost sight of where he came from. In all of his work, perhaps in the *Carol* (and also *The Chimes*) most of all, he attempted to speak up for a vast multitude that was far worse off than he had ever been.

This same irony—the fact that his work was reaching the mass audience that he wanted to help, albeit in a vulgarized version from which he received little or no financial compensation—was even more clearly in evidence in the burst of theatrical adaptations that followed the *Carol's* publication. It is here that the story of the *Carol's* considerable pre-cinema life begins.

By the time that *A Christmas Carol* arrived on the scene in late 1843, the practice of adapting a popular novel for the stage had become fairly common. Dickens himself had a passionate interest in the theatre throughout his entire life, and undoubtedly saw many such adaptations prior to beginning his own writing career. The practice of dramatizing Dickens had also become fairly common, with some stage versions appearing before a novel had finished its serial appearance, and multiple productions often competing for the public's attention. Unfortunately, Dickens lacked the kind of copyright protection that is available to writers today, and his works were freely pillaged by enterprising playwrights. As a result, his stories were often vulgarized and trivialized beyond recognition; he also rarely received any share of the profits that they generated. He did, however, quickly realize that it was impossible to prevent all unauthorized adaptations and thus sometimes offered certain playwrights various forms of assistance with their adaptations, thus creating a quasi-official version that he hoped would leave the rest of the pack in its wake.

As an indication of his early popularity,

it is interesting to note that one of Dickens's very first pieces, "The Bloomsbury Christening" (reprinted in *Sketches by Boz*), was very loosely dramatized not long after it first appeared in print. And, of course, theatrical adaptations from *Pickwick* were part of the phenomenally popular reception afforded Dickens's first novel. (Regarding the explosion of "Boz mania" that surrounded *Pickwick's* release, the distinguished Dickens scholar Robert L. Patten tells us, "There were Pickwick hats, canes, cigars, fabrics, coats, song books, china figurines, Weller corduroys and jest books, and Boz cabs. There were imitations, plagiarisms, parodies, sequels, extra illustrations, Pickwick quadrilles, stage piracies and adaptations."[3]) Some of Dickens's other pre–*Carol* works had also received considerable attention from the playwrights, with *Nicholas Nickleby* and *Oliver Twist* emerging as early favorites.

We see, then, that the commercialization of the *Carol* was by no means without precedent, and it comes as no surprise to find that three theatrical adaptations premiered on February 5, 1844: Edward Stirling's *A Christmas Carol, or, Past, Present, and Future*, C. Z. Barnett's *A Christmas Carol; or, The Miser's Warning*, and Charles Webb's *Old Scrooge; or, The Miser's Dream*; by mid–February, five more productions appeared. (Discussions of these early plays can be confusing since a number of title variations have been recorded, a situation which can also make the already difficult task of determining whether one is dealing with an original play, or yet another production of an existing play, even more difficult.)

Of this group, the Stirling production was the only one that claimed to have been approved by Dickens; and in a letter to his friend John Forster, Dickens actually gave it a tolerable "review": "…better than usual, … but heart-breaking to me. Oh Heaven! if any forecast of this was ever in my mind! Yet O. Smith [as Scrooge] was drearily better than I expected. It is a great comfort to have

that kind of meat underdone; and his face is quite perfect."[4] Interestingly, the Webb version was initially more popular than the "official" Stirling version; it appears to have been the basis for at least four of these early productions.[5]

Before touching on the subject of theatrical adaptations, tribute must be paid to H. Philip Bolton's remarkable *Dickens Dramatized*, a prodigious reference work which chronicles roughly 3,000 productions of Dickens's works that have appeared between the years 1834 and 1984. (As Bolton himself makes clear, this figure is very conservative!) While this work is particularly strong regarding theatrical versions, Bolton makes the case for the significance of all types of adaptations:

> The dramatic adaptation of his [Dickens's] novels and stories has probably been the single most effective means of spreading his fame far throughout the world, and down to the lowest, largest, and least literate classes. The record of the plays, films, radio and television productions from his novels is probably the best single measure of his popular posterity.[6]

In light of this initial burst of activity on the boards, and of the *Carol's* enormous popularity and longevity, it can be rather shocking to discover that after the mid–1840s there was a marked decline in the number of *Carol* adaptations. One finds, in fact, only a relative handful of revivals prior to the turn of the century. Thus the *Carol* was actually one of the least dramatized of Dickens's works, even failing to garner much interest in the 1870s when, following his death, there was a tremendous resurgence of interest in dramatizing Dickens.

Of his *Christmas Books*, *The Cricket on the Hearth* was by far the most widely and successfully dramatized in Dickens's lifetime; its theatrical popularity, in fact, extended well into the twentieth century. (As a book, *Cricket* was not well liked by the critics, but it did enjoy great popular success and out-sold both its predecessors in the Christmas Book genre, the *Carol* and *The Chimes*.) Along with its fairy-tale aura, *Cricket* contains a good deal of what might be termed domestic melodrama, and it is interesting to note that it was this domestic aspect — i.e., the Cratchits — that many Victorians felt was the real focus of the *Carol*. That being the case, it is indeed surprising that the *Carol* was not adapted more often in the nineteenth century.

In this context, it is possible that Dickens may have stolen some of his would-be competitor's thunder by making *A Christmas Carol* the definitive item in his repertoire when he decided to embark on a very successful second career of public readings from his works. The term "readings" can actually be a bit misleading, because Dickens did much more than simply get up in front of a crowd and read a book. To a great extent, much of what he did can be looked at in the light of his love of the theatre and acting; his interests in this area can be traced back to childhood. He also wrote several plays and supervised and acted in a number of ambitious amateur productions throughout his lifetime and, by all accounts, was a very good actor. What apparently took place at these readings was an actual performance, a dramatic interpretation with Dickens bringing each character to life via a skillful blending of vocal characterization and physical expression.

For several years Dickens had been in the habit of favoring small groups of friends with private readings (in essence a "sneak preview") from new works. Significantly, it was the *Carol* that he chose for his subject when he gave his first public reading, for charity, in December of 1853. It was also the focal point of his presentation when he began reading professionally (for pay) in the spring of 1858, as it was for his farewell performance shortly before his death in 1870. After a process of continuous shortening of his text, Dickens eventually arrived at a

version of the *Carol* that lasted about ninety minutes, although contemporary reports tell us that no two performances were ever exactly the same.

The definitive source of information on all of Dickens's readings is Philip Collins's meticulously edited *Charles Dickens: The Public Readings*. Readers should also see his *A Christmas Carol: The Public Reading Version*, a fascinating facsimile edition of Dickens's own "prompt-copy" from which he read.[7] As testament to just how well received Dickens's *Carol* reading was, Collins tells us that he performed it 127 times in his reading career, second only in number of performances to *The Trial from Pickwick* which was a much shorter item and was, in fact, frequently paired with *The Carol* to form the definitive Dickens program. Significantly, Dickens also drew heavily upon his other Christmas works, primarily the *Christmas Stories*, for source material in many of his other readings.

As the text of the reading version indicates, Dickens eliminated most of the *Carol's* overt social criticism and focused more on what might be called its dramatic possibilities, with the Cratchits' memorable Christmas dinner serving as its center. Nevertheless, this necessary condensation did nothing to diminish the *Carol's* power. There is also much evidence to suggest that its message was in no way muted or compromised: For example, one American factory owner was so moved by witnessing Dickens's *Carol* reading that he decided to end his practice of opening his business on Christmas Day.[8] As Phillip Collins notes, "Reporters often asserted, too, that audiences left the hall, after hearing the *Carol*, better moral beings; unlike the other Readings, there was about this one an element of a rite, a religious affirmation."[9]

Apart from whatever competition may have been generated by the readings per se, many commentators have suggested that the dearth of early theatrical *Carols* can be at least partially explained by a general reluctance on

Depiction of Dickens's last public reading of the *Carol* shortly before his death. From March 19, 1870, issue of *The Illustrated London News*. Courtesy Dickens House Museum.

Oct. 23, 1901 THE SKETCH. 27

TWO CHRISTMAS-DINNER SCENES FROM "SCROOGE,"
AT THE VAUDEVILLE.

Ebenezer Scrooge   Tiny Tim   Bob Cratchit   Mrs. Cratchit   The Ghost of Jacob Marley
(Mr. Seymour Hicks).   (Master George Bernes).   (Mr. Compton Coutts).   (Miss Florence Lloyd).   (Mr. Harbottle Dixon).

"MR. SCROOGE, THE FOUNDER OF THE FEAST!"

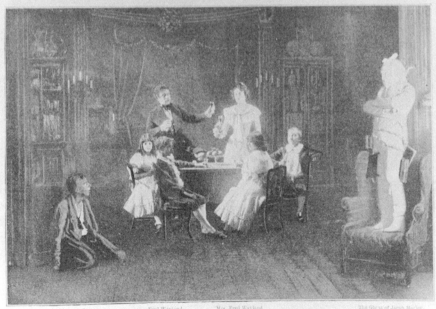

Ebenezer Scrooge.   Fred Wayland   Mrs. Fred Wayland   The Ghost of Jacob Marley
                               (Mr. Stanley Brett).   (Miss Hilda Antony).

"HERE'S THE OLD BOY'S HEALTH—UNCLE SCROOGE!"

From Photographs by Alfred Ellis and Walery, Baker Street, W.

the part of the Victorian public to embrace the dramatization of sacred material — and there is no question that for many readers in this period, the *Carol* was indeed considered a sacred text. This feeling was perhaps best summed up by one Edwin Charles, who, in a heartfelt 1909 letter to the editor of *The Dickensian*, objected to the *Carol's* upcoming appearance at London's Coliseum music hall: "I have no objection to music-halls, but I do not think they are fitted, either by the necessities of their programme or by their environment, for the exploitation of sacred subjects. I regard *A Christmas Carol* as a sacred subject, and I believe there are thousands of other Dickens worshippers who think with me in that respect. It is a sermon, amplifying and exemplifying Holy Writ itself, telling all in a practical and material manner of the newer and higher and holier duties of man to man which Christ came down on earth to teach."[10]

In a general sense, the fact that this sort of grumbling was taking place as late as 1909 suggests that the concept of the *Carol* as a sacred text was a deeply entrenched belief among many "Dickens worshippers." However, its expansion into the music hall seems to provide proof that the *Carol* was also wide open to interpretation, and that it had begun to spread its popular wings in the nearly four decades that had passed since Dickens's death.[11]

The most significant indicator of this new wave of popularity was its reemergence in the theatre via J. C. Buckstone's *Scrooge*, one of the most important of all plays derived from the *Carol*.[12] This adaptation premiered in London on October 3, 1901, at the Vaudeville Theatre. Interestingly, however, it was not the main event on the evening's theatrical bill of fare. Instead, Buckstone's one-act *Scrooge* was a warm up or curtain raiser for Basil Hood's three-act comedy *Sweet and Twenty* which had been playing at the

Vaudeville since April. Nevertheless, *Scrooge* caught the attention of the royal family, and a few weeks later a command performance was given at their Norfolk residence of Sandringham.

In condensing the story into a tight one-act in which the focus is kept very much on Ebenezer Scrooge, some interesting changes are in evidence. Scrooge's living quarters and office are combined at one location; the familiar pair of charity solicitors is replaced by one who is identified as Mr. Middlemark (he reappears in the Christmas Future vision and jokes with a Mr. Worthington about Scrooge's unlamented passing); and, most significantly, the traditional ghosts of Christmas Past, Present and Future do not appear. Instead, Jacob Marley's ghost presents all the visions to Scrooge. *The Illustrated London News* noted:

> Patrons of the Vaudeville Theatre should make a point of seeing its first piece — for here is an adaptation of Dickens's "Christmas Carol," which preserves the broad human sentiment of the original. Moreover, they will discover whence came the idea for "The Message from Mars" — the idea of a miserly egoist, converted by supernatural dream-pictures of his own unimportance and others' miseries. [The reference is to Richard Ganthony's 1899 play *A Message from Mars*, which is discussed in Chapter Nine.] The mechanism of the story may seem childish in the playhouse; but Mr. J. C. Buckstone has done his dramatization so neatly that the little parable should draw tears from the most stony-hearted. "Scrooge," too, provides some interesting acting: that of Mr. Holbrook Blinn, who makes a very sonorous Marley's Ghost; that of Mr. Seymour Hicks, whose thoughtful impersonation of Scrooge would be truly admirable if the actor could only govern his voice — it is rarely that of an old man — and avoid hysteria.[13]

Opposite: **Advertisement for J. C. Buckstone's *Scrooge* with Seymour Hicks. From October 23, 1901, issue of *The Sketch*.**

The Era was considerably harsher in its assessment of Hicks's performance:

> Expectation was rife as to how Mr Seymour Hicks would play the leading character. It was his first attempt in a part of this kind, and a bold venture. The task proved too difficult for his ability, and his representation of old age was not at all convincing; indeed, his Scrooge was obviously juvenile, and as a character impersonation decidedly amateurish.[14]

Nevertheless, *Scrooge* was the vehicle through which the popular actor Seymour Hicks became one of the most prominent Scrooges of this, or any other, era. This theatrical revival took place more or less concurrently with the infancy of the motion picture, and it is interesting to note that the premiere of the Buckstone play was followed a few weeks later by the first of many filmed versions of the *Carol*. (This first cinematic *Carol*, called *Scrooge; or Marley's Ghost*, is discussed in the next chapter. And, as we shall see, Seymour Hicks starred in film versions of the *Carol* in 1913 and 1935, both of which were entitled *Scrooge*. However, while all three draw heavily upon the Buckstone play, none represents a verbatim transfer of the play to the screen.)

As mentioned above, this period found the *Carol* alive and well not only in the theatre, but also in the less respectable arena of the music hall. The term *music hall* is used to describe a form of popular entertainment that emerged in England in the first half of the nineteenth century. Basically the equivalent of American vaudeville, it was the dominant form of popular entertainment in the late nineteenth and very early twentieth centuries. The term is also used to describe the physical place where this entertainment was presented; in the early days the music hall was basically part of a pub, while later halls were essentially large theatres.

The appeal of the music hall was largely that it offered an urban, working class audience a place to gather, to drink, and to see and hear a variety of indigenous popular entertainment — particularly comedians and comic or irreverent songs. (In Edwin Charles's letter quoted above, he feared that future generations would not take kindly to the *Carol* having been "put on as a music-hall turn between a comic song and a conjuring act.") In their youth, Charlie Chaplin and Stan Laurel performed in the halls; and, although not easily available in this country, American audiences can get a taste of earthy music hall humor in the films of such music hall stars turned film stars as George Formby, Gracie Fields, and Max Miller.

While the music halls were not designed to be a forum for the staging of dramatic productions (there was, in fact, early legislation which prohibited a direct encroachment onto the turf of the legitimate theatre), dramatic sketches and highlights from drama and literature eventually became a popular part of the music hall repertoire. In this context, Seymour Hicks brought his own version of the Buckstone play into the music hall in the form of a considerably condensed one man tour-de-force which focused entirely on the character of Scrooge.

The other major Scrooge of the day was Bransby Williams, whose association with Dickens, and in particular the character of Scrooge, was virtually a lifelong phenomenon. Speaking at a 1955 dinner honoring the 143rd anniversary of Dickens's birth, Charlie Chaplin remembered seeing Williams perform and recalled the event as "enlivening a young boy's interest in literature" (Chaplin was eight years old at the time). "I stood there enthralled," Chaplin said, "as I watched a world for the first time, a new world of romance, mystery and wonderment, enacted by a very handsome gentleman imitating characters from Charles Dickens."[15]

Williams appeared as Scrooge as early as 1896, and by the very *Carol* conscious year of 1901 he was busy in the halls. Of his performance at The Tivoli *The Era* noted: "A touch of sentiment is imported to the bill by

Top: Bransby Williams as Scrooge ca. 1905. Courtesy Dickens House Museum. *Bottom:* Advertisement from January 4, 1902, issue of *The Era.*

Mr Bransby Williams, who as the Scrooge of Dickens's 'Christmas Carol' preaches the lesson of charity in a forcible way. With a cunning make-up as the old skinflint, Mr Williams delivers his lines with dramatic excellence, while the dignity of the regenerated miser is impressively suggested."[16] *The Era* was also in attendance at the London Pavilion: "A happy revival ... is *Scrooge*, in which monologue Mr Bransby Williams has compressed the pith and purpose of Charles Dickens's 'Christmas Carol.' The lesson of charity and goodwill cannot be repeated too often. It is always worth hearing, especially when it enables one to renew acquaintance with Mr Williams's Scrooge — an impersonation that is hardly second in merit to his Sydney Carton or his aged grandfather in 'The Old Curiosity Shop.'"[17]

The script of Williams's solo version of the *Carol*, which runs about four pages in length, can be found in his 1913 book entitled *My Sketches from Dickens*. He refers to it as a monologue, as opposed to his even shorter character sketches. However, in spite of its brevity, it is a remarkably effective piece which is clearly intended to convey the basic essence or idea of the *Carol* by triggering a response from those who know the complete story. As he tells us in his introduction: "In 'Scrooge' (which can be done as a recital) there is first the idea of the man — endeavoring to show the hard-faced, bitter old miser before his dream, the horror and fear during the dream, and then the great change in face, body and voice, etc., after the dream; in fact, the contrast to the opening should be a beaming, merry old gentleman."[18]

Williams was also one of the very first to make a recording based on the *Carol*. His 1905 Edison cylinder recording, entitled *The Awakening of Scrooge*, is a remarkably effective compression of the reborn Scrooge's memorable "morning after." As we shall see, Williams also figured in landmark British film and television productions of the story. Other important interpreters of Dickens

in this period, although not necessarily "Scrooge specialists" like Hicks and Williams, included Thomas Bentley and Tom Terriss; both, especially Bentley, would also try their hand at bringing Dickens to the screen. (In recent years, the "one man show" approach to the *Carol* has been brilliantly revived, but on a much more sophisticated level, by English actor Patrick Stewart.)

Over the next few decades, theatrical adaptations (and, of course, films) regularly appeared, but the greatest number of adaptations are found after World War Two. In fact, the last twenty-five to thirty years have witnessed an astonishing avalanche of theatrical *Carols*, usually with music and songs, so many that it is impossible to count them all. These productions range from the recent extravaganzas at The Paramount, Madison Square Garden in New York, to numerous national and regional touring companies that offer up their own interpretations every season, to countless quasi-professional and amateur productions that are staged every December in high school auditoriums and local playhouses. A fascinating cluster of theatrical adaptations, all of which are discussed later, even found its way onto television from the late-seventies through the mid-eighties. (This group of televised plays includes adaptations that were staged at three of the nation's most prestigious theatrical venues, Ford's Theatre in Washington, D.C., the Guthrie Theater in Minneapolis, and the American Conservatory Theatre in San Francisco; all three were aired nationally. It also includes one that was broadcast locally from Kent State University in Ohio, and another that was staged, and later broadcast nationally, at a Minneapolis church. And, as part of this practice of merging art forms, one finds two operas and a ballet version in this period as well.)

What is interesting is that amidst all the theatrical *Carols* that have proliferated in what we might call the modern era of its life on the stage, no single adaptation or script

A Christmas Carol (1994): Walter Charles as Scrooge (left) and Jeff Keller as Marley's Ghost in spectacular musical version staged at The Paramount, Madison Square Garden, in New York. Courtesy Photofest.

has emerged as definitive in the way that Lionel Bart's *Oliver!* has with *Oliver Twist*. In a sense this is probably best in that it helps keep the story open to exploration and fresh ideas. In reference to one of his *Carol* readings, Dickens once wrote: "I never beheld such a rapturous audience. And they — and the stage together: which I never can resist — made me do such a vast number of new things in the Carol, that Arthur [Arthur Smith, manager of Dickens's reading tours] and our men stood in amazement at the Wing, and roared and stamped as if it were an entirely new book, topping all the others. You must come to some good place and hear the Carol. I think you will hardly know it again."[19] That is the challenge faced by all modern adapters: to look for something "new" in the *Carol*. And for the modern audience, there is always the hope that an enterprising playwright, a creative

director, a brilliant actor, or a visionary set designer will find it.

If one had to come up with a single word that would provide a convenient umbrella description of the various pre-cinema incarnations of the *Carol* that have been sampled thus far, it might be fair to say that they are all theatrical in nature. Plays, music hall sketches, and readings (by Dickens or another) primarily involve one or more human beings getting up in front of an audience and presenting a "living" interpretation of the story. There is, however, one final means of expression to be considered in the extensive pre-cinema life of the *Carol*. It was theatrical in the sense that it was presented to a live audience, and that it required the involvement of at least one person or performer to make it happen. (It should be added, however, that in many cases, that one person was a great showman.) But, its foundation, its modus operandi — in truth, its heart — was highly cinematic. It is the source of some of the most fascinating and yet virtually unknown Dickensian adaptations ever produced, and the medium that exerted the most direct influence on the fledgling motion picture industry that we will meet in the next chapter. It is the predecessor of the movies and television and videos that we take so much for granted today. Its name? The magic lantern.

The forerunner of our modern slide projector, the magic lantern can be traced back to the mid-seventeenth century. Its invention has traditionally been attributed to the German Jesuit Athanasius Kircher; recent scholarship, however, credits the Dutchman Christian Huygens with being the first to actually produce a working projector. But what is most interesting for our purposes is just how quickly the magic lantern's potential for "putting on a show" was realized. In the 1660s the Dane Thomas Rasmussen Walgensten began touring Europe with his magic lantern exhibitions, the first in a long tradition of traveling lanternists. And by the end of the eighteenth century the Belgian Étienne Gaspard Robert (aka Robertson) brought magic lantern entertainment into the big time with his "Fantasmagorie," which, long before the birth of horror films and Alfred Hitchcock, thrilled and chilled audiences with horrific images and dazzling special effects.

Few of us today realize that long before the advent of motion pictures, people were accustomed to gathering in theatres, town halls, schools, churches, and tents to watch a succession of images that, in one way or another, told a story; the magic lantern made this possible. Similarly, long before the advent of television, they also gathered in the parlors of private homes, and it is interesting to note that in Angus Wilson's *The World of Charles Dickens* we learn that Dickens was exposed to the magic lantern at a very early age. From young Charles's nurse, Mary Weller, we learn that "little Charles was a terrible boy to read," and that "sometimes Charles would come downstairs and say to me, 'Now Mary, clear the kitchen, we are going to have such a game,' and then George Stroughill would come in with his Magic Lantern, and they would sing, recite and perform parts of plays."[20] We are reminded here that books and theatre (and the basic need to have some fun in life) were powerful influences, primordial forces, throughout Dickens's life. There is no evidence to suggest that he was in any way directly influenced by the magic lantern, but it is interesting to think of this early meeting, a felicitous crossing of paths between a boy and an optical device, both of whom would go on to become great storytellers. (In the context of his journalism, Dickens does make reference to other pre-cinematic devices such as the Diorama and the Panorama, but there do not appear to be any corresponding references to professional magic lantern shows in any of his public or private writings. It seems inconceivable, however, that he did not see at least one professional magic lantern show as an adult.)

For present purposes, it is also interesting to note that the home of a young writer was among those illuminated by the magic lantern in the last century. On the last day of December 1842, Dickens wrote to his American friend Cornelius Felton, and among the topics covered were his plans for an upcoming party: "The actuary of the National Debt couldn't calculate the number of children who are coming here on Twelfth Night, in honor of Charley's [his eldest child's] birthday, for which occasion I have provided a Magic Lantern and divers other tremendous engines of that nature."[21] (Whether Dickens hired a professional lanternist or handled the projectionist's chores himself with an amateur model lantern is unclear. However, throughout his life he was what might be termed a "hands on" entertainer and, given his well-documented skill as an actor and a public reader of his own works, there is every reason to believe that he would have made an excellent magic lanternist had he chosen to do so. He was also an accomplished magician, and this letter goes on to detail that the highlight of the evening would be an exhibition of his conjuring skills. A fascinating account of the relationship between the magician and both the magic lantern and the cinema will be found in Erik Barnouw's *The Magician and the Cinema*.[22])

The basic idea behind the magic lantern is simple: An image that has been fixed on a transparent surface is projected onto a screen by means of a light source and a series of lenses. It bears a striking resemblance to the basic idea behind the motion picture projector. And as with motion picture technology, there was a constant process of refinement, particularly in the areas of improved optics and sources of illumination, all of which contributed to a bigger and brighter projected image.

We pause here to note that the magic lantern was not the only front on which the battle to achieve pictures that moved was being waged. Indeed, even a cursory overview of the history of nineteenth century science and technology reveals that the subject was addressed elsewhere — and often more consciously and directly — throughout the entire century. However, the seemingly simple question of "Who invented the movies?" requires an answer that is anything but simple. For present purposes, let us simply note that the quest basically took interested parties down two separate paths — sometimes parallel, sometimes intersecting.

On the one hand, we have the birth and development of photography: Start with the pioneering work of Wedgwood, Niépce, Daguerre and Fox Talbot in the first half of the century. Around mid-century it became possible to fix a photographic image on

transparent glass plates, a development that was not lost on magic lanternists. Late in the century, the development of flexible roll film supplied one of the last and most important pieces of the puzzle.

On the other hand, we have the work of various inventors and optical or mechanical thinkers and tinkerers: Start with Roget's discussion of the persistence of vision and then witness the succession of ingenious precinematic devices that it inspired, such as the Thaumatrope, the Phenakistoscope, the Zoetrope, the Praxinoscope, and others. And to the pioneering work in motion analysis of Marey and Muybridge, add the efforts of those who struggled (usually in vain) to produce workable cameras and projectors: Lumière, Le Prince, Edison, Dickson, Friese Greene, et al.

These two paths would converge, and then merge, in the last twenty years or so of the century. The result of this merger would eventually become known as the movies. The point here, however, is that while the magic lantern was indeed a major player in the pre-history of the movies, developments in magic lantern techniques and technology, like so many other things discussed in this book, did not take place in a vacuum.[23]

And now back to our magic lantern show: Also contributing greatly to the ever-increasing sophistication and entertainment potential of magic lantern shows were constant improvements to the slides themselves. Most early slides were long strips of wood-framed glass containing several images that were painted directly onto the glass; eventually, however, the single-subject slide became the norm. Improvements in painting techniques and materials resulted in images of astonishing complexity and beauty, and, as noted above, by the mid-nineteenth century advancements in still photography made it possible to project actual photographic images that had been fixed on glass

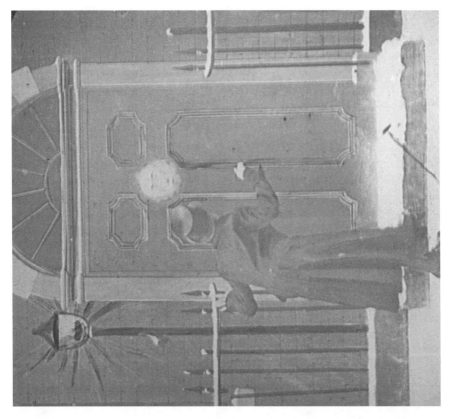

Pages 52–54, *Marley's Ghost* (Twenty-five slide life model version of the "Carol" produced by Frederick York, England, 1880; slides were hand colored at time of initial release). *Above left:* Scrooge's office on Christmas Eve. *Right:* Scrooge sees Marley's Ghost in the doorknocker.

Above left: Scrooge and Marley's Ghost. *Right:* Scrooge and the Ghost of Christmas Past.

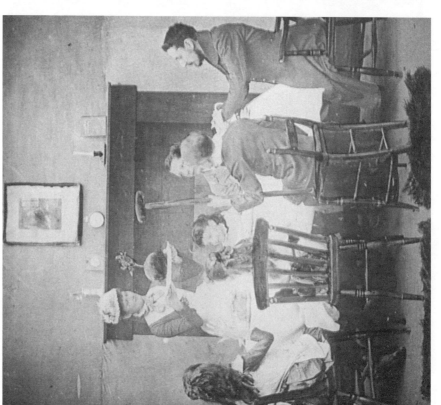

Above left: The Cratchits' Christmas dinner. *Right:* Scrooge and the Ghost of Christmas Future.

slides. Underscoring the magic lantern's potential to educate as well as entertain, this latter development enabled audiences to enjoy views of foreign lands and exotic locales that few could ever hope to visit for themselves. Perhaps most importantly of all, many of these slides were animated — i.e., they moved.

In this context — the context of motion — the most obvious weapon in the magic lanternist's arsenal was the mechanical slide. For example, a variety of geared and levered slides enabled windmills to turn and children on swings to swing, and slip slides depicted movement by sliding a movable piece of glass across another that remained stationary. Chromotrope slides produced spectacular kaleidoscopic effects and, pre-dating the psychedelic visuals made possible in the 1960s and 1970s with liquid overhead projection, tank slides produced swirling masses of moving color by injecting colored dyes into specially designed slides filled with water. Thus projected images and movement were linked together long before the birth of the movies.

But for anyone who finds this connection vague or indirect, please note that many visual effects and storytelling techniques that are generally assumed to be the exclusive province of the motion picture, and later television, were actually inherited from the magic lantern. The familiar pan or panning shot, for example, in which the camera moves horizontally from left to right or right to left, was easily achieved by pulling (slowly and smoothly!) a long horizontal slide through the projector. And in the nineteenth century, expanding technology also enabled the lanternist to achieve sophisticated visual effects, such as the dissolve in which one image slowly fades out as another fades in, by using two projectors in tandem. Similarly, the use of two projectors made it possible to cut directly from one slide to the next in much the same way in which a film director cuts from one shot to another. Later, the spectacular biunal and triunal models

enabled the lanternist to achieve such effects (and much more) with a single projector. For the expert lanternist armed with an assortment of conventional and mechanical slides and a triunal projector, the creative possibilities were virtually endless, and all types of magic lantern shows were successfully staged throughout the world.

However, within the context of pre-cinematic literary adaptations, two types of slides — both of the non-mechanical variety — are of particular interest. The first were known as life model slides. As the name suggests, this approach eschewed the common practice of projecting an artist's rendering, or even conventional photographic slides. Instead these slides used live models (in effect actors) who, anticipating the methods utilized by early motion picture producers, were photographed on sets with painted backdrops. While never very successful in America, life model slides were extremely popular in England and, underscoring the direct connection that exists between the magic lantern and the early cinema, some slide manufacturers eventually branched into motion picture production. The Yorkshire firm of Bamforth and Co., Ltd., for example, which began producing slides and postcards in 1870, was arguably the most important of these pioneering producers. Of the many types of life model slides that were available, adaptations of well known stories and works of literature were very popular. *A Christmas Carol* and *The Cricket on the Hearth* were among those brought to life in this manner.

In spite of the obviously cinematic "look" of the life model approach, the most subtly cinematic lantern slides were those produced in Philadelphia, in the late nineteenth and early twentieth centuries, by the firm of [Casper W.] Briggs and Company from original drawings by the American artist and illustrator Joseph Boggs Beale. Beale's original artwork, which was specifically designed and intended to be viewed as a projected image, was photographed, reduced and then

Pages 56–58, *Marley's Ghost* (Briggs and Company, United States, from original artwork by Joseph Boggs Beale, ca. 1908; slides were hand colored at time of initial release. Courtesy the Beale Collection). *Top:* Scrooge sees Marley's Ghost in the doorknocker. *Bottom:* Christmas Past, Fezziwig's party.

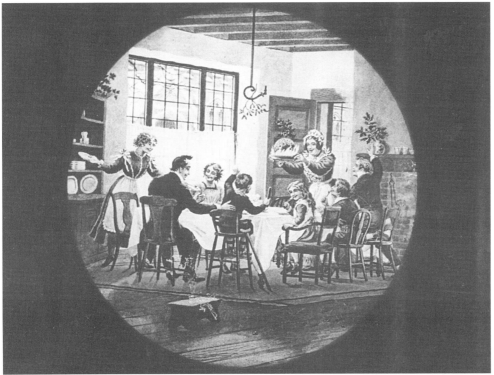

Top: **Scrooge meets the Ghost of Christmas Present.** *Bottom:* **The Cratchits' Christmas dinner.**

Top: Scrooge and the Ghost of Christmas Future. *Bottom:* A new Scrooge on Christmas morning; note the smiling doorknocker.

Magic Lantern special effects: In Christmas Past, Scrooge looks on as his younger self finds companionship in a book (below). When slide of Ali Baba (above) is superimposed over top portion of image, the effect suggests the young boy's imagination at work. Such effects could be achieved with the use of two magic lanterns, or with biunal or triunal models. (A triunal model is pictured at left.) All images courtesy the Beale Collection.

transferred onto glass slides; from there, multiple copies were hand colored and then sold.

Briggs had a plan that was both ambitious and farsighted: to build the world's foremost library of slides based on well known historical, literary, and biblical stories and themes. Moreover, he wanted to avoid the constraints inherent in most earlier illustrated readings. Previously, the general practice in the United States, when illustrating a poem or story, was to utilize a single scene or image (on some occasions two or three) that in some sense conveyed the essence of a work; the effect was not unlike that produced by the frontispiece of a book. With this practice, lanternists were generally restricted to short works or heavily abridged selections from longer ones. Briggs, however, was interested in telling a complete narrative through a sequence of anywhere from eight to twenty-four images. As magic lantern historian and modern day lanternist Terry Borton puts it: "The existing images were episodic; they did not *tell a story* with a visual beginning, middle, and end. The existing images froze a moment in time; Briggs wanted the story itself to move, to be, as it were, a 'movie.'"[24]

And move they did, though not with the absolute movement made technically possible by motion pictures. Instead, Beale infused his illustrations with a decidedly cinematic sense of composition and exposition, as well as an obvious familiarity with the style and conventions of contemporary theatre. His images, in tandem with the lanternist's reading, moved with the kind of narrative progression associated with watching a motion picture. To put it another way, through an implosion of words and images, a narrative, indeed a movie, was created in the mind of each individual viewer. In this context, a Beale version of the *Carol* entitled *Marley's Ghost* appeared toward the end of the magic lantern era ca. 1908; it consisted of twenty-five slides (or, to put it in cinematic terms, twenty-five shots).

As a footnote to this discussion of magic lantern *Carols*, it is interesting to note that decades later — in the 1940s and the 1960s to be precise — two popular American magazines offered a brief return of sorts to the magic lantern era. In 1944, *Life* ran what it called a "photographic essay" in which a condensed version of the story was illustrated with a series of black-and-white photographs depicting various scenes from the story; Lionel Barrymore was Scrooge in this most unusual adaptation. And in 1964, *The Saturday Evening Post* offered a very similar treatment, this time with color photographs, in what it called "an original photographic version" of the story; Trevor Howard starred as both Scrooge and Marley. In both cases we find, in effect, modern, life model versions of the *Carol*.[25]

The magic lantern was nearly two hundred and fifty years old when it reached its heyday in the 1890s — a decade that also witnessed the formal introduction of "the movies." While specialists in this area have always been aware of the magic lantern's relationship to the motion picture, that relationship has traditionally been thought of in the context of developments in technology: The magic lantern — i.e., the physical hardware used to throw light upon a screen — is an obvious (and obviously older) relative of the motion picture projector. However, current film scholarship reminds us that the magic lantern told stories, and that the storytelling techniques that it pioneered had a profound influence on the cinema that followed. Film historian Charles Musser, who has been at the forefront of shedding important new light on this aspect of early cinema, suggests that the true significance of the magic lantern will not be found in a history of mechanical and optical devices, but rather in what he calls a history of *screen practice*: "In such a history, cinema appears as a continuation and transformation of magic lantern traditions in which showmen displayed images on a screen, accompanying them with voice, music, and sound effects."[26] However, as so often happens, this kind of continuation and transformation, this progress, came with a price tag. The cost in this case was the death of the magic lantern.

As noted above, motion pictures as we know them burst onto the world stage in the latter part of the nineteenth century. The December 28, 1895, presentation by Louis and Auguste Lumière in Paris is generally cited as the "official" premiere. This new form of entertainment developed and expanded rapidly, although its success and longevity were by no means guaranteed from the start. Nevertheless, by the end of the first decade of the twentieth century, the motion picture had evolved from a novelty shown on single-viewer Kinetoscope machines to a staple of the American entertainment diet shown in storefront theatres known as Nickelodeons; and the lavish picture palaces of legend lay just around the corner.

But the magic lantern did not go out quietly. As the new film theatres became more and more popular, so too did song slides, which were used to interpret and illustrate contemporary popular songs. Just as MTV hopes to entice today's viewers into buying cassettes and compact discs, song slides were intended to sell sheet music. We continue to be reminded that very little, if anything, is new. Today MTV offers audiovisual interpretations of the latest hits; *Soundies*, musical shorts viewed on "jukebox" machines via 16mm film, did it in the 1940s; and the magic lantern did it before that.

Of course the magic lantern itself never actually died out completely. Its offspring, the modern slide projector, has grown and evolved throughout the twentieth century. It is true that, whether for entertainment or educational purposes, slides are constantly being threatened by other media; film and video are the two prime offenders here. And yet, the slide show endures: In the face of the camcorder revolution, images from last year's trip to Disneyland continue to illuminate living room walls across the country, while at the other end of the spectrum ultra-sophisticated multi-image shows, employing banks of computer controlled Kodak Carousel projectors, electrify audiences with a stunning blend of high-tech sight and sound. But, sad to say, few of us today are aware that the "old-fashioned" magic lantern did it first; and, as noted earlier, fewer still realize that it gave us the first audiovisual Dickens adaptations — including, of course, the first such adaptations of the *Carol*. In doing so, the magic lantern paved the way for the film and television *Carols* that we look forward to each December. For that story, as the Ghost of Christmas Past said to Scrooge in what most observers agree is the greatest of all filmed *Carols*, we do but turn another page.

Silent Film

*Among the barren wastes of the talking films there occasionally occur
passages to remind one again of the profound and suggestive power
of the silent film to evoke an ideal world of beauty, to release unsus-
pected floods of music from the gaze of a human countenance in its
prison of silver light.*

Joseph Cornell

If only things happened in real life the way they do in the movies! If they did, then this section would begin with a proclamation that the very first motion picture ever made was an adaptation of Charles Dickens's *A Christmas Carol*; or, short of that fortuitous coincidence, that the first cinematic adaptation of a Dickens work was a version of the *Carol*. Well, however one chooses to define what qualifies as the first motion picture ever made, we do know that it was not drawn from the *Carol*. However, regarding the latter possibility, we *almost* hit the bulls-eye, because in November of 1901 the British film pioneer Robert W. Paul released a version of the *Carol* entitled *Scrooge; or Marley's Ghost*. Interestingly, it was released concurrently with another Dickensian adaptation entitled *Mr Pickwick's Christmas at Wardle's*.

The film which appears to win the prize for the first Dickensian adaptation on screen was an 1897 American Mutoscope production, entitled *Death of Nancy Sykes* [sic]; the second Dickensian film appears to be an 1898 British effort, also from Robert W. Paul, entitled *Mr Bumble the Beadle*. It is not surprising that the first Dickens films would be drawn from *Oliver Twist*. After all, if we accept the premise that the *Carol* is Dickens's most popular and best known work, a strong case can be made for *Oliver Twist* as second in terms of overall popularity and recognition value with the general public. In surveying the decades that have passed since their initial publication we do, in fact, witness the *Carol* and *Oliver* battling it out at various times for supremacy in terms of their respective "adaptability" by other media.

To attempt a chronological survey of the various motion picture adaptations of the *Carol* that have proliferated over the years, it is of course necessary to begin with the earliest known version, which, as we have just seen, was released in 1901. However, since this puts us very close to the beginning of film history — a period that is either virtually unknown or grossly misunderstood by non-devotees of the silent film — it might be advisable to lay a little groundwork before proceeding.

The note of uncertainty that is present in the preceding paragraphs — the first Dickensian film adaptation *appears* to be *Death of Nancy Sykes*; the first *known* version of the *Carol* was *Scrooge; or Marley's Ghost*—is not there by accident. If we define "the movies" as moving images projected on a large screen in front of a paying audience, then the movies have been with us for just over one hundred years. Also, the movement to recognize film as an art, and to document, preserve, exhibit and study it as such, has been in full vigor for about thirty-five to forty years now. And yet even at this late date there is much that we simply don't know about the early days of film history, and the primary reason for this is the simple fact that most of the films no longer exist. That being the case, it is both difficult and dangerous to make definitive claims about film firsts. It is, for example, a brave film historian who would claim that a particular film contains the "first" close-up, or for that matter the first anything, because there is always the chance that an earlier and previously unavailable film will turn up and prove him wrong.

Then, as now, motion pictures were a commercial commodity; their ultimate function was to lure an audience into laying down its money, and once the last penny had been squeezed out of a film, there was usually little or no thought given to preserving it for posterity. Throughout the silent era thousands of films simply disappeared for a variety of reasons.

Virtually all films intended for the theatrical marketplace were shot and released on 35mm film; this has always been the professional standard and is identical in width to the film used in the still cameras that most of us are familiar with. However, prior to the early fifties, these films were released on cellulose-nitrate film stock — commonly referred to as nitrate film — which is highly susceptible to both fire and chemical decomposition. The sad result is that a staggering number of silent films have literally gone up in smoke and flames or deteriorated, first into a gelatinous mass of foul-smelling goo, and then into a pile of dust. Compounding this problem was the fact that many films were routinely destroyed to free up storage space or to recover the particles of silver that they contained.

But in spite of the fact that so many silent films are not available for viewing, much research has been accomplished on this period of film history. There have, for example, been more definitive books written about the silent period than about any other era of film history; and by searching through reviews and notices in newspapers and trade publications, copyright records, and the surviving records and catalogs of the production companies themselves, film archivists and scholars have been able to compile an astonishing amount of documentation as to exactly what was made even if the actual films themselves no longer exist.

Nevertheless, despite this excellent documentation, we have no way of knowing how many titles may have eluded the net of even the most meticulous researchers. As such, we may learn someday that somewhere someone produced a version of the *Carol* in 1897 or 1900; but until that happy day arrives, let the record show that the first filmed version of Charles Dickens's *A Christmas Carol* was a 1901 British effort entitled *Scrooge; or Marley's Ghost*.

What was the film like? Before answering that question a little more groundwork is probably in order because however much information the experts may compile, the silent film remains shrouded in mystery and misinformation for most people. Ask the proverbial man on the street what he thinks of silent movies — if indeed he has ever thought of them at all — and a very predictable litany of negativity is sure to follow: crude, primitive artifacts from another age that have no relation to the ultra-sophisticated films that we know today; a quaint conglomeration of herky-jerky exaggerated motion, resplendent in scratchy, fuzzy, black-and-white — and all to the tune of a tinny tinkling piano. And of course let's not forget the silly pratfalls, or the naive heroine, perpetually helpless and preyed upon by an evil, mustachioed villain. Such is the stuff that myths are made of, but in the case of the silent film, the myths bear no relation whatsoever to the truth.

The fact is that most of the rules by which movies are made were written and defined in the silent era. The films, including the very earliest ones, were as clear and sharp as anything made today. When we see an "old-time movie" that is soft or fuzzy, too light or too dark, or filled with scratches, it simply means that we are looking at a poor copy that may be several generations removed from the original.

Silent films were generally not black-and-white. Throughout this period a variety of methods were employed to add color to the films. It was first added by hand, meticulously painted frame by frame; later an elaborate stencil process was employed. Beautiful effects were also achieved by tinting and toning the films with hues that matched the prevailing mood or content of a scene — blue for night, shades of red for a battle or a passionate love scene. Perhaps the most common "look" was a rich amber tone, not unlike the sepia-toned photographs of great-grandpa that now reside in many family archives. Experiments were also carried out with actual color cinematography, including early versions of the Technicolor process that

eventually brought full color to the movies in the 1930s.

Also worth dispensing with is the notion that silent films moved too fast. In truth, their look and rate of movement was perfectly normal. Complications arise, however, because there was not a standard speed at which silent films were shot and projected; speeds could generally vary from twelve to eighteen frames per second although they tended to get a bit faster as the period wore on. Further complicating matters for the modern viewer is the fact that many directors shot portions of the same film at different speeds in order to achieve a desired effect — the most obvious, perhaps, being speeded up motion for a *deliberately exaggerated* comic effect.

Where problems have traditionally arisen is that modern audiences usually see silent films projected on a modern projector that is capable of running only at today's standard speed of twenty-four frames per second, a speed established for technical reasons when sound films were perfected. (Variable speed projectors are available today, but it is a safe bet that the average college, school or library will not be using one.) Hence, most of today's viewers believe that silent films moved at an unreal pace, a falsehood given even more credence by the fact that when silent films are shown on television, the even faster video speed of thirty frames per second can make them look even more ridiculous.

Fortunately, there has been a tremendous surge of interest in silent films in recent years, and new technology has made it possible for many titles to be released at their proper speed on video tape and laser disc. The short of it is that when one sees a silent film that is obviously moving too fast, it is simply being shown at the wrong speed; there is nothing wrong with the film and one should not draw any conclusions as to the look or pace of silent films in general.

And finally, let's dispense with the obvious: Silent movies were never silent. (This

CHRISTMAS, 1901.

NEW AND SEASONABLE FILM SUBJECTS.

SCROOGE;

OR,

MARLEY'S GHOST

AS PLAYED BEFORE

THE KING AND QUEEN,

BY ROYAL COMMAND,

AT SANDRINGHAM.

IN TWELVE ANIMATED TABLEAUX.

1. Christmas Eve at Scrooge and Marley's. Scrooge, whose partner, Marley, has been dead some years, is engaged in his office. His ill-paid clerk, Bob Cratchitt, is endeavouring to keep warm. Scrooge's nephew vainly invites him to dinner on Christmas Day. A charity collector meets with a rebuff.

2. Scrooge, going to his street door, finds the knocker turns into the head of Marley, and then disappears again

Advertisement for the first filmed version of the *Carol*. From December 21, 1901, issue of *The Era*.

is a critical point because when an uninitiated audience is shown a silent film without music, the results can be disastrous: at best a film's tempo can be ruined, and at worst a final nail is driven into its coffin by confirming the assumption that all silent films were dull and tedious affairs.) Nor was their accompaniment limited to the afore-

mentioned tinkling tinny piano. There was always *at least* a piano, or perhaps a trio or quartet of musicians. Later came the legendary organs that could shake the rafters of even the largest picture palaces, and for special occasions full orchestral accompaniment was an option. It is also worth noting that for special exhibitions live sound effects were sometimes added in the theater and that, prior to the formal introduction of sound in 1926, there were periodic attempts to create talking or sound films throughout the silent era. And finally, it should be remembered that the musical accompaniment was not there to provide a little innocuous background noise; it was, instead, an integral part of the total *experience* of the film. Frequently reflecting or commenting on action or emotion on the screen, as well as enhancing the film's overall rhythm and pace, music comprised half of the intricate pas de deux of sight and sound that was the "silent" film.

Why this detour into such essentially technical waters? Because while the primary mission of this chapter is to document the what, when and where of silent *Carol* adaptations, these pages will also attempt to convey some sense of what these films were like. Generally speaking, the easiest way to find out what an old film was like is to get your hands on a copy and watch it, something that is much easier to do than it used to be thanks to the electronic wonders of home video and cable television. Unfortunately some silent *Carols* appear to be lost, and those that have survived often remain sequestered in archives and private collections and are therefore inaccessible to all but the most intrepid *Carol* search parties. Under these circumstances, it seems that the best way to begin discussing what these silent *Carols* were like is to begin with what they were not like—i.e., they were not the crude and primitive artifacts mentioned above.[1]

Having said that, it must be acknowledged that motion picture technique underwent a process of constant discovery, experimentation and refinement throughout the silent period. As a result, when looked at out of context, a *Carol* made in 1901 can indeed appear crude and primitive when compared with one made in 1916. Such is the case with the first cinematic *Carol*, Robert W. Paul's aforementioned *Scrooge; or, Marley's Ghost*, and any discussion of it must bear in mind that it was the progeny of a strange new marriage of art and industry that was less than a decade old.

At 620' in length, or a running time of about eleven minutes, this first *Carol* was a comparatively ambitious film by 1901 standards. Sadly, no complete prints are known to exist, but a partial print has survived and is preserved at the British Film Institute. (To be specific, 323', or just over half of the film, has survived; the missing material constitutes two sizeable chunks of celluloid, one from the beginning and another from the end of the film.) This "partial *Carol*" runs for about five and one-half minutes and picks up the story just after Bob Cratchit has let someone out of Scrooge's office on Christmas Eve, and just before he and Scrooge leave for the night; it ends abruptly at the beginning of a scene showing the death of Tiny Tim. While it is always difficult (and risky) to judge a film based on incomplete evidence, this author has seen the surviving footage and can report that the first cinematic adaptation of *A Christmas Carol* was both interesting and very well done indeed.

It is noteworthy that with this initial filming begins the frequently employed practice of changing the title to *Scrooge*. As noted in Chapter 4, J. C. Buckstone's play *Scrooge* tended to define the story for the theatre and music hall in this period, and it seems safe to assume that Paul was aware of it. In a broader sense, the frequent change of title can also be attributed to the well known ability of the film industry to exploit an obvious commercial possibility, in this case the fact that by the turn of the century the character of Scrooge had long since become firmly established as a highly visible

and recognizable cultural icon. It also allows the filmmaker, and later the exhibitor, to focus on the presence of a popular star such as Seymour Hicks, Alastair Sim or Albert Finney.

When viewing the available footage, it quickly becomes apparent that Paul's film follows the structure of the Buckstone play very closely. (A detailed synopsis of the film that was printed in an entertainment publication called *The Era* has been very helpful in filling in the missing pieces of this *Carol* and supports the view that the film was clearly inspired by the play; this synopsis has been reprinted in its entirety in Michael Pointer's *Charles Dickens on the Screen*.[2]) The film, for example, follows the play's lead in having Scrooge fall asleep in his quarters, thus suggesting that all that follows is a dream. However, the most significant point of reference here is that the film, like the play, dispenses with the Ghosts of Christmas Past, Present and Future, and instead has Marley's Ghost present all the familiar visions to Scrooge.

With just a little critical analysis and comparison of the play, the surviving footage, and the synopsis from *The Era*, further evidence can be found. For example, *The Era* tells us that "the next visitor, who is collecting subscriptions for a Christmas dinner for the poor, meets with no better reception [than that previously given to Scrooge's nephew Fred], and after Bob has received a severe scolding and instructions not to be late in the morning, he is sent off home."[3] This is precisely where the incomplete *Carol* begins: Bob Cratchit has just finished closing the door behind someone, but we don't know who. The key point here is that *The Era* tells us that it was a visitor, and not visitors, who was taking up a collection for the poor; this appears to coincide with the fact that the Buckstone play had earlier combined the two familiar charity solicitors into one character named Middlemark.

Yet one can also point to some fairly significant differences: In the play, for example,

Robert W. Paul's 1901 *Scrooge; or Marley's Ghost* with unidentified player as Scrooge; player is definitely not Seymour Hicks who was then playing Scrooge on stage. Courtesy British Film Institute.

Scrooge's place of business and living quarters appear to be at the same location, and this is where all of the action takes place. The film, on the other hand, has Scrooge take the familiar walk home, and encounter Marley's face in the familiar door knocker, before settling down for the night. And the film later shows us nephew Fred's joyous Christmas dinner, whereas the play does not.

One can go on and on with such comparisons, but the question can be summed up by saying that while the film is clearly and largely based on the Buckstone play, it *is not* an exact transposition from stage to screen. (It should also be noted here that while dialogue titles were not in use at this time, the film does contain a number of explanatory title cards which provide information and help to "set the stage" at various points. Nevertheless, the film clearly assumes some degree of audience familiarity with Dickens's original text, and perhaps even with the very recent Buckstone play.)

Apart from the question of its origins, the film, *as a film*, is quite good. From a technical standpoint, the photography is crisp and clear, and the cinematic techniques, such as dissolves and at least one wipe, are competently handled. It also features some very basic but effective special effects work in presenting Scrooge's ghostly visions. (In addition to being an inventor, and arguably England's most important film pioneer, the film's producer Robert W. Paul was a trick film specialist; significantly, Walter R. Booth, who is credited with the film's actual direction, was a magician as well as a specialist in trick and comic films. An illustrated discussion of Paul's technique in this and other films can be found in F. A. Talbot's *Moving Pictures: How They Are Made and Worked*.[4])

In terms of its entertainment value, or its overall aesthetic impact, the film is fairly impressive when looked at in context, and its static camera and painted backdrops serve to remind us that an unmistakable theatricality was part of the context in which the cinema functioned in 1901. The influence of the theatre can be seen in the acting as well. But all things considered, the *Carol's* seemingly endless life on screen was off to a fine start.

A quick word on the length and running time of these early *Carols*: The first motion pictures were generally very short, in many cases just 50–100 feet in length. Such films might run anywhere from a minute to a minute and a half, depending on the exact projection speed. A case in point is the aforementioned *Mr Bumble the Beadle*. According to Denis Gifford's *The British Film Catalogue 1895–1970*, a monumental reference work for which anyone even remotely interested in British films (and Dickensian adaptations!) must be eternally grateful, this film was a mere 60 feet long, a length which would obviously allow for just the slightest glimpse between the covers of *Oliver Twist*. Gifford describes the film as a period comedy in which the "Beadle courts a workhouse matron"[5]; from this account we can probably assume that the film draws on Chapter 23 of *Oliver* in which Mr. Bumble and Mrs. Corney take tea beside the fire.

As this film appears to be among the missing, we cannot say for sure how effectively this episode comes across. Some early films were remarkably adept at conveying the essence of a scene with just a minute or so of action, while others tended to be more tableau-like in their approach. But it is interesting to note both how early the new medium was turning to Dickens, and how much the producers appeared to assume that audiences of the day would be familiar with the source material. As noted earlier, this British effort was preceded by the American *Death of Nancy Sykes*; this appears to have been a reenactment of a vaudeville sketch, and even allowing for the fact that it draws on one of the most famous incidents in the entire Dickens canon, audience familiarity with Dickens was undoubtedly assumed here as well.

Generally speaking, films tended to get longer as the new medium marched into the new century, eventually arriving at a standard length of one reel. Such films are often referred to as "one-reelers," a reel being defined as 1000 feet of 35mm motion picture film which, at the slower projection speeds of the day, would generally run for about fifteen to twenty minutes. However, reference to the *standard* length of 1000 feet is not intended to suggest that at some point all films suddenly became uniform in length. In these early years films of all lengths continued to appear, some longer and some shorter than 1000 feet. As films became increasingly sophisticated and ambitious — primarily through the efforts of D. W. Griffith — two and three reel films began to become standard items as well.

For present purposes, the main point is that filmmakers were soon able to cram an astonishing amount of story and action into fifteen or twenty minutes of screen time — a block of time that is not unlike today's half-hour television format, minus the commercials. Within this context, all kinds of "story" films, including some extremely ambitious literary adaptations, became possible. By the end of the first decade of film production in this century, the *Carol*, *Oliver Twist*, *The Pickwick Papers*, *Nicholas Nickleby*, *The Old Curiosity Shop*, *The Mystery of Edwin Drood*, *The Cricket on the Hearth*, *David Copperfield* and *Bleak House* had been tapped by filmmakers; many more adaptations would follow.

It is also worth noting that Dickens was in good company in these early adaptations as a wide range of literary lights, ranging from Shakespeare and Tolstoy to Longfellow and Hugo, were drawn upon by filmmakers who were artistically ambitious — and smart enough to realize that there was a sizeable, pre-sold market for works based on prestigious literary sources. (The issue of literary adaptations became more complex when, after several years of litigation, and in a decision that Dickens would no doubt have approved of, Kalem's unauthorized 1907 version of Lew Wallace's blockbuster novel *Ben-Hur* was declared to have been guilty of copyright infringement. The case established that authors and publishers have a right to grant permission for film adaptations — and a right to be compensated.)

The British industry once again drew on the Christmas chapters in *Pickwick* with the 1904 production of *Gabriel Grub the Surley Sexton*, but the next *Carol*, and the first American one, came from Essanay in 1908. While there appear to be no extant copies of the film available for examination, the following plot synopsis, which has been transcribed exactly as it appeared in *The Moving Picture World*, indicates some interesting changes and additions to the story:

ESSANAY FILM MFG. CO.

CHRISTMAS CAROL—Scene 1 shows the miser Scrooge passing down a London street the morning before Christmas, on his way to his counting house. So much is he detested that no one speaks to him, until a beggar approaches, asks for alms, and is angrily stricken to the ground. A spirit appears and tells the miser that the beggar will again appear that night.

Scene 2 shows Scrooge approaching his counting house, and as he is entering, the beggar again appears before him. He places his hands before his eyes to shut out the apparition, and when he looks again the figure has vanished.

Scene 3 shows the interior of the counting house, with Bob Cratchett [sic], the clerk, and Fred, the nephew of Scrooge, attending to their duties. Fred announces that he has just been married. His bride, together with the crippled boy, Tiny Tim, enter the office. Looking out the window, they discover the approach of Scrooge, and at the advice of Fred the ladies conceal themselves. Scrooge enters and is told of Fred's marriage. He kisses the bride, but immediately regretting his action, orders them out of the office. They plead for a Christmas holiday, to which Scrooge eventually consents. The spirit appears and leads Scrooge from the office.

Scene 4 shows a merry throng on a London street, with a stranger scattering money to the children who gather about him. The spirit leads Scrooge to the throng, who shun him as he endeavors to speak to them at the command of the spirit.

Scene 5 shows the cripple at the lodgings of Scrooge, and the latter entering, still led by the spirit.

Scene 6 shows the beggar warming himself by the fireplace, while Scrooge in anger attempts to strike him, when he is transformed into the image of the dead partner of the miser. Horror-stricken, Scrooge sinks into a chair, and looking into the fireplace seeks a vision of his boyhood days. With a cry he sinks to the floor. The spirit again compels him to look into the fireplace, where he sees a vision of his forsaken sweetheart, as well as that of himself as a young business man. Thoroughly overcome, he falls to the floor exhausted but the spirit again raises him with a command to follow him from the office.

Scene 7 shows the meager home of the Cratchetts where, at the command of the spirit, he showers money upon the ill-paid clerk and his happy family, and is again led away.

Scene 8 shows the Christmas festivities at the home of Fred, the nephew of Scrooge. Fred toasts his uncle, but the company refuses to drink to the toast. Scrooge, concealed in the recess of the window, notices this, and coming forward, showers them with money, promising that hereafter he will lead a different life.

Scene 9 shows the spirit and Scrooge in the lodgings of the latter, where Scrooge falls upon his knees in prayer.

Scene 10 is Christmas Day. Scrooge gives a banquet to all his house can hold, including Fred, the Cratchetts and his friends, where he promises that in the future he will live to achieve the happiness of others.[6]

The year 1910 produced two *Carols* for the Christmas trade, one from the American Edison studio, and the other from the Italian Cines studio. Unfortunately the Italian effort, called *Il sogno dell' usuraio*, appears to be lost, but coming from one of Italy's most important early studios, it is a film that one would dearly love to see. *The Bioscope* published this account of the film in England, where it was released as *Dream of Old Scrooge*:

> This is a film portrayal of one of Charles Dickens' most famous characters. The various scenes are well worked out, and make an interesting subject. It is Christmas Eve, and old Scrooge is shown in his office, attending to his numerous clients. To all he is the same — cold, hard and grasping — unless, perchance, a wealthier individual than usual is ushered in by his half-starved, wholly underpaid clerk, Bob Crachitt [*sic*]. At length the office is shut, Crachitt has departed, and Scrooge, having eaten and drank his fill at a cafe, sits in his easy chair in his attic and falls asleep. Before him appear three figures, representing the Past, the Present, and the Future respectively. Past first shows him his early boyhood days, then Present his various clients, and people he has had dealings with. The widow and orphan he has so often passed in the cold streets, and then a glimpse of Bob Crachitt's home, where, in spite of poverty, true happiness dwells. The Future shows him as he will be, lying on his death bed, while people rob him of his wealth. With a start, Scrooge wakes up and tremblingly opens his safe. He is relieved to find that all is secure, but his dream has touched him, and he sallies forth to atone in some measure for his previous hard-heartedness.[7]

Fortunately the Edison film has survived, and it is surprisingly good. The praise is qualified here because the Edison Manufacturing Company is not the first studio that normally comes to mind when thinking of the best or most sophisticated films of this period. It was a prolific source of Dickensian adaptations in these early years, but its films were generally unambitious and unpolished when compared with much of the competition, particularly those films from Biograph and Vitagraph.

While the basic thrust of the Edison *Carol* is very much true to Dickens, some interesting changes are in evidence from a structural standpoint. It opens at Scrooge's place of business where we meet his cheerful nephew, the charity solicitors and, of course, Bob Cratchit; however, the film is similar to the famous J. C. Buckstone play in that the core of the film's action takes place in Scrooge's living quarters. Also, after the initial appearance of Marley's Ghost, the film compresses the familiar trio of ghostly visitors into a single spirit called The Spirit of Christmas. And the approach here is interesting in that for the visions of Christmas Past, Present and Future, the film does not take Scrooge (and the viewer) to the visions; instead the visions are all shown to Scrooge while he remains in his quarters. While there is nothing spectacular about the technical work here, it is nevertheless very well done; in essence, we see the ghostly apparitions overlapping Scrooge's dreary sleeping quarters. The effect is almost as if Scrooge were watching a holographic presentation of his life — and without ever having to leave the comfort of his bedroom.

Perhaps the only significant departure from Dickens's text worth noting is that a certain expansion of the role of Scrooge's nephew is clearly in evidence: One of the visions shown to Scrooge is that of his nephew being rejected by his sweetheart for lack of money. However, all ends well on this front when, on Christmas morning, the reborn Scrooge presents his nephew with a letter informing him that he has been made a business partner and can now marry. (In

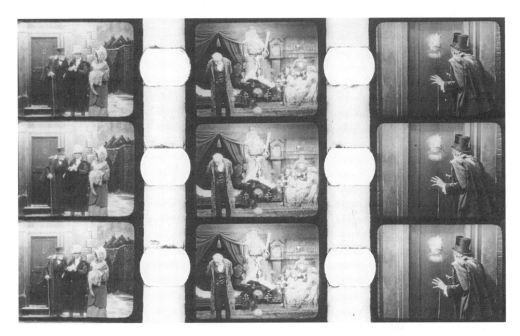

Three scenes from Edison's 1910 *A Christmas Carol*, starring Marc McDermott as Scrooge. From a rare three-strip 22mm print produced for viewing in the home via the Edison Home Projecting Kinetoscope. Courtesy Kirk Bauer Collection.

Dickens's original text the nephew is already married when the story opens.) Anticipating the finale of MGM's 1938 adaptation, the young lovers join Scrooge at Bob Cratchit's home for a general outpouring of Christmas cheer. The film ends with Tiny Tim on Scrooge's shoulder and everyone toasting, "God bless us every one."

All in all, the film manages to tell its story in a reasonably effective manner, although it is certainly not helped by the kind of static camera and overall staginess mentioned earlier. Nevertheless, as *The Moving Picture World* noted in its review of the film cited below, a familiarity with the original book was not a prerequisite to understanding or appreciating the film. This is probably true, although whatever success the film enjoys in this regard is due primarily to the source material rather than the skill of those involved with the film. The *Carol* as written is broken up into five distinct and relatively brief segments from which the "essence" can be distilled rather easily. And as we have

seen, *A Christmas Carol* was then, as it is now, one of the most popular and best loved books of all time; as such, even those who were not well read were aware of it and the unique place that it occupied on the cultural and iconographical landscape.

Not surprisingly, the Edison company was rather well pleased with its holiday offering. Its *Kinetogram* informed those in the trade that "the story is impressive and wonderfully effective in its dramatic and sympathetic appeal, and photographically will probably rank with the very highest productions that the Motion Picture world has yet seen. The visions and ghosts possess an unsubstantiality which is new and beautiful in the extreme."[8] Of far more importance was *The Moving Picture World's* assessment: "It is useless to undertake a description of this film. It is Dickens' story put into motion pictures and so cleverly reproduced that the characters actually live before one. ... whether one has read the original or not there will be no difficulty in understanding the picture. It is one of the best releases of this company for a long time."[9]

The film was also very well received in England where it was released the following year at Christmas time. *The Bioscope* called it "a wonderfully human portrayal ... lacking none of those lovable, sympathetic touches which characterized the great novelist's works. It is a true work of art, and will undoubtedly rank with the very highest productions that the moving picture world has yet seen."[10]

Significantly, favorable reception of the film was not limited to the trade press. *The Dickensian*, official publication of the recently formed Dickens Fellowship, announced, "A special private view has been given by the Edison Company of an elaborate cinematograph representation of *A Christmas Carol*, which will not be seen publicly in London till a fortnight or so before Christmas. It is wonderfully well arranged and reproduced, and will no doubt be a great favourite wherever it is shown."[11]

While this author's viewings of Edison's *A Christmas Carol* suggest that it is not quite as wonderful as the above reviews might lead one to believe, it was nevertheless a solid effort, and the age of cinematic *Carols* was well under way. Six years would pass before Scrooge next emerged from an American studio, but America had by no means deserted Dickens. It is particularly interesting to note that while the *Carol* was on hiatus, some of Dickens's other Christmas writings found their way onto American screens: In this period we find two versions of *The Cricket on the Hearth* (a Russian *Cricket* also chirped in the mid-teens), one of *The Chimes* (*The Chimes* rang in England as well) and, most surprisingly, two films drawn from Dickens's *Christmas Stories*—*Mrs. Lirriper's Lodgers* and *Mrs. Lirriper's Legacy*. Frequent adapters of Dickens's works, Edison and Vitagraph also turned to *The Pickwick Papers* during this period, but did not draw upon the Christmas chapters. The Thanhouser Company also produced several Dickens adaptations in this period, but did not touch any of his Christmas writings.

In the context of all these Dickensian Christmas films, it is important to note that silent era filmmakers, like filmmakers of today, were by no means limited to Dickens and the *Carol* for source material. For example, *The American Film Institute Catalog* indicates that from 1897 through 1910 over forty non–Dickensian Christmas films were produced or distributed in this country with titles ranging from *A Dutch Soldier's Christmas Box* and *The Christmas Goose* to *Christmas: From the Birth of Christ to the Twentieth Century* and *Little Peter's Christmas Day*. Nevertheless it must have been difficult for many filmmakers not to have Dickens somewhere in mind when planning a Christmas film; may we not, after all, assume that the producers of such films as *Rag Picker's Christmas*, *A Street Waif's Christmas* and *An Outcast's Christmas* had at least a passing acquaintance with Dickens?[12] What is unfortunate but in retrospect not surprising, is that no one in this early period turned to the *Carol* as a vehicle for serious social commentary. There was no shortage of serious "problem films" in the first two decades of this century, but as far as genuinely serious — i.e., truly faithful — adaptations of the *Carol* are concerned, the situation would not be rectified for many years to come.[13]

While the American studios were exploring other areas of the Dickens canon, their British counterparts offered two new *Carols*, in 1913 and 1914. (In 1912 a British short entitled *Leaves from the Books of Charles Dickens* also appeared in which Thomas Bentley portrayed a number of Dickensian characters. Bentley was a frequent interpreter of Dickensian characters on the stage, as well as the director of several Dickens films. Whether or not this film dealt with the *Carol* could not be determined as of this writing.) Since the last *Carol* in 1910, great changes had taken place in the film industry, the most significant of which was the transition to feature-length films. While one

Scrooge (1913): The reformed Scrooge (Seymour Hicks) dines with the Cratchits on Christmas Day. That's mistletoe in Scrooge's hand—and he's about to get a kiss from Mrs. Cratchit! Courtesy British Film Institute.

and two reel films continued to flourish, the feature-length film was establishing itself as the staple of the public's motion picture diet. (A feature-length film is defined as a film of four or more reels in length; this would provide a running time of one hour or more. While one can cite many important earlier examples of the feature-length film, 1912 is generally considered to be the year that marks the start of the transition to features.)

At 2500' (2.5 reels) in length, or a running time of about forty minutes, the Zenith Film Company's 1913 *Scrooge* was the first film to approach a feature-length treatment of the story. However, the film's prime claim to fame is the presence of Seymour Hicks, who according to an opening credit had already played the title role for over 2,000 performances; as we shall see in the next chapter, Hicks featured prominently in the first feature-length sound version of the

Carol as well. Hicks also adapted the story for this film, and clearly based his conception on the J. C. Buckstone play with which, as noted in Chapter Four, he had been closely associated for many years.

Some minor additions are in evidence in the early going: a poor woman enters Scrooge's office asking for money, and later a young boy runs through the office while taunting Scrooge. We also see the character of Middlemark giving away food to the poor before making his call on Scrooge's office. But, once again, the film is essentially an adaptation of the J. C. Buckstone play, which was still being performed at this time. Interestingly, Buckstone himself appears in the role of Middlemark.

On a certain level this film provides an important record of one of the stage and screen's most famous Scrooges in his prime. Unfortunately, in all other respects the film is a major disappointment. While it is not as appallingly bad as Sarah Bernhardt's *Queen Elizabeth* or James O'Neill's *The Count of Monte Cristo*, it must be relegated to the list of dismal films that attempted to record famous stage stars for posterity.

The chief problem here is that the film is exceedingly theatrical in design and execution. (Even though filmmaking technique had made enormous strides in the nearly two decades that had passed since the Lumière Brothers' first public exhibition in 1895, there were still plenty of filmmakers around who hadn't learned a thing.) While there are some exterior scenes early on, the bulk of the film is dominated by the interior of Scrooge's office and living quarters (again combined), with the action recorded by a mostly static camera. The overall effect, of course, is not unlike the experience of watching a live play.

The aura of the theatre surrounds the film's performances as well, with a complete lack of subtlety and an abundance of broad gesturing wiping out any possibility of character development in several key roles; Hicks is the prime offender here. The problem is compounded by the depiction of Scrooge as a stereotypical miser who even falls asleep while fondling a bag of coins. Nevertheless, the combination of Hicks and Scrooge seems to have offered a guarantee of box office success. *The Bioscope* noted that "Mr. Seymour Hicks has played the part of Scrooge for so long, and has found it such a favourite with the public, that there can be little doubt as to its success when introduced to the larger public of the picture theatres"[14] and that "Scrooge is certainly one of Mr. Hicks' cleverest impersonations, and the film cannot fail to be largely popular."[15] (It is also worth noting here that this is the strangest looking Scrooge to date: in this film he is dressed very shabbily, suggesting more a member of Fagin's den of thieves than a prosperous man of business, and he also appears to be in desperate need of a bath!)

Interestingly, signs of trouble are evident in a cluster of surprising gaffes that appear before the narrative even gets started: An opening credit tells us that we are about to watch "Dicken's [sic] 'Christmas Carol.'" Then, a few moments later, another title tells us that we are about to see Charles Dickens in his library at Gad's Hill, which is all well and good except that we then cut to an exterior shot, not of Dickens's Gad's Hill home, but of two men in twentieth-century attire entering his birthplace at Mile End Terrace, Portsea. Further problems ensue when we cut to the obviously artificial interior of the library in which we find none other than Charles Dickens himself restlessly searching for inspiration. An idea comes to him, and he sits down and begins writing *A Christmas Carol*. Sounds nice, but there are two problems: The Dickens that we see is not the handsome, clean-shaven young author of *A Christmas Carol*, but rather the bearded, older Dickens that most people are undoubtedly familiar with. And even if it were the "right" Dickens, he could not have written the *Carol* at Gad's Hill since the story was written and first published in 1843, and Dickens did not purchase his Gad's Hill property until 1856.

There are other lapses that could be mentioned, but calling attention to all the errors might amount to pedantry or the pursuit of trivia. Suffice it to say that there is evidence of haste and what can only be called a general ineptitude at the core of this film — one cannot help wondering aloud how someone like Hicks, whose name was virtually synonymous with that of Ebenezer Scrooge, could not have noticed.

On a more upbeat note, the film's unique opening does provide a rare opportunity to see Dickens "in person" on screen. A few television productions have focused in one way or another on Dickens, his world and his work — most notably, perhaps, the memorable *Dickens of London* (1977) which contains an interesting overview of the events leading up to the *Carol's* writing. The NBC 1951 adaptation of the *Carol* starring Ralph Richardson features an introduction and

Scrooge (1913): "Charles Dickens" receives a bolt of inspiration as he sits down to write the *Carol*; player is unidentified. Courtesy British Film Institute.

epilogue by Dickens himself. We also see the author hard at work on his first *Christmas Book* in the Guthrie Theater's stage adaptation of *A Christmas Carol* which was first televised in 1982. And, believe it or not, an animated Dickens appears in the 1972 Rankin/Bass adaptation of *A Christmas Tree*. But the imaginative uses of Dickens as a character extended even further: In 1963, the popular western series *Bonanza* added a twist to the existing body of Dickens scholarship by informing us that on his second trip to America, Dickens carried his battle for international copyright protection as far west as Nevada; while it is doubtful that Dickens would have anything good to say about this episode as history, it is probably safe to assume that he would approve of its title, *A Passion for Justice*. And on the big screen, he was among the luminaries passing through *The Best House in London* (1969).

Despite these occasional cameos, however, Dickens's extraordinary life has not been given the full Hollywood treatment — rather surprising, given that the "biopic" has always been a motion picture staple. One can speculate on what might have been — imagine, for example, a late thirties Dickens biography, with Robert Donat in the title role, sandwiched between his memorable work in *The Citadel* and *Goodbye, Mr. Chips*.

The following year London Films followed up Hicks's disappointing *Scrooge* with its own much shorter version (1340') called *A Christmas Carol*. The return to Dickens's original title is significant, perhaps, in that the film follows the basic approach laid out by Dickens, rather than the Buckstone play, in telling its story. This approach is most evident in the absence of Middlemark, and the return of the Ghosts of Christmas Past, Present and Future. Charles Rock turns in a

A Christmas Carol (1914): Scrooge's office on Christmas Eve. Left to right: Fred (Franklyn Bellamy), Bob Cratchit (George Bellamy), Belle (Edna Flugrath) and Scrooge (Charles Rock). Courtesy British Film Institute.

fine performance as Scrooge, as does an excellent supporting cast which includes American actress Edna Flugrath in a part identified as Scrooge's niece. (She accompanies Scrooge's nephew on his famous Christmas Eve visit, and from the context of the story, one assumes that she is indeed the nephew's wife.) She was the sister of actresses Viola and Leonie Flugrath, both of whom appeared in the 1910 Edison *Carol* discussed earlier, and who achieved considerable success in silent films as, respectively, Viola Dana and Shirley Mason. While the film is not easily available to the general public, sharp-eyed viewers can get a quick glimpse of it in the 1990 syndicated television special *Christmas at the Movies* in which it is mistakenly referred to as a 1917 production.

While it would not have taken much to improve on Hicks's lifeless effort of the previous year, this 1914 *Carol* is actually quite good on its own terms. In addition to the high quality of the acting, it is a very good looking film. Everything is extremely well lit and photographed, and while it does employ a mostly static camera, director Harold Shaw keeps his concise adaptation moving at a brisk pace while still managing to do justice to the various vignettes chosen to tell his story. In this regard, there are no major innovations to report, but as in most versions, one can point to minor differences that briefly attract our attention. The most interesting addition along these lines comes in the familiar scene where Scrooge notices the bell in his chambers beginning to swing and ring, announcing the approach of Marley's Ghost. Here we actually see Marley on a flight of stairs below Scrooge's quarters, pulling on the other end of a rope that is attached to the bell!

The film was well received by *The Bioscope*:

> It was inevitable that such a work, breathing the very spirit of the Christmas season as everyone would wish it to be, and offering such possibilities to the scope of the camera, should have been exploited before, and we have had several versions of the story more or less satisfactory. It is not too much to say that Mr. Harold Shaw's adaptation is far and away the best that has yet been presented. The story, which is admirably concise, follows the book in all essentially dramatic and pictorially effective details, the omissions being those vexed social questions which, however excellent as a means to point a moral by force of contrast, may be considered by many to hamper the novelist's delightful humour and playful fancy. This Mr. Shaw, with the assistance of a most excellent company, succeeds in conveying with great effect, and the result is a film story of unquestionable charm and sympathetic interest.[16]

The film is actually quite balanced in its approach and does not overlook its responsibilities regarding those "vexed social questions." An added scene in which Scrooge sharply rebukes a female beggar on the street, for example, manages to make a quick but effective point. Scrooge and friends would not appear in another short for almost a decade and, all things considered, this may well be the best of all extant miniature *Carols* from the silent era.

By virtue of these several short *Carols*, it would appear that by the mid-teens the story had become a cinematic standard. When it returned to American screens in 1916, it was in the form of the silent era's only feature-length version. With what is arguably the most substantial variation on the story's original title, the film was released by Bluebird Photoplays as *The Right to Be Happy*. Sadly, the film appears to be lost, but there can be no doubt that by this time both the story and its audience deserved the more expansive treatment that the feature film made possible. (This film was five reels in length; depending on its exact footage and projection speed, it would have run in the neighborhood of seventy-five minutes.)

Rupert Julian, who is best known as the director of the original version of *The Phantom of the Opera*, directed *The Right to Be Happy* and also starred as Scrooge. Bluebird was an interesting but minor studio, and from this and its generally undistinguished cast, we can probably infer that this was at best an interesting but minor film — and we can only wish that a top-shelf feature version had been produced in this period, with perhaps John Barrymore or Henry B. Walthall appearing as Scrooge.

Apart from the fact that we cannot judge the film for ourselves today, it is always frustrating when contemporary reviewers don't seem to have agreed on a film's worth. *The Moving Picture World*, the best and most important early trade paper as far as film coverage is concerned, gave the film solid marks:

> But it is true that while this picture is most appropriate to the Christmas season, it can be presented at any season of the year with the same pleasing effect. The production has the genuine Dickens spirit, and the characters are well portrayed. Sometimes in ensemble scenes we are conscious, for instance, of the spirit of the boisterous American girl, rather than the subdued and dignified feminine of the England of Dickens' day, but dealing with generalities, we are pleased.
>
> The role of Ebenezer Scrooge is skillfully handled by Rupert Julian, and a better portrayal of the character of Bob Cratchit, Scrooge's intimidated clerk, could not be desired than that given us by John Cook. Claire McDowell appears to good advantage in the role of Mrs. Cratchit, and little Francis Lee as Tiny Tim.

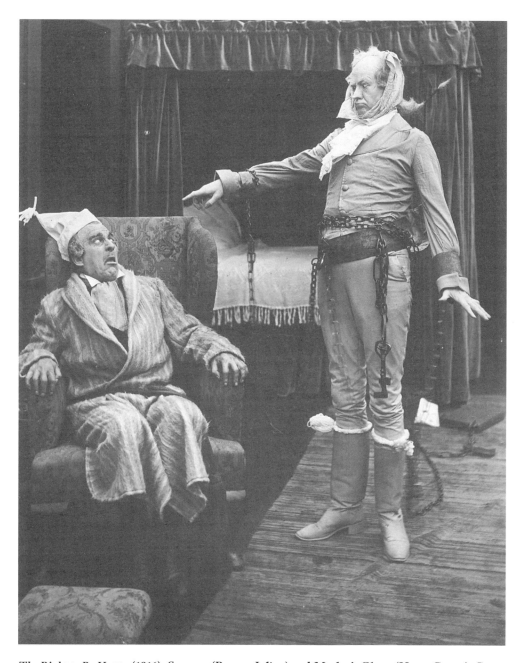

The Right to Be Happy (1916): Scrooge (Rupert Julian) and Marley's Ghost (Harry Carter). Courtesy Museum of Modern Art.

While this production may not compare altogether favorably with some Dickens' [sic] productions we have seen that have been made on English soil, still there is little fault to be found with it. Adults will be pleased with it and children will be delighted with this adaptation of the story of the regeneration of an old grouch.[17]

However, *The New York Dramatic Mirror* was largely unimpressed:

While "The Right to Be Happy" is a pretty and highly moral little play, it cannot be regarded as a faithful screen interpretation of the immortal "Christmas Carol" by Dickens. The thousand, almost imperceptible details which make up what we vaguely call "atmosphere" are conspicuous by their absence and the scenes and characters fail utterly to suggest the quaint classic which has been associated with the Christmas season as inevitably as holly or mistletoe. For one thing, the Christmas scenes in this production are staged under a blazing California sky amid the luxuriant green foliage of Mid-Summer and without the slightest suggestion of anything resembling snow. Now "A Christmas Carol" without snow is like "The Garden of Allah" without sand or "Faust" without fire and brimstone and it would take a masterpiece of direction and composition to compensate for this inconsistency alone. The interior scenes are better, but they too have a modern touch and suggest more a house-party masquerading as Dickens's characters than the old illustrations which Cruikshank has immortalized. [The reference here is to George Cruikshank, whom the reviewer has apparently confused with the *Carol's* original illustrator, John Leech. Cruikshank did provide the original illustrations for *Oliver Twist*, as well as some found in *Sketches by Boz*.]

By far the best piece of acting was done by John Cook as Bob Cratchit. He is unmistakably a "Dickens type" and gave a convincing and artistic picture of the wistful, timid little clerk. Rupert Julian as Scrooge was a disappointment—his makeup and mannerisms were exaggerated.

The story itself is in almost perfect scenario form as it stands *and will undoubtedly appeal to those who do not associate it too closely with the original "Christmas Carol." Exhibitors should not over emphasize the play's relation to Dickens, but bill it simply as a charming story which teaches goodwill to men* [emphasis added].[18]

It is interesting to note that both reviews touch (the latter much more directly) on how difficult and expensive it can be to mount a convincing period drama that is set in a foreign country. While surviving stills from the film suggest that its interiors and costumes were at least adequately realized, there can be no doubt that creating convincing exteriors on a limited budget—especially in southern California—was a much more complex task. Nevertheless, and notwithstanding the *Mirror's* curious admonition italicized above, the *Carol* has a way of surviving even the most inadequate attempts at adaptation. And it is also true that audiences approach a *Carol* adaptation, not necessarily with expectations of what that adaptation *should be* like, but definitely with an awareness of what the original story *is* like. In short, Dickens is always there to help us fill in the blanks. As *Exhibitors Herald* noted in its review, "There is not a bit of doubt but what this picture will appeal to motion picture patrons since nearly everybody is familiar with the story."[19]

The Right to Be Happy was, again, the silent era's only feature-length *Carol* adaptation. (For the record, it might be more accurate to say that it was the silent era's only formal or "straight" feature-length *Carol* adaptation; feature-length productions of *My Little Boy* and *A Message from Mars* did appear, but these qualify as *Carol* variations and, as such, are treated in Chapter 9 and the filmography.) This seems particularly odd in light of the fact that numerous Dickens features were produced in this period, and not just from America and Great Britain; Germany, Hungary and Denmark also contributed feature-length treatments. It is also interesting to note that of Dickens's fifteen novels, all but two (*Nicholas Nickleby* and *Martin Chuzzlewit*) were adapted at least once into silent feature films. And when one adds feature-length adaptations of *The Chimes* and *The Cricket on the Hearth* to this equation, the relative lack of interest in the *Carol* is downright shocking.

It is particularly unfortunate that British interest in the *Carol* was confined to the short subject, since the British industry was faced with a constant struggle for survival throughout this period and one would like

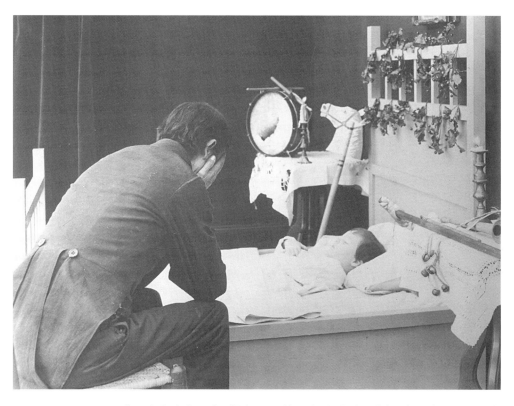

The Right to Be Happy (1916): Bob Cratchit (John Cook) at the bedside of Tiny Tim (Francis Lee). **Courtesy Museum of Modern Art.**

to think that a solid version of a pre-sold classic like *A Christmas Carol* would have succeeded at home — and might have found its way onto American screens as well, a market that was generally denied to British silents. (The problems confronting the British film industry in the silent era were many, but it is always worth mentioning that it was under a constant state of siege by the American industry, and to this day Britain remains the most unjustly neglected and unfairly maligned of all the countries that were active in the silent era.[20])

However, in this context, it is also worth looking at the other side of the coin. There were many who felt that the British industry had always relied far too heavily on adaptations from the theatre and literature, the gist of this view being that a constant recycling of "the classics" discouraged new talent and fresh ideas. By the mid and late twenties, vital new blood was being pumped into the British industry with the arrival of people like Alfred Hitchcock, Michael Balcon and Anthony Asquith, but there remained no shortage of literary adaptations. Dickens dramas continued to appear, usually among the short subjects.

The next *Carol* was indeed a British short subject, entitled *Scrooge*. It appeared in 1922, this time as part of a twelve film series from Master Films bearing the intriguing title of *Tense Moments with Great Authors*. English actor and playwright Henry V. Esmond appeared in the title role. Along with *Scrooge*, Dickens was represented by two drawn from *Oliver Twist—Fagin* and *Nancy—* and *A Tale of Two Cities*. Other titles included *Les Misérables*, *Vanity Fair* and the ever popular *East Lynne*.

Contemporary reviews of the series were quite favorable. *The Bioscope* noted that the

Scrooge (1922): Scrooge (Henry V. Esmond) hears Marley's Ghost approaching. Courtesy Library of Congress.

films were "admirably produced, with the atmosphere of the period, country and author faithfully preserved," and went on to predict that "these carefully chosen selections from literary masterpieces will appeal alike to those who are intimate with the books, and will be gratified to see the characters so reverently brought to life, and the others, who from such excellent short entertainments, will surely desire a better acquaintance with the authors."[21] *The Kinematograph Weekly* concurred: "Artistic merit is present in these abbreviated versions of world-famed books and raises them far above the average. They are aptly termed tense, for a somber tone characterizes the series, while impressions of horror can be derived from most of the sketches they contain."[22] And with what can probably be considered the ultimate compliment to this kind of film,

The Kine continued: "As thumbnail impressions they are very good indeed."[23]

Until very recently, this *Scrooge* had been considered a lost film. However, one of the happiest results of the research for this book is that the Library of Congress agreed to make a viewing copy of an unidentified short *Carol* that had been languishing for years in its nitrate film vaults. It was unidentified because its original titles had been removed, and new ones inserted in their place, in the mid-twenties. Once the film was viewable, it became possible to compare its contents to what was known about various lost *Carols*. For example, a comparison with the reviews quoted earlier eliminated the possibility that it was the 1908 Essanay version or the 1910 Italian version. This left the 1922 British film as the leading contender, a suspicion that was confirmed by the British Film Insti-

Scrooge (1923): Scrooge (Russell Thorndike) and Marley's Ghost (Forbes Dawson). Courtesy British Film Institute.

tute's Luke McKernan, who, by consulting still photographs from other films in which Henry V. Esmond appeared, was able to establish that our Scrooge here was indeed Esmond and that this film was in fact the lost 1922 British short.

Unfortunately, it is not possible to offer a totally accurate assessment of the film because what survives appears to be an abridgement rather than a complete print; the original film was 1280' in length, whereas the print at the Library of Congress is about 825'. It appears that the film may have been edited by an American distributor, perhaps so that it could be more conveniently marketed as a one-reeler. This is troublesome for present purposes, because while short versions of the *Carol* are heavily truncated to begin with, one can only guess as to what was cut from the film's original release

version. In any event, the surviving version is an interesting but unremarkable affair which offers no new insights into the familiar story.

It opens at Scrooge's office (a rather neat and well-polished place) where we briefly meet Bob Cratchit and Scrooge's nephew, both of whom might be said to personify the now somewhat archaic show business term "juvenile"; by contrast, Esmond is quite haggard and sour as Scrooge. The charity solicitors do not appear, and the scene quickly shifts to Scrooge's chambers where a rather cranky Jacob Marley delivers his familiar warning. At this point additional cutting becomes very apparent as the film bypasses the Christmas Past sequence entirely and cuts right to a brief scene of Scrooge and the Ghost of Christmas Present observing the Cratchit family. It then cuts to an exterior shot of the Ghost of Christmas Present handing Scrooge over to his counterpart from the future; the final spirit then shows Scrooge his tombstone and, before we know it, the reformed Scrooge is happily bouncing about his rooms on Christmas morning. He sends a turkey to the Cratchits, greets his nephew on the street, and, next morning at the office, playfully doubles his faithful clerk's salary.

It should be clear from this description that this *Carol*, at least in its surviving form, presents a very rushed and obviously incomplete version of the story. It is, however, well-acted, and its production values are generally quite good. From this evidence it seems safe to assume that, in its original form, the film was an effective if unspectacular distillation of the *Carol*.

The kind of "package" approach found in the *Tense Moments with Great Authors* series was popular; other series included *Tense Moments from Great Plays*, *Master Song Scenas*, and *Tense Moments from Opera*. (As they were comprised of *silent* films, the latter two would appear to have been particularly ambitious undertakings.) The next *Carol*, also entitled *Scrooge*, appeared in 1923 as part of a series entitled *Gems of Literature* from the British and Colonial Kinematograph Company. In this adaptation, Russell Thorndike appeared in the title role; he was a younger brother of actress Dame Sybil Thorndike, a successful author (of the *Dr. Syn* books), and a very busy actor, primarily on the stage and frequently in Shakespearean roles, for over half a century. Prior to this film, he had played Scrooge on the London stage in his own adaptation of the *Carol* entitled, simply enough, *A Christmas Carol*.

At less than two reels in length (1600'), this was yet another compact *Carol*; fortunately it has survived and proves to be a very effective little film. It opens along the standard lines with Scrooge and his clerk disagreeing on what the temperature of the office should be, the visit by his nephew, and the visit by just one charity solicitor.

However, an interesting touch is added when Scrooge dashes outside his office and vigorously wallops a young caroler over the head with a rather substantial ledger book; and to insure that the message was received, the boy is chased off with an angry shaking of his fist.

The scene soon shifts to Scrooge's residence where he is quickly confronted by the spirit of his former partner. Much of Marley's dialogue, with its explicit social criticism, is left intact here and the overall effect is quite powerful. The visits of the three Christmas Spirits are of course greatly condensed, but each one offers some interesting departures from the norm. The Ghost of Christmas Past shows Scrooge just one vision, that of his former sweetheart; recalling the approach of the earlier Edison film, the vision is played out before him in his own quarters. The Ghost of Christmas Future takes him directly outside, to his grave. But the most interesting variation comes when the Ghost of Christmas Present, who shows Scrooge nothing of the present holiday, rather bluntly rebukes him, saying, "No! You cannot tempt me to remain, for you have no love for your fellow men — only love for yourself!"

The film's closing section shifts to Christmas Day at Scrooge's nephew Fred's house, where we find Topper wooing Mrs. Fred's sister with considerable flair, and Scrooge himself seeking reconciliation with his family. The film's ending adds its most satisfying and creative touch by transposing the speech in which the reformed Scrooge raises his clerk's salary from the office to Scrooge's home, and in a fadeout clearly intended to invoke John Leech's illustration from the *Carol's* original edition, Scrooge and Bob Cratchit toast each other and the holiday in front of a blazing fire.

After an advance screening of some of the titles in the *Gems of Literature* series, *The Kinematograph Weekly* observed that "These films constitute another fairly successful addition to the number of short subjects now available to [film] exhibitors. Of the four selected for the Trade show [the others were *The Mistletoe Bough*, *Curfew Must Not Ring Tonight* and *The Dream of Eugene Aram*], "Scrooge" is well in advance of the others with regard to entertainment value."[24] *The Kine* also put Scrooge's reformation into sharp perspective by noting, "Shocked at his own character as thus revealed, he [Scrooge] hurries next day to his nephew's, and, for the first time in his life, behaves like a human being."[25] It also minced no words regarding the star's performance: "Russell Thorndike as Scrooge is immeasurably better than he is as Eugene Aram. In the latter role he is theatrical and overacts badly."[26]

A viewing of the film confirms that Thorndike's Scrooge was very well done indeed. And while the film does have a certain stagebound aura about it (in this sense, it sometimes has the look of a much older film), it was a remarkably faithful and flavorful distillation of the story. It was also the screen's last silent *Carol*. Ebenezer Scrooge would next appear on screen for Christmas of 1928, but by this time the silent film was disappearing fast. The movies had learned to talk.

The Talkies

"You're Norma Desmond. You used to be in silent pictures. You used to be big."
"I am big. It's the pictures that got small."

William Holden and Gloria Swanson
in *Sunset Boulevard*

Among aficionados of the silent film, Norma Desmond's famous remark needs no explanation. Those who have not seen many, or any, silent films, will simply have to take her word for it: The cinema lost more than it gained with the transition to sound. In any event, the boundaries of the silent era can be generally, and very conveniently, staked off and labeled 1895 on one side and 1930 on the other; this constitutes, roughly speaking, the first third of film history. But, however useful, such generalizations are inevitably misleading. As noted in the previous chapter, experiments with sound took place throughout the silent period, and there were periodic bursts of activity on both sides of the Atlantic that often resulted in the release of a group of short films utilizing an early sound system of one sort or another.

(Also, it should never be forgotten that Thomas Edison, whose name is certainly the most widely recognizable of all the early film pioneers, originally thought of motion pictures as an adjunct to his already successful phonograph.)

Significant technical progress in the areas of sound recording and amplification was made by the mid–1920s and the transition to sound formally began in 1926 with the release of the lavish John Barrymore vehicle *Don Juan*. Utilizing Warner Bros.' sound-on-disc Vitaphone process, the film featured a synchronized musical score with sound effects. The sound-on-disc approach, however, proved to be impractical and rapidly gave way to the sound-on-film approach (optical sound) that was spearheaded by Fox's Movietone process. The next major step forward came the following year with the release of Warner's *The Jazz Singer*. Contrary to being the first talking picture as is generally reported — the impression often given is that the talking film was instantly established, and that the silent film instantly disappeared, with the appearance of this single film — *The Jazz Singer* is actually a silent film with synchronized musical score, songs, and just a few words of dialogue. The first all-talking synchronized sound film came a year later with the release of *The Lights of New York*, also from Warner Bros.

There was then a concurrent phasing in of the sound film, and a phasing out of the silent film, that lasted about five years. Interestingly this transitional period witnessed the release of some of the silent screen's greatest achievements; films like F. W. Murnau's *Sunrise* and King Vidor's *The Crowd* come to mind. During this period a variety of hybrid films also appeared that were part silent, part sound, and some were released in dual versions since many theaters were slow to invest in the new sound equipment. But by mid–1930 the silent film was essentially dead. Chaplin remained the last holdout, releasing *City Lights* in 1931 and *Modern Times* in 1936; both were silent films utilizing a synchronized musical score with sound effects.

Apart from feature films, one of the most interesting (and ultimately very important) aspects of this transitional period is that film producers were suddenly able to exploit, in a reasonably successful manner, a whole new range of possibilities by filming subjects that were previously impossible, or at least impractical, such as musical performances or dramatic readings. For example, along with *Don Juan*, the famous premiere of the Vitaphone process also included several musical shorts ranging from tenor Giovanni Martinelli's selection from *I Pagliacci* to Roy Smeck's Hawaiian guitar and ukulele. What is important here is that many major stars — from the theatre, music hall, vaudeville, opera, and so forth — were recorded for posterity on film. These films did not always

capture a performer in his or her prime, and some can be rather stiff and unentertaining, but in many cases they provide the only visual and aural record of a given performer. This was the context in which the first sound adaptation of the *Carol* appeared.

This first sound *Carol*, entitled *Scrooge*, was one of a pair of 1928 sound shorts, both running nine minutes in length, from Great Britain's British Sound Film Productions that drew upon Dickens; the second, *Grandfather Smallweed*, was adapted from *Bleak House*. Both films starred Bransby Williams who, as noted earlier, was very much a Dickens specialist. Unfortunately, no copies of this *Scrooge* are known to exist, nor does it seem to have been reviewed anywhere. It is therefore impossible to comment on it with any kind of authority, other than to say that it appears to have been a transposition of Williams's famous music hall turn as Scrooge. (As noted in Chapter 4, in 1905 Williams made an Edison cylinder recording entitled *The Awakening of Scrooge*, one of the first known recordings based on the *Carol*. He also made a three-part 1912 recording called *Scrooge from a Christmas Carol*, with the individual titles *Before the Dream*, *The Dream*, and *The Awakening*. Both are lively affairs which undoubtedly convey something of the flavor of his famous music hall performances. Based on this experience, it is difficult not to speculate that this first sound film version must have been an interesting and effective production. It is also interesting to note that, in his later radio and recorded interpretations of Scrooge, Lionel Barrymore sounds very much like Williams!)

As noted earlier, it is surprising that the silent era produced only one feature length version of the *Carol*, 1916's *The Right to Be Happy*. This film did, however, begin a general trend of at least one major production (either film or television) appearing every fifteen to twenty years. This brings us to the mid–1930s where we find not one but two new versions: the 1935 British *Scrooge* with Seymour Hicks and MGM's 1938 *A Christ-*

mas Carol with Reginald Owen. (There was actually a third *Carol* of sorts produced in this period, an unusual 1934 British short entitled *A Dickensian Fantasy*, in which a man's faith in human nature is restored after dreaming of characters and incidents from *A Christmas Carol*. Interestingly, Sam Weller of *Pickwick Papers* fame also appears in what technically qualifies as the first sound *Carol* variation. See filmography for details.)

But before considering these films it is important to note that, like their literary source, they did not appear in a vacuum; they were, in fact, part of an impressive (and primarily American) cycle of 1930s Dickens adaptations. If one discounts Paramount's 1931 *Rich Man's Folly*— an absurdly truncated adaptation of *Dombey and Son* which transposes the story to contemporary New York— the thirties Dickens cycle began at Monogram, arguably the most interesting and ambitious of Hollywood's poverty row studios. Their 1933 adaptation of *Oliver Twist*, with child star Dickie Moore very effective in the title role, is not well known today but is a remarkably flavorful and enjoyable film in spite of its limited budget and production values.

Universal contributed a pair of interesting and very underrated films with its *Great Expectations* (1934) and *Mystery of Edwin Drood* (1935). Because these novels emerged from what is often referred to as Dickens's later and darker period, one can see why Universal, by this time the established master of richly atmospheric horror films, might have been attracted to them. Indeed it is difficult not to compare the graveyard scenes in *Great Expectations* with those found in any number of other Universal films, nor is it too much of a stretch to sense a *Phantom of the Opera* quality in their handling of *Drood*; Universal had produced the legendary silent *Phantom* with Lon Chaney a decade earlier. In this context, such earlier works as *Oliver Twist* and *The Old Curiosity Shop* might have proved interesting material for Universal as well. On the surface it might also seem surprising that the studio did not explore (or

exploit) the obvious "ghost story" angle present in some of Dickens's Christmas works. The *Carol* is, of course, the most obvious possibility, with Dickens's text offering numerous opportunities for some genuinely horrific imagery. However, the powerful social commentary present in the *Carol*, and say *The Chimes* and *The Haunted Man*, was not really Universal's metier. It is worth noting too that in spite of the fact that the horror film has been a staple throughout the sound era, there have been surprisingly few serious ghost stories filmed.

However, if there is a sense of missed opportunity or unfulfilled promise in this area, it surely lies with MGM, whose flawless 1935 versions of *David Copperfield* and *A Tale of Two Cities* have never been equaled. Indeed if there was one studio that had the requisite resources, talents and "polish" to do justice to all of Dickens's works, it was unquestionably MGM, and it is most unfortunate that the studio did not launch an extended series.

Along these lines, Edward Wagenknecht relates an interesting and very revealing story in his classic book on the silent film, *The Movies in the Age of Innocence*. In the context of a discussion of actress Margaret O'Brien, he writes: "Some years ago, when Dickens still seemed to have some vogue in Hollywood, I suggested to Lionel Barrymore, who, I knew, loved Margaret as much as I did, that he try to get M-G-M to do *Little Dorrit* for her, with himself as William Dorrit. Barrymore thought well of the idea in both aspects and went nobly to work but got nowhere. As he wrote me, you can't tell what 'those people' are thinking even when they seem to be agreeing with you."[1] By "those people" Barrymore presumably meant studio management, who possessed the taste and insight necessary to sanction films like *David Copperfield* and *A Tale of Two Cities*, but also possessed an astonishing capacity for stupidity and shortsightedness.

It would be fair, though, to question how effectively or faithfully Hollywood might have treated certain of Dickens's works. How much, for example, of the grim social commentary of *Bleak House*, or the complex combination of humor and biting satire in *Martin Chuzzlewit*, would have made it to the screen intact? Hollywood was indeed capable of producing strong films in this period, as witnessed by such titles as *I Am a Fugitive from a Chain Gang*, *Dead End* and *Fury*. And apart from Dickens, it was also capable of producing faithful adaptations from literary sources as disparate as *Of Mice and Men* and *Gone with the Wind*. However, as we will see with MGM's *Carol*, compromise was more often the rule than the exception, and notwithstanding the sheer brilliance of its two 1935 efforts, it is not unreasonable to assume that a certain formulization and general whitewashing would have taken place with much of the Dickens canon.

And on the other side of the water, the only Dickens feature to emerge from a British studio during this period, apart from *Scrooge*, was Thomas Bentley's 1934 version of *The Old Curiosity Shop*. Bentley specialized in interpreting Dickens on both stage and screen, and this was his third filming of the story of Little Nell. It ranks among the very best of all Dickensian adaptations, but is virtually unknown in America. Intelligently adapted, it is also a good looking, beautifully naturalistic film. As the distinguished film historian William K. Everson has observed, the film used "exteriors and actual buildings and locations that had not changed one whit since Dickens' day," in addition to "at least one masterly new set, the ramshackle waterfront dive wherein the climax is played out."[2] When one factors in its marvelous cast, headed by Hay Petrie as Quilp, it stands out as one of the most underrated—or again, more to the point, sadly unknown—Dickens adaptations. (In this period, a German *Little Dorrit*, and a French *Cricket*, also appeared.)

The 1935 *Scrooge* with Seymour Hicks was produced at Britain's Twickenham Film Studios under the auspices of its colorful head Julius Hagen and was capably, if unspectacularly, directed by Henry Edwards who had been a popular actor and director in British silents. The participation of Hans Brahm as production supervisor is also noteworthy; as John Brahm he went on to a lengthy career as a director in American film and television and is perhaps best known for the memorable thrillers *The Lodger* and *Hangover Square*.

As its title suggests, Seymour Hicks (now Sir Seymour) is very much on center stage. Recalling his earlier association with the *Carol* on both stage and screen, this *Scrooge* is best remembered as yet another important record of one of the most famous Scrooges of all time. However, when one looks closer, the film ultimately disappoints; it contains some interesting but minor flourishes and bursts of originality, but never forms a truly substantive whole.

Its weaknesses begin with Hicks. In keeping with the film's overall leaden pace, this Scrooge reveals an undeniable lack of energy and drive as he goes about his business. Conversely, the Scrooge that Charles Dickens created had some spunk. There is a certain gusto and relish, and a perversely appealing charm, with which Dickens's Scrooge cracks wise about decreasing the surplus population, or claims that there is more of gravy than of grave about Marley's ghost. Apart from a couple of sarcastic remarks which do come across quite well, this side of Scrooge, which Alastair Sim would later render with such perfection, is noticeably absent in Hicks's performance. It must be said, however, that when Hicks's reformed Scrooge awakens on Christmas morning, he is considerably more energetic and almost childlike; one senses that he appreciates how close he came to sharing Marley's fate and that he is truly grateful for the second chance that he has been given. (And it must also be said that notwithstanding its deficiencies, Hicks's performance in this film represents a marked

Scrooge (1935): Scrooge (Seymour Hicks) and Bob Cratchit (Donald Calthrop) disagree about the need for more coal. **Courtesy Museum of Modern Art.**

improvement over his previous cinematic effort in 1913.)

As anyone who has seen a few adaptations of the *Carol* has surely noticed, it is not all that unusual to encounter a weak or less than perfect Scrooge. Where real problems can arise, however, is when such a Scrooge is presented in tandem with a weak or less than perfect script. Such is the case with the 1935 film. Apart from the young Scrooge's parting with his fiancée, a familiar episode drawn from the book which is actually expanded upon in this version, we are told nothing of his past. Why he is what he is remains something of a mystery; we can, however, infer that he simply enjoys being a miser — he is certainly not doing anything with his money that would make his life more pleasurable or any easier.

But even a poorly defined or developed Scrooge can be overlooked or at least

accepted. The film's real weakness is one shared by many other versions, namely that it bowdlerizes the story that Dickens wrote by eliminating virtually all of its social commentary and criticism. There is no question that the film's Bob Cratchit, beautifully and effectively played by Donald Calthrop, is poor and ill-treated. However, with only one significant exception, there is little suggestion of the widespread social injustice that Dickens was attempting to address.

This exception is a curious one, presumably inspired by a portion of a line that appears in Stave One just after the charity solicitors leave Scrooge's office. In the midst of one of Dickens's many descriptive montages, the book tells us that "the Lord Mayor, in the stronghold of the mighty Mansion House, gave orders to his fifty cooks and butlers to keep Christmas as a Lord Mayor's household should."[3] In the film we see a lengthy and briskly paced sequence which begins with fancy carriages pulling up to the Lord Mayor's residence and their fortunate occupants going inside for an elaborate banquet. A moment later, a footman chases away a young beggar, while back inside we are given a delightful glimpse of jolly cooks and bakers preparing a great feast for my lords and ladies. Next, we are shown one of the chefs tossing food (presumably some sort of scraps) to a group of children who have been watching the preparations through barred windows from out on the street. After a cut to Scrooge's solitary meal in a dreary tavern, the Lord Mayor proposes a toast and all sing "God Save the Queen." The sequence winds down with a cut back to the street children who join in the song, then back inside where the singing continues, and finally to Scrooge as he leaves the tavern no more cheerful than when he entered it and clearly isolated from any semblance of holiday spirit or communal celebration.

On one level, this sequence may well be the film's high point; it is certainly its most original. Indeed, one of the great moments in the life of any serious *Carol* aficionado comes with the recognition in a new version of a scene or bit of business from the book that has rarely, or in some cases never, been drawn upon before. For example, most adaptations show us Scrooge's return to his unhappy school days with the Ghost of Christmas Past, but how often do we see the visit by Ali Baba?

And how often do we see Scrooge and the Ghost of Christmas Future's vision of the young couple who, however guiltily, rejoice in the miser's death? The short answer is: not often. Interestingly, this *Carol* does follow Scrooge and the Ghost of Christmas Present on their journey to a lonely lighthouse and a solitary ship at sea, and yet these fascinating vignettes are almost always ignored by film and television. Just as the same Dickens works tend to be adapted over and over and over again, while

others remain untouched for decades, so it is that one tends to find the same incidents and bits of business included in most versions of the *Carol*—and the same ones continually overlooked.

In this regard, one must again applaud the film for a truly astonishing burst of originality in its expansion of this very minor reference in Dickens's text. And the concept of contrasting the opulent feast inside with the presumably poor and hungry children being tossed scraps outside is about as effective a visual synthesis of the *Carol's* message as one could possibly imagine. (Parallel editing for the purpose of conveying this type of message is, of course, not always subtle, but it can be most effective; in film, it can be traced back deep into the silent era. Arguably, the most important early example will be found in D. W. Griffith's famous 1909 film of social commentary, *A Corner in Wheat*, in which scenes of a lavish banquet are contrasted with shots of the poor standing in line for bread. However, as Edward Wagenknecht points out in *The Movies in the Age of Innocence*, Griffith is drawing on Frank Norris's original text here; thus we are reminded that the technique is literary and not cinematic in origin.[4]) Unfortunately, the power of the entire sequence is ultimately undermined when the children join in singing "God Save the Queen." One can perhaps view this as a suggestion that the nation really was one and at peace with itself, at least at Christmas. Such an interpretation may have been welcomed by many in the economically and politically troubled 1930s, but it is totally at odds with what Dickens wrote. He was, of course, concerned with children who were poor and hungry; but in his vision these children were not singing "God Save the Queen." The clearest statement of what he had in mind can be found at the end of Stave Three.

It is worth noting here that further evidence of this *Carol's* derogation of duty with regard to Dickens's social criticism exists in its handling of the end of Stave Three—

i.e., it does not show us the two children named Ignorance and Want. To its credit, it does include a slightly modified version of the Ghost of Christmas Present's blistering rebuke of Scrooge's crack about the surplus population — "Man, if man you be in heart, not adamant, forbear that wicked cant," and so forth. (Many adaptations, including some of the best, omit this speech — a significant omission in that it lays some important groundwork for the Ghost's later revelation of Ignorance and Want.) And yet the Christmas Present sequence fades out with an image of the Ghost heartily laughing along with the merrymakers at the home of Scrooge's nephew, and no mention of what, in the final analysis, may well be the most important portrait of children ever created by Dickens.

But in spite of what can only be called a basic lack of substance in its handling of the *Carol's* more serious aspects, there is actually much to recommend this version. It adds another creative touch, for example, by including a scene (not found in Dickens's text) in which, in the Christmas Past sequence, Scrooge's fiancée witnesses the young Scrooge callously dismissing a young couple who ask for more time to repay a debt. And it shows us that poignant but often neglected moment in which Scrooge sees that his former sweetheart has become a happy wife and mother — but not with him. One also notes that the film takes a very unusual approach in its presentation of Scrooge's ghostly visitors. For example, other than a brief glimpse in the famous doorknocker scene, Jacob Marley is not shown; he is visible to Scrooge, but the audience only hears his voice. The Ghost of Christmas Past (always the most difficult spirit to depict faithfully) is seen as a vaguely discernible human form with a bright, glowing exterior; and the Ghost of Christmas Future is seen only as a shadow. Only the Ghost of Christmas Present — a particularly corpulent Ghost of Christmas Present — is presented in the traditional manner.

It is also a very good looking film. Its rich, shadowy cinematography and lighting not only create atmosphere and mood, but also both hide and enhance its modest production values. In this regard the opening portion of the film (that corresponding to Stave One in the book) is particularly impressive. Figures and buildings are bathed in a skillful mixture of shadow and fog, and although the film is shot in black-and-white one can feel the cold, and the "palpable brown air," closing in.

The film is also noteworthy for some very authentic looking sets. Scrooge's place of business, for example, is every bit as dark, dingy and dilapidated as one might suppose it to be. Indeed it has the look of a place run by someone too miserly to invest in a broom or a coat of paint in spite of the fact that, for all intents and purposes, his entire life is spent there. The home of Bob Cratchit and family is also recreated with great authenticity and respect for the spirit of what Dickens wrote and intended; there is no question that this is the home of a "poor man's child." This is important because some adaptations — the 1938 MGM *Carol* being a case in point — present us with an incongruously prosperous looking Cratchit residence.

All in all, the 1935 *Scrooge* can be a difficult film to come to terms with. For sentimental reasons alone, one wants to love Seymour Hicks's Scrooge, and yet he is overshadowed by one of the screen's best and most understated Bob Cratchits. It can also be a difficult film to assess accurately and fairly since it is difficult to see — at least in America — as its makers intended it to be seen. Whether one views a 16mm film print, or more likely a video tape where quality control problems can be even more acute, this *Scrooge* usually circulates in very poor quality copies that bear little resemblance to the film that premiered in 1935. Also, the film was originally released in England with a running time of seventy-eight minutes and was cut slightly when distributed in America by Paramount. This was, sad to say, a

A Christmas Carol (1938): Reginald Owen as Scrooge. Courtesy Museum of Modern Art.

common practice, and as a result many great British films are known in America only in abridged (and frequently retitled) versions, a situation which has effectively ruined many films for American audiences. Over the years, various distributors have cut *Scrooge* even further so that when viewed today, again usually on home video, one is seeing a version that may be lacking anywhere from ten to twenty-five minutes of its intended running time. (In the past, various 16mm film condensations have circulated that cut the total running time to thirty—and even as little as ten—minutes in length!)

In its original form *Scrooge* is, once again, a very good looking and effectively atmospheric film. Unfortunately, what most people see and remember is a very murky and choppy *Carol*, an experience which tends to perpetuate many of the popular misconceptions and exaggerate many of the bona fide problems connected with British films of the 1930s. For quality and completeness, readers are urged to seek out the version once distributed by the legendary Blackhawk Films/Video Collection.

As a footnote, it should be noted that while *Scrooge's* deficiencies far outweigh its merits, the film in its complete form ends with a surprisingly inspired flourish. Though most of the cut versions end after the reformed Scrooge makes amends with Bob Cratchit on the morning after Christmas—sending him home to be with his family and joyfully proclaiming, "God bless us, every one!"—the complete film includes a closing scene in which Scrooge enters a church and joins Bob Cratchit and the rest of the congregation in singing "Hark! The Herald Angels Sing." Presumably inspired by a brief mention (in Stave Five) that Scrooge went to church on Christmas morning, and notwithstanding the fact that Scrooge's creator was not an advocate of formal organized religion, it is an epilogue of which Dickens himself might well approve.

As we cross the Atlantic for the next major *Carol* of the thirties, it is worth mentioning that British films of this period were made in an atmosphere that was completely different from that of their American counterparts. While it had no shortage of filmmaking talent on both sides of the camera, the British industry simply could not match the kind of money that Hollywood, with its larger market and subsequently larger profits, was able to pour into its films. Most British films had to be rather low budget affairs which generally lacked the polish and technical perfection of Hollywood films. When the first American *Carol* of the sound era was made at the greatest of all film studios, no such constraints were in place.

Having said this, one must be careful not to assume that MGM's 1938 *A Christmas Carol* is the kind of top-of-the-line blockbuster for which this studio is so well known. As indicated by its compact running time of 69 minutes, and its capable but undistinguished direction by Edwin L. Marin, who tended to specialize in moderately budgeted secondary features for MGM, it is very much a B film. But if it is not the kind of high-gloss A production that is virtually synonymous with this particular studio, audiences knew that even an MGM B promised to be a highly polished, skillfully produced, thoroughly entertaining film. In this regard, the film does not disappoint.

Indeed, if one remains focused on that word "entertaining," there is much to recommend this version of the *Carol*. Particularly impressive are its opening sequences in which we are introduced to all the principal characters. The sets recreating the busy streets of London on Christmas Eve are beautifully realized and we immediately take notice of an excellent supporting cast. In particular, a very prominent role is afforded to Scrooge's nephew Fred, amiably played by Barry Mackay, and Gene Lockhart's charming performance as Bob Cratchit lingers in memory long after the film has ended. (Lockhart was also very effective in weasley villain roles, and one cannot help thinking that he would have made a marvelous Uriah Heep.)

And what of Reginald Owen's Ebenezer Scrooge? Owen, an Englishman active in Hollywood since the beginning of the sound era, is justly remembered as a truly great character actor. However, his Scrooge is much shallower than the one that Dickens created and he is simply unconvincing a good deal of the time. In fairness, Owen was a rather youngish fifty-one when the film was made, and the attempt to age him by fitting him with a bald wig did nothing to enhance his credibility.

The role of Scrooge was originally intended for Lionel Barrymore, whose health

Lionel Barrymore as Scrooge in a CBS publicity photo released on December 17, 1938, in anticipation of the December 23, 1938, radio broadcast of the *Carol* on *The Campbell Playhouse*. Photo
may be from an earlier CBS broadcast; for the 1938 broadcast, Scrooge was played by Orson Welles.
Courtesy Photofest.

problems prevented him from appearing in the film. His unavailability was particularly unfortunate since he was on his way to becoming something of a national institution via his radio performances as Scrooge.[5] He did, however, appear in a promotional film entitled *A Fireside Chat with Lionel Bar-* *rymore* in which he tells the audience of the upcoming production of *A Christmas Carol*, and of the fact that Scrooge will be played by Reginald Owen; no reference is made to the fact that he will not be appearing in the production. This "chat" runs just over two and one-half minutes in length and is simply a promotional preview for the film that was shown in theatres to whet the collective appetite of the public. There was nothing unusual about this type of preview of coming attractions, known as a trailer; however, it was unusual for a trailer to be given a specific title like this, and to be so "personalized"—i.e., it clearly exploits Barrymore's connection with the role of Scrooge.

But while he undoubtedly would have made a better Scrooge, there is no reason to assume that Barrymore's would have been a definitive Scrooge—or even a great one. Indeed if one examines his vast repertoire of crusty old curmudgeons, a twinkling eye and heart of gold can usually be found just beneath the surface—which is all well and good, but it is not really what Dickens had in mind. (One might want to note the obvious exception here of his Mr. Potter in Frank Capra's *It's a Wonderful Life*; this is a genuinely mean individual.) But even if Barrymore had played Scrooge, it is likely that he would have been working with the same script and that the result would have been essentially the same film. Which brings us to the subject of this *Carol's* shortcomings.

The basic problem—and it *is* a problem—is that the film offers a drastically declawed version of Dickens's tale by removing virtually all of its social commentary and criticism. A hint of where the film is going (or rather isn't going) comes with the visit of Marley's ghost, played by Leo G. Carroll. After a rather bland series of speeches to Scrooge, accompanied at one point by a particularly syrupy musical score, the phantom departs through a window without showing Scrooge the suffering woman and child or the lamentations of the spirits who have lost the power to help them.

Thus the tone is set early on, but clear evidence of the film's de facto abandonment of Dickens's text can be found throughout the sequence with the Ghost of Christmas Present. The most interesting example occurs early in the treatment of that powerful moment when the Ghost turns Scrooge's

famous crack about "decreasing the surplus population" against him. In the book, as Scrooge and the Ghost observe the Cratchits' Christmas dinner, Scrooge asks if Tiny Tim will live. The Ghost replies: "If these shadows remain unaltered by the future, none other of my race will find him here. What then? If he be like to die, he had better do it, and decrease the surplus population."[6] In the film, the conversation (which takes place at the end of a memorable sequence outside a church, just before going to observe the Cratchits) is somewhat altered; the Ghost's response to Scrooge is "But what of it. If he be like to die, he better do it and decrease the population." The omission of the adjective *surplus* before the noun *population* is most telling and completely, albeit almost subliminally, undercuts the power of the Ghost's rebuke just as Scrooge's initial remark in Stave One would have been considerably less cruel and callous had Dickens written just *population* instead of *surplus population*. Oddly enough, in the film's handling of the earlier scene with the charity solicitors wherein Scrooge utters the famous remark, Scrooge does say *surplus population*. It is possible that the later omission is simply an example of the kind of minor gaffe that can go unnoticed in even the most carefully prepared and executed film; the film had in fact been rushed through production in the fall of 1938 so that prints would be available for distribution in time for its relatively short holiday run.[7] Indeed signs of haste are evident throughout the film, most obviously in its rather rushed or hurried pace. However, the preponderance of examples of this kind of sanitizing of Dickens's text suggests that this was not an accidental omission.

The Cratchits' Christmas dinner also receives a coat of MGM's famous gloss. A very well dressed Cratchit family celebrates in a very comfortable and well furnished home, replete with neatly folded napkins and matching glassware at the dinner table; the two tumblers and the custard cup without a handle are nowhere in sight. Then as the dinner winds down, in an astonishing reversal of the scene that Dickens wrote, it is Mrs. Cratchit (cloyingly played by Gene Lockhart's wife Kathleen; their daughter June also appears as one of the Cratchit children) who enthusiastically proposes a toast to Mr. Scrooge! And for anyone still unconvinced as to the message that this squeaky clean *Carol* wishes to impart, witness the end of the sequence with the Ghost of Christmas Present, which fades out not with a horrific glimpse of allegorical children named Ignorance and Want, but with an apparently reformed Scrooge laughing and proclaiming, "I love Christmas."

But in spite of what can accurately be termed a flagrant dereliction of duty in ignoring the complete story that Dickens wrote, there is still much to recommend this version. What one tends to remember most fondly is its warmth. Its opening scenes, for example, establish a lovely mood of Christmas Eve anticipation, and in spite of the Cratchit's rather well-fed bourgeois appearance, the depiction of their intense love of Christmas and of each other is undoubtedly the film's major strength. This is an important point because, at various stages in the *Carol's* history, there has been considerable debate (both popular and scholarly) as to whether the character of Scrooge and his reformation or the joyous holiday celebration of the Cratchit family should be the real focus of the story. Dickens, of course, managed to combine both sides of this debate — in a sense corresponding to the *Carol's* two "co-authors" mentioned earlier — into a seamless and almost magical whole. But then, Dickens was a genius. All one can reasonably expect of any adaptation is that it attempt to achieve some sort of balance between these two sides of the story.

The best adaptations do this, and occasionally much more. Unfortunately, however, most fall short of the mark. Yet it is interesting to consider how much we still care about these lesser *Carols*. And no matter

how much Christmas charity one might wish to apply to the equation, the two thirties versions must ultimately be counted among the lesser *Carols*. They are good films, perhaps, but far from great. And yet they still manage to leave their mark; images, impressions and isolated vignettes take their place at the Christmas feast and contribute to what might be termed our total *Carol* consciousness. This author can recall, for example, spending many frantic moments one day searching through various editions of *A Christmas Carol* for that marvelous moment when Scrooge's nephew, during that famous Christmas Eve visit to his uncle's office, offers Bob Cratchit a heartfelt glass of holiday cheer: "It's a wine, Bob. A cheering, warming, goodly wine that'll race through your veins with little torches. It's port, Bob, the fifth essence of the Christmas Spirit." As one might imagine, a well-deserved period of self-chastisement followed my eventual realization that these lines came not from the *Carol* that Dickens wrote, but from the version that MGM filmed. But looking back I can temper my chagrin with the realization that countless others have undoubtedly had similar experiences, and, like me, wouldn't have had it any other way.

Surprisingly, forty years would pass before Hollywood next turned to Dickens, but two American films from outside the Hollywood mainstream carried the Dickensian banner into the decade of the forties. One was a short adaptation of the *Carol* filmed with an 8mm home movie camera by a young boy in Toledo, Ohio, in 1940. This boy, Gregory Markopoulos, would later achieve international fame as one of America's greatest avant-garde filmmakers (see filmography for details). And on a much more ambitious level, but still representing MGM's antithesis in terms of filmmaking resources and "polish," we find David Bradley's 1940 experimental version of *Oliver Twist*; in this decade he also produced experimental versions of *Peer Gynt* and *Julius Caesar*, both of which starred a young Charlton Heston.

As we shall see in the next chapter, the *Carol* was very much alive and well on television in the forties; however, apart from the Gregory Markopoulos film, which was of course not intended for commercial consumption anyway, it was ignored by American and British film makers. (Does this in any way "explain" *It's a Wonderful Life*? Was there a gap waiting to be filled?) Nevertheless, one big screen *Carol* did appear in this decade. It did not come from America, nor did it come from that other frequent *Caroler*, Great Britain. This *Carol*—one of a surprisingly small number to come from outside of America and Great Britain — came from Spain, in 1947, in the form of a feature-length theatrical film entitled *Leyenda de Navidad*. (The title translates as *Legend of Christmas* or *Christmas Legend*.) For many years this film was thought to be lost, perhaps considered the Holy Grail of cinematic *Carols*. However, one of the happiest consequences of the research for this book is that a lone 16mm print (it was originally filmed in 35mm) of *Leyenda de Navidad* surfaced in Spain and has been seen by this author. While the film may not be an absolute masterpiece, it is, nevertheless, an excellent adaptation that is filled with many delightful surprises.

The film was written and directed by Manuel Tamayo, a prolific writer and director who was, in fact, making his directorial debut with this film; he had debuted as a writer in 1941. (He would later work extensively in Spanish television where, in 1966, he adapted another version of the *Carol*, also entitled *Leyenda de Navidad*.) While essentially unknown outside of Spain, he received a modicum of international fame as co-writer of the noted 1955 feature *Tarde de Toros*.

In this *Carol* Tamayo's work is first-rate in both areas, with script and directorial style exhibiting many interesting creative touches. The film is also very well acted in both lead and supporting roles, with Jesús Tordesillas turning in an excellent performance as a miser who, for this version, wears a beard and has been rechristened William Scrooge.

No attempt will be made here to discuss the film in the context of the Spanish cinema of its time, as pre–1950s Spanish cinema is essentially unknown outside of Spain. (Luis Buñuel is arguably the only Spanish filmmaker who started out in this period and went on to achieve any degree of international recognition; however, it must be remembered that he usually worked outside the commercial mainstream and that most of his films were made outside of his native Spain.) Until fairly recently, in fact, Spanish cinema has never received anywhere near the kind of international attention and recognition that is routinely showered upon its filmmaking neighbors in Western Europe — Great Britain, France and Italy are, perhaps, the relevant reference points here.

It is also worth noting that those Spanish films that have gained attention outside of Spain in recent years generally tend to be of the "art house" variety, a situation which is all well and good, but which can present a distorted, or at best incomplete, picture of a nation's cinematic culture and tastes. Suffice to say that *Leyenda de Navidad* is the product of a nation whose cinematic past is long overdue for serious international study and recognition.

And as for the film itself: In terms of its visual style, *Leyenda de Navidad* is a good looking film, although it must be noted that the surviving print is worn and faded. Thus it is difficult to make any definitive judgments about its cinematography or its overall "look." In a general sense, it has the look of many low to moderately budgeted Hollywood and British films of the thirties and forties. Or, to be a bit more specific, one might say that it recalls both the 1935 and 1938 *Carols* discussed earlier, with perhaps an emphasis on the former due to the condition of available copies of both films.

In terms of the story, the film is very faithful to the spirit and basic thrust of

Leyenda de Navidad (1947): **Jesús Tordesillas as Scrooge (on right) and the Ghost of Christmas Present (Manuel Requena). Courtesy Filmoteca Española.**

Dickens's original text. To begin with, it is set in a reasonably convincing if unspectacular recreation of Dickens's London, with the story opening at the familiar offices of Scrooge and Marley. In this regard, the only significant changes in evidence are that Scrooge has several clerks working for him, with Bob Cratchit apparently serving as a kind of doorman, and that Messrs. Scrooge and Marley took over the business from their former employer, a benevolent gentleman named Tackleton, who, in this version, replaces the character of "old Fezziwig." (The decision not to update the story to modern times, or to transpose it to Spain, is interesting in that period films set in a foreign country are generally more expensive to produce than films with a contemporary or native setting. It may be that a basic respect for Dickens's original story is in evidence here, although, as we shall see, the film does take liberties in other areas.)

What liberties the film does take come in the form of some surprises which, as noted above, are very delightful indeed. For example, in the sequence with Marley's Ghost, the spirit's arrival is not announced with the familiar clanging of bells or the clanking of

chains, nor with the sound of footsteps approaching from below. Instead, as Scrooge greedily counts the contents of a bag of coins, he hears an accusatory cry of "bandido" (bandit) from behind him. He turns around to discover that a lifesized portrait of Marley that hangs over a fireplace has come to life. Scrooge helps him down with the aid of a ladder and then receives the customary tidings that will eventually bring about his reclamation. During the course of their conversation, Marley abruptly disappears and then reappears to the accompaniment of a humorous whistle-like sound effect. The overall effect is to establish a certain lightness of tone at the outset.

This approach continues in Scrooge's encounters with the Ghosts of Christmas Past and Present as well. Both are presented as well-dressed gentlemen of about Scrooge's own age. For example, the Ghost of Christmas Past climbs up the face of Scrooge's building (and not without a struggle) and enters through the bedroom window, and the Ghost of Christmas Present playfully sneaks up on Scrooge as he lies in his bed. Even the various comings and goings of Scrooge and the spirits have a subtly humorous aura about them as they appear from behind curtains and enter and exit through windows; Scrooge and the Ghost of Christmas Present even enter his nephew's home through a large fireplace (while we don't see it happen, they have presumably come down the chimney). Even the Ghost of Christmas Future — in this version he is a tall gaunt man clad in black cape and top hat; we see his face, but he does not speak — has Scrooge enter the site of one vision through a free-standing clothes closet. However, none of this is meant to suggest that the film should in any way be interpreted as a comedy or parody. On the contrary, it is a straightforward adaptation, but one which manages to employ a unique and subtle lightness of touch. For finding a fresh approach to a very familiar storyline, writer-director Tamayo is to be commended indeed.

Certain other changes are also in evidence, but they bear more directly on the film's thematic content. It would be fair to say that this version emphasizes Scrooge's personal reformation rather than the larger issues of poverty and social injustice. The film does contain Scrooge's famous encounter with the charity solicitors, but it omits the appearance of Ignorance and Want. While the omission of these allegorical figures is a serious fault in any version, it is perhaps not a fatal flaw in this film because of an important incident that occurs during Scrooge's journey with the Ghost of Christmas Past. In a unique and genuinely touching scene, Scrooge sees himself and his sister as children sitting together before a fireplace, listening to their grandfather tell them the story of the first Christmas. As the grandfather narrates, his words are illustrated by a montage of manger figures that helps to tell the story. While several versions do include some of the religious references that can be found in Dickens's original text, this was the first cinematic adaptation to directly embrace the explicitly religious underpinnings of the story. (Very few versions have done so since, the 1983 production of *The Gospel According to Scrooge* being the most obvious exception; see filmography for details. See also the 1978 animated version of *The Stingiest Man in Town*, the American Conservatory Theatre's

Spanish poster for *Leyenda de Navidad* (1947).

1981 *A Christmas Carol*, and the 1985 British *Christmas Present*.) One could argue that this scene informs everything that follows, creating an implicit acknowledgment of the call for morality, charity and social justice that Dickens made so directly in the *Carol*.

The performance of Jesús Tordesillas as Scrooge is both subtle and introspective, qualities which contribute greatly to the credibility of this scene. His Scrooge is genuinely moved by this reminder of the true meaning of Christmas, and he has clearly begun the painful process of thinking — and regretting. *Leyenda de Navidad* was perhaps not the screen's first "psychological *Carol*," but it contains some important suggestions of things to come.

To underscore its emphasis on Scrooge's personal odyssey and personal reformation, *Leyenda de Navidad* brings its telling of the story to a close in a most felicitous manner. As in virtually all adaptations, it is established that Scrooge was once in love, but that his quest for wealth and success drove a wedge between himself and his sweetheart; she is identified here as Mary, and is very well played by Lina Yegros. The familiar parting takes place in the Christmas Past sequence. In the Christmas Future sequence, however, we learn that Mary has never forgotten Scrooge. In a unique expansion of the scene where the phantom shows Scrooge his own lonely tombstone, we see Mary mourning at the grave. All ends well, because when the reformed Scrooge wakes up on Christmas morning, part of his process of making up for lost time and past mistakes is to think about his former sweetheart. He goes out into the world with a new lease on life — he has even shaved his beard (an outward sign, perhaps, that he is a new man)— and stops by the office to make amends with his employees who *had not* been given the day off; he also asks Bob Cratchit about Mary. (He also buys Bob a turkey that is still very much alive and well!) Bob tells him where she can be found, a reconciliation takes place, and Scrooge and Mary later appear at his nephew's home full of good cheer and ready, one would assume, to live happily ever after in their remaining years. In every sense, Scrooge's life has come full circle.

In the midst of so many British and American adaptations, this Spanish effort reminds us that both Dickens and his "Ghostly little book" were, and are, enormously popular throughout the entire world. This being the case, it is not surprising that in any era Dickens is rarely off screen for very long. As a practical matter, *Leyenda de Navidad* stands apart as a fascinating "one-shot" film in that it is neither American nor British in origin. However, the late forties does in fact find us at the start of another cycle of Dickensian adaptations, this time all British, at the center of which is yet another *Carol*. For many it is THE *Carol*: Renown Pictures' 1951 *Scrooge* (retitled *A Christmas Carol* for American release) with Alastair Sim.

This important burst of interest in Dickens began with what is generally regarded as the finest of all Dickensian adaptations, the 1946 *Great Expectations* directed by David Lean. (There are, in fact, many who would count this among the greatest British films ever made.) Lean followed it up two years later with an *Oliver Twist* that is also unlikely to be improved upon. Both films made effective use of their highly stylized sets and magnificent cinematography, and can be counted among the most intensely atmospheric films ever made. What distinguished these adaptations from most of their predecessors, apart from the presence of a master filmmaker at the height of his craft, was their extraordinary faithfulness to Dickens's books. They were, and still are, magnificent accomplishments.

These films tend to be the standard against which all Dickensian films are measured. At the risk of oversimplification, they can be said to have signaled a willingness to deal with a side of Dickens that was largely absent in previous adaptations. Extremely faithful films had of course appeared earlier; MGM's *David Copperfield* and *A Tale of Two Cities* immediately come to mind. And a good case can be made that the 1934 version of *The Old Curiosity Shop* paved the way for Lean's approach in terms of its overall tone. But the Lean films brilliantly managed to highlight the dark side of Dickens's world, with its attendant intensity and psychological depth. The result was a unified vision that effectively mirrored Dickens's own.

Wedged in between the two Lean films, Alberto Cavalcanti's 1947 adaptation of *Nicholas Nickleby*, for Ealing Studios, is a film that has been unfairly overlooked and overshadowed over the years. Like the book, it is very dark when it has to be, and very funny when it has to be. Sir Cedric Hardwicke as a particularly sinister Ralph Nickleby and Stanley Holloway as a delightfully eccentric Crummles stand out in its marvelous ensemble cast. Like Bentley's 1934 *The Old Curiosity Shop,* this film has simply never received the recognition that it is due.

In 1952, Renown followed up its *Carol* with an excellent adaptation of *The Pickwick Papers* featuring a perfect Pickwick in James Hayter, and an equally perfect Jingle in Nigel Patrick. While the film bypasses the Christmas episode at Dingley Dell in its condensation of Dickens's sprawling story, it is something of a minor gem and deserves to be more widely known and appreciated. And by being a bit liberal in defining its boundaries, one can close out this cycle with the 1958 Rank production of *A Tale of Two Cities,* a film which, in spite of the seemingly perfect casting of Dirk Bogarde as Sydney Carton, ultimately disappoints and seems to stand a bit apart from the others.

When discussing film adaptations, as when discussing the books themselves, one must be cautious not to overemphasize the "dark side" of Dickens. Nevertheless there can be no doubt that the postwar world was a darker and more dangerous place. Nor is there any question that this reality began to find its way onto the screen. Sharp realistic films depicting a variety of serious social problems were suddenly possible. In Hollywood, in fact, they were positively in vogue: *The Best Years of Our Lives, The Lost Weekend, Pinky, The Search, Gentleman's Agreement, The Snake Pit, Home of the Brave, The Men.* And the film noir, with its complex world of psychologically tortured heroes and anti-heroes, and its dark, brooding, suffocating urban landscapes, was well into its golden age. In Britain, the period of Free Cinema, kitchen sink realism and Angry Young Men was still a few years off, but films like *It Always Rains on Sunday, Odd Man Out, The Third Man, The Lost People, Brighton Rock, Frieda,* and even an Alastair Sim comedy like *Hue and Cry* suggest a few new wrinkles in the landscape. And when attempting to sketch a picture of postwar American and British cinema, one should not overlook the influence of Italian neorealism and films like *Shoeshine* and *The Bicycle Thief.* So why not, for once, a serious attempt to deal with the *Carol* as Dickens wrote it?

The result of this "dealing with" Dickens in a faithful manner was a film that has come to be generally regarded as the definitive film version, and it is worth noting that until the appearance of Clive Donner's 1984 adaptation with George C. Scott, there was not even a hint of serious competition from television. As is the case with any great film, a number of factors contribute to its overall excellence, but ask anyone what makes it so good and the usual response will be the presence of the one and only Alastair Sim as Ebenezer Scrooge. In fact, references to the "Alastair Sim version" do more than distinguish it from the "Seymour Hicks version," the "Reginald Owen version," or any other version. For most *Carol* aficionados, Sim is the definitive, transcendent Scrooge, and reference to the "Alastair Sim version" implies a kind of metaphysical certitude associated with no other version.

The Scottish born Sim was fifty-one years old when the film was made, but in keeping with its naturalistic approach, no drastic attempt was made to make him look older as MGM had done with Reginald Owen. Instead, one of the screen's great comic character actors was essentially allowed to be himself. With a wonderfully expressive face and eyes, a rich mellifluous voice, and an almost indescribable penchant for droll wit, irony and eccentricity, Sim was both a unique personality and a fine actor; it is unfortunate that general audiences in America tend to know him only though this film, and perhaps *The Belles of St. Trinians.* His deadpan response of "Why?" to the charity solicitors' request to help the poor, or his bewildered reaction when he first sees the Ghost of Christmas Present, are classic Sim. As brilliant as his performance is, however, it never dominates the film. Instead, it is seamlessly integrated into a near perfect distillation of the story.

But the character of Scrooge is far more than just a vehicle for a bravura performance.

What really matters is how the film illuminates and significantly expands upon a theme that is for the most part only implicit in Dickens's text: Scrooge's past. We are not expected to simply assume that Scrooge is a greedy old goat who rather enjoys his lot in life. This *Carol*, like none before it, seeks to explain Ebenezer Scrooge. The sequence with the Ghost of Christmas Past is in fact the longest in the film, and the aura of the past (and past mistakes) colors the rest of it as well. And yet a solid sense of balance is always in evidence; although the movies had recently discovered the box-office potential of modern psychoanalysis, the makers of *Scrooge* wisely avoided any temptation to turn this film into a Freudian field day. As *The Commonweal* observed: "...the English have made a new film version which stems from the original novel. Psychology-wise moderns can read what they want to into this story of Scrooge's conversion ... but in any case the emphasis in the film is where it should be — on Scrooge, instead of on the prettier and more sentimental episodes revealed by the spirits."[8] And, to pick up on a point made in this review, one must also remember that in dealing with Scrooge's past the film is ultimately, and quite simply, being faithful to the letter — and, even more so, to the implications — of Dickens's original text. When his five major Christmas stories were collectively published in 1852 as *Christmas Books*, Dickens wrote in his introduction that "the narrow space in which it was necessary to confine these Christmas Stories, when they were originally published, rendered their construction a matter of some difficulty, and almost necessitated what is peculiar in their machinery. I never attempted great elaboration of detail in the working out of character within such limits, believing that it could not succeed."[9] Quite so, but nevertheless he does supply enough information (some of it autobiographical) to suggest that Scrooge is indeed a very complex character.

At a fairly compact eighty-six minutes in length, the film wastes no time in getting down to business — the business of exploring Scrooge's past. Its opening portion, that corresponding to Stave One in the book, is in fact a remarkably concise summary of the text which skillfully gathers momentum as it establishes the basic facts of time, place and character. We first see Scrooge leaving what is undoubtedly his home away from home, the London Exchange, for his real home, the offices of Scrooge & Marley. Along the way he callously dismisses a poor man who owes him money and chases away a group of young carolers. Everything in these opening moments is geared toward telling us who and what Scrooge is; the very streets that he walks through are dark and lonely reflections of himself. And the sparse, gray office in which he greets the charity solicitors and his nephew, while neither as nice as Owen's nor as shabby as Hicks's, is clearly the home of someone too preoccupied with business to notice or care about his surroundings.

The bleak tone of this opening is relieved only once, in a charming vignette introducing Tiny Tim, in which we find him gazing rapturously into a storefront window filled with a wondrous assortment of authentic Victorian toys, many of the elaborate mechanical variety. The scene is a magical synthesis of many of our standard expectations of what a Victorian Christmas is supposed to look like, and also serves to underscore the influence of the Christmas revival discussed earlier. Significantly, it also reminds us of the harsh realities of Christmas in Dickens's day as we witness the look on Tiny Tim's face when a beautiful boat is removed from the window, obviously a gift for another, more fortunate, little boy.

This scene is also interesting in that it is arguably the only serious attempt in any version to duplicate the kind of montage effect that Dickens utilizes so brilliantly in his text. The toyshop scene is not Dickens's, but it does recall the marvelous display of succulent Christmas delicacies that were "heaped up on the floor, to form a kind of throne" when Scrooge meets the Ghost of Christmas

Scrooge (1951): Alastair Sim as Scrooge. Courtesy Museum of Modern Art.

Present.[10] One also thinks of Scrooge and the Ghost's life-affirming trek through the bustling streets of London on Christmas morning, and of how images of ordinary commodities — chestnuts, onions, lemons, figs — are woven together to form a tantalizing tapestry of holiday bounty.

In a very real sense, the film's treatment of Christmas Past — Scrooge's past — begins with the appearance of Marley's ghost, brilliantly played by Michael Hordern in this small but pivotal role. (Sim and Hordern would later lend their distinguished voices to the same roles in Richard Williams's classic 1971 animated version of the *Carol*; see Chapter Seven. And in one of the best-kept secrets in the annals of *Carol* adaptation — at least in America — Hordern eventually got to try his hand *as Scrooge* in a 1977 British television production; see filmography.) In

fact, if one wishes to find a defining moment in this film, it occurs when Marley is explaining the purpose of his visit to the as yet unrepentant Scrooge. Scrooge sees fit to defend Marley's previous life of avarice and greed on the grounds that Marley was "always a good man of business." In a slight abridgment of Dickens's text, Marley responds in a wailing, pain-soaked cry that speaks volumes of the tortures of the damned: "Business! Mankind was my business..." And for anyone still unsure as to the approach this *Carol* will be taking, Marley's visit concludes with a truly disturbing vision of the phantoms (Marley included) who are tortured by their inability to help the poor woman and child who sit huddling in the cold night air. In spite of its few requisite touches of humor — no one delivers Scrooge's crack about Marley being "more of gravy than of grave" quite like Alastair Sim — the entire sequence with Marley's Ghost is chilling and not easily forgotten.

The sequence with the Ghost of Christmas Past is again the longest in the film, and it is here that many of the fragments of information that Dickens provides (or in some cases merely suggests) are dusted off and expanded upon. In the original text, for example, we are shown two of young Scrooge's many lonely holidays at school. In the first we find Scrooge, just like the young Dickens, taking refuge in his books, and one can readily understand the old man's tears and description of his younger self as "Poor boy!"[11] In the second, his younger sister Fan comes to take him home for Christmas, saying, "Father is so much kinder than he used to be, that home's like Heaven! He spoke so gently to me one dear night when I was going to bed, that I was not afraid to ask him once more if you might come home; and he said Yes, you should."[12] The film condenses this sequence into one visit (featuring a considerably older Scrooge and Fan) and yet we learn much about Scrooge's early life when Fan tells him, "Everyone loves you very much. You must forgive papa and forget the past." And in another expansion of the text, our picture of Scrooge is sharpened even further when we are told that Scrooge's father blamed him for his mother's death, just as Scrooge blames his nephew for Fan's death.

Interestingly, for a film that is generally considered to be an extremely faithful adaptation, this *Carol* goes beyond merely expanding on ideas or themes suggested by Dickens and actually makes some significant changes and additions. Fortunately, these alterations underscore rather than compromise Dickens's message by demonstrating to Scrooge, and to us, that his actions have had far-reaching consequences. For example, the Ghost of Christmas Past takes Scrooge to his sister's deathbed, where he sees his younger self angrily storm off after rejecting both Fan's baby and her husband. But the scene does not end here; instead the camera lingers and we hear the dying Fan, who thinks that her brother is still there, say to him, "Promise me you'll take care of my boy." One may or may not care to speculate as to what this tells us about Fan's relationship with her husband, but one has to assume that Ebenezer would have respected her wishes — if only he had not left as he did, if only he had heard her.

An equally creative and powerful moment occurs with the Ghost of Christmas Present when Scrooge is shown the fate of his former sweetheart, identified in this version as Alice. In Dickens's text, Scrooge learns that she is happily married and has been blessed with a large and delightfully boisterous flock of children; this memorable vignette provides Scrooge an understandably painful opportunity to contemplate what might have been. But in the film Scrooge learns that Alice has not married. Instead he observes her spending Christmas Day at a shelter, tending to the needs of the poor. Obviously Alice has gone on to lead a very good and useful life, but the look in her eyes tells us, and Scrooge, that she has known great pain and loneliness. (One is reminded here of the heartrending moment in Orson Welles's 1942 adaptation of Booth Tarkington's *The Magnificent Ambersons* in which we learn, regarding Aunt Fanny, brilliantly played by Agnes Moorehead, that "just being an aunt isn't … really the great career it may sometimes seem to be."[13]) In this scene, as in the earlier one at Fan's deathbed, Sim's Scrooge conveys an appropriate sense of anguish and regret as he contemplates the results of his selfish and misguided decisions: the nephew, his beloved sister's flesh and blood, that he has chosen not to know; the wife and lover that he never had.

This approach — this filling in the blanks in Scrooge's past — provides us with a very complex and richly textured Scrooge who contrasts sharply with the kind of cardboard villain found in many lesser versions. It also serves as the foundation for Sim's interpretation of the role, for if we look beyond his deliciously eccentric surface, this Scrooge is a very believable human being. Like most of us at one time or another, he has been scarred by painful experience, by life. Thus scarred, he is vulnerable, defensive, frequently afraid, and, therefore, very real.

It is important to remember, though, that Scrooge's life is not the sole dimension of the film. It may indeed be the screen's first psychological *Carol*, but director Brian Desmond-Hurst and screenwriter Noel Langley (who was one of the screenwriters of *The Wizard of Oz*) have skillfully integrated both Scrooge and his past into a beautifully balanced effort. Whether seeing the film for the first or the fiftieth time, one is also struck by its memorable blend of Victorian bric-a-brac, beautifully atmospheric cinematography and music, and a host of superb supporting performances. In a sense it is superfluous praise to mention the supporting players in a film like this, since one tends to take flawless ensemble playing for granted in British films. But the Cratchits of Mervyn Johns and Hermione Baddeley, Kathleen Harrison's expanded role as Scrooge's housekeeper, Glyn Dearman as Tiny Tim and George Cole as young Scrooge all stand out in memory. And is there a film buff anywhere who doesn't cherish the moment when the undertaker, played by Ernest Thesiger (another great British eccentric, particularly memorable as Dr. Praetorious in *Bride of Frankenstein*) meets Scrooge outside the bedroom where Jacob Marley lies dying:

SCROOGE: You don't believe in letting the grass grow under your feet, do you?
UNDERTAKER: Ours is a highly competitive profession, sir.

The presence of another stalwart British player, Jack Warner, is also particularly interesting because his character of Mr. Jorkins was created specifically for this film. Now one may well question the need to add a new character, but Jorkins does make a significant contribution by luring young Scrooge away from his place of employment at Fezziwig's to a higher paying position in his own company, where Scrooge meets his future partner, young Jacob Marley. But what is most important is how Jorkins injects a contextual note into the film that is absent in virtually all other versions and that informs, but does not directly figure into, Dickens's original text—namely the unrelenting juggernaut of change unleashed by the Industrial Revolution. When we first meet Jorkins, in a conversation overheard by the young Scrooge, he tries to convince Mr. Fezziwig to sell off his business: "Come, come, Mr. Fezziwig, we are good friends I think, besides good men of business. We are men of vision and progress. Why don't you sell out while the goin's good? You will never get a better offer. This is the age of the machine and the factory and the vested interests. We small traders are old history, Mr. Fezziwig, dodos." And later, when Scrooge and Marley first meet at Jorkins's firm, the following exchange takes place:

MARLEY: The world is on the verge of new and great changes Mr. Scrooge. Some of them, of necessity, will be violent. Do you agree?
SCROOGE: Oh, I think the world's becoming a very hard and cruel place, Mr. Marley. One must steel oneself to survive it and not be crushed under with the weak and the infirm.
MARLEY: I think we have many things in common, Mr. Scrooge.
SCROOGE: I hope so, Mr. Marley.

The Scrooge of Desmond-Hurst and Langley, like Dickens's Scrooge, is not a factory owner, nor does he appear to have any direct ties to what we would today call big business. Nevertheless he is at least partly the product of a process, and a mindset, that Dickens felt was at odds with humanity itself. He would of course deal with this issue more directly in other places: a decade later in *Hard Times* or just months later in a speech given in the industrial city of Birmingham in which he stated, "For it surely cannot be allowed that those who labour day by day, surrounded by machinery, shall be permitted to degenerate into machines themselves; but, on the contrary, they should be able to assert their common origin in that Creator from whose wondrous hands they came, and unto whom, responsible and thinking men, they will return."[14] The character of Jorkins is another example of how this film ingeniously manages to tinker with Dickens's text while at the same time remaining extremely faithful to it.

There is, then, a larger context in which the film's handling of Dickens's message operates, and though it differs from most other adaptations, the more familiar tools are utilized as well. In fact, the film is filled with many shocking images which slam home Dickens's points, such as the horrifyingly real presentation of the allegorical children Ignorance and Want which segues into the stunning appearance of a truly frightening Ghost of Christmas Future. Or one can point to the visit to Old Joe's rag-and-bottle shop where Scrooge's housekeeper and laundress and the undertaker sell his belongings after his death; complete with wretched tubercular children, it is every bit the foul and slimy place that Dickens describes. One can of course contrast this kind of imagery with the film's handling of the *Carol's* happier side. The Cratchit family is warm and loving; Scrooge's nephew is overflowing with genuine good will; and the reformed Scrooge's euphoric cavorting on Christmas morning, or on the following morning when he catches Bob Cratchit coming late to work, is positively infectious. But again, as with the *Carol* that Dickens wrote, a seemingly effortless balance is in evidence. One cannot help being moved by its celebration of the special joy that is unique to the Christmas season, and by its powerful affirmation of how good life can be; nor is

one likely to forget its depiction of those two children, Ignorance and Want.

Interestingly, reaction to the film was rather mixed at the time of its initial release; and, in America at least, it has earned its formidable reputation primarily through television. The usually reliable *Variety* positively hated the film and, in what must surely rank as one of the most dunderheaded reviews of all time, even went so far as to claim that Alastair Sim "stalks through the footage like a tank-town Hamlet."[15] In the overall assessment of the film the reviewer was no more perceptive: "It is a grim thing that will give tender-aged kiddies viewing it the screaming-meemies, and adults will find it long, dull and greatly overdone. There's certainly no Yuletide cheer to be found in this latest interpretation of Charles Dickens' Christmas classic."[16]

At the other end of the spectrum, *The New York Times* was most perceptive in its commentary: "In short, what we have in this rendition of Dickens' sometimes misunderstood 'Carol' is an accurate comprehension of the agony of a shabby soul. And this is presented not only in the tortured aspects of Mr. Sim but in the phantasmagoric creation of a somber and chilly atmosphere. These, set against the exhibition of conventional manifests of love and cheer, do right by the moral of Dickens and round a trenchant and inspiring Christmas show."[17]

The Christian Century's remarkably concise one-sentence review not only hits the nail squarely on the head but also shares some of the *Times*'s feelings almost word for word: "The Dickens classic presented not with cheerful holiday gloss, but as a *somber, often chilling* study of a misanthrope's painful regeneration, set realistically against a background of poverty, social injustice and ghostly shadows."[18] *Harrison's Reports* was very much on the same page: "Though it does have its somber moments it ends on so cheerful a note that one cannot help but leave the theatre in a happy mood."[19]

Those worried about the screaming-meemies can always have an order of *Carol*

Lite by watching the Reginald Owen version — and indeed there are, and always have been, those who prefer the kind of fluffy holiday fare served up by MGM in 1938. Trouble is, Dickens's "Ghostly little book" *is* rather somber and chilling at times; like it or not, that's the way he wrote it. For this reason and many others, it is hard to imagine that Dickens could be anything but pleased with the "Alastair Sim version."

Nearly two decades passed before the next major *Carol* hit the big screen, this time as a musical. In the intervening years, most of the attention came from television, including several musical versions, although a handful of interesting theatrical and educational shorts did appear. But at last came the 1970 British production *Scrooge*, one of the very best — and certainly most underrated — versions of *A Christmas Carol*. Period. The list of truly great cinematic and television *Carols* is a very short list indeed, and this film deserves a place on it.

This *Scrooge* appeared in an interesting context. To begin with, it was part of what might be called the last wave of the traditional movie musical. Specifically, it was part of that cycle of big-budget super-musicals whose roots can be traced back to the fifties, but which were really a phenomenon of the sixties and portions of the seventies. Many of them them began life as a book, while others first appeared on the stage. They ranged from the spectacularly successful (*The Sound of Music, Mary Poppins, My Fair Lady, Oliver!*) to films which, for one reason or another, did not succeed (*Half a Sixpence, Star!, Darling Lili, Doctor Dolittle, Chitty Chitty Bang Bang, Goodbye, Mr. Chips, Paint Your Wagon*).

For present purposes, the most important subdivision within this cycle of films is a truly fascinating burst of Dickensian musicals comprised of *Oliver!* (1968), *Scrooge* (1970) and *Mr. Quilp* (1975). (As an interesting footnote to this group, add the 1974 adaptation of *Great Expectations* starring Michael York, Sarah Miles and James Mason; it was originally planned as a musical, but released in a straight dramatic version. This was one of several Dickensian adaptations to be released theatrically in England, and as a television film in America.) *Oliver!*, a screen adaptation of Lionel Bart's 1962 stage musical, is generally regarded as a superb film. *Mr. Quilp* is based on *The Old Curiosity Shop*; it is quite a good film, but one which has fallen into undeserved obscurity since its initial release. Anthony Newley was well cast in the title role, and also supplied music and lyrics.

This was indeed the era of the high-stepping, widescreen, super-duper musical — but some films, including the Dickensian musicals, did attempt to ground the basic unreality of the musical in a very real, and occasionally grim, world. *Scrooge* is a case in point; the generally exuberant *Oliver!* also manages to retain a measure of the original novel's social criticism, and the ending of *Mr. Quilp* is downbeat and very unmusical. But for the most part, their ultimate goal was to accomplish, and on a virtually unprecedented scale, what musicals do best: deliver a brief (but hopefully memorable) respite from reality.

But this was also an era when many films were reflecting their politically charged and socially conscious times. In British films, this approach is generally traced to the Angry Young Men who broke important new literary and theatrical ground in the fifties. (One can, however, cite *many* earlier examples of gritty realism in British films like *Doss House* [1932] and *Love on the Dole* [1941].) This movement also spawned a stunningly fresh burst of films in the late fifties and sixties which were socially conscious, exceedingly realistic in approach and subject matter, and essentially critical of government and society in general: *Look Back in Anger, Room at the Top, The Entertainer, This Sporting Life, The Loneliness of the Long Distance Runner*. In *Saturday Night and Sunday Morning*, *Scrooge's* star Albert Finney made a lasting impression with his brilliant performance as

Arthur Seaton, an unhappy and unpleasant young factory worker. And, of course, by the time of *Scrooge* in 1970, full-scale empire-bashing was positively in vogue: *If...*, *The Charge of the Light Brigade*, etc.

A socially conscious, and indeed in many respects radical, book like *A Christmas Carol* would thus seem to have been a natural choice for adaptation in 1970. And as many of the problems addressed in the *Carol* had not changed much since 1843, one can imagine Dickens's justifiably angry voice having considerable appeal. In this context, one might reasonably assume that if a major *Carol* was going to be made at this time, it would be revisionist in its approach and that it would use the book's social and political dimensions as a launching point for an assault on some specifically contemporary issues. However this is not the case, and the reason probably lies, at least in part, in the fact that Dickens's solutions were moral rather than political. There *is* a decidedly secular tone about the film that would certainly be in keeping with its times, but then again there is a crucifix on the mantle in the Cratchit residence, and at no time does Bob seem to have any basic problem with the economic system in which he ekes out a living. In short, at no time is there a departure from Dickens's basic message, nor is there an attempt to lampoon or undercut that message in any way.

It is perhaps surprising that no major counter-culture *Carol* appeared in this period with, say, Malcolm McDowell as an aggressively disgruntled Bob Cratchit. In any event, the 1970 *Scrooge* is pretty conventional in its *Carol* approach. Its only real departure from Dickens's text, apart from the fact that people are singing throughout, is that it takes us even deeper than any previous version into the heart and mind—the past—of Ebenezer Scrooge.

This *Scrooge* wastes no time in introducing us to the title character in the presence of Albert Finney, who, being in his mid-thirties at the time, was clearly too young to fit the traditional picture of Ebenezer Scrooge. Nevertheless, Finney's is a thoroughly convincing portrayal thanks to a restrained hand in the application of his makeup. (In contrast, compare Henry Winkler's absurdly heavy makeup in the television film *An American Christmas Carol*, the end result of which is a seriously compromised *Carol*; see filmography.) While Finney did have to endure the application of some elaborate makeup, the effects are subtle and he remains very natural looking with a receding hairline and a few touches of gray simply suggesting age. He was also able to draw effectively upon his theatrical training and incorporate various vocal inflections and physical mannerisms which helped to suggest that he was an older man. And yet there remains an unmistakable impression that this is a younger Scrooge than we are accustomed to, and this works to the film's advantage. Instead of seeing the almost stereotypically *old* curmudgeon who has already reached the end of the line when the film opens, Finney's Scrooge is still in the process of self-destructing. His teeth may be yellowing, his hands and fingernails may be perpetually dirty, and he is clearly growing nastier by the hour—and yet there is a sense that, if he chooses to, he could still have many good years ahead of him. This sense adds a particularly poignant dimension to the film, for this is a *Carol* very much concerned with wasted youth and lost opportunity.

Significantly, one of the most important tools, perhaps the most important, by which this musical *Carol* sheds light on Scrooge's character is also generally perceived to be the film's weakest element: the songs. Even among those who are kindly disposed toward the film, there is usually a consensus that the songs are simply not very good. But while it is true that the film did not produce any real showstopping hits—the kind that take on a commercial life of their own outside of the film—such criticism is completely off the mark. The music and songs were provided by Leslie Bricusse, who also contributed an

Scrooge (1970): Albert Finney as Scrooge. Courtesy Museum of Modern Art.

excellent screenplay, and *Scrooge* is as good an example as one is ever likely to find of a musical in which the songs are seamlessly integrated into the body of the film. They are, in effect, simply part of the screenplay.

The critical point of reference here is the generally accepted maxim that in a proper musical the songs keep the plot moving; a song which stops the narrative dead in its tracks while people are singing is the proverbial kiss of death. Quite so, but the point is moot since that is simply not what happens in this *Carol*. The film (like many British films of this period) is very much a two-hour mood piece, and while it does contain a couple of toe-tappers, like "Thank You Very Much" and "December the Twenty-Fifth," the primary function of the songs is to convey information, comment on action and

character, and contribute mightily to the film's frequently melancholy mood and bittersweet tone. Where this musical differs from the norm is in the way most of the songs quietly go about their business in a subtle manner that is generally at odds with our assumptions about what a musical is supposed to be like. But do all musicals have to be bold, brassy affairs? To paraphrase the opening of L. P. Hartley's 1953 novel *The Go-Between*, which also serves as the opening of its memorable 1970 film adaptation, "The musical is a foreign country: they do things differently there." Can we not then, every once in a while, be reasonably expected to accept a somewhat different kind of musical? (For the record, the film was nominated for best original song score, and "Thank You Very Much" for best original song, though it failed to win in either category. It also received well-deserved nominations, but no Oscars, for Art Direction/Set Decoration and Costume Design.)

In this version, Finney's Scrooge has undoubtedly suffered the kind of psychological beatings delineated earlier in the Alastair Sim film (and over a decade later in the George C. Scott version). But in his scenes with the Ghost of Christmas Past, played by an exquisitely droll and sarcastic Dame Edith Evans, he also conveys a much deeper and broader sense of isolation and alienation than found in any other version. When he and the Ghost arrive at his old school, for example, he views his former classmates happily enjoying a wagon ride and singing Christmas songs. Looking at them, he tells the Ghost, "I could never join in those Christmas parties." And at the party at Fezziwig's, he is clearly a wallflower who responds to the Ghost's question of why he did not join the dance by flatly stating, "Because I couldn't do it."

But he is reluctantly persuaded to dance, a haunting slow-motion dance, the object of his affection in this case being Fezziwig's daughter Isabel, nicely played by newcomer Suzanne Neve. As the old Scrooge looks on at these happier days he sings, with unmistakable pain in his voice, "You, you were new to me ... you were everything." And the song trails off with him singing, "I let you go away..." In this lonely and alienated young Scrooge one might choose to find some reflection of the times in which the film was made; one might find a similar reflection — as in "Do your own thing" — in Isabel's declaration (sung) that "Happiness is whatever you want it to be." Perhaps. But above all, a profound sense of loss is in evidence here as Scrooge contemplates his lonely past and his even lonelier present and future. Armed with this knowledge of his past, we can readily understand how he was earlier able to sing "I hate people" with such conviction. However, this Scrooge is no cardboard Victorian lonely guy. He is real; he is recognizably human; he

is every young boy who cannot muster the courage to ask a pretty girl to dance. In this sequence the film forges a link with the audience, offering emotions that, whether we care to admit it or not, most of us remember from some point in our own past.

While the film paints a lasting impression of what Scrooge's life has been like, it does not shirk its responsibilities in other more traditional areas. The scenes with Bob Cratchit and his family convey the requisite warmth and sincerity, his nephew's Christmas spirit will not disappoint anyone, and the "December the Twenty-Fifth" production number at Fezziwig's party is a rollicking affirmation of the fun and fellowship that are an integral part of the "Dickens Christmas."

This side of the Christmas feast is clearly proclaimed by Kenneth More's engaging performance as one of the very best (possibly the best) Ghosts of Christmas Present. He picks up where Evans's Ghost of Christmas Past left off by injecting a delightfully playful tone into the film: "Come over here, you weird little man," he tells Scrooge when they first meet. He then urges Scrooge to (literally) taste and enjoy the milk of human kindness. And is there not some echo of Dickens's own voice in his hearty song, "I Like Life?"

While Dickens's social criticism is implicit throughout the film, More's Ghost is the primary channel through which it directly enters at strategic moments. He takes Scrooge to observe the Cratchits' Christmas dinner, during which we hear Tiny Tim sing, "On a beautiful day that I dream about, in a world I would love to see..." Is this just the inevitable syrupy, sappy number that most musicals usually get around to? Or is there not some echo here of a voice that tried to speak up for tortured, suffering children? Did Oliver Twist, or his little friend Dick, or that nameless urchin from *The Haunted Man*, or Jo the crossing-sweeper from *Bleak House*, ever have such dreams?

Scrooge The Musical (1992): Anthony Newley as Scrooge in Leslie Bricusse's stage adaptation of his earlier screenplay on which the 1970 Albert Finney film was based. Courtesy Photofest.

Surprisingly, Scrooge's sojourn with the Ghost of Christmas Present does not conclude with the vision of the two urchins, Ignorance and Want. Nevertheless the film does a remarkable job of crystalizing Dickens's message at the end of this sequence when the Ghost tells Scrooge: "There is never enough time to do or say all the things that we would wish. The thing is to try to do as much as you can in the time that you have. Remember Scrooge, time is short and suddenly you're not there anymore."

The other principal channel of social criticism is Scrooge's old partner, Jacob Marley. This film accomplishes the neat trick of using Marley as a framing device: He appears right on schedule at the beginning of the film to set the wheels of Scrooge's reformation in motion, *and*, as part of Scrooge's vision of the future, Marley is on hand to greet him when he arrives at his final resting place — in Hell. (This is one of a small handful of *Carols* that literally shows Scrooge — as well as the viewer — what the ultimate punishment for his crimes will be.)

Alec Guinness's Marley, however, is like no other Marley before or since. He is wry, droll, fey, self-deprecating; he is playful, and at times delightfully irreverent, but at no time does he cross over into satire or parody. Apparently having the time of his life with the role, Guinness even adds a weird, disjointed motion to his walk, and when he is annoyed by Scrooge's initial resistance, he rises up and hovers over his former partner with chains and cash boxes banging. He also neatly condenses Marley's dialogue from the original text — "Mankind should be our business, Ebenezer, but we seldom attend to it" — and goes flying off (with Scrooge) among the floating phantoms outside the window who are identified as "these inhabitants of Hell." In the later scenes in Hell, the black humor is delicious as Scrooge is wrapped in an outrageously large chain and, in payback for his treatment of Bob Cratchit, deposited in his frigid, ice-bound quarters where he'll be "the only man in Hell who's chilly." As noted earlier, one always hopes to find some new angle or fresh idea in every *Carol*, and Guinness's Marley is surely about as original an interpretation as one can possibly imagine. This Marley is, in a word, very funny — but, true to Dickens's original conception, there is rage behind his humorous facade.

Setting aside the thematic aspects, one is actually first drawn in by the film's considerable visual appeal. It was the first theatrically released version to be filmed in color and the results were quietly spectacular. At times, atmospheric shadows effectively evoke the downside of Christmastime in Dickens's day, and Scrooge's quarters are appropriately bleak and gray. And at other times, as during Bob Cratchit's walk home with his children on Christmas Eve, the look is rich and nostalgic, the colors muted but warm and inviting. This sequence is particularly memorable in that it recalls Dickens's brief but vivid description of the bustling London streets in Stave One; it even includes an homage (presumably intentional) to the 1951 version as the Cratchit children gaze wondrously into a toy shop window.

This was, and still is, the *Carol's* only exposure to the widescreen Panavision lens, and at times the broader canvas is utilized very effectively to convey a sense of the sheer size and depth of London, or to allow singers and dancers a chance to really spread out and kick up their heels. The rousing "Thank You Very Much" and the film's finale are particularly effective in this respect. (*Scrooge* has been released in a letterboxed version on laserdisc which preserves its original widescreen aspect ratio. Short of a 35mm theatrical revival, this is the best way to experience this extraordinary film.[20])

All in all, this *Carol* is one of those wondrous collaborative efforts that proves that "big" films can work. Along with Bricusse's songs (and screenplay) the work of veteran director Ronald Neame, who was co-producer and co-scenarist of the classic 1946 British version of *Great Expectations*, cannot be faulted. Ronald Searle's wonderfully evocative titles at the beginning, and Oswald Morris's outstanding cinematography throughout, also contribute greatly to what must be judged one of the two or three best looking *Carols*. And there is its marvelous cast, headed by Albert Finney's distinctive interpretation of Scrooge. All of which add up to a memorable, but, sadly, very underrated film.[21] Interestingly — and fortunately! — the Leslie Bricusse screenplay, music and lyrics have been revived in a recent British stage production entitled *Scrooge The Musical*. It premiered at the Alexandra Theatre in Birmingham on November 9, 1992, with long-time Bricusse collaborator Anthony Newley in the title role. An excellent original cast album is available on compact disc.[22] And a 1970 promotional film entitled *What the Dickens Have They Done to Scrooge?* offers a behind the scenes look at the film's production. At almost ten minutes in length, it is able to transcend the nonsense that one usually finds in a conventional trailer, and features some very interesting commentary from Neame, Finney and Searle on their approaches to Dickens.

Since Finney's 1970 *Scrooge*, there have been no theatrically released *Carols*, at least no "straight" versions (*Mickey's Christmas Carol* and Bill Murray's *Scrooged* are addressed elsewhere). It would appear, given the marketing priorities of today's film industry, that any future adaptations will likely come through television. In keeping with the theory of a new major *Carol* appearing every fifteen to twenty years, it was indeed television that brought the last one to American audiences, in 1984, with George C. Scott starring as Scrooge; in England, however, this version was released as a theatrical motion picture. A new version also appeared on French television in this same year.

But who knows? Who, for example, could have predicted that in 1988 we would be treated to a six-hour, theatrically released adaptation of one of Dickens's most infrequently adapted works, *Little Dorrit*? The motion picture industry is (at least once in a while) quite unpredictable, and may well feel that only film can do justice to a new *Carol* for the new millennium.

Television

I believe television is going to be the test of the modern world, and that in this new opportunity to see beyond the range of our vision we shall discover either a new and unbearable disturbance of the general peace or a saving radiance in the sky. We shall stand or fall by television—of that I am quite sure.

E. B. White

Clearly, the time for being amazed by television has long since passed. Like the air that we breathe, and the ground that we walk on, it is simply there; and there are many of us who would undoubtedly do without a refrigerator or indoor plumbing before parting with our television set (or sets). Technological advancements are simply taken for granted: Five-hundred channels in the palm of my hand? A forty-inch screen in the bedroom? My favorite sitcom broadcast in stereo, and then channeled though my very own digital audio surround processor? Of course. But, dammit, why didn't I have these things ten years ago?

And yet, in spite of its pervasive role in contemporary life and culture, how many of us ever think about television's origins and history? Citizens of a certain age may

remember RCA's demonstration at the New York World's Fair in 1939, an event which is generally referred to as the "official" launching point of the new medium. And there is, as many historians of early television have pointed out, a vague assumption out there that television was simply an advancement or "step up" from radio. But, as with the history of motion pictures, there is no easy explanation: Just as no one person (or nation) singlehandedly invented movies, no one individual (or nation) invented television. In the former case, one must sort out a host of names and give each his due: Edison, Dickson, Friese-Greene, Muybridge, Lumière, Jenkins, Armat, to name just a few. For the latter, names like Nipkow, Jenkins (again), Baird, Farnsworth and Zworykin merely scratch the surface.

In spite of television's immediacy and apparent modernity — we go to the movies, but we live with television — most people would undoubtedly admit to knowing even less about television history than they do about motion picture history.[1] The man on the street is far more likely to know something about Thomas Edison, and to have at least a vague awareness that he was somehow connected with the invention of motion pictures, than he is to have even heard of Philo Farnsworth, let alone his image dissector tube. Since this is the case, and since television long ago eclipsed the movies as the primary means of *Carol* dissemination, a bit more background might be in order.

As far as the connection with radio is concerned, for present purposes it is enough to simply note that while the early years of television are inextricably bound to the radio industry in many ways — the commercial dimension for one, and the division of the broadcast day into neatly prearranged blocks of time into which certain *types* of programming can be easily inserted for another — their technical relationship is indirect. In his definitive history of television technology, *The History of Television, 1880 to 1941*, Albert Abramson sets the record straight:

> The visual arts — the motion picture and television — are actually two sides of the same coin. Yet they came from different roots. The motion picture had arisen from a combination of photographic techniques combined with mechanical means for propelling a strip of light-sensitive emulsion through a camera; and after suitable processing, the developed strip of images being driven through a viewing device of one sort or another. Television evolved from the field of electrical communication, a direct descendant of the electrical telegraph, the telephone and finally "facsimile" or the transmission of still pictures.[2]

In the final quarter of the last century work began in earnest on both television and motion pictures. Technically, however, television took much longer to become a practical, working reality. Nevertheless, by the 1920s serious television experimentation was well underway, and by late in the decade the battle to bring sight (as well as sound) into the home was being waged on two competing fronts: mechanical television and electronic television.

In 1928, some of the most important experimental broadcasting began at General Electric's facility in Schenectady, New York. It was here, on September 11, that the first television drama was broadcast. An adaptation of J. Hartley Manners's 1899 melodrama *The Queen's Messenger* was chosen for this auspicious occasion, primarily because it was a one-act play with only two characters, which would be relatively easy to stage.

Adaptations of plays and literary standards continued popular, and in some cases scenes or highlights from current Broadway hits were broadcast. A few original stories created specifically for television appeared, but there was a definite reliance on established material that was in some sense presold and was also in the public domain. (Bransby Williams — of theatrical Scrooge fame — appeared before the camera of British pioneer John Logie Baird in this early part of the experimental period, but to date there is no evidence that he recited or performed anything from the *Carol*.)

Over the course of this experimental period — a span of time which lasted about twenty years, from the late 1920s to the late 1940s — the entertainment and information dimension of television was really a secondary consideration. Television was a working reality, but still highly experimental and, when compared to motion pictures, very crude. The priority of each broadcast was to take advantage of an opportunity for research and development in technical/engineering areas; nevertheless it is important to note just how quickly television embraced drama (or, for that matter, entertainment programming in general) in this experimental period. In this context, it should also be noted that, in

England, the BBC produced what appear to have been the first Dickensian television broadcasts, drawn from *The Pickwick Papers*, in 1936 and 1938. Consequently, and contrary to the popular assumption that television was "born" in the late 1940s with Milton Berle the attending obstetrician, this period represents television's true infancy. The so called "Golden Age" of the late 1940s through the late 1950s, when television was mostly live and mostly from New York, might more accurately be termed the medium's healthy adolescence. (A groundbreaking examination of the role of dramatic productions in this experimental period will be found in William Hawes's *American Television Drama*.[3])

The early 1930s witnessed both the decline of mechanical television and the rise of its electronic cousin. (Although it was actually the first successful working television system, the mechanical approach, which bore a certain resemblance to various Victorian era optical devices in that it utilized a cumbersome spinning wheel in its scanning process, quickly proved to be a dead end.) Interestingly, there were also many demonstrations of large screen television in this period, and underscoring the manner in which it was perceived in some quarters as a novelty item rife with potential and ripe for exploitation, one can find several reports of television demonstrations in the early 1930s among *Variety's* vaudeville reviews.[4] But in spite of frequent announcements that television was just around the corner, or that it had in fact actually arrived, electronic television (i.e., television as we know it today) still required considerable research and development over the final two-thirds of the decade; consequently, the FCC was reluctant to authorize commercial television until all of its component pieces were in place. Without FCC authorization, television broadcasting remained in the experimental stage, and relatively little of the broadcasting that took place was intended for consumption by the general public. However,

by early 1939, when RCA decided to unveil television at the New York World's Fair, it had achieved a level of technical quality which guaranteed that consumers would be willing to invest in the new television sets that would soon be rolling off the assembly line — and that advertisers would be anxious to strike up a conversation with those consumers.[5]

In his definitive study of early television, *The Great Television Race: A History of the American Television Industry 1925–1941*, Joseph H. Udelson points out that commercial broadcasting could have begun in 1939 but that disagreements within the nascent industry over technical standards prevented its authorization.[6] In 1941, the first commercial license was granted at last, to NBC's station WNBT, and television seemed ready to take off. However, World War Two presented a final obstacle and just a handful of stations kept the new medium alive, on a still essentially experimental basis, until after the war; in England, BBC television was shut down completely during this period. But after the war, television, like all healthy adolescents, wasted no time in celebrating its new freedom — and in testing its boundaries. Commercial television, for better or worse, had arrived.

What about the televised *Carols*? When was the first one? How many have there been? Most of us have seen recent *Carols*, like the George C. Scott version, or any number of animated versions that have flooded the market since Mister Magoo's initial holiday appearance in 1962; but early television, like silent movies, represents uncharted territory for most of us.

We will never know for sure what most of the early television *Carols* were like because, like many of their cinematic counterparts, the majority of them no longer exist. As noted earlier, much of our film history has fallen prey to the dangers associated with nitrate film, as well as the indifference of the corporations that made or own the films themselves. Similarly, much of television history is unavailable for viewing today. As with film, serious efforts at television preservation are a fairly recent phenomenon; indeed it is surprising how much relatively recent programming from the 1960s and 1970s appears to be lost. In the case of television, however, nitrate film stock is not the problem.

While bearing in mind the distinction between television's infancy versus its adolescence, one might generally regard all television prior to the late 1950s (when most production left New York and headed west) as "early television."[7] And in terms of the preservation of early television programming, the main problem lies in the fact that videotape, which we take so much for granted today, was not in use through most of this period. Evolving naturally from the development of magnetic recording tape, serious experimental work on the development of videotape began in the late 1940s; by the late 1950s, various workable systems were being phased in by the television networks. Some programming did originate on film, but much was simply aired "live" and never intended to be seen again.

In this period television programs could be recorded through the use of kinescope recording, a system of making a film copy directly off the cathode ray tube via a motion picture camera. In most cases, 16mm motion picture film was used. In theory, it would have been possible to preserve all television programming in this manner, and while such recordings yield results that are inferior to a program that was shot directly on film, they are obviously better than nothing at all. Unfortunately, kinescopes were not always made, and those that were made were not always preserved. Nevertheless, enough early television has survived, ranging from the best to the worst, to give later generations a representative sampling of what the fledgling medium was like. And as with

motion pictures, "lost" programming continues to turn up from time to time.

To put it mildly, there have been many television versions of the *Carol*. Indeed, as a survey of the filmography will indicate, it is fascinating to note just how quickly the story was embraced by the new medium and turned into a veritable institution quite early in the game. In this sense, the *Carol's* ubiquity on television parallels the longevity of certain vaudeville routines, or the manner in which certain plays became untiring warhorses that could be trotted out again and again and yet never wear out their welcome.

But again, most of the early television *Carols* no longer exist. Many of the more recent ones, from the 1960s and 1970s for example, exist only in network vaults or various archives and are very difficult, if not impossible, to see. Sadly, the networks rarely reach into their vaults and air the vintage programming that does exist. (Home video, however, has begun to make such material more accessible in recent years.) Under these circumstances, the best we can do here is to discuss in detail just a handful of the most noteworthy extant television versions — in effect a "Best of Television *Carols*" which can be looked at against the larger picture contained in the filmography.

The first televised *Carol* appears to have aired in New York on December 22, 1943, on DuMont's experimental station W2XWV. (Of course it is impossible to state that this was positively the first dramatization of the *Carol* to appear on television. All one can say with certainty is that, in spite of extensive searching, nothing earlier has turned up — so far.) Not only was it the first documentable televised *Carol*, it was also, according to *Radio and Television Weekly*, "believed to be the longest and most elaborate studio play yet presented over television." Probably one reason the production was called "elaborate" was the care lavished on both interior and exterior settings. For the interiors, according to *Radio and Television Weekly*, "An impressive array of antique furniture, scenery and props" were being made ready in the DuMont studio. For the exteriors, "carefully selected movie films" showing famous London landmarks would be woven into the production to create the proper atmosphere. *Radio and Television Weekly* continued: "Much attention is being paid to unique lighting effects whereby to obtain fantastic scenes, particularly for the ghosts in the story. Also, there will be novel camera angles and effects. Appropriate incidental music will round out this most ambitious telecast presentation in the best Yuletide fashion."[8]

And while it is always risky to judge a production based on advance publicity — the glowing terms in the *Radio and Television Weekly* article suggest a press release, and press releases are notoriously unobjective to say the least — a review of the actual broadcast suggests that it was in fact a very impressive production. According to *The Billboard*, it was "probably the station's most ambitious undertaking in the dramatic field to date."[9] *The Billboard*'s very favorable appraisal continued:

> George Lowther directed a group of players known as the Montebanks in Christmas Carol, adapted for tele by William Podmore. Podmore, who also played Scrooge, headed a cast which included Don Randolf, Consuela Lembke, Ralph Locke, Noah Julian, Roger DeKoven and Lon Clark.
>
> Title and credits were handled in movie fashion, and play opened with a view of the book. Camera panned up to reveal Noah Julian reading from the classic: faded him out and Scrooge into view. Reading was resumed as bridge when scope of present tele technique and studio space limitations made actual tele presentation impossible.
>
> Authentic scenery, props and costumes of the period contributed to realistic story-telling. The various ghosts were properly eerie and earth-detatched, thanks to lighting that created a faintly fluorescent effect and camera work that drained them of any hint of solidity.

> Podmore carried the entire production. Supporting players, however, all turned in good performances.[10]

The following year, when DuMont's call letters were changed to WABD, two broadcasts in the days before Christmas indicate that it still had plenty of holiday spirit. Its December 19, 1944, bill of fare included a short drama which appears to qualify as the first televised *Carol* variation entitled *Christmas, 1944*. As William Hawes points out in *American Television Drama*, WABD made its facilities available in this period to outside groups that were interested in experimenting with television drama.[11] In this context, *Christmas, 1944* was actually produced by WOR radio, in anticipation of a move into television, as part of its *Video Varieties* series.

Unfortunately, little is known about this production from a dramatic standpoint, although from its title we can undoubtedly infer that it was a contemporary Christmas story. For present purposes it is perhaps enough to simply note that *The Billboard* called it "a very bad play about Christmas and a Scrooge-like character."[12] *The Billboard*'s review of this program also indicates that it was an interesting but apparently unsuccessful example of technical experimentation within the context of "putting on a show":

> Bob Emery's *Video Varieties* was devoted entirely to an interesting but impractical experiment Tuesday night, an attempt to put dialog on a disk and have the actors work in pantomime. As is the case with almost all video experiments, there is a strong tendency to rationalize mistakes and hope for the best. Here, however, it is impossible. The elimination of studio noise, which, we presume, was the reason for the waxing, is not a great enough advantage to compensate for the strained, unnatural, zombie-like performances that result. ... The performers were oft-times off-cue, and they were unable to do the job really well because

A Christmas Carol (1948): NBC television production with Dennis King as Scrooge and Harry Sothern as the Ghost of Christmas Past. Note boom microphone. Courtesy the New York Public Library for the Performing Arts.

of the psychological difficulty of opening one's mouth and saying nothing as well as the tendency to overact when one element of the drama is missing.[13]

The following night, December 20, 1944, WABD moved from a *Carol* variation to a full-fledged *Carol* adaptation. Unfortunately, this production does not seem to have been previewed or reviewed anywhere, so there is little that can be said about it beyond the fact that its running time of thirty minutes suggests that it was the grandaddy of the many compact, and usually quite perfunctory, television *Carols* that would follow.[14] (As an interesting footnote, it is worth mentioning here that DuMont's chief rival at the time, NBC-owned WNBT, also made a major contribution to a busy week of New York based holiday programming with a

screening of Sir Seymour Hicks's 1935 *Scrooge*.)

These early productions, appearing during the war years when television was barely alive and still highly experimental, kicked off a string of televised *Carol* adaptations and variations that would remain virtually unbroken until the 1960s. In fact, as a glance at the filmography will indicate, the late forties and early fifties constituted a very fertile period for *Carol* adaptation, particularly on American television. There were, for example, a number of thirty and sixty minute adaptations, including one put on by a group of Chicago high school students and another that was performed by marionettes. Of this group, only two seem to have survived: a rather dismal 1949 effort with Taylor Holmes, and an interesting but hardly classic 1951 version with Ralph Richardson; the

A Christmas Carol (1954): An idealized "Dickens Christmas" from CBS television production starring Fredric March as Scrooge. Courtesy Photofest.

former appears to be the oldest extant "straight" televised version of the *Carol*. There were also two adaptations, in 1945 and 1949, of a *Carol* variation entitled *The Strange Christmas Dinner*. The latter production has survived and appears to be the oldest extant television *Carol* variation. And on the BBC, an eighty-year-old Bransby Williams starred in the first major British effort.

When contemplating the televised *Carols* of this period we can only speculate as to which was the best, or which ones qualified as major *Carols*, because most are simply unavailable for viewing. About the best we can do is to cite the first *known* major *Carol*, and for this we can point with some precision to the night of December 23, 1954, when CBS television's *Shower of Stars* variety hour broadcast a new Dickensian holiday offering entitled *A Christmas Carol*.

However, this was not just another rehashing of the familiar story. It was the first fullfledged musical version of the *Carol*, and it seems very likely that in an overall sense, it was also the most elaborate television adaptation of the story up to that time. To this day, by whatever standards one chooses to apply, it remains a very impressive production.

The CBS network pulled out all the stops on this one. To begin with, *Shower of Stars* was usually broadcast live; this entry was filmed — and in color. While the production is modest in terms of the number of sets utilized, the fact that it was filmed rather than broadcast live undoubtedly contributed to its very smooth, realistic and polished look. The opening scenes, for example, take place in a very effective recreation of a busy London street. Sadly, since there were not many color receivers in use at this time, few viewers were able to appreciate the results of its being filmed in color. As *Daily Variety* noted: "It's unfortunate most viewers saw it in black-and-white, for the colored hues in "Carol" were striking and added immensely to the overall effect."[15] Unfortunately, color copies of this version do not appear to have survived. Nevertheless, the black-and-white 16mm film prints and video copies that circulate today reveal a very good looking production.

A two-time Oscar winner and an accomplished star of stage and screen for decades, Fredric March starred as Scrooge. Although he did not join in the singing, March was an extremely versatile actor and his performance, as always, was excellent. In fact, this Scrooge can be faulted in just two areas, both of which March presumably had no control over. The first is a grotesquely distorted and oversized nose which, at times, suggests some of the more extreme incarnations of Fagin much more than Scrooge. The second comes as the story nears its fadeout: There is an excruciatingly long close-up of Scrooge as he sits at the Cratchits' table on Christmas Day listening to a song from Tiny Tim. *The Billboard* was impressed with this scene, noting that March "was best in a close-up shot of long duration wherein, thru facial expression only, he movingly put across Scrooge's transformation into a new personality."[16] March was in fact an actor of immense subtlety and sensitivity, one of those performers who could speak volumes with the most minute gesture or change of expression, and it is clear here that his reformed Scrooge, while happy, is reflecting on what a fool he's been in the past. But while a good point is made, the shot just goes on faaar toooo looooooong.

Heading a solid supporting cast, Basil Rathbone appeared as Jacob Marley. Long one of Hollywood's finest actors, particularly in suave, villainous roles — his Murdstone in MGM's *David Copperfield* is beyond brilliant, and one also remembers his Marquis St. Evremonde in that studio's *A Tale of Two Cities* — Rathbone is perhaps best known as the screen's definitive Sherlock Holmes. He was also no stranger to the "Dickens Christmas" and made two subsequent television appearances as Scrooge. Rounding out the major supporting players, Bob Sweeney registers well as one of the more timid Bob Cratchits, and Ray Middleton, who appears as Scrooge's nephew Fred *and* the Ghost of Christmas Present, is overflowing with gusto in each role. Alert viewers will also catch a glimpse of a young Bonnie Franklin; she, and sister Judy, can be counted among the young Cratchits.

Heavyweight talent was assembled behind the scenes as well. The Pulitzer Prize–winning American playwright Maxwell Anderson, who had previously collaborated on musicals with Kurt Weill, provided the adaptation and lyrics, and the distinguished American composer Bernard Herrmann, whose film credits include Orson Welles's *Citizen Kane* and *The Magnificent Ambersons* as well as several films for Alfred Hitchcock, composed a memorable score. The script offers no new insights into the story or its central characters, but is always literate and intelligent. Its lyrics and music might even be termed *more* literate and intelligent than one would expect to find in a work aimed at a broad, mainstream television audience. In fact, from the perspective of the popular audience that would have been tuned in to this production, one might say that it has a certain classical or operatic flavor. The only clearly "pop" tune present is the Ghost of Christmas Present's very upbeat "A Very Merry Christmas" with which Middleton's Ghost — this production breaks with tradition and presents the Ghost as a rather paunchy Robin Hood look-alike — attempts to reintroduce Scrooge to the joys of the holiday. (The idea of the same actor playing both Scrooge's nephew and the Ghost of Christmas Present is a good one, in that the nephew, as written by Dickens, is clearly the embodiment of Christmas spirit. A similar point is made by having the Ghost of

A Christmas Carol (1954): Scrooge (Fredric March) and the Ghost of Christmas Present (Ray Middleton) in CBS television production. Courtesy Photofest.

Christmas Past, and Scrooge's former fiancée Belle, played by the same actress.)

Apart from the notorious "long shot" referred to above, producer-director Ralph Levy, whose credits from this period include *The Jack Benny Show* and the pilot for *I Love Lucy*, keeps things moving at a brisk pace.

The economical use of sets helps here. For example, the entire sequence with the Ghost of Christmas Past takes place at Fezziwig's party which, in this version, has been moved to Fezziwig's rather lavish home. First we join in the dancing and general merriment; then Belle and young Scrooge gush over

The Stingiest Man in Town (1956): Scrooge (Basil Rathbone) and Bob Cratchit (Martyn Green) in publicity photo for NBC television production. Courtesy Photofest.

each other in a duet of "What Shall I Give My Girl for Christmas?"; and then, rather abruptly, we find Belle admonishing Ebenezer for his change of heart toward her and the world.

For the most part this is a very upbeat *Carol*. The original's social criticism is not ignored, but it is not dealt with in a major way either. It is worth mentioning, though, that the early scene between Marley's Ghost and Scrooge is quite powerful — particularly when Marley fades away moaning, "Oh God, Oh God." It is a chilling moment which conveys, as do few other versions, the depth of the anguish and regret felt by Scrooge's old partner. This tone continues as Scrooge, instead of seeing the familiar phantoms outside his window, is haunted inside his quarters by an eerie, chanting chorus that leaves him cowering in terror in a corner.

There is also a brief return to this darkness of tone as the story begins to wind down. At the end of the visit to Bob Cratchit's house, where Scrooge and the Ghost of Christmas Present have been observing the holiday festivities, Scrooge looks through a window and sees a black bird perched in a bare tree. Both the bird and the tree stand out in sharp relief against an ominous gray sky. (The Ghost of Christmas Yet to Come does not appear in this production. The inference we are drawn to is that the black bird has replaced the familiar hooded phantom.) The camera moves us through the window and reveals a distorted, highly stylized graveyard set in which Scrooge, as the eerie chorus returns, finds both his and Tiny Tim's grave. Scrooge's night with the spirits is thus brought to a close in an unexpectedly innovative manner — and with a decidedly expressionistic flourish.

All things considered, this version is an excellent adaptation of the familiar story. It breaks no major new ground, and yet it gets our attention with any number of imaginative touches. Moreover, it deserves to be judged without the condescension that frequently informs most discussions of early television. It is in other words, a *good production* — not just a good production for early television. And like all good versions, it contains a defining moment which effectively crystalizes Dickens's message. In this one, the reformed Scrooge makes a quick stop at his nephew's home while on his way to the Cratchits' on Christmas Day. With a definite bounce in his voice he declares: "Fred, I'm rejoining the human race. Save me some mince pie, I'll be back in an hour or so." Dickens himself couldn't have said it better.

This *Carol* was very well received and was subsequently rebroadcast in the United States and in England. Its success may have at least partially inspired another musical extravaganza, the 1956 production of *The Stingiest Man in Town*, with Basil Rathbone in the title role. In the best of all possible worlds, this version would be next in line for a lengthy discussion, for it unquestionably qualifies as a major *Carol*. Unfortunately, we do not live in the best of all possible worlds, and *The Stingiest Man in Town* has been unseen since its live broadcast on NBC's *The Alcoa Hour* on December 23, 1956.

Nevertheless, there has been tremendous interest in this production over the years. For serious *Carol* aficionados, it is yet one more adaptation that must be seen as a simple matter of principle, with the presence of a singing Basil Rathbone only adding to the sense of urgency. And there is also the fact that a soundtrack record album, featuring all of the music and songs, was released in conjunction with the broadcast. Many people who have heard the album, but who have never seen the production on which it was based, are anxious to complete their experience of this particular *Carol*. There are undoubtedly also many people who saw the broadcast in 1956 and are anxious to see it again (several such people have made their wishes known to this author). In short, there is no question that *The Stingiest Man in Town* represents the television counterpart of *Leyenda de Navidad* which was discussed in the last chapter — i.e., it is the Holy Grail of television *Carols*.

This author has been able to view a partial copy of the production that is preserved at the Library of Congress, and to approximate a reconstruction of the rest of it by drawing on the record album, as well as its script and contemporary reviews. But the fact still remains that the complete program has apparently gone unseen for the last forty years. That being so, it would be unfair to attempt a serious critique of *The Stingiest*

Man in Town in the context of this chapter on "major *Carols*"— to, in effect, judge it— based on incomplete evidence. For this reason, rather than interrupt the flow of this chapter any further with a litany of explanations and qualifications, additional commentary on this elusive adaptation will be found in the filmography.

Some interesting non-musical variations also surfaced in the mid to late fifties which are touched on in Chapter Nine, and additional musical versions from Canada and Great Britain lay just around the corner. However, the next major television *Carol* (which also happens to be a musical)— indeed the next major *Carol* period— came from an unlikely source.

In his 1958 survey of filmed *Carols* entitled *Dickens' "A Christmas Carol"* Robert C. Roman remarked:

> It was announced recently that Ronald Searle, the British caricaturist, was planning a cartoon version of *A Christmas Carol* in association with "some of the men who produced the Mr. Magoo cartoons." Christopher Fry was mentioned as a possible adapter, and Alec Guinness as a voice for Scrooge. ... A Searle satire of *A Christmas Carol*, based on a Fry adaptation, sounds like disintegration at work in Western Christendom.[17]

This particular *Carol* never materialized. Searle did become a "*Carol* player," however. In 1960 he illustrated a new edition for Perpetua Books, and, as noted earlier, in 1970 he not only designed the titles for the Albert Finney musical version, but also appeared in a short film aimed at promoting it. And as for the men who produced the Mister Magoo cartoons...

Let's get right to the point here: On the night of December 18, 1962, one of the best and most enjoyable of all *Carol* adaptations premiered on NBC. I refer to *Mister Magoo's Christmas Carol*— and let no one make the mistake of underestimating or denigrating this version because it happens to be a cartoon. Unfortunately, most animated *Carols*, of which there have been many in recent years, are perfectly wretched affairs which insult both Dickens and their audience— a particularly egregious offense since most of the animation produced in the last forty years or so has been specifically targeted at children. But Quincy Magoo's turn as Ebenezer Scrooge, along with Richard Williams's version discussed below, offers proof positive that one can discuss an animated work in the context of a "best of" discussion. In other words, animation does not have to be shunted off onto some obscure sidetrack (on which we will also find the documentary and the avant-garde or experimental film) simply because it is a different form of expression that non-specialists conveniently assume to be somehow inferior to more conventional or "straight" approaches.

What makes this one so special is the fact that it was produced by UPA (United Productions of America), one of the most innovative and influential animation studios in history. The UPA studio was formed in the mid–1940s by a group of like-minded animators, many of whom had previously worked for Walt Disney, who were tired of traditional approaches to animation and wanted to branch out in a new direction. At this point in time, the Disney studio had long since established itself as the leader in animation. Its cartoons, both shorts and features, benefited from huge budgets and the best in facilities and talent; Disney animators also strove for, and achieved, an amazingly realistic look to their films thanks to detailed, mood-enhancing backgrounds, incredibly smooth lifelike motion, and great depth within each frame.

The UPA animators found this type of animation too constraining. Instead of trying to make cartoons as lifelike as possible, as Disney had done, they wanted to explore and work within the inherently abstract nature of the medium. Essentially, they wanted to celebrate rather than deny the obvious fact that no matter how hard one might try, there is no way around the unreality of animation.

It should be noted here that UPA was not the only animation studio that found its own way of keeping up with the Disneys. Lacking the resources that Disney was able to pour into its product, others, particularly the animation branches of Warner Bros. and MGM, found that it was possible to create their own identity by departing from the Disney model. The road chosen was pure slapstick — physical, sometimes violent, sometimes surreal, and always very funny. This is not to suggest that Disney cartoons were not funny, but it would be fair to say that they were always more reserved than their competitors. Even Donald Duck at his most rambunctious seems pretty staid when compared to the wild, crazy, Marx Brothers–like world inhabited by Bugs Bunny, Daffy Duck, Wile E. Coyote and even Tom and Jerry. As Don Nardo puts it in his outstanding introduction to animation entitled *Animation: Drawings Spring to Life*, "Instead of trying to outdraw Disney, they attempted to be funnier. And they succeeded."[18] Or put another way, comparatively speaking, a Mickey Mouse cartoon might be likened to a visit to the theatre or the opera, whereas time spent with Bugs or Daffy more closely resembled a trip to the local vaudeville or burlesque house.

The UPA productions represented an even more radical departure from the standards set by Disney. They eschewed virtually all of the traditional rules of animation. Attempts to create a realistic looking world, with characters that moved realistically in it, were jettisoned in favor of a highly stylized two-dimensional world. These films pioneered what is generally referred to today as "limited animation." In such cartoons the characters do not move smoothly and fluidly;

Mister Magoo's Christmas Carol (1962): **The one and only Quincy Magoo from UPA's legendary animated version of the** *Carol*. **Courtesy Photofest.**

instead they are frequently static and only parts of their bodies may move, in an unreal manner. This type of animation is cheaper to produce since it requires fewer drawings to complete an action, but in the highly skilled hands of UPA's artists, it was used as part of a comprehensive stylistic approach. Their work was highly influential on the direction that television animation would take in the 1960s, but it should not be confused with the extremely limited — and

Carol for Another Christmas (1964): The Imperial Me (Peter Sellers) presides over an apocalyptic Christmas Future. Courtesy Photofest.

lifeless — animation that has dominated in recent decades.

Backgrounds in this style were sparse, or sometimes not present at all, and weird, disjointed shapes and angles were everywhere. Frequently both impressionistic and expressionistic in style, the UPA look might be termed modern art in motion. It must also be noted that its sophisticated cartoons tended to focus on human characters and real situations, and were frequently used as effective vehicles for social commentary. In England, one can find parallels in the work of the husband and wife team of John Halas and Joy Batchelor, as well as in some of the illustrations and cartoons of Gerard Hoffnung; some of Hoffnung's work was

posthumously animated by Halas and Batchelor but, sadly, Hoffnung did not live long enough to branch into animating his work for film or television.[19]

With this background in mind, no one should be surprised to hear that *Mister Magoo's Christmas Carol* is a visual treat. Moreover, in spite of an opening credits admission that it is "freely adapted from" the *Carol*, let the record show that it is also an astonishingly faithful adaptation of the story. One sees the inevitable compression and omissions of course, and for some reason the Ghost of Christmas Present appears before the Ghost of Christmas Past, but the only real liberty taken adds considerably to its charm: In this version, we are introduced to the nearsighted Mister Magoo as a Broadway performer on his way to the theater to star in a production of *A Christmas Carol.* En route he belts out a brassy number telling us how good it is to be "back on Broadway." Depending on how one feels about loud, brassy show tunes, this is arguably the only low point in the production. For the most part, though, the excellent songs — heavyweight talent here too, with music by Jule Styne and lyrics by Bob Merrill — are flawlessly incorporated into Barbara Chain's solid script. Once at the theater, the actual *Carol* begins as a play within a play; we even see the stage a few times from the audience's point of view. (It should perhaps be noted here that the one and only Mister Magoo made his first appearance for UPA in 1949. He went on to become their most successful character, winning two Oscars in the 1950s.)

Once again, a quality script is at work here, providing us with an innovative, fun-filled *Carol* which still manages to remain true to Dickens. There is, for example, no whitewashing in evidence in Jacob Marley's speech to Magoo's Scrooge, and the visit to young Scrooge's lonely holiday at school, in which he sings, "Millions of grains of sand in the world, why such a lonely beach?" is genuinely touching. The song "Winter Was Warm," sung by Scrooge's fiancée after their breakup in Christmas Past, also raises a surprisingly bittersweet note — surprising perhaps for a cartoon, but not at all inconsistent with what Dickens wrote.

Wisely, Magoo's handlers decided to play the *Carol* portion of the production pretty straight; it never becomes a parody or spoof. Our hero's nearsighted shtick, and the great Jim Backus's priceless W. C. Fields–like mumbling and muttering, are largely reserved for the opening and closing scenes which frame the *Carol* proper. In the last of these scenes, Magoo, while taking a curtain call, quite literally brings down the house. It's a fitting ending to one of the most energetic and fun *Carols* ever made.

Television's love affair with the *Carol* continued throughout the sixties, although there were a few individual years that do not appear to have produced any new adaptations. And while *Mister Magoo's Christmas Carol* was the only bona fide classic to emerge from this decade, a couple of interesting variations appeared in 1964 that are worth noting. A Canadian musical version called *Mr. Scrooge* was highlighted by the intriguing casting of stage star Cyril Ritchard in the title role, and on American television, Rod Serling's nightmarish *Carol for Another Christmas* brought Dickens into the atomic age (see filmography for details on both). As noted in the previous chapter, a new adaptation of *Leyenda de Navidad* appeared on Spanish television in 1966. Unfortunately, this version was unavailable for viewing during the course of research for this book. It is worth noting, though, that literary adaptations were very popular on Spanish television in this period, and there is every reason to believe that this *Leyenda* may have been a substantive adaptation. Nevertheless, for serious *Carol* aficionados, the sixties will forever be synonymous with the name of Quincy Magoo.

However, as great as *Mister Magoo's Christmas Carol* is, Richard Williams's *A Christmas Carol* is widely considered the best animated version. Since it was made for television (it was produced in England for ABC), it also qualifies as one of the very best televised *Carols* overall. Like the UPA effort, it is a brilliant exercise in style; but unlike the near-surreal world inhabited by Quincy Magoo and friends, the approach here is what might be termed a highly stylized realism that mirrors John Leech's original illustrations from the first edition of the *Carol.* This remarkable little film, which runs a mere twenty-six minutes, premiered on ABC television on December 21, 1971. Appearing, as it did, close on the heels of a terribly lackluster animated *Carol* from Australia, it provided a refreshing and much

A Christmas Carol (1971): Bob Cratchit and Tiny Tim in Richard Williams's animated classic. Courtesy Photofest.

needed reminder of just how good animation can be.

The key to this version's success undoubtedly lies with the fact that it was brought to life by two of the greatest names in animation history: Chuck Jones and Richard Williams. Jones, who served as the project's executive producer, began his career in the 1930s and was one of the guiding forces behind Warner Bros.' legendarily zany cartoon unit. Representing the next generation, Williams's work reveals a more eclectic but equally inspired approach. His first major success was a nearly twenty-minute long effort called *The Little Island*; the first British cartoon to be produced in Cinemascope, it was also steeped in symbolism and social commentary, and won a British Film Academy Award in 1958. More recently, he masterminded the staggering animated magic

of *Who Framed Roger Rabbit?* (1987).

As a comparison with the original Leech illustrations will indicate, Williams and company made a conscious effort to duplicate the steel engraving technique that was utilized in Dickens's day.[20] Williams had previously duplicated this look in the animated portions of Tony Richardson's 1968 revisionist version of *The Charge of the Light Brigade*. But in addition to insuring the authenticity of *how* the film looked, exhaustive research was conducted to insure that *what* was depicted — buildings, furniture, clothing, etc. — was as authentic and accurate as possible. This approach resulted in a richly textured and meticulously detailed film, the overall impact of which, when combined with its skillful mixture of both subtle and intense colors, is simply stunning.

Stunning is also an apt word to describe a dazzling camera style that literally propels us through the story at breakneck speed. It opens, for example, high above the rooftops of London; then, via what can only be called a bravura tracking-shot, we are first transported into its labyrinthine streets, and then into the offices of Scrooge and Marley. We have, quite literally, descended into another world: the dark netherworld in which Ebenezer Scrooge is very much at home. There are also several instances in which transitions of time or place are handled in a similarly unconventional (and spectacular) manner. One is conscious here of a master filmmaker at work — in this case, a filmmaker who is also an animator. Indeed, comparisons to the style frequently exhibited by Orson Welles — exuberant, exhilarating, perhaps a bit flamboyant, but never ostentatious—would not be out of order.

This version also distances itself from most other animated *Carols* via the distinguished cast that came together to give voice to Dickens's characters. Sir Michael Redgrave, the most understated and underrated of the great British theatrical lions, provides a very restrained and subtle narration, and two of the principals from the classic 1951 live-action version, Alastair Sim and Michael Hordern, were reunited in the creation of a new classic. As noted earlier, Hordern was positively brilliant in his brief appearance in the earlier film, and his reprise of Marley adds immeasurably to an already rich texture.

And what more is there to say about Alastair Sim? Alastair Sim is, quite simply, Alastair Sim; and, for all practical purposes, Alastair Sim is Scrooge. His voice is clearly older, but still as unique and effective as ever, and his presence here is no gimmick masquerading as an homage. At times, though, it is clear that tribute is being paid to the earlier film apart from the simple presence of Sim and Hordern. Compare, for example, the mannerisms of the animated Scrooge, particularly when seated at his desk, to Sim's earlier performance. And this version's drawing of Old Joe, who buys up the deceased Scrooge's belongings in Christmas Future, is a dead ringer for the wonderful Miles Malleson who played the role in the earlier film.

The only thing that one can possibly complain about with this version is that it is not long enough; one can only regret that it wasn't produced as a feature-length film. In this sense, it shares some of the problems found in all versions that attempt to tell the story in less than sixty minutes, namely that a great deal of material must be compressed or omitted altogether. But in spite of these omissions and compressions, it is still one of the most faithful of all adaptations; the warmth of the "Dickens Christmas" is present in all the right places, and its particularly

nightmarish visualization of those troublesome children named Ignorance and Want assures us that the *Carol's* strong social commentary has not been given short shrift. It even manages to include many of the lesser known vignettes contained in Dickens's original text that are seldom, if ever, dealt with when the story is adapted to another medium. For example, we follow the Ghost of Christmas Present and Scrooge as they observe how Christmas is kept at a remote lighthouse and on a lonely ship at sea. And during their visit to the Cratchit household, the film picks up on what is only a portion of a sentence in Dickens's text in which we are told that the Cratchit family "had a song, about a lost child traveling in the snow, from Tiny Tim; who had a plaintive little voice, and sang it very well indeed."[21]

All things considered, this production remains the standard against which other animated *Carols* must be judged; and it certainly deserved its 1972 Oscar for best animated short subject. It is interesting, though, to play devil's advocate for a moment and wonder aloud if it isn't almost too good, or too intelligent, an adaptation. Its distillation of the story is so concentrated, its pace so quick, and its overall approach so subtle, that it seems to require a pretty solid familiarity with the original text in order to be fully appreciated. Indeed, one has to wonder how it would fare side by side with other animated *Carols*, in a demonstration arranged for a general audience— i.e., an audience that contains no Dickens or animation specialists. This may sound like elitism, or cynicism, or both, but neither is intended. We must simply recognize the fact that this kind of animation—for the sake of argument let's call it "artsy," a term that could also be applied to the UPA style in certain contexts—is totally at odds with the kind of sludge that has dominated the field for nearly four decades now. This may be the reason why, in spite of an outstanding and well-deserved critical reputation, this *Carol* is not and never has been the

perennial television favorite that it deserves
to be; nor is it available to the home video
market in a top-quality copy, as it most certainly should be.

After this 1971 effort, all manner of *Carols* continued to appear at a regular pace
throughout the decade. With just one exception (*The Passions of Carol*), all were produced for television. Some were animated,
and virtually all were variations of one sort
or another (and, as such, are covered in
Chapter 9 or the filmography, or both). This
pattern continued throughout the eighties
with most *Carols* coming via television,
although we also begin to note the appearance of direct-to-home-video releases. Some
of these *Carols* were interesting, some were
indifferent, and at least one (*Mickey's Christmas Carol*) was a major disappointment.

The eighties, however, was a particularly
significant decade in that it offered not one
but two productions that meet our criteria,
however imprecise they may be, of what
constitutes a major *Carol*. Both appeared
in 1984, and each came as a complete surprise in a decade which, as far as Dickensian adaptations are concerned, was filled
with surprises: Who could have predicted
1988's gigantic *Little Dorrit*? Or the even
more gigantic stage production of *Nicholas
Nickleby*, an extravaganza which eventually
found its way onto television and home
video? Or thought that among the many
Carols that appeared in the eighties, a serious retelling of the familiar story would
appear from a country other than America
or Great Britain? And who would have
thought that yet another version, regardless
of its place of origin, would emerge as a new
classic?

The non–American, non–British version,
entitled *Christmas Carol*, appeared on T F 1
television in France on Christmas Day 1984.
In calling attention to the fact that it is a
"foreign" *Carol*, no disrespect or chauvinism
of any kind is intended. Quite the contrary:
As with the Spanish *Carols* discussed earlier, this one is most welcome and appreci-

ated. It is simply a statistical fact that in spite
of the *Carol's* universal message and its enormous popularity throughout much of the
world, the overwhelming majority of film
and television adaptations have come from
English speaking nations, primarily America and Great Britain. Also, in the interest
of fairness to this particular *Carol*, as well as
full disclosure to the reader, this author must
state for the record that he does not speak
French. This being the case, the type of
extensive analysis that has been attempted
with other versions cannot be offered here —
but in its place, there follow some general
impressions of what is, without question, a
Carol to be reckoned with.

Actually, since the mechanics of the story
are so well known, this *Carol* is easy enough
for even a non-francophone to follow. Fur-
thermore by paying attention to body language, facial expressions, and tone of voice,
as well as the music and overall visual style
of the film, one can in fact appreciate it on
a fairly sophisticated level. (This author has
also received feedback and translations of
specific scenes from a specialist in French
language and culture.)

Even within this limited methodology it
is possible to state without hesitation that
this *Carol* is a fascinating adaptation filled
with many interesting surprises. To begin
with, the story has not been updated in any
way, nor has it been transposed to France;
the period and the setting are Dickens's
England. And in addition to the issue of
period and setting, one quickly notices that
this *Carol* features, to the best of this author's
knowledge, the only redheaded Scrooge to
date in Michel Bouquet who turns in an
excellent and very subtle performance.

In terms of its basic construction, nothing has been changed that in any way affects
the thematic substance of the story, although
a few creative touches are in evidence. For
example, the story itself is actually framed by
two incidents not found in Dickens's original text. It begins with Jacob Marley's
funeral at which we first encounter a Scrooge

who is clearly more concerned with getting back to business than he is with mourning for his dead partner. (The story then flashes forward to the famous Christmas Eve described by Dickens.) And for its finale, the story fades out at Scrooge's funeral, at which we see a grown-up Timothy Cratchit (still using a crutch) mourning the death of someone who had clearly become a close friend. Also noteworthy is Scrooge's encounter with the Ghost of Christmas Past, at the beginning of which he is transported, along with the large canopy bed in which he is sitting, to the middle of a pasture near the school that he attended as a boy. This "traveling bed" device is not repeated; nevertheless it is a delightfully unique way for Scrooge to begin his journey into the past. As *Télérama* noted in its review: "His [The Ghost of Christmas Past's] magic pulls Scrooge back to the village of his youth and transforms his canopy bed into a magic carpet."[22] And when Scrooge encounters his younger self at the school (a particularly cold, bleak and dilapidated place), he glances out a window and sees his old friend Ali Baba passing by, making this version one of a handful in which we actually see one of the fictional characters who were brought to life through Scrooge's boyhood reading.

But again, no substantive changes are in evidence here in terms of this *Carol's* relation to Dickens's original text; it is, in fact, a fairly straightforward adaptation. It does, however, break new ground in opting for an extremely low-key acting style in all major roles. While the reformed Scrooge is appropriately happy, indeed almost giddy, when he wakes up on Christmas morning, he is very quiet, restrained and introspective throughout much of the production. While we have seen introspective Scrooge's before, Bouquet's performance could well be termed definitive in this context. Of particular interest is the scene in which the Ghost of Christmas Past shows Scrooge the breakup of his relationship with his former sweetheart. As an extremely heated exchange

takes place between the two young lovers, the elder Scrooge just watches. He says nothing, and his face is expressionless. Yet Bouquet skillfully conveys the sense of a man who is seeing and hearing everything, and who is intensely aware of the price that he has paid for his past selfishness and foolishness.

Equally noteworthy are the various spirits who call upon this Scrooge, beginning with a bearded Jacob Marley who addresses his former partner in calm, measured tones which, paradoxically, are very disquieting since we have come to expect a certain amount of fire and brimstone from this particular spirit. The depiction of the three Christmas spirits, however, is particularly interesting. The Ghost of Christmas Past, for example, is a rather androgynous young man whose soothing speech almost seems designed to lull Scrooge to sleep, and the Ghost of Christmas Future is a very androgynous young woman who, in a nod to tradition perhaps, says nothing at all. Most surprising, however, is a Ghost of Christmas Present who, while clad in red (but not a bright red), is as far removed from the traditionally jovial essence of Christmas joy and bounty as one can possibly imagine. Instead, he appears here as a rather elegant man, perhaps in his early sixties, whose tone with Scrooge — even while revealing a particularly heartrending vision of Ignorance and Want — is, for the most part, gentle and almost paternalistic. (Only once does this spirit become angry with Scrooge: This is one of the very few versions to include that moment when Scrooge accuses the spirit of wanting to close bakeries and places of recreation for the poor on Sundays. In response, the spirit sharply rebukes Scrooge by telling him to instead blame those who do evil in the name of religion or through some hypocritical notion of what is right and proper. Scrooge is properly rebuked, but in a novel twist, he restores the spirit's good humor by sprinkling him with some of his own incense or "magic dust.")

These unique interpretations of the familiar Christmas spirits are matched by an equally unique approach in other areas. From a visual and aural standpoint, the production is richly atmospheric — and yet very subtly so. The overall look is dark, but it is not the almost film noirish darkness of the 1951 version with Alastair Sim. Here the dark shadows merge with muted colors, and overcast skies, and snow covered London streets that reflect an eerie bluish moonlight. And an evocative, and at times ethereal, score adds yet another layer of vaguely perceptible mystery. In this context, one also notes that after the initial use of Scrooge's "traveling bed," the transitions from one vision to the next are seamlessly, almost magically, smooth: In Christmas Past, for example, Scrooge gazes through a window at old Fezziwig's and observes his younger self feeling happy and in love. After a while, as the party begins to fade out, he becomes conscious of something behind him. He turns and finds that he is now standing in a garden, witnessing the breakup of his romance. And when the Ghost of Christmas Present invites Scrooge to touch his robe so that they may begin their journey, the room suddenly fills with fog, and where a wall had been just a moment before, they step directly out into a busy London street.

The overall effect here is that the sequences with the Christmas spirits — in essence, the core of the story — possess a lyrical, dreamlike, otherworldly quality that is hard to describe but even harder to overlook. While this could not be called a surrealistic *Carol*, it definitely takes a fascinating and subtle step or two in that direction at times. One is in fact reminded more than once, particularly in the Christmas Present sequence, of the classic 1946 French film adaptation of *Beauty and the Beast*. (Which raises an interesting thought: Think, just try to imagine, what Jean Cocteau might have done with the *Carol*.)

Unfortunately, this *Carol* is not commercially available — even in France! One hopes that this situation will be rectified someday as it deserves to be exposed to a wider international audience where it can take its rightful place on that relatively short list of *Carol* adaptations that manage to be both faithful and innovative. In the final analysis, viewers fluent in the French language will have to pass judgment as to whether it deserves to be called a classic. What is certain, however, is that another version appeared in 1984 — and how remarkable it is that two substantial adaptations would surface in the same year — that very quickly established itself as a bona fide modern classic.

The *Carol* in question, entitled *A Christmas Carol*, was first broadcast on December 17, 1984. It has since come to be widely known as the "George C. Scott version." It was filmed in England and is technically considered a British film; however, as noted earlier, it was released theatrically in England, and shown on television in America. As such, it could just as easily have been discussed in the previous chapter. However, since this book is written from the perspective of an American, let's approach it as a television production. Either approach, however, is still fairly consistent with the theory of a new major production appearing every fifteen to twenty years: If thought of as a theatrical film, it comes along fourteen years after Albert Finney's *Scrooge*, and if thought of as a television production, it appears thirteen years after Richard Williams's animated version.

When this one first appeared, most *Carol* purists probably approached it with a certain degree of trepidation, fearing perhaps a revisionist *Carol* that would do too much revising. It turned out, however, to be a magnificent production that confirmed that there was hope for quality filmmaking in the eighties and beyond. To begin with, it is stylishly directed by Clive Donner. As a director, he is one of those individuals whose career is marked by a consistent pattern of unevenness, and a rather quirky selection of subject matter; nevertheless, he is noted for

A Christmas Carol (1984): The Ghost of Christmas Present (Edward Woodward) and Scrooge (George C. Scott). Courtesy Photofest.

having a sense of visual flair and style that is clearly in evidence here, as it is in his 1982 production of *Oliver Twist* which also stars George C. Scott. (Working in tandem with Donner's visual panache, first-rate production values are in evidence throughout this *Carol*; it is a very good looking film.) Don-

ner's credits also include work for the stage and television, but in the present context it is worth noting that he broke into films as an editor, and that among the many notable British films that he edited in the 1950s was *Scrooge*—the "Alastair Sim version."

It is also important to note early on in

this discussion that, along with Scott's excellent performance as Scrooge, the film benefits immeasurably from one of those powerhouse ensemble casts for which British films are so famous: Frank Finlay, David Warner, Susannah York, Nigel Davenport, Michael Gough, Edward Woodward, et al. It is, in this respect alone, a joy to watch. And yet it is not just another one of those "less than meets the eye" television adaptations of a popular literary classic, the kind that is content to get by on costumes, scenery and British accents. Its insightful script by Roger O. Hirson provides the framework for one of the most thoughtful and provocative *Carols* ever. This is, in short, a *Carol* of great style *and* substance.

As the opening credits roll, there is yet another visit to a Victorian toyshop window; a nice touch, but the point is, wisely, not belabored. We also note the presence of a fairly substantial fog; it is nowhere near the kind of intensely thick fog described by Dickens in the opening pages of Stave One, but it is a detail usually overlooked by *Carol* adapters. The film wastes no time, though, in presenting its version of Ebenezer Scrooge. He has all the customary qualities that we have come to expect in any decent interpretation of the role, but as we see in his very elaborate humiliation of Bob Cratchit for using too much coal, he is also a bit of a martinet; and as we see in his confrontation with the charity solicitors, which here takes place at the Exchange rather than in Scrooge's office, he has a particularly well-developed penchant for sarcasm and smirking arrogance. As written by Hirson, this Scrooge is thoughtful, calculating, and extremely self-absorbed. He also possesses the kind of intelligence, intensity, and aggressiveness that are synonymous with George C. Scott. Indeed this Scrooge frequently confronts and challenges the spirits, and even attempts to strike bargains as if he were their equal; and when looking at the various visions he does not cower on the sidelines, but frequently gets up close and

confronts them as directly as possible. Without question, one will have to look long and hard to find a more cerebral or self-assured Scrooge, or one with a greater capacity for rage.

This then is a *Carol* dominated by an extraordinarily complex Scrooge. It is also, arguably, the ultimate example of a *Carol* that takes some substantial liberties with Dickens's text — primarily in terms of the additional information provided about Scrooge's background — while simultaneously remaining very faithful to it. For example, Scrooge is identified here as a grain merchant, as opposed to the usual depiction of a generic businessman or stereotypical miser. This sets the stage for a particularly callous Christmas Eve business transaction in which Scrooge is clearly unmoved when told that his money-gouging tactics will result in the poor not being able to afford the price of bread. One is again reminded of D. W. Griffith's *A Corner in Wheat* which focuses on another greedy grain merchant; it also reminds us of the consequences of such hard-hearted policies.

The most significant new information about Scrooge comes, of course, during his sojourn with the Ghost of Christmas Past. Although played by an obviously human Angela Pleasence, this is the closest that any live-action version comes to even suggesting the first phantom as written by Dickens; she even carries the extinguisher-cap or "bonnet" that Dickens describes, another detail that most versions choose to omit. As we have seen, this is not the first adaptation that attempts to explain Scrooge, but this one does so with a disarming bluntness that is virtually unprecedented. Immediately upon seeing his younger self at school, this Scrooge tells us that "his mother is dead" and that "his father holds him a grudge." (As in several other versions, Scrooge's father apparently blames the child for his wife's death during childbirth.)

Scrooge then sits down right next to his younger self who, as described by Dickens, is shown engrossed in a book. But there are no tears here, nor the sorrowful lament of "Poor boy!" found in Dickens's text. This Scrooge dismisses the ghost's suggestion that the boy has no real friends, and that the solace found in books is no substitute for human contact: "Robinson Crusoe not real? And Friday? And the parrot, with green body and yellow tail, not real? He made do, this boy." However, the real revelation comes when, after the familiar scene in which sister Fan comes to take her brother home for Christmas, we actually see Scrooge's father waiting for him with a coach outside the school. Unfortunately, there is no evidence that he is "so much kinder than he used to be." Instead, Nigel Davenport's brief cameo as the elder Scrooge presents an unsettling portrait of a cold, distant and, one suspects, genuinely disturbed individual. The whole scene echoes with chilling irony as Scrooge remarks, "My father was a very [he pauses here for a second, searching for the right word] stern man."

Again, this was not the first film or television *Carol* to open a psychological Pandora's Box. The Sim film did most of the initial spade work, and the Finney version went considerably further down the road. (As suggested earlier, Finney's is arguably the most alienated and lonely Scrooge yet filmed or televised; Scott's is far more angry and resentful.) Clearly, one can trace a psychological escalation that links these versions, culminating here in the most intense and complex Scrooge yet seen. It is important to remember, though, that while Dickens provided none of these details, there is nothing inconsistent here with what he intended. Indeed, it is possible to arrive at a quick distillation of just what he intended, and of what these films are on some level trying to say, by paraphrasing the words of George Orwell quoted earlier in Chapter Three: "Treat the child decently, and he or she will grow up to be a decent adult." Dickens's fiction is filled with children who have been ill-treated in one way or another, as well as with adults who, in one way or another, have survived such childhoods and become perfectly rotten adults; it does not, for example, require too vivid an imagination to conjure up an image of what Bill Sikes's childhood was like. Scrooge, however, is arguably the most significant example of the long-term consequences of such treatment. As another Scrooge puts it — in Warren Graves's 1978 *Scrooge*, one of the best modern stage adaptations (see filmography regarding its 1978 Canadian television adaptation) — when describing what his life was like when he was finally allowed to leave his lonely existence at school and return home: "They found me to be a cold, dark child. Was it any wonder? I had learned to live in a cold, dark place."[23]

While there is no question that the inclusion of Scrooge's father is a major stroke of inspiration, it should be noted that it works as well as it does because it is brief, subtle, and intelligently handled. One must fear, however, that it is only a matter of time before future adaptations from less skillful hands begin to hammer us with gruesome details of the horrors visited upon young Scrooge by his father. However, in the context of this father and son relationship, there is another *Carol* that must be mentioned, particularly since it appeared *before* the Scott version, namely the adaptation by Dennis Powers and Laird Williamson that has been staged by the American Conservatory Theatre in San Francisco since 1976, a special production of which appeared on cable television in 1981. (Since a line had to be drawn somewhere, stage adaptations are not discussed at length in this book. However, since this production did find its way onto television, it warrants at least a mention here on technical grounds alone. Truth be told, though, it warrants much more than that as the televised version is a brilliant and truly insightful production. Sadly, it was broadcast when access to cable television was not nearly as widespread as it is today, and it has never been released on

Scrooge (1978): Jacob Marley (Drew Borland) and Scrooge (Warren Graves) in televised version of Graves's Canadian stage production of the *Carol*. Courtesy Warren Graves.

home video; as such, it ranks among the most underrated, indeed the most unknown, of all extant televised *Carols*. See filmography for details.)

In the ACT version, in the Ghost of Christmas Past sequence, we find young Scrooge and Belle talking while ice skating on a beautiful, starlit Christmas night. When Belle suggests that a desire to prove himself to his father lies behind her fiance's hunger for success in the world of business, he attempts to deny it by saying: "He doesn't even know I'm alive. He'll probably never mention my name again, except in some drunken reproach. Well, let him if he please. What do I care? As for me he no longer exists. He might as well be dead." And when Belle insists that the problem is indeed Scrooge's tormented relationship with his father, and that he has never forgotten his cruelty, Scrooge replies: "Yes I have forgotten. I have forgotten my father. I have for-

gotten I ever was a child. [At this point he breaks down and cries.] I only remember the cold, the endless hours of work, and the beatings." Startling information indeed; while we do not actually see Scrooge's father, we learn disturbing details that one can only infer from the Scott version. And yet these revelations do not overwhelm us, nor do they leave us drowning in armchair psychology and psycho-babble. This young Scrooge is understandably hurt, angry, resentful, bitter — and the moment works as well as it does because, as with the appearance of Scrooge's father in the Scott version, it is brief, subtle, and intelligently handled.

Returning to the Scott version, however interesting and original the presence of Scrooge's father is, of far greater significance is the direct confrontation of hard core economics that is also implicit in Dickens's text. The Christmas Eve business transaction referred to above sets the stage here. Its

A Christmas Carol (1981): William Patterson as Scrooge in televised version of The American Conservatory Theatre's stage production of the *Carol*. **Courtesy Photofest.**

effect is as powerful as if we had seen Scrooge physically stealing a piece of bread from a hungry child. Then, also in Christmas Past, we see that the cause of young Scrooge's breakup with Belle was not the general change of heart usually referred to, but rather a conscious decision to assign a higher priority to his business interests. (We learn that Scrooge's father left him a small inheritance; Belle wanted to marry right away, but he preferred to wait and instead took the money and "laid the foundations of financial success.") As Paul Davis so aptly puts it: "In Victorian terms he has opted for Malthusian prudence. In contemporary terms he could be characterized as deciding between family and career, a far more ambiguous and difficult choice than that between marriage and miserliness."[24]

The sequence with the Ghost of Christmas Present continues this discussion of economics, but, in no sense does it skimp on its presentation of the festive side of Christmas described by Dickens. Scrooge and the ghost take a brief stroll through the streets and take in the sights and sounds of a busy marketplace. Scrooge remarks, "There's a lot of buying, isn't there?" and the spirit replies, "Oh Ebenezer, is that all you can see?" And the celebration at the Cratchit residence presents what may be the warmest and most sincerely felt depiction of this familiar scene. Worthy of particular mention here are the performances of Susannah York and David Warner as the Cratchits. Both are among the finest and yet most underappreciated players of their generation; in this case, one remembers Susannah York as a most attractive Mrs. Cratchit, and it is a remarkable film indeed in which a character played by David Warner can be described as gentle or even nice.

But, once again, the spectre of economics is felt here as it is in no other version. When Scrooge hears that his nephew has offered young Peter Cratchit a job at what he (Scrooge) considers an exorbitant rate of pay, he becomes indignant; and when he remarks, "It's a very small goose." The spirit turns and shouts in his ear: "It's all Bob Cratchit can ahfoad." (This is not an upper-class spirit.) (As mentioned when discussing the Albert Finney film, one can make the case that Kenneth More made the best Ghost of Christmas Present, but one would hate to have to choose between him and Edward Woodward, who is simply brilliant here in capturing all sides of Dickens's phantom. In this contest, Francis de Wolff's interpretation in the Alastair Sim *Carol* deserves honorable mention; his Ghost of Christmas Present lacks none of the warmth and heartiness with which Dickens imbued the character, although he is quite reserved when compared to either More or Woodward.)

The juxtaposition of events in this scene is interesting and revealing. After receiving a crushing rebuke from the spirit for his infamous crack about the surplus population (the spirit's lines are delivered in a searing, angry close-up: "So perhaps in the future you will hold your tongue until you have discovered what the surplus population is..."), this resilient Scrooge is still able to respond to Bob Cratchit's "founder of the feast" toast with chest-thumping bravado. "He's made a point, Bob Cratchit has," says the miser. "Without me there would be no feast. No goose at all. My head for business has furnished him employment."

Even at the end of the Christmas Present sequence, this Scrooge continues to prove a tough nut to crack. While he *is* weakening, he remains essentially unmoved by a vision of homeless families huddling for shelter under a bridge and cooking meager suppers over open fires. And when the spirit shows him a particularly gruesome vision of Ignorance and Want, he responds with, "Cover them, I do not wish to see them." This vision of the hungry and homeless, quite literally out on the streets, is, sadly, an accurate image from both Dickens's day and our own; it is a powerful addition to the story. It does, however, become a bit preachy (something Dickens *does not* do in the *Carol*) when a young father responds to his wife's inquiry as to whether or not they have enough wood to last the night: "Ay, it'll last through. At least there's one thing still free in this country." And a moment later he looks nobly at his hands and declares his willingness to work. Despite the obvious contextual relevance here, is it possible that a gratuitous swipe at Ronald Reagan or Margaret Thatcher is also on the agenda?

For anyone so inclined, it is possible to find other things to carp about in this *Carol*. For example, despite Scott's truly excellent performance, his English accent is simply not very good and its use is wisely kept to a minimum. One might also note the use of shimmering, soft light and a yellowish tint to suggest or add period flavor in places; such visual effects can easily become tiresome clichés. But on the whole there is very little to complain about in this *Carol*, and a great deal to praise. One is impressed, indeed disturbed, by its omnipresent economic dimension — and by its complex and very realistic Scrooge. And it is because this Scrooge is so much a reflection of real life that he can disturb us more than any other Scrooge to date. He is not evil, but he has been hurt and changed by evil. And he counters by making himself a master of all kinds of self-deluding sophistry and denial. For reasons that are ultimately impossible to define, the Alastair Sim version will always remain, for most of us, the best *Carol*; but, for the manner in which it holds up a mirror and challenges us to look at ourselves and our world, the George C. Scott version may well be the most important one. And let the record show that this very modern *Carol* avoids the pretentiousness and chic nihilism found in so many contemporary films that strain to be modern and relevant. Its creators understood that the ingredients necessary to give their *Carol* its cutting edge had already been discovered by Dickens, over a century earlier. As such, this *Carol* opts for Dickens, rather than Freud or some contemporary guru, for its denouement: In a subtly moving scene at his nephew's house on Christmas morning, the reformed Scrooge is anxious to put the past behind him. He has family and friends now, and a lot of happy, productive living to get on with. "God forgive me for the time I've wasted," he tells nephew Fred and his wife. Enough said.

No truly major *Carol* has appeared on television (or film) since the George C. Scott version debuted in 1984. Interestingly, the producers of this version, perhaps realizing that they have a classic on their hands, have wisely avoided the perils of overexposure; it has only recently been released on home video, and it is not televised every year like most other major *Carols*. This latter point goes a long way toward helping it retain some degree of specialness. (Remember how special *The Wizard of Oz* used to be when its appearances on television were carefully limited?)

There have actually been a number of other *Carols* since 1984, but for the most part they stand apart from the type of productions that have been the focus of this and previous chapters. Instead they join a parade of fascinating one-shots, parodies, and more

animation — to say nothing of assorted variations and abominations — which, as we will shortly see, can be traced back to Dickens's own day.

A Television Postscript

The previous chapter on sound film adaptations ended with speculation that the next major *Carol* might be a theatrically released film version. It appears, however, that it will indeed be television that ushers in the new millennium with a new major *Carol*. As this book goes to press in 1999, production is underway on a new television adaptation starring Patrick Stewart as Scrooge. And while it is obviously impossible to comment on it at this point, one can comment on some of the circumstances that surround it. To begin with, it appears that the theory of a new major *Carol* appearing every fifteen to twenty years will hold true once again. More importantly, however, Stewart has recently earned a place on that relatively short list of all-time great Scrooges thanks to his powerful one-man stage interpretation of the *Carol* and the subsequent audio recording that it inspired. As such, there is every reason to believe that this new television version will be a major *Carol* in every sense of the word. Stay tuned...

PART THREE

Dickens's Other Christmases

The very fact that Dickens returned again and again to the theme of Christmas, from Sketches by Boz *at the beginning of his career to the unfinished* Mystery of Edwin Drood *more than thirty years later, indicates that it had a more than casual significance for him.*

Katherine Carolan

While Dickens's "Ghostly little book" continues to be a source of endless interest and fascination, and while we look forward to each new adaptation, it is unfortunate that it has tended to overshadow his other Christmas-related works. Indeed, while it is difficult to imagine that more than one or two people in a thousand will not in some sense be familiar with the *Carol*, it is just as difficult to imagine that more than one or two will have even heard of *The Haunted Man* or *Mrs. Lirriper's Lodgings*.

It is not surprising, then, that there have been relatively few adaptations of Dickens's other Christmas works. Notwithstanding the obvious fact that many great films and television programs of all kinds have been produced over the years, the overall track record of the film and television industry is one of mediocrity and staggering stupidity. One might also add a propensity for playing it safe. Thus new *Carols* and *Olivers* continue to pile up, but one can grow very old waiting for a new version of *Barnaby Rudge* or *Dombey and Son*. In such a climate, it is an adventurous writer indeed who would approach the average film or television producer with a script of, say, *The Chimes*; and with just a little dramatic license — and perhaps an image in mind of the stereotypically crass, cigar-chomping mogul of old — one can readily imagine the typical response: "What the hell is this *Chimes*, where's the kid with the crutch?"

The following is an overview of Dickensian Christmases in which Jacob Marley and the Ghosts of Christmas Past, Present and Future do not appear.

Christmas Books

The success of *A Christmas Carol* initiated a practice that would continue almost
every year until Dickens's death: the creation
of a special "present" for his readers at
Christmas. It must be noted, however, that
on more than one occasion the creation of
this annual "present" is known to have put
Dickens's Christmas spirit to the test as the
smaller story became more of an obligation — rather than an expression of seasonal
joy and social concern — which kept him
from working on one of his novels. The
Carol (1843) was followed by *The Chimes,
The Cricket on the Hearth, The Battle of Life*
and *The Haunted Man*. Interestingly, the
Christmas holiday itself is directly addressed
in only the first and last of these works.

In 1852, these five short books were gathered together and published as *Christmas
Books*. The two-volume edition readily available in paperback from Penguin Classics
(first published by the Penguin English
Library in 1971), which features extensive
and authoritative commentary and notes by
the distinguished Dickens scholar Michael
Slater, is indispensable.[1]

The Chimes

Appearing in 1844, *The Chimes* was the
Carol's immediate successor in the Christmas Book genre. Written while Dickens was
living for a time in Italy, it is nevertheless
another very English product of the Hungry
Forties. The time, however, is New Year's
Eve, and like its predecessor this story contains a heartfelt plea for charity and broth-
erhood. The supernatural motif is employed
in the form of the spirits of the bells in an
omnipresent church tower. The book also
continues the *Carol's* vigorous assault on the
rampant social injustice of Dickens's day,
although in a much more explicit and con-
frontational manner. While much of its
social criticism, including some of Dickens's
most ferocious satire, is very topical, it still

delivers another timeless sledgehammer
blow.

Details on *The Chimes's* topical references
and background (which include such topics
as suicide and infanticide, as well as the
question of whether the poor have any right
to live at all) are documented in Michael
Slater's introduction and notes to the Penguin Classics edition referred to above, as
well as in his important essay *Dickens's Tract
for the Times*. Another valuable discussion of
this unjustly neglected work will be found in
Edward Wagenknecht's *Dickens at Work: The
Chimes*.[2] The story has attracted a modest
amount of attention on stage[3], but as for
audiovisual adaptations there is, sadly, little
to report on. Apart from an interesting pair
of silent efforts, it is positively astonishing
that it has been ignored for so long by film
and television. It would seem a particularly
appropriate subject for the BBC or American public television.

The Cricket on the Hearth

Dickens's Christmas offering in 1845
revealed a distinct change of pace from its
predecessors. It is essentially a domestic
melodrama which takes place in winter *after*
the holidays. The supernatural does not
figure directly in the proceedings, and social
criticism is noticeably absent. As its subtitle
A Fairy Tale of Home suggests, it is a quiet
little story, filled with warmth and charm, at
whose core is a fairy tale quality that is hard
to define but unmistakably present. Perhaps
its most interesting characters are the gentle toymaker Caleb Plummer and the servant Tilly Slowboy, yet another of Dickens's
memorable domestics. One would love to
see both playing out their parts on the larger
canvas of a Dickens novel.

Despite a poor critical reception, *Cricket*
was popular with the public and, from the
standpoint of its initial sales, is believed to
have been the most successful of the five
Christmas Books. It is known to have spawned
several theatrical productions within weeks

of its initial publication and was popular on the stage well into the twentieth century.[4] While one suspects that it is not widely read these days, it has inspired a fair number of audiovisual adaptations. It attracted the attention of D. W. Griffith, as well as early French and Russian filmmakers, and television has also turned to the *Cricket* with versions ranging from an early Grace Kelly vehicle to an animated musical. If nothing else, the range of these adaptations would seem to confirm that, apart from the *Carol*, the *Cricket* is the only *Christmas Book* that has managed to establish and sustain any sort of commercial life of its own.

The Battle of Life

There is a general consensus among critics and scholars that this 1846 effort is the least successful of the *Christmas Books* and that it ultimately gravitates to a resting place outside the comparatively close-knit circle of the other four. (To a lesser extent, the *Cricket* can also be viewed as a bit of an outsider.) To begin with, it takes place in the eighteenth century and, most importantly, is devoid of Christmas, the supernatural, and social criticism. It is essentially a sentimental story of familial devotion, focusing on a young woman who sacrifices her own happiness so that her sister can marry a man that they both love. If there is any sort of Christmas connection to be found, it is in the fact that it might be interpreted as a minor conversion tale: The sister's rather cynical father is deeply impressed by the love that his daughters bear one another and, in the end, seems resolved to see more good in the world and to take the gift of life a bit more seriously.

The Battle of Life has received a modest amount of attention from the theatre, primarily in the last century.[5] Not surprisingly, perhaps, there appear to have been no film or television adaptations and, as H. Philip Bolton points out, only one radio dramatization has been recorded.[6] While

unquestionably one of his minor works, like anything written by Dickens it is not without interest and small pleasures. In the final analysis, however, Michael Slater's observation that it is a "savagely foreshortened Dickens novel"[7] is unquestionably right on target.

The Haunted Man

In the fall of 1847 Dickens was hard at work on *Dombey and Son* and reluctantly concluded that another *Christmas Book* was out of the question for the upcoming holiday season; thus this final entry in the series did not appear until December 1848. After what might be termed the digressions of *The Cricket on the Hearth* and *The Battle of Life*, *The Haunted Man* returns to the seasonal setting, the supernatural dimension, and the explicit social criticism found in *A Christmas Carol* and *The Chimes*.

The resulting work is probably the most underrated of all of Dickens's Christmas writings. Its theme focuses on Dickens's belief that our spiritual health and happiness in the present is inexorably linked to our willingness to face and "deal with" the painful side of our past. A familiar theme of course, and in a sense, Dickens comes full circle with this book. Its main character, Redlaw, is ultimately converted through the direct intervention of the supernatural; Dickens recalls the Cratchits via his depiction of the poor but loving Tetterby family; and there is a chilling depiction of a wild, savage, starving young urchin, picking up where Dickens left off at the end of the *Carol's* Stave Three.

The Haunted Man appears to have inspired the fewest stage adaptations of all the *Christmas Books*, with most of them coming in the last century.[8] Surviving records tell us that at least two of them were spectacular affairs, with a flying ghost in one production, and in another, a ghost in the form of an image reflected via an offstage light source. Surprisingly, there appear to have

been no film or television adaptations even though, like *The Chimes*, this one cries out to be introduced to new audiences through an intelligent adaptation.

This lack of interest is particularly unfortunate because the story was produced during a particularly important and revealing phase of Dickens's career. Its closing line — "Lord Keep my Memory Green"[9]— is not only a fitting coda for his work in the Christmas Book genre, but, in a sense, perhaps even an apt summation of all that he hoped to accomplish (at least personally) through his work. And, as many commentators on Dickens have pointed out over the years, it is surely no coincidence that he would soon be embarking on his most sustained exercise in autobiography, *David Copperfield*.

Christmas Stories

When Christmastime rolled around in 1849, Dickens was immersed in *David Copperfield*. In the fall of 1850 he was not only laying his "favourite child" to rest, but had also assumed the pressures of publishing a weekly periodical, *Household Words*. Even a seemingly inexhaustible fount of energy and genius like Dickens was forced to decide that there would be no more *Christmas Books*. A far more manageable task would be to produce shorter seasonal works, which would be published in the pages of *Household Words*, and its successor *All the Year Round*. At least one such story appeared annually from 1850 through 1867; several were written in collaboration with Wilkie Collins. The first major collection of the *Christmas Stories* appeared shortly after Dickens's death.

As all Dickens lovers can readily attest, a dozen or so major novels will be found at the summit of his monumental body of work; for many, *A Christmas Carol* will be found there too. But the rewards hiding

in the fascinating nooks and crannies that make up the lower reaches should not be overlooked. The *Christmas Stories*, which today must surely be counted among Dickens's least familiar material, are a prime case in point. Like the *Christmas Books* they vary in the degree to which they have anything to do with Christmas per se, and as Margaret Lane points out in her excellent introduction to the Oxford Illustrated Dickens edition of the *Christmas Stories* the warmth and nostalgia of the early entries soon gives way to a steadily darkening tone.[10]

A Christmas Tree was the first and most famous of these stories; it is often included in Christmas anthologies. Here, in microcosm, is yet another classic "Dickens Christmas." It is rich in detail and holiday trimmings, and the tone is most definitely warm and nostalgic. And yet, being a free-flowing meditation upon a lifetime of memories that are embodied in, and associated with, the Christmas tree, an undeniable note of melancholy is present. Is it mere coincidence that it was written by the same man who had just finished *David Copperfield*, and not long before had written, "Lord Keep my Memory Green," and who, not long afterwards, would celebrate his fortieth birthday? (In this vein, it is probably worth noting that Dickens's 1851 Christmas contribution to *Household Words* was entitled *What Christmas Is as We Grow Older*.)

To see just how quickly the tone of these stories does indeed begin to change, one need only compare *A Christmas Tree* with Dickens's 1853 holiday effort *Nobody's Story*, a sharply satirical piece which amounts to nothing less than an indictment of the "haves" who mistreat the "have nots" in this world. Truly stunning in its directness, this is a piece worthy of mention whenever the subject of Dickens's social criticism is raised. Sadly, it is effectively lost between the

Opposite: **Dickens's last words in the Christmas Book genre: "Lord Keep my Memory Green" by Clarkson Stanfield. From** *The Haunted Man.* **Courtesy Dickens House Museum.**

covers of the *Christmas Stories* and seems destined to remain unknown to general readers. And while it is always dangerous to make too much out of apparently obvious connections between Dickens's works, it is interesting that *Nobody's Story* was written just after the conclusion of *Bleak House*, and that *Hard Times* and *Little Dorrit* lay not far ahead.

There is no question that the *Christmas Stories* should be counted among Dickens's minor writings, but this does not mean that their comparative obscurity is deserved. Nor does it make them unsuitable for adaptation, for in fact they have been tapped by film and television a surprisingly high number of times. "The Signalman" episode from *Mugby Junction* has emerged as a particular favorite in this regard. However, the 1972 animated version of *A Christmas Tree* must surely rank as one of the most surprising Dickensian adaptations to date. It does vaguely pick up on a few images or ideas that are suggested in Dickens's text, but it is not a serious attempt to film the story. Instead it descends into ridiculous cartoon fare involving children trying to recover the "essence of Christmas" that has been stolen by a giant and an evil magician; the storyline even includes an animated "appearance" by Dickens himself. It is worth noting here that while H. Philip Bolton reports only a smattering of interest in the *Christmas Stories* from the stage, Dickens frequently drew upon them in his public readings, as did the late Emlyn Williams in his one-man Dickens show.

For present purposes, it is interesting to think of the *Christmas Stories* in cinematic terms. One might, in fact, liken them to the so-called B films produced in the glory days of Hollywood. These films were modest in their conception and scope, and, to some extent, rather specifically targeted in terms of their intended audience. But as every film buff knows, they were rarely without interest. Like those movies, the ranks of Dickens's *Christmas Stories* are filled with real sleepers, like *Nobody's Story*; brilliantly created and executed characters, like Mrs. Lirriper, who transcend the modest vehicles in which they are entrapped; and minor classics like *A Christmas Tree*.

The Pickwick Papers

As mentioned in Chapter 1, *The Pickwick Papers* is one of the best loved and most widely read works in all of literature. And yet, within the context of Dickens criticism, one is frequently reminded that it is episodic, fragmented and generally lacking in structure when compared to his later, more sophisticated works. Indeed, in his various prefaces to the book, Dickens himself freely acknowledged its loose construction. However, for most readers *Pickwick* transcends such analysis and stands on firm ground as something very special indeed.

There have been many productions of *The Pickwick Papers* in just about every medium imaginable, but there is something about it that seems to resist a definitive interpretation; indeed, as far as the stage is concerned, one suspects that it will require a production of at least twice the size (and length) of the now legendary Royal Shakespeare Company production of *Nicholas Nickleby*.[11] As far as film and television is concerned, the 1952 British version is, as noted earlier, an excellent film, but one suspects that it will be a very different kind of film — and a very special one — that truly captures the essence of *Pickwick*. And even the extended length offered by the multi-part television format has never quite managed to do justice to its vast canvas and seemingly endless supply of memorable characters and incidents. Along these lines, we must surely regret that among the many unrealized projects of Orson Welles was an adaptation of *The Pickwick Papers* in which he considered featuring W. C. Fields as Mr. Pickwick. (Welles did produce *Pickwick*, as well as the *Carol* and other Dickensian tales, on radio.) Even a cursory viewing of *Citizen Kane*, particularly its first half, reveals a stunning freedom, originality, and confidence in its construction; a keen eye for characterization and detail; and a bubbling sense of energy and humor — all of which suggest that Welles was probably very much in touch with the heart and pulse of *The Pickwick Papers.*

Film and television versions of *Pickwick* have ranged from numerous shorts and a feature in the silent era, to lengthy treatments from England and Italy in the television era. In many cases these adaptations have focused on a key, more or less self-contained, episode; the famous trial of Mr. Pickwick is most often singled out in this regard. A few, including an interesting short made expressly for the educational film market, have focused specifically on the Christmas chapters.

Sketches by Boz

Not surprisingly, the various "sketches by Boz" have been virtually untouched by film and television. Vitagraph's 1913 one-reel version of *Horatio Sparkins,* and a 1956 production entitled *The Mating of Watkins Tottle,* which was broadcast live on NBC's *Matinee Theatre,* appear to be the only adaptations to date. The sketches have, however, received a bit more attention on the stage and on radio.

While there has always been some measure of critical disagreement about the extent to which the sketches can be viewed as a direct foreshadowing of the mature Dickens, they do indeed offer many fascinating previews of what was to come and are certainly possessed of their own unique life and energy. The more impressionistic sketches would obviously be difficult to dramatize, but it is unfortunate that more attempts have not been made. Early television, with its incredible wealth and diversity of thirty and sixty minute dramas (not to mention its frequent reliance on easily accessible literary classics that were in the public domain) would perhaps have been the ideal time and

place, although today's public television would also seem to suggest a safe haven for this type of material. In this context, an adaptation of *A Christmas Dinner* would not be at all out of the question. (A similar case can also be made for an adaptation of *A Christmas Tree* from the *Christmas Stories.* Its essentially abstract nature might at first suggest an unfilmable work. However, as the stunningly beautiful 1987 television adaptation of Dylan Thomas's *A Child's Christmas in Wales* demonstrates, it is indeed possible to film a work that is largely comprised of poetic imagery.)

Master Humphrey's Clock

Not surprisingly, Dickens's short-lived periodical does not appear to have inspired any film or television adaptations of any kind, let alone any that focus on the "Christmas episode" discussed in Chapter 1; however, H. Philip Bolton does list ten early theatrical productions which, even if in name only, boast some connection with *Master Humphrey.*[12] There have been several film and video versions of *The Old Curiosity Shop* and *Barnaby Rudge,* both of which were originally published within the pages of the *Clock;* however, like the novels themselves, they stand apart from the quickly abandoned framing device of the character of Master Humphrey.

Dickens's Last Christmases

Dickens' Last Christmases is the title of Katherine Carolan's seminal 1972 article which reminds us that in the last decade of his life — the period that produced the so-called "dark novels" — Dickens touched on the subject of Christmas in the context of two major works: *Great Expectations* and his unfinished final novel *The Mystery of Edwin Drood.*[13] However, as this article makes clear, these holidays are not the stuff from which our popular image of the "Dickens Christmas" has been fashioned. Indeed, they very much mirror that steadily darkening tone already noted in the *Christmas Stories*.

In *Great Expectations*, for example, a summary of the Christmas festivities would look something like this: A young boy, Pip, starts his Christmas Eve by being assaulted and threatened in a graveyard by an escaped convict. He then goes home, where he is beaten and verbally abused, forcefed a healthy dose of Tar-water, and sent to bed. On Christmas morning — a damp, cold, foggy Christmas morning — he steals food from his sister's kitchen and returns with it to the graveyard to give it to the convict. Later, at dinner, he is terrified that the theft will be discovered; he is given the most unappetizing scraps of meat to eat; and he is mercilessly tormented by a pack of particularly pompous and nasty adults (Joe, of course, excepted) who even compare him to a pig. The day is rounded off with a chilling trek through the muddy marshes at the end of which he witnesses two escaped convicts fighting like rabid animals. He then returns home, barely awake, where he is given a "heavy thump between the shoulders"[14] and quite literally dragged upstairs to bed.

In *The Mystery of Edwin Drood*, there is very little action that is directly related to Christmas. Instead we are dealing here more in terms of tone — and this tone is anything but merry. There is, for example, a vague but noticeable tension in the air as two leading characters (Rosa Bud and Edwin Drood) break their engagement, another (Neville Landless) prepares to "get out of town" on Christmas morning, and still another (John Jasper) continues to act in what can only be called a rather creepy and suspicious manner. In the second paragraph of the book's fourteenth chapter, where most of the Christmas references occur, we find *Drood*'s most substantial account of what Christmas in the city of Cloisterham is like. Just over half of this paragraph is devoted to a descriptive montage of the holiday goings-on in the streets of the city. Whether Dickens

intended it or not, this passage immediately demands comparison with the enchanting descriptions of Christmas bounty found in the *Carol*. Dickens tells us that "red berries shine here and there"[15] and that "lavish profusion is in the shops,"[16] and yet the predominant color or tone of what he goes on to describe is gray, and its look is more than a little bit shabby. Indeed, as Katherine Carolan observes, "Christmas in Cloisterham has a strangely modern air."[17]

Audiovisual adaptations of these two works have generally tended to minimize (or in some cases ignore) any connection with Christmas; nevertheless, one can also point to a couple of instances where an interesting bit of minor expansion is in evidence. In the case of the definitive David Lean version of *Great Expectations*, for example, there appears to be some sort of greenery in evidence at Pip's home, but otherwise the film makes absolutely no reference to the holiday setting. Conversely, the 1989 miniseries clearly acknowledges the holiday and even adds a scene in which Pip brings some food out to a group of carolers that have stopped outside the forge. The version that most accurately captures the content, and spirit, of *Great Expectations*' rather depressing holiday is probably the 1981 adaptation from the BBC.

The Mystery of Edwin Drood has been adapted far less often, and only two versions are readily available for assessment. The appropriately somber 1993 British adaptation places the story in summer, rendering the question of Christmas moot. The 1935 Hollywood version, however, does a nice job of conveying the general tone of the book in this regard. While it does not show us anything of how Cloisterham is decked out for the holiday, there is a brief scene in which we follow a group of carolers about the city on Christmas Eve. The mood here is what might be termed quasi-gothic film noir, and that is precisely what any decent adaptation of *Drood* should be. The "Christmas angle" is briefly noted, almost subliminal; and yet an alert viewer, with only a casual knowledge of Dickens, cannot help but noticing that something is wrong. This is not what is supposed to come to mind when one thinks of Dickens and Christmas.

The question of what happened to the joyous Christmases of *Pickwick* and the *Carol* is complex to say the least, and one must ultimately look to the detailed chronological picture contained in a full-length biography in order to see how all the pieces fit together. However, in broad terms, Dickens is generally thought to have grown increasingly pessimistic, regretting, perhaps, that while his books were still very popular, their various messages seemed to be falling on deaf ears. His later years were filled with all manner of personal troubles as well: In 1858, for example, he separated from his wife with whom he had been unhappy (dissatisfied may be a better word) for many years. (Not long before this he met Ellen Ternan, with whom he maintained a close, albeit fairly secretive, relationship until the time of his death.) And in the last decade of his life, the 1860s, the passing of his mother (with whom he was not close), three brothers, one son, and a number of close friends insured that the spectre of death was never far out of sight; indeed, in 1865, he narrowly escaped death himself in a railway accident in which several of his fellow passengers were killed and many more injured. He also suffered from a variety of physical ailments and was frequently in great pain, and he suffered great anxiety about money, and about his relationship with his public. Such worries, in fact, caused him to maintain an exhausting schedule of physically demanding public readings, including a grueling American tour in 1867-68.

In trying to sum up these late Dickensian Christmases, that "strangely modern air" just referred to with regard to *Edwin Drood* comes to mind once again. In the case of *Great Expectations*, it permeates the house on Christmas morning when Mrs. Joe is too busy putting on a great show of cleaning, and otherwise preparing for the farcical feast that will take place later in the day, to accompany Joe and Pip to church. How many of us have not, at least once in our lives, gotten so caught up in our Christmas "duties" that the holiday quite literally passes us by, leaving us feeling nothing but tired?

Is it possible that Dickens saw this coming much earlier than *Great Expectations*? Did he recognize it when the "Dickens Christmas" was just a few years old? As noted earlier, *The Haunted Man* (1848) is undoubtedly Dickens's most underrated Christmas work. In it we are introduced to the Tetterby family who, like the Cratchits, are poor; and, like the Cratchits, they are used to "making do" all year round, Christmas being no exception. One evening, after returning from shopping, Mrs. Tetterby confesses to her husband:

> ...this being Christmas-time, when all people who can, make holiday, and when all people who have got money, like to spend some, I did, somehow, get a little out of sorts when I was in the streets just now. There were so many things to be sold — such delicious things to eat, such fine things to look at, such delightful things to have — and there was so much calculating and calculating necessary, before I durst lay out a sixpence for the commonest thing; and the basket was so large, and wanted so much in it; and my stock of money was so small, and would go such a little way....[18]

These feelings pass very quickly; she regrets them, and gives thanks for what she does have, her family most especially. Nevertheless, they make a quiet impression on the reader, and on the "Dickens Christmas" — and their "strangely modern air" lingers. There may not be pessimism per se at work here, but let's at least call it creeping disillusionment.

However, it is the presence of that wild young urchin alluded to earlier in *The Haunted Man*, a work which appeared just five years after the *Carol*, that must surely be taken as a bad sign. In his important 1951 essay entitled *Dickens's Christmas Books*, John Butt asks: "And the boy labeled 'Ignorance' in *A Christmas Carol*, what has he become? He has become in *The Haunted Man* a clearly recognizable savage slum child."[19] And, as Professor Butt goes on to point out, we will encounter this boy again, just a few years later, in the form of Jo in *Bleak House* (1852–53).

But before the appearance of *Bleak House*, Dickens would make what may well be his strongest statement on the matter in *A December Vision*, a chilling, apocalyptic piece of journalism which appeared shortly before Christmas of 1850. In it he reminds us that the Spirit of Death will eventually come for us all, and that those who have failed to act against evil and injustice will have much to answer for. On the subject of children we are told:

> I saw a Minister of State, sitting in his Closet; and round about him, rising from the country which he governed, up to the Eternal Heavens, was a low dull howl of Ignorance. It was a wild, inexplicable mutter, confused, but full of threatening, and it made all hearers' hearts to quake within them. But, few heard. In the single city where this Minister of State was seated, I saw Thirty Thousand children, hunted, flogged, imprisoned, but not taught — who might have been nurtured by the wolf or bear, so little of humanity had they within them or without — all joining in this doleful cry. And, ever among them, as among all ranks and grades of mortals, in all parts of the globe, the Spirit went; and ever by thousands, in their brutish state, with all the gifts of God perverted in their breasts or trampled out, they died.[20]

Over the course of roughly ten years, then, Dickens sounded an alarm, each time much louder, as a briefly glimpsed allegorical figure became a nameless but unforget-table child of the streets, who in turn multiplied into thirty thousand nameless children of the streets and then gave way to a significant character in a major novel. Clearly it had not escaped his attention that the moral transformation so fervently called for in the *Carol* was rather slow in coming about.

And yet, to return to the 1860s, it must be said that all is not pessimism, nor doom and gloom, in these two late glimpses of Christmas. As Katherine Carolan very astutely points out, the wretched dinner endured by Pip is but one of two Christmas dinners in *Great Expectations*: "For all its bizarre circumstances, the breakfast Pip takes to Magwitch on Christmas morning is more in keeping with the spirit of the holiday than his sister's dinner."[21] Indeed. (Surprisingly, this aspect of Magwitch's Christmas dinner has usually gone unrecognized in the numerous film and television adaptations of this story. However, in the 1934 Universal version, Pip finds Magwitch in the cemetery on Christmas morning, standing, with outstretched arms, in front of a large stone cross; and underscoring the scene's obvious symbolism, a burst of inspirational music briefly rises up on the soundtrack.) And what of Joe's response to Magwitch, when the convict takes the blame for stealing Mrs. Joe's precious savoury pork pie: "God knows you're welcome to it.... We don't know what you have done, but we wouldn't have you starved to death for it, poor miserable fellow-creatur."[22] Even at this early point in the narrative, the reader doesn't need to be reminded that Joe is as kind, decent, and humble a man as can possibly be imagined; nevertheless, is there not some measure of hope to be found in this elegantly simple articulation of Christian charity?

And is there also some sense in which *Great Expectations* can be viewed as another Dickensian tale of reformation? Pip does, after all, come to regret, and eventually rectify, his mistakes; and while one suspects that life will always remain rather bittersweet for him, it appears that the reformed Pip will be living happily ever after as the story trails off. And do we wish to make anything of the fact that, at the start of the last chapter, Dickens tells us that Pip returned to his old home, after eleven years in India, "upon an evening in December, an hour or two after dark"?[23] (The 1974 version of the story starring Michael York has Pip returning on Christmas Eve.) The ground is rather shaky here, and it is well to remember that *Great Expectations* is a *very* complex novel; central questions of good and evil are being asked, and things do not happen for obvious reasons.

It may be more profitable to remember that while we hear Pip's story told in the first person, Dickens is speaking through other characters as well. Consider, for example, Mr. Jaggers's hypothetical explanation to Pip of the circumstances under which he, as an attorney specializing in criminal matters, took charge of the young child Estella many years earlier:

> Put the case that he [Jaggers's hypothetical self] lived in an atmosphere of evil, and that all he saw of children was, their being generated in great numbers for certain destruction. Put the case that he often saw children tried at a criminal bar, where they were held up to be seen; put the case that he habitually knew of their being imprisoned, whipped, transported, neglected, cast out, qualified in all ways for the hangman, and growing up to be hanged. Put the case that pretty nigh all the children he saw in his daily business life, he had reason to look upon as so much spawn, to develop into the fish that were to come to his net — to be prosecuted, defended, forsworn, made orphans, bedeviled somehow.[24]

Dickens scholars have pointed out that the events of Pip's early years, and therefore of Estella's early years, take place somewhere in the first third of the nineteenth century.[25] Thus Jaggers is describing here many of the same problems and conditions which, as we have seen, bore so directly on the writing of the *Carol*. There is an unmistakable intensity, almost a bitterness, about the tone of Jaggers's remarks that seems to suggest that Dickens is still aware of, and disgusted by, such things in the early 1860s and that, to some extent at least, they helped to fuel his growing pessimism. And yet, once again, all is not doom and gloom, for the grim litany spelled out above is relieved when Jaggers continues: "Put the case, Pip, that here was one pretty little child out of the heap who could be saved."[26] And so, as we know, this seemingly heartless lawyer did indeed pluck the young Estella from that heap of doomed children.

In searching for signs of optimism in *Great Expectations*, one is tempted to pounce on the fact that, at the last minute, Dickens substituted what can only be called a conventional "happy ending" for one which was much more consistent with the predominantly melancholy tone of the rest of the book.[27] However, is there a more subtle message to be found in Jaggers's account of what, for all we know, may have been the only truly decent thing he ever did in his life? Can we hear Dickens saying that, although society may appear to be rotten to the core, and that his message of almost twenty years earlier has been largely ignored, all is not lost? Can we hear him saying, "Put the case that no matter how true and disheartening these things may be, the individual can, and must, still try to *do something*." The Christmas world of *Great Expectations* is clearly not the same world that Scrooge's nephew charged through with such confidence and good cheer; nevertheless, some echoes, however faint, of the old "Carol philosophy" can still be heard.

And what, ultimately, are we to make of Dickens's very last writing on the subject of Christmas? If one had to describe it in one word, it can at best be called depressing. In addition to the rather dreary festivities described in the second paragraph of *Drood's* "Christmas chapter," and its "strangely modern air," what else happens over the holiday in Cloisterham? Instead of the requisite dusting of Christmas Eve snow, the town is ravaged by a fierce storm of wind and rain — and the population spends its Christmas Day investigating, or otherwise preoccupied with, the mysterious disappearance of Edwin Drood. And can we not assume that the town's collective Christmas spirit was dampened even further by the possibility that foul play might be involved in this disappearance?

There is simply no getting around the fact that this is a very dark and disturbing episode, in a very dark and disturbing book. However, before leaving this subject, it is worth taking a look at the paragraph that begins *Drood's* "Christmas chapter":

> Christmas Eve in Cloisterham. A few strange faces in the streets; a few other faces, half strange and half familiar, once the faces of Cloisterham children, now the faces of men and women who come back from the outer world at long intervals to find the city wonderfully shrunken in size, as if it had not washed by any means well in the meanwhile. To these, the striking of the Cathedral clock, and the cawing of the rooks from the Cathedral tower, are like voices of their nursery time. To such as these, it has happened in their dying hours afar off, that they have imagined their chamber-floor to be strewn with the autumnal leaves fallen from the elm-trees in the Close: so have the rustling sounds and fresh scents of their earliest impressions revived when the circle of their

lives was very nearly traced, and the beginning and the end were drawing close together.[28]

It seems that people are still coming home for Christmas. And is that the Ghost of Christmas Past's voice that one hears between the lines: "Christmas Time! That man must be a misanthrope indeed, in whose breast something like a jovial feeling is not roused — in whose mind some pleasant associations are not awakened — by the recurrence of Christmas."[29] And again: "Happy, happy Christmas, that can win us back to the delusions of our childish days."[30] And yet again:

> And I *do* come home at Christmas. We all do, or we all should. We all come home, or ought to come home, for a short holiday — the longer, the better — from the great boarding-school, where we are for ever working at our arithmetical slates, to take, and give a rest.[31]

Without attempting for one second to deny the darkening tone of Dickens's later years and work, nor the dark events that follow this opening paragraph in Cloisterham, it might, for present purposes, be enough to simply focus on a prematurely old man. He is sick and tired — to some extent through his own fault, but sick and tired none the less — and he knows that the circle of his own life is very nearly traced. However, as Katherine Carolan has observed in the epigraph which began this chapter, Christmas still has "a more than casual significance for him."

Variations on
a Theme by Dickens

Numbers of unknown fiddlers, hearing of the success of Mr. Dickens's opera, rush forward fiddle in hand, of the very same shape by the very same maker. "Come and hear our partition," they say....

William Makepeace Thackeray

The film and television adaptations considered thus far — even those that have animated, psychoanalyzed or musicalized the *Carol*— all qualify as essentially faithful representations of the story that Dickens wrote. However, as we have seen, substantive adaptations don't come along all that often. And yet we have suffered no shortage of audiovisual *Carols* in recent years. Indeed, one is hard pressed to locate many postwar Decembers in which there has not been at least one new manifestation of the familiar story. The postwar era, of course, coincides with the period in which television has been among us.

However, it can still come as a bit of a shock to even the most devoted *Carol* completists — those of us who will not rest until every extant version has been dutifully tracked down, and every rumor of a new one investigated thoroughly — to note the astonishing number and diversity of sequels, continuations, parodies, updatings, variations, etc., etc., that have proliferated over the years. From a practical standpoint, one can also include here the many minor versions, both live-action and animated, that attempt to play it straight with the *Carol* but, through a paucity of budget or inspiration, usually fall rather short of their mark.

However, setting aside the issue of quantity, we are not shocked by the basic *idea* of all these variations on a theme by Dickens; on the contrary, we have come to expect them. As such, many diverse voices join in the celebration as Alastair Sim and

159

The Odd Couple (1970): Tony Randall (left) and Jack Klugman star in one of many television sitcom *Carol* variations. Courtesy Photofest.

George C. Scott mingle with Alvin the Chipmunk, Scrooge McDuck, the Jetsons, the Muppets and the Flintstones. And there are numerous twentieth-century updatings of the *Carol*, with business-suited Scrooges (male and female) who remind us that its message is indeed timeless. We have also had a cowboy *Carol*, a country music *Carol*, a pornographic *Carol*, a *Carol* to teach us the value of conserving energy, and *Carols* for the classroom and the boardroom.

Count also the numerous spoofs and humorous skits that have been a television staple for the last forty or so years. If it is true that, sooner or later, every actor worth his salt wants to have a go at Hamlet, then it also seems true that, sooner or later, most television sitcoms will feel obliged to have a little fun with the *Carol*. Vaudeville has been dead for a long time now, and the once familiar refrain of "Slowly I turned..." is all but

forgotten; however, its electronic cousin carries on, with "Bah! Humbug!" a very reliable component of its verbal repertoire. (And while on the subject of electronic variations, please note that among the many straightforward dramatic adaptations produced on radio over the years, one can also find the *Carol* being kidded by Burns and Allen as well as the gang at *Duffy's Tavern*, updated to the hardboiled world of Dick Powell's *Richard Diamond, Private Detective*, and transposed to the old West by James Stewart's *The Six Shooter*. And please also note that among the many straightforward recordings of the *Carol* that have been released over the years, particularly the years before the tape and compact disc era, one will find humorous interpretations by an interesting assortment of talents ranging from Howdy Doody and Mickey Mouse to Stan Freberg, Rich Little and Lord Buckley.)

The Muppet Christmas Carol (1992): Scrooge (Michael Caine) and Bob Cratchit (Kermit the Frog). Courtesy Photofest.

Count too the occasional frontal assault, like Bill Murray's mean-spirited *Scrooged*, or a number of recent animated atrocities (not surprisingly, Beavis and Butt-head lead the pack here) in which gentle lampooning is supplanted by deconstruction — if not outright destruction. In spite of its enormous popularity, not everyone likes the *Carol*, nor does everyone necessarily agree with its various messages and assumptions. The viewer is well advised to question the motives of filmmakers and producers when judging *Carols* such as these.

And what of those instances in which

even a hint of *Carol* iconography makes a full-fledged adaptation unnecessary? What of those countless mean, miserly individuals, like the recurring character of Ben Weaver on *The Andy Griffith Show*, who operate their Scrooge franchises in countless television shows? An early example of television's interest in this type of *Carol* variation is NBC's 1945 broadcast of Margaret Cousins's short story entitled *The Strange Christmas Dinner*.[1] The focus here is on the grumpy proprietor of a dingy Times Square restaurant who refuses to give his employees a day off for Christmas. (To make matters worse, he also insists on serving pigs' feet for Christmas dinner!) However, he is given a crash course in Christmas spirit by his only holiday customer — a mysterious, oddly dressed stranger who turns out to be none other than Charles Dickens himself! Interestingly, NBC produced a second adaptation of this story in 1949. This latter version is an engaging Christmas treat which features a fine performance by Melvyn Douglas as Charles Dickens. (See filmography for details.)

While the mean miser has indeed become a television mainstay, he has also been known to turn up in the occasional feature film. For example, there were two silent versions of Richard Ganthony's 1899 play *A Message from Mars* in which a very Scrooge-like astronomer is shown the error of his ways by a visitor from the red planet. The first, which was made in England in 1913, may in fact qualify as the first filmed *Carol* variation; the second came from America in 1921. Now, since H. G. Wells's *The War of the Worlds* was published in 1898, it is probably safe to assume that Dickens was not the only author who influenced this story; nevertheless, the "*Carol* connection" is unmistakable.[2] In between these two films there was the 1917 Bluebird Photoplays production of *My Little Boy*. (As noted in Chapter 5, Bluebird had already produced *The Right to Be Happy*, a formal *Carol* adaptation, the previous year.) Drawing on both

the *Carol* and Eugene Field's poem *Little Boy Blue*, the story introduced viewers to a wealthy old grouch whose objection to his nephew's marriage causes the two to become estranged. (As in the "Carol," the nephew is named Fred.) A few years later, the old man dreams that he has accidentally killed the nephew's son on Christmas Day. Upon waking, and realizing that it was just a dream, he repents and embraces both his family and the holiday.

And what of the ultimate Scrooge wannabe, Mr. Potter, in Frank Capra's 1946 classic *It's a Wonderful Life*? As noted earlier, Potter is a genuinely mean individual. He is, in fact, more aggressively mean and overtly dishonest than any depiction of Scrooge, including Dickens's, to date. He does, after all, literally steal money from George Bailey; for all his faults, we cannot call Dickens's Scrooge a criminal in any legal sense of the word. Nevertheless, in its depiction of this character the film unquestionably relies on an awareness of the *Carol* and its attendant imagery, going beyond the fact that Potter is played by Lionel Barrymore, the actor whose name, for an American audience in 1946, was virtually synonymous with that of Ebenezer Scrooge.

There is, of course, no direct connection between the *Carol* and *It's a Wonderful Life*, and yet the former inevitably seems to crop up as a primary point of reference in any discussion of the latter. Many in fact feel that Capra's film has overtaken Dickens's book (and its various film and television incarnations) and become both the definitive Christmas story and the definitive Christmas film. At the very least, a consensus seems to have emerged that *It's a Wonderful Life* is a quintessentially American Christmas story — in effect, the American *Carol*. Nevertheless, the extent to which the *Carol* informs the film cannot be overstated, particularly when one considers the fact that it is known to have been one of the filmmaker's favorite books.[3]

It is perhaps enough to simply remind ourselves that for all of *It's a Wonderful Life's* vast charm and sheer brilliance, the template for this type of story was manufactured in 1843 by a young man named Charles Dickens.

Returning to television, let us not forget those thirty-second conversion plays, otherwise known as television commercials, in which a mean looking individual who may or may not be identified as Scrooge is transformed through the intercession of the Christmas marketplace. If a brand new (insert product name here) can get a smile out of old Scrooge, shouldn't you have one too? The line that separates tribute and exploitation blurs considerably, and with remarkably few exceptions, such *Carols* and mini–*Carols* are usually a great deal of fun.

But fun notwithstanding, the task of collating and coming to terms with these film and television *Carol* variations is no easy task. A chapter on this subject, one might

An American Christmas Carol (1979): **Henry Winkler as twentieth-century Scrooge Benedict Slade. Courtesy Photofest.**

imagine, would comprise a lengthy and detailed discussion that would meticulously weigh the pros and cons of all known variations. The air is filled with all sorts of interesting questions: Is *Br'er Rabbit's Christmas Carol* a more faithful telling of the story than *Mickey's Christmas Carol*? Does *An American Christmas Carol* do a better job of transposing Scrooge and company to the twentieth century than, say, *Skinflint* or *John Grin's Christmas*? Of the many recent high-brow *Carol* variations, which was most effective: the opera, the mime show, or the ballet? And who is the best female Scrooge to date? Is it Susan Lucci as Ebbie Scrooge in *Ebbie*; Cicely Tyson as Ebenita Scrooge in *Ms. Scrooge*; or Mary Stuart as Carol Screwge in *The Passions of Carol*?

It soon becomes apparent that a chapter will not suffice; a book length study could be devoted to resolving such tantalizing questions. Someday, undoubtedly, such a study will appear. Until then, the world's *Carolers* will have to construct their own pantheon of *Carol* variations. The filmography that comprises roughly the final third of this book places them in the overall context of *Carol* adaptations, and is intended to provide a useful point of reference in this regard. However, the task of seeking out and evaluating these variations is often its own reward, and somehow one never tires of asking, "What have they done now with (or to) the *Carol*?" A far more useful pursuit might be to view these variations as part of the process of "responding to" the *Carol*, and to continue to be amazed at what a truly universal story — an utterly indestructible story — Dickens wrote.

But when and where (and why) did all this tinkering begin? As we have seen, the first cinematic adaptation of the *Carol* appears to have been produced in 1901, yet we have also seen that *Carol* adaptations, most definitely predate the cinema. *Carol* variations predate the cinema as well. However, a thorough analysis of the *Carol's* influence on subsequent Christmas literature and other media is a formidable task that is beyond the scope of this discussion. Nevertheless, that influence has been considerable, and it is important for today's space age *Carolers* to be at least generally aware of the fact that, like the *Carol* itself, the endless variations that we take so much for granted today were not, and are not, created in a vacuum. Instead, they are an offshoot of a grand tradition — a grand *literary* tradition — of interpreting, exploiting, and in one way or another responding to, Dickens's "Ghostly little book." And with an eye toward doing no more than familiarizing ourselves with the lay of the land, this notion of responding to the *Carol* is perhaps the best place to start.

The responses have always come in many forms, and as we have seen with the notorious piracy from *Parley's Illuminated Library* as well as the initial burst of theatrical adaptations,[4] they came very quickly. These were the first of what might be termed the direct responses, that large and unending body of work that runs the gamut from inspired variation to outrageous ripoff, from affectionate parody to vicious satire. Consider just a random sampling from Dickens's own lifetime: In 1844, the prolific American writer Joseph Holt Ingraham produced *Santa Claus, or The Merry King of Christmas: A Tale for the Holidays*, in which an omniscient narrator whisks the reader through the streets of a city (apparently Boston) on Christmas Eve to look in on the lives of both rich and poor.[5] There are no Scrooge and Cratchit surrogates present in this story, but its debt

to the *Carol*, including much in the way of stinging social criticism, cannot be ignored. And, from England, one finds W. M. Swepstone's *Christmas Shadows* from 1850, a politically and economically charged tale in which a Scrooge-like character is converted by allegorical ghosts named Starvation and Conscience.[6] Then there is Horatio Alger's 1863 story entitled *Job Warner's Christmas*; in this version it is not the supernatural, but a Cratchit-like bank clerk's act of Christmas Eve charity, that transforms yet another Scrooge-like man of business.[7] And in 1865 Bret Harte produced one of his finest "Condensed Novels" entitled *The Haunted Man* in which he drew upon the *Christmas Books* (specifically *A Christmas Carol* and *The Haunted Man*) to create a brilliant and loving parody, not of the *Carol* per se, but of Dickens's writing style in general.[8]

These *Carol*-inspired works appeared during Dickens's lifetime. However, after Dickens's death, the story continued to serve as a pattern and a springboard for new efforts, perhaps the most interesting early example of which was Louisa May Alcott's charming if sentimental 1882 short story entitled *A Christmas Dream, and How It Came True* in which a spoiled little girl learns a valuable lesson about Christmas, and about life, after reading the *Carol*.[9] And later, as Paul Davis has noted, one finds the story being used even more creatively when it becomes both a political sounding board and a vehicle for humor: "'Irreverent' parodies, imitations using the *Carol* as a framework for political or social commentary, seem to have begun in 1885 in *Punch*. In the following two decades parodies of the *Carol* appeared regularly in the Christmas issues of *Punch* and other popular magazines."[10] This process, in tandem with the concurrent movement into the music halls and cinemas, ensured that by early in this century the *Carol* was one of the most brilliant (and reachable) points of light in the pop culture firmament. And the writers, journalists, humorists, and political cartoonists have

Left: **Susan Lucci as Ebbie Scrooge in** *Ebbie* **(1995).** *Right:* **Cicely Tyson as Ebenita Scrooge in** *Ms. Scrooge* **(1997). Courtesy Photofest.**

never stopped reaching out to the *Carol* when in need of the "Ghost of an Idea."

However, it should be noted that the *Carol* was also largely responsible for creating a climate in which responses of a more general nature were not only possible but expected and, from the point of view of the professional writer, potentially profitable. These might be termed the indirect responses. As we have seen, a long and rich tradition of Christmas-related literature predated the *Carol* in England. Dickens was aware of this legacy, and it certainly helped to inform the atmosphere in which he labored in the last quarter of 1843. And the basic idea so closely associated with the *Carol's* initial appearance — that of producing "something special" for the holiday — was not without precedent. Prior to the *Carol's* debut, publications known as annuals or gift books regularly appeared at Christmas. These were basically collections of verse, fiction, essays and illustrations designed to make an attractive holiday gift; in modern terms, they might be likened to the Christmas anthologies and special issues of popular magazines that appear without fail every December. However, in the *Carol*, Dickens created something new and very special indeed, something which (in his hands at least) rushed to the forefront of an ongoing process of defining and redefining the celebration of Christmas. It was, in fact, nothing less than a new literary genre: the Christmas Book.

As defined by *A Christmas Carol*, a Christmas Book was an attractively packaged, original piece of fiction that was published in time for holiday consumption. It was much shorter than a novel, even a short novel; but longer than a short story, even a long short story. This comparative brevity is an important point in that, in an age without radio or television, it could be read or listened to in one evening. (Today, one can listen to an unabridged recording of the *Carol* in about three hours.) Thus the Christmas Book provided Victorian readers and listeners with a complete, self-contained experience — not unlike today's practice of settling down on the couch for a couple of hours and watching a new made-for-TV Christmas movie. And finally, and arguably most importantly, the Christmas Book (at least as initially defined by the *Carol*) had a direct connection and relevance to the holiday in terms of its content and theme.

The Christmas Book has never disappeared. Indeed we seem to be in the midst of a Christmas Book renaissance in recent years. (Particularly noteworthy is a poignant short story by the late great actor Richard Burton that has been published as *A Christmas Story*, one of the best Christmas Books in recent memory; and there is James Finn Garner's *Politically Correct Holiday Stories* which contains a priceless *Carol* parody, as well as Richard Paul Evans's enormously successful *The Christmas Box*. The latter is a particularly interesting case in that it is credited with reintroducing modern readers to William Dean Howells's 1892 story entitled *Christmas Every Day*.[11]) And yet the real heyday of this literary genre was short; its popularity began to taper off only a dozen or so years after the *Carol's* debut. Nevertheless, that debut started a substantial cultural and commercial bandwagon on its way, and (to borrow a metaphor from Thackeray) any number of fiddlers were eager to hop on board and strike up a tune.

Of course not all these fiddlers were minor talents. In fact, we might even say that to some extent Dickens himself responded to the *Carol* by writing four more *Christmas Books* as well as numerous pieces of shorter fiction for publication at the holiday. Also, as we have seen, Dickens's post–*Carol* Christmas writings vary considerably in the extent to which they have anything at all to do with Christmas. Dickens thus implicitly granted considerable latitude to

anyone else interested in diving into the heady waters of the Christmas marketplace.

In this context, the only other fiddler to enter the Christmas Book sweepstakes who was comparable in stature to Dickens was William Makepeace Thackeray. Best known to general readers as the author of *Vanity Fair* and to film buffs as the author of the work which inspired Stanley Kubrick's 1975 masterpiece *Barry Lyndon*, Thackeray wrote and illustrated five Christmas Books of his own: *Mrs. Perkins's Ball* (1847), *Our Street* (1848), *Doctor Birch and His Young Friends* (1849), *The Kickleburys on the Rhine* (1850) and *The Rose and the Ring* (1855). However, it must be noted that unlike many Christmas Book authors, Thackeray was no literary mercenary out to divert some of Boz's thunder (and royalties). He was keenly interested in all types of literature and had addressed the subject of Christmas literature before the *Carol* appeared. However, unlike Dickens, Thackeray was chiefly concerned with middle and upper middle class people and situations. His Christmas Books, while they do contain certain "lessons," eschewed the kind of social criticism and concerns that were such an integral part of Dickens's best work in the genre. Also, like much of Dickens's work in this vein, they frequently have nothing to do with Christmas per se. Instead, to use his own description of what constitutes a proper Christmas Book, Thackeray's can be broadly categorized as "fire-side Christmas pantomimes."[12] Add too that they are charming, sophisticated and unjustly neglected entertainments. If given a chance, modern readers will find them pleasant company on quiet evenings at home over the holidays.

There were other fiddlers too, some of them indeed unknown; others were quite accomplished, but in comparison with Dickens or Thackeray, they are remembered as lesser lights. They too contributed their Christmas Books (both good and bad) and, like Dickens himself, their shorter Christmas stories. Among the lesser but good

Christmas Books one can count works like *The Snow Storm* (1845), *New Year's Day* (1846) and *The Inundation, or Pardon and Peace* (1848) by the now all but forgotten Mrs. Catherine Gore. Also worthy of mention in the context of quality, and as a reminder of the new genre's commercial dimension, is John Ruskin's charming fantasy *The King of the Golden River*; as S. A. Muresianu has noted, this one was written as a children's book before the *Carol* appeared, but was not actually published until several years after the *Carol*, when it was marketed at Christmas as a Christmas Book.[13] Along with Thackeray's *The Rose and the Ring*, it is one of the few non–Dickensian Christmas Books from this period to have achieved any degree of long-term familiarity among general readers.

Returning to the direct responses, and at the other end of the quality spectrum, one finds the anonymously authored *Christmas Eve with the Spirits, or, The Canon's Wanderings through Ways Unknown, with Some Further Tidings of Scrooge and Tiny Tim*, a work worthy to stand atop any list of all-time bad Christmas Books. Appearing in 1870, well after the new genre had peaked, this rather heavy-handed (and heavily didactic) tale of an ineffective clergyman who is shown various visions of earthly problems and heavenly rewards represents one of the most blatant acts of trespassing on the *Carol's* turf in this or any other period. It is particularly interesting, though, in that its "highlight" is a continuation of the *Carol's* timeline that shows us Scrooge on his deathbed attended to by an adoring, and no longer tiny, Timothy Cratchit. While one suspects that its moral and religious fervor is sincere, it would require an unusually heavy dose of Christmas charity to categorize this, and many other similar works, as anything but bad imitations of the *Carol*. Nevertheless, it is an important work in that it provides an opportunity for anyone who finds the *Carol* (or Dickens in general) to be overly sentimental, mawkish, or preachy, to be reminded of

just how good a Christmas Book the *Carol* really is.

It is fitting perhaps, certainly interesting, that a work like *Christmas Eve with the Spirits...*, arguably the absolute nadir of literary *Carol* variations, appeared in the year of Dickens's death. Indeed, one can only wonder about his reaction to what has been done with — and to — his work ever since. Nevertheless, and notwithstanding the fact that the *Carol* was indeed viewed by many as a "sacred text," a process of popularization, including all manner of parody and variation, began in earnest in the second half of the nineteenth century. More than a century later, this process shows no signs of abating.

Writing several years after Dickens's death, the great Victorian novelist Anthony Trollope, who although he wrote no Christmas Books did contribute several enjoyable short stories for the holiday, offered some interesting and important perspective on the subject:

> While I was writing *The Way We Live Now*, I was called upon by the proprietors of the *Graphic* for a Christmas story. I feel, with regard to literature, somewhat as I suppose an upholsterer and undertaker feels when he is called upon to supply a funeral. He has to supply it, however distasteful it may be. It is his business, and he will starve if he neglect it. So have I felt that, when anything in the shape of a novel was required I was bound to produce it. Nothing can be more distasteful to me than to have to give a relish of Christmas to what I write. I feel the humbug implied by the nature of the order. A Christmas story, in the proper sense, should be the ebullition of some mind anxious to instill others with a desire for Christmas religious thought, or Christmas festivities, — or, better still, with Christmas charity. Such was the case with Dickens when he wrote his first two

Christmas stories. But since that the things written annually — all of which have been fixed to Christmas like children's toys to a Christmas tree — have had no real savor of Christmas about them. I had done two or three before. Alas! at this very moment I have one to write, which I have promised to supply within three weeks of this time, — the picture-makers always require a long interval, — as to which I have in vain been cudgeling my brain for the last month. I can't send away the order to another shop, but I do not know how I shall ever get the coffin made.[14]

Trollope's commentary here, like so much of his fiction, is both insightful and prescient: he acknowledges Dickens's central role in defining what a Christmas Book should be, while also acknowledging the fact that what came after in his lifetime was not up to the standard set by Dickens's earliest *Christmas Books*; and he also anticipates much of what has been written for Christmas since Trollope's death in 1882. Christmas fiction had indeed become more popular than ever in the *Carol's* wake and, like the holiday itself, was expected to appear on schedule. And so it did — and does; the fiddlers and coffin makers have never been out of work.

And yet it is obviously wrong to conclude that everything that has been written (and, for that matter, filmed or televised) for Christmas in the last century and a half has been lacking in value or honesty; the record clearly indicates otherwise. Critics and anthologists, for example, have frequently made the case that the best Christmas fiction is that in which the story is only indirectly about Christmas, or one in which the holiday serves as merely a background or framework for other issues; Herman Melville and Thomas Hardy are among those frequently called upon to prove this point.[15] Without

question, the Christmas story can be viewed as a kind of universal frame, a stage upon which various universal — and yet deeply personal — dramas are played out. In the introduction to her scintillating anthology of contemporary Christmas fiction entitled *A Literary Christmas*, Lilly Golden asks:

> For mistletoe and ho-ho-ho aside, what is Christmas if not a time when the nuances of our lives are magnified, when our worlds are illuminated and laid bare? And what is a short story if not a revelation of some truth about ourselves, some insight into the human heart?[16]

Applying these guidelines to Dickens, and setting aside the aroma of plum pudding and roast goose, is the *Carol* not the story of a life — and the life of a nation — laid bare? And setting aside the unlikely, if ingenious, method by which Scrooge's reformation is brought about, is there not some reflection of Scrooge in the human heart? In all our hearts?

Dickens accomplished many things in his first *Christmas Book* — including pulling off the neat trick of placing the holiday itself (with all of its requisite sentiment) in the center of that universal frame, while at the same time avoiding the syrupy slope down which so many other literary (and cinematic) *Carolers* have slid.[17] In so doing, he also set a standard, and set the stage, for the ongoing spectacle of Christmas fiction that continues to this day. And whether those contributing to the deluge have chosen to slavishly copy the *Carol*, or to parody it, or to deliberately avoid anything that could even remotely be called Dickensian, it is difficult to imagine any *Caroler* who is not well aware of the *Carol's* unique place in the history of Christmas literature, and who has not felt, in one way or another, the presence of Charles Dickens standing in the spirit…

Epilogue

There were not many white Christmases in our part of Wales in my childhood—perhaps only one or two—but Christmas cards and Dickens and Dylan Thomas and wishful memory have turned them all into white.

Richard Burton

Richard Burton's words here serve as yet another reminder of the central role that the *Carol* has played in shaping our modern vision of Christmas, and in a very subtle way, they wisely caution us to keep our feet on the ground when reaching out for the "Dickens Christmas." Good advice indeed, for sooner or later, we all learn that a "Dickens Christmas," complete with all the trimmings, is no sure thing. And, as we have seen, Dickens's own Christmas visions grew steadily darker in the closing years of his life. For that matter, it has been documented that while Dickens's early Christmases were in fact white, snow in England at Christmas is not the norm.

Are we to conclude then that the "Dickens Christmas" was, and is, just the product of wishful thinking? Mere illusion? Pure humbug? Perhaps, but then again, what is wrong with wishing for snow at Christmas? And who among us, through just a little casual reshuffling of facts, has not transformed the Christmases that were into the Christmases that should have been?

Like Christmas itself, the *Carol* is, above all, about hope — and we surely cannot blame Dickens if we let the hope that is renewed every December slip through our fingers before the New Year is very old. With hope comes the knowledge that Scrooge *was* better than his word, and that Tiny Tim *did NOT* die, and that one could do far worse than to invest another ninety minutes in a tenth or twentieth viewing of the "Alastair Sim version."

Filmography

Author's Note: What follows is a chronological listing of film, television and video adaptations of *A Christmas Carol.* I once entertained the hope that it would be unequivocally accurate and absolutely complete up to the point of publication. I have grown quite a bit older, and I hope a bit wiser, since that ridiculous thought first entered my head. All I can say now is that it is the most extensive listing of *Carol* adaptations published to date, and that, at best, it is an interim report. I would also like to acknowledge that several items relative to British and French television were brought to my attention through Michael Pointer's *Charles Dickens on the Screen.* Any information regarding errors of omission or commission will be most welcome.

This filmography has no subdivisions for film, television/video, or other categories. The intention is to provide a seamless overview that the reader can follow in a continuous chronological order. This arrangement makes trends and patterns easily discernible, particularly with regard to the dominance of either film or television in any given year or decade. And, as noted earlier, this filmography is intended to serve as a backdrop against which the major *Carols* discussed at length in Part Two can be viewed.

Not all entries represent full-fledged *Carol* adaptations or variations. Some are just loosely inspired by the *Carol*, while others constitute "in name only" borrowings, and others still are not adaptations but rather programs about the *Carol.* Including them all is the best way to demonstrate both the wide range of interest in the *Carol* and the wide range in the seriousness with which it has been approached over the years.

Each entry follows essentially the same format: The title is followed by the producer or production company or broadcast network, year of release or broadcast, country of origin, running time, and a designation of color or black and white (b/w). (Whenever possible, I have tried to list the precise running time of a given production. However, please note that in the case of some *Carols* that appeared on commercial television, a round number like thirty or sixty minutes includes commercials.) In some cases a distributor's name will follow the production company in parentheses, and in the case of silent films, length is expressed in feet and no designation is made for color or b/w. This basic information is then followed by cast and production credits.

Inevitably, the amount of available information varies greatly from one title to another. There are many for which only the barest details are available, and others for which an absolute mountain of information exists. In every case, however, I have done my utmost to annotate the filmography entries with specific information and commentary about each production. Productions that are discussed at length in Part Two are marked with an asterisk; in most cases, the

in-text discussion serves as annotation for these entries.

Whenever possible, the annotation consists of personal reaction to *Carols* that I have actually seen. Some warrant just a line or two, others several paragraphs. In the case of *Carols* that I have not been able to see, I have attempted to provide a quote from at least one representative review. Please note, however, that many *Carols* have not been reviewed; this is particularly true of television versions. There are some entries for which no annotation was possible.

SCROOGE; OR, MARLEY'S GHOST*

Robert W. Paul 1901 Great Britain 620'
Director: Walter R. Booth.
CAST: Unknown.
*See discussion in Chapter 5.

A CHRISTMAS CAROL*

Essanay 1908 USA 1000'
Production Credits: Unknown.
CAST: Thomas Ricketts.
*See discussion in Chapter 5.

A CHRISTMAS CAROL*

Edison 1910 USA 1000'
Supervision [Producer]: J. Searle Dawley. Director: Some question exists as to who directed this film. The prolific pioneer director J. Searle Dawley has traditionally been cited as its director. Ashley Miller, who wrote a 1928 play entitled *Mr. Scrooge,* and who was involved in the early motion picture industry, has also been credited. And finally, Einar Lauritzen and Gunnar Lundquist's *American Film-Index 1916–1920* (Stockholm: Film-Index, 1984), p. 561, credits John H. Collins with both the film's direction and scenario. This information is contained in the section which provides additions and corrections to their earlier volume entitled *American Film Index 1908–1915* (Stockholm: Film-Index, 1976); in this volume they had credited the film's direction to Dawley and no writer was cited. As these books are a very reliable reference source, based primarily on meticulous researches through *The Moving Picture World,* the fact that Collins was credited as an addendum would seem to suggest that the authors found some specific evidence on which they based their decision to revise their earlier work. Whatever evidence Lauritzen and

Lundquist found has proved untraceable, but it is worth noting that Collins spent many years at Edison, beginning in 1905; thus it is entirely possible that he may have directed this particular film.

CAST: Marc McDermott (Ebenezer Scrooge); Charles Ogle (Bob Cratchit); William Bechtel; Carey Lee; Viola Flugrath; Leonie Flugrath.

*See discussion in Chapter 5. Thanks are due to film historian Anthony Slide for his identification of major cast members.

IL SOGNO DELL'USURAIO*

Cines 1910 Italy 675'
Production & Cast Credits: Unknown.
This appears to be the only Italian version of the *Carol.* Also known as *Il sogno del vecchio usuraio; Dream of Old Scrooge; Old Scrooge.*
*See discussion in Chapter 5.

A MESSAGE FROM MARS

United Kingdom Films 1913 Great Britain 4000'
Producer: Nicholson Ormsby-Scott. Director: J. Wallett Waller. Screenplay: J. Wallett Waller.
CAST: Charles Hawtrey (Horace Parker); E. Holman Clark (Ramiel); Crissie Bell (Minnie); Frank Hector (Arthur Dicey); Hubert Willis (Tramp); Kate Tyndale (Aunt Martha); Evelyn Beaumont (Bella); Eileen Temple (Mrs. Clarence); R. Crompton (God of Mars); B. Stanmore (Wounded Man); Tonie Reith (His Wife).

Adapted from Richard Ganthony's 1899 play. While not an "official" *Carol* variation, the source material unquestionably owes something to Dickens.

"The film, which is in four reels, opens in the Council Chamber of the Kingdom of Mars, where one of their number, fallen from his high estate, is upon his trial, and sentence is eventually passed upon him to proceed to earth and reclaim a lost soul. [The lost soul in question turns out to be the Scrooge-like Horace Parker, played by Charles Hawtrey, in a reprise of his role from the original 1899 London stage production.]"—*The Bioscope*, July 31, 1913, p. 360

*See reference in Chapter 9.

SCROOGE*

Zenith Films 1913 Great Britain 2500'

Director: Leedham Bantock. Screenplay: Seymour Hicks.

CAST: Seymour Hicks (Ebenezer Scrooge); William Lugg; Leedham Bantock; J. C. Buckstone; Dorothy Buckstone; Leonard Calvert; Osborne Adair; Adela Measor.

*See discussion in Chapter 5.

A CHRISTMAS CAROL*

London (Fenning) 1914 Great Britain 1340'

Director: Harold Shaw. Screenplay: Harold Shaw.

CAST: Charles Rock (Ebenezer Scrooge); Edna Flugrath (Belle); George Bellamy (Bob Cratchit); Mary Brough (Mrs Cratchit); Franklyn Bellamy (Fred); Edward O'Neill (Jacob Marley); Arthur Cullin (Christmas Past); Windham Guise (Christmas Present); Asheton Tonge (Christmas Future).

*See discussion in Chapter 5.

THE RIGHT TO BE HAPPY*

Bluebird Photoplays, Inc. 1916 USA 5 reels

Director: Rupert Julian. Screenplay: Elliott J. Clawson. Cinematographer: Stephen Rounds.

CAST: Rupert Julian (Ebenezer Scrooge); John Cook (Bob Cratchit); Claire McDowell (Mrs Cratchit); Francis Lee (Tiny Tim); Harry Carter (Jacob Marley); Emory Johnson (Fred, Scrooge's nephew); Roberta Wilson (Caroline); Francelia Billington (Scrooge's sweetheart); Mrs Titus (Miss Fezziwig); Wadsworth Harris (Ghost of Christmas Past); Dick Le Strange (Ghost of Christmas Present); Tom Figee (Ghost of Christmas Future).

*See discussion in Chapter 5.

MY LITTLE BOY

Bluebird Photoplays, Inc. 1917 USA 5 reels

Director: Elsie Jane Wilson. Screenplay: Elliott J. Clawson from a story by Rupert Julian. Cinematography: Stephen Rounds.

CAST: Ella Hall (Clara); Zoe Rae (Paul);

Emory Johnson (Fred); Winter Hall (Uncle Oliver); Harry Holden (Joe); Gretchen Lederer (Clara's mother).

A *Carol* variation inspired by Dickens's story and the poem *Little Boy Blue* by Eugene Field. The poem concerns a little boy who has died, and the toys that await his return. It should not be confused with the Mother Goose nursery rhyme that begins with the line "Little Boy Blue, come blow your horn."

"It was a happy thought on the part of Elliott J. Clawson to combine Charles Dickens' 'A Christmas Carol' and Eugene Field's 'Little Boy Blue' in a five-part photoplay for the Bluebird brand. Both story and poem are noted for their heart interest, and Elsie Jane Wilson, who directed the production, has handled it with sympathetic understanding. The entire cast show the same appreciation of their work, and a charming screen story, told with great charm, is the result. From 'A Christmas Carol' has been borrowed the characters of old Scrooge and his nephew. They are brought down to the present, however, and the older man is turned into a 'grouch' in place of being a miser. He is now known as Uncle Oliver, and refuses to have anything to do with his nephew when the young fellow marries against his will. Six years later Fred determines to ask his uncle to spend Christmas with him and meet his son, Paul, who is known in the family as Little Boy Blue. Oliver grudgingly consents, and is more grouchy than ever when he arrives on Christmas Eve. After trying to make everyone as miserable as possible he goes to bed and has a dream that makes a new man of him."—*The Moving Picture World*, December 22, 1917, p. 1802

"'My Little Boy' is a composite version of Charles Dickens' 'Christmas Carol' and Eugene Field's 'Little Boy Blue.' And, although it possesses the element of child appeal, the story is so lacking in dramatic power that it frequently fails to be interesting. Those uncritical souls, however, who care little for the plausible and are easily diverted, will find enough perhaps to make the time spent worth while."—*The New York Dramatic Mirror*, December 15, 1917, p. 18

NOTE: See additional reference in Chapter 9.

A MESSAGE FROM MARS

Metro Pictures 1921 USA 6 reels/5,187'

Director: Maxwell Karger. Screenplay: Arthur J. Zellner; Arthur Maude. Cinematography: Arthur Martinelli.

CAST: Bert Lytell (Horace Parker); Raye Dean (Minnie Talbot); Maude Milton (Martha Parker); Alphonz Ethier (The Messenger); Gordon Ash (Arthur Dicey); Leonard Mudie (Fred Jones); Mary Louise Beaton (Mrs. Jones); Frank

Currier (Sir Edwards); George Spink (The Butler).

The second film adaptation of the Richard Ganthony play, this time updated to the post–World War One period.

"The moral tone of the picture is high, the story teaching the gospel of unselfishness, exemplified by the conversion of the most egotistical man on earth by a Martian sent to earth for that purpose."—*The Moving Picture World*, April 2, 1921, p. 518

"[Maxwell] Karger has some especially beautiful street stuff, supposed to be scenes in London during the Christmas season, and the atmosphere of England's metropolis is wonderfully well preserved."—*Exhibitors Herald*, April 30, 1921, p. 65

NOTE: See additional reference in Chapter 9.

SCROOGE*

Master Films (British Exhibitors' Films) 1922   Great Britain   1280'

Producer: H. B. Parkinson. Director: George Wynn. Screenplay: W. C. Rowden.

CAST: H[enry] V. Esmond (Scrooge).

From the "Tense Moments with Great Authors" series.

*See discussion in Chapter 5.

SCROOGE*

B & C (Walturdaw) 1923   Great Britain 1600'

Producer: Edward Godal. Director: Edwin Greenwood. Screenplay: Eliot Stannard.

CAST: Russell Thorndike (Ebenezer Scrooge); Nina Vanna (Alice); Jack Denton (Bob Cratchit); Forbes Dawson (Marley).

From the "Gems of Literature" series.

*See discussion in Chapter 5.

SCROOGE*

British Sound Film Productions   1928 Great Britain   9m   sound   b/w

Director: Hugh Croise. Screenplay: Bransby Williams.

CAST: Bransby Williams (Ebenezer Scrooge).

*See discussion in Chapter 6.

A DICKENSIAN FANTASY

Gee Films (Mackane) 1934   Great Britain 10m   b/w

Producer: David Mackane. Director and Adaptation: Aveling Ginever. Photography: Geoffrey Faithful.

CAST: Lawrence Hanray (All Characters).

Theatrically released short subject.

According to the *Monthly Film Bulletin*, the film opens with a shot of a man reading—presumably *A Christmas Carol*, since he then "soliloquises as to whether the spirit of Scrooge, Sam Weller [of *Pickwick Papers*], Tiny Tim and Bob Cratchit are abroad in the world to-day and concludes that they are not." Nodding over his book, he dreams of both Scrooge and Weller, "and then his dream continues to a modern parallel of the scene between Scrooge and Cratchit in which the latter is threatened with dismissal, and also of the final scene of reconciliation." He wakes up and announces, as bells chime in the background, that the Spirit of Christmas lives.

The *Monthly Film Bulletin* found the work "pleasantly entertaining," but warned that the film would be "most appreciated by modern audiences who know their Dickens." Overall the reviewer found the production "good," the acting "adequate," and the "musical accompaniment ... for the most part, too loud."—*Monthly Film Bulletin*, March 1936, p. 37

SCROOGE*

Twickenham Film Distributors   1935   Great Britain   78m   b/w

Producer: Julius Hagen. Director: Henry Edwards. Scenario: H. Fowler Mear. [Note: Various sources also cite Seymour Hicks as a contributor to the screenplay; however, he is not credited in the film.] Production Supervisor: Hans [John] Brahm. Photography: Sydney Blythe; William Luff. Art Direction: James A. Carter. Supervising Editor: Jack Harris. Film Editor: Ralph Kemplen. Sound Recording: Baynham Honri. Assistant Direction: Arthur Barnes; James Davidson. Original Score and Musical Direction: W. L. Trytel. Costumes: L. & H. Nathan. Coiffure: Charles.

CAST: [Sir] Seymour Hicks (Ebenezer Scrooge); Donald Calthrop (Bob Cratchit); Robert Cochran (Fred); Mary Glynne (Belle); Garry Marsh (Belle's Husband); Oscar Asche (Spirit of Christmas Present); C. V. France (Spirit of Christmas Future); Athene Seyler (Scrooge's Charwoman); Maurice Evans (A Poor Man); Mary Lawson (His Wife); Barbara Everest (Mrs. Cratchit); Eve Grey (Fred's Wife); Morris Harvey (Poulterer); Philip Frost (Tiny Tim); D. J. Williams (Undertaker); Margaret Yarde (Scrooge's Laundress); Hugh E. Wright (Old Joe); Charles Carson (Middlemark); Hubert Harben (Worthington). [Note: Some versions of the film list Marie Ney as the Spirit of Christmas-Past.]

*See discussion in Chapter 6.

A CHRISTMAS CAROL*

MGM 1938   USA   69m   b/w

Producer: Joseph L. Mankiewicz. Director:

Edwin L. Marin. Screen Play: Hugo Butler. Musical Score: Franz Waxman. Recording Director: Douglas Shearer. Art Director: Cedric Gibbons. Associate Art Director: John Detlie. Set Decorations: Edwin B. Willis. Costumes: Valles. Character make-up created by: Jack Dawn. Photography: Sidney Wagner. Film Editor: George Boemler.

CAST: Reginald Owen (Ebenezer Scrooge); Gene Lockhart (Bob Crachit [sic]); Kathleen Lockhart (Mrs. Crachit [sic]); Terry Kilburn (Tiny Tim); Barry Mackay (Fred); Lynne Carver (Bess); Leo G. Carroll (Marley's Ghost); Lionel Braham (Spirit of Christmas Present); Ann Rutherford (Spirit of Christmas Past); D'Arcy Corrigan (Spirit of Christmas Future); Ronald Sinclair (Young Scrooge).

NOTE: Production and cast credits listed above are as they appear in the film. For a much more thorough listing of credits see Patricia King Hanson, executive ed., *The American Film Institute Catalog: Feature Films 1931–1940, Film Entries A–L* (Berkeley: University of California Press, 1993), p. 347.

*See discussion in Chapter 6.

A CHRISTMAS CAROL

Gregory Markopoulos 1940 USA 5m b/w

CAST: Gregory Markopoulos (Ebenezer Scrooge); Andrew Markopoulos; Elaine Markopoulos; with childhood friends.

Gregory Markopoulos, who would go on to become one of America's foremost avant-garde filmmakers, made this film at age eleven or twelve in his hometown of Toledo, Ohio. It was filmed (at 18 frames per second) with an 8mm Keystone home movie camera. In the forties, Markopoulos also made short films based on *Wuthering Heights*, *For Whom the Bell Tolls*, and *Green Mansions*. This appears to be the first known film version of the *Carol* by an amateur film maker.

NOTE: Information on this most elusive *Carol* comes from John G. Hanhardt and Matthew Yokobosky's *Gregory J. Markopoulos: Mythic Themes, Portraiture, and Films of Place* (New York: Whitney Museum of American Art, 1996).

A CHRISTMAS CAROL*

W2XWV [DuMont-TV] 1943 USA 60m b/w

Director: George Lowther. Teleplay: William Podmore.

CAST: William Podmore (Ebenezer Scrooge); Don Randolf; Consuela Lembke; Ralph Locke; Noah Julian; Roger DeKoven; Lon Clark.

This experimental broadcast took place on Wednesday, December 22, 1943, at approximately 9:30 P.M. It was the finale of a two-hour broadcast that was preceded by an hour of music, a short film, a discussion of the war. and commercials.

NOTE: *The Billboard* review of this *Carol* quoted in Chapter 7 does not cite a broadcast date. However, the date is cited in the following: *The New York Times* (December 22, 1943, p. 39); *New York Herald Tribune* (December 22, 1943, p. 29).

*See discussion in Chapter 7.

CHRISTMAS, 1944*

WABD [DuMont-TV] 1944 USA 30m b/w

Producer: Bob Emery.

Carol variation that was broadcast on Tuesday, December 19, 1944 at 8:45 P.M. As noted in Chapter 7, it was produced as part of WOR radio's *Video Varieties* series, but was staged at, and broadcast by, WABD. In addition to *The Billboard* review quoted in Chapter 7, see television schedule in the following: *The New York Times* (December 19, 1944, p. 37); *New York Herald Tribune* (December 19, 1944, p. 29).

*See discussion in Chapter 7.

A CHRISTMAS CAROL*

WABD [DuMont-TV] 1944 USA 30m b/w

CAST: Carl Eastman (Bob Cratchit); Helen Jerome (Mrs Cratchit); Bobby Hookey (Tiny Tim); Evelyn Juster (Martha); Beverly Benson (Peter). [Note: Existing sources do not reveal who played Scrooge in this production.]

This broadcast took place on Wednesday, December 20, 1944, at 9:30 P.M. See television schedule in the following: *The New York Times* (December 20, 1944, p. 35); *New York Herald Tribune* (December 20, 1944, p. 29). See also a photograph of this production in *The New York Times* (December 24, 1944, Section 2).

*See discussion in Chapter 7.

THE STRANGE CHRISTMAS DINNER

NBC-TV 1945 USA 45m b/w

Producer/Director: Fred Coe. Technical Director: Al Protzman. Teleplay: Fred Coe. Sets: Bob Wade. Narrator: Bill Woodson.

CAST: Grandon Rhodes (Charles Dickens); John Souther (Herman Grubb); George Matthews [a role described by *The Billboard* as "a Maxie Rosenbloom type"]; Celia Babcock (hat check girl); Ed Hussey; A. P. Kaye; Alan MacAteer; John Martin; Dave Davis; Artie Semon; Lee Molnar; Kevin McCarthy; Bob Tobin.

Telecast (live) by WNBT in New York on December 9, 1945. As noted in Chapter 9, this was the first of two adaptations of a Margaret Cousins short story that originally appeared in *Good Housekeeping* magazine; see entry for 1949 version below. The story concerns one Herman Grubb, the Scrooge-like owner of a New York restaurant who refuses to give his employees a day off for Christmas. He is reformed, however, by a mysterious stranger who turns out to be none other than Charles Dickens himself!

Variety gave the production a very favorable review, noting that "producer Fred Coe added much to the show's merits by bringing films of Times Square and references to modern Broadway goings-on to help set the story's locale. Cast, topped by Grandon Rhodes as Dickens and John Souther as Grubb, was uniformly good, and Bob Wade's set was an almost perfect facsimile of a second-rate Broadway chop house."—*Variety*, December 12, 1945, p. 39

The Billboard, however, was not impressed with the production, nor with the later legendary Fred Coe: "The only thing strange about it is why it was scanned [televised] at all. There is only one director in a thousand who can both write, or adapt, and produce his own scrivening. Fred Coe isn't the one. There was a charming note to the story, the idea of Charles Dickens coming back to earth to discover that Scrooge lives on thru all eternity, but it took so long to reach the dinner scene climax that nobody gave a continental damn. There was no peace on earth for men of good will among the viewers."—*The Billboard*, December 15, 1945, p. 41

NOTE: *The Billboard* review goes on to mention that the story was well acted and that it was narrated. However, it did not feel that the narration was a positive addition to the story: "This is one story that should have been told without a narrator. What developed should have come forth from the men and women who peopled the play, not from an omnipotent voice who pulled the story strings." It also takes issue with a line in the script which refers to *The Billboard* as "a circus mag," an apparent reference to the fact that at this stage of its history, the circus was among the many forms of entertainment covered by *The Billboard*. This, and a couple of other points mentioned in the review, suggest that there may have been some kind of a feud brewing between Fred Coe and *The Billboard*. However, for present purposes it also seems to indicate, as does the *Variety* review quoted above, that the production developed a minor point that is mentioned but not explicitly dealt with in the original story, that being a certain "show biz" subtext in which unemployed actors and writers are seen as regular patrons of the restaurant.

A CHRISTMAS CAROL

WBKB-TV 1945 USA 30m b/w
Producer/Director/Teleplay: Beulah Zachary.
Cameras: Rachel Stewart; Esther Rajewski.

CAST: Norman Pellegrini (Ebenezer Scrooge); Raymond Groya (Scrooge's nephew); James Wade (Bob Cratchit); June Schmidt (Mrs. Cratchit); Dave Koukal (Marley's Ghost); Bruce Fields (Scrooge as a small boy); Marian Erickson (Mrs. Fred); Marilyn Fisher (Mrs. Dilber).

Presented on December 20, 1945, as part of a one-hour variety broadcast. The *Carol* portion featured students from Chicago's Taft High School. It was one of a series of experimental broadcasts involving students from various Chicago high schools.

"This show marked the end of an experiment, the last of an unfortunate series of amateur programs for the video medium. After 12 segments in the same vein the obvious conclusion to be drawn is that television was never meant for the non-professionals.

"This particular attempt was somewhat better than previous trys, with double-dissolve technique for the ghost business expertly done. ... Adaptation for video, which consisted largely of cutting, was whipped up efficiently by Miss Beulah Zachary."—*Variety*, December 26, 1945, p. 33

The Billboard noted that this *Carol's* amateur cast "did some excellent acting that was of a professional level." It continued: "Direction of this portion of the program was by Beulah Zachary. Work of the actors and actresses did much to make the show a success, but Miss Zachary's work added plenty. Typical of what the direction did was one shot in which she used a double dissolve to present Marley's ghost and Scrooge in conversation. Shot of the ghost was dissolved in and superimposed on a door. Effect gave the impression of the ephemeral qualities of the ghost."—*The Billboard*, December 29, 1945, pp. 10 & 12

CHRISTMAS NIGHT

BBC-TV 1946 Great Britain 60m b/w
Devised and Produced by: Philip Bate. Story told by: Hubert Foss. Music by: Vaughan Williams.

Carol variation broadcast on December 25, 1946. This appears to be the first treatment of the *Carol* on British television. It is not a formal adaptation, but rather, as the *Radio Times* described it on p. 37 of the issue cited below, "a fantasy" and "a family fireside story" told with music, ballet and mime.

"The season would not be complete without a flavour of Dickens, to whom the festive season owes so much. Philip Bate has chosen part of *A Christmas Carol* on which to base his fantasy

Christmas Night. He will be introducing Scrooge and company in ballet and mime, and a highlight of the programme is expected to be a musical version of Mrs. [sic] Fezziwig's Ball."—*Radio Times*, December 20, 1946, p. 35

LEYENDA DE NAVIDAD*

Panorama Films (Balart) 1947 Spain 70m b/w

Producer: Jose Maria Alvarez. Director: Manuel Tamayo [aka Manuel Tamayo Castro]. Story and Script: Manuel Tamayo Castro. Cinematography: Enzo Serafin; Joaquin Llopis. Music: Juan Duran Alemany. Costumes: Sastreria Penalba. Makeup: Manuel Manteca. Sets: Salvador Mateu. Editor: Antonio Canovas.

CAST: Jesús Tordesillas (Scrooge); Lina Yegros (Mary); Emilio Santiago (Bob Cratchit); Angel Picazo (Jack); Ramon Martori (Jacob Marley); Manuel Requena (Ghost of Christmas Present); Fernando Aguirre (Ghost of Christmas Past); Jose Jorner (Ghost of Christmas Future); Charito Montemar (Elizabeth); Joaquin Soler Serrano.

NOTE: Various sources list this film as either 80 or 89 minutes in length, but the 16mm print seen in research for this book runs about 70 minutes. It is possible that the film was abridged for television or non-theatrical distribution.

*See discussion in Chapter 6.

A CHRISTMAS CAROL

WABD [DuMont-TV] 1947 USA 60m b/w

Some question exists regarding major production credits for this version. The *Variety* review quoted below cites James L. Caddigan as the producer and director, but does not provide a credit for the adaptation or script. However, the *Televiser* review quoted below credits David P. Lewis as producer, director and writer. The latter claim is supported by an advertisement in *The New York Times* (December 24, 1947, p. 32), which notes that this *Carol* was adapted for television and directed by David Lewis. Technical Director: Frank Bunetta. Sets: Rudy Lucek. Sponsor: Kaiser-Fraser Corporation.

CAST: John Carradine (Ebenezer Scrooge); Ray Morgan (Nephew; Narrator); Bernard Hughes; Eva Marie Saint; Somer Alder; Sam Fertig; Helen Stenborg; Jonathan Marlowe; David Carradine.

Live telecast from DuMont's station WABD on December 25, 1947. The *Variety* review quoted below indicates that this New York–based production was also fed to Philadelphia, Baltimore and Washington, D.C.

"There have been many dramatic versions of this Dickens work amongst which this enactment registered as being of the stiff and formal group. Formal? Well, with a tinge of the classroom recitation. It put the playing in a slow key from which there was no rescue.

"For current television it was an ambitious production effort comprising 12 sets and 22 people. Most of the sets were either small backdrops or flat pieces."—*Variety*, December 31, 1947, pp. 18 & 28

"[This] version's slow, drawn-out opening became tedious, particularly since John Carridine's [sic] Scrooge lacked conviction. He was too ready to be kind—never the nasty, selfish, money-grubbing tyrant of Dickens....

"Most effective bit was the nephew–Scrooge scene. Ray Morgan as the nephew did a job. He was also good as the narrator."—*Televiser*, January 1948, p. 27

NOTE: A photograph from this production showing John Carradine's Scrooge in his office, with a DuMont camera in the foreground, will be found on page 19 of the January 1948 issue of *Televiser*. While it is dangerous to draw any definitive conclusions about the "look" of this *Carol* based on one photograph, it appears to confirm *Variety's* comments above regarding the sets.

A CHRISTMAS CAROL

NBC-TV 1948 USA 60m b/w

Producer: Fred Coe. Director: Fred Coe. Teleplay: Samuel Taylor.

CAST: Dennis King (Ebenezer Scrooge); Frank M. Thomas (Marley's Ghost); Harry Sothern (Ghost of Christmas Past); Loring Smith (Ghost of Christmas Present); James [Mac?] Coll (Bob Cratchit); Judson Rees; Valerie Cossart.

Philco Television Playhouse live telecast of December 19, 1948. Also featured was a filmed epilogue with Bing Crosby and the Mitchell Boys Choir singing "Silent Night."

"The familiar "Christmas Carol" story was mainly powered by Dennis King's brilliant performance as Scrooge. King projected the role so forcibly that it broke out of the small screen limitations into a three-dimensional portrait with a terrific emotional kick. ... There were some incidental flaws in the camera angles but these did not materially detract from the overall impact. More serious, however, was the repetitious use of a tricky photographic effect for the ghostly flights through time and space."—*Variety*, December 22, 1948, p. 32

NOTE: The Billy Rose Theatre Collection of the New York Public Library has a large selection of photographs relating to this *Carol*. A look at these photographs reveals that this was a very good looking, well-mounted production.

DICKENS' CHRISTMAS CAROL

ABC-TV   1948   USA   60m   b/w

Producer: Leonard Steinman.

CAST: The Rufus Rose Marionets, under the direction of Rufus and Margo Rose. [Note: Rufus Rose was Howdy Doody's off-camera operator.]

Live telecast by ABC television in New York on December 24, 1948.

"Here was at once the most novel and ambitious Yule season presentation on video....

"Considering the hour-long manipulation of the wooden figures and the lack of any emotional impact ordinarily contributed by live performers, it managed with an unusual degree of success to capture the spirit and moral of the classic tale. All told, more than a dozen marionets, beautifully modeled in the traditional manner, were put through their paces, and if the actual manipulation could have stood some perfecting, the production itself outweighed this crudity." — *Variety*, December 29, 1948, p. 33

DICKENS' CHRISTMAS CAROL

WCBS-TV   1948   USA   60m   b/w

This local broadcast, featuring a version of the *Carol* by a Baltimore children's group, aired on Christmas Day of 1948 between 6 P.M and 7 P.M. *The New York Times* (December 25, 1948, p. 26) indicates that WCBS also broadcast "Film Theatre: Dickens' 'A Christmas Carol'" from 1 P.M to 2 P.M this same day. Details have proved elusive, but this was likely a broadcast of a theatrically released (and in this case abridged) film version. The 1935 version of *Scrooge*, for example, was shown frequently on television in this period.

THE STRANGE CHRISTMAS DINNER

NBC-TV   1949   USA   60m   b/w

Teleplay: Fred Coe, Joe Less. Note: Although a complete kinescope of this production exists and was screened for this research, unfortunately, production credits (other than major cast members) do not appear to have been included in the broadcast. It was presumably produced and directed by the legendary Fred Coe who also spearheaded NBC's 1945 version (see entry above).]

CAST: Melvyn Douglas (Stranger/Charles Dickens); Vaughan Taylor (Alfred Stubbs); Ralph Riggs (Charlie Stubbs); Frank Tweddell (Frank); Daniel Reed (Adolphus); Bill Story (Mike); Melle Matthews (Josie); Elaine Ellis (Ruth). [Note: An unbilled John Marley appears in a bit as an unemployed writer.]

Philco Television Playhouse telecast live on December 18, 1949.

As noted in Chapter 9, this was NBC's second offering of Margaret Cousins's short story about the very Scrooge-like owner of a shabby New York restaurant who refuses to give his employees a day off for Christmas. While he appears to have a particular dislike for Christmas, he is also depicted as a generally miserable person who treats everyone with contempt throughout the year; he has also cut off contact with his daughter because she married an actor. The twist here is that this modern Scrooge's reformation is not brought about by ghostly visitors, but rather by a mysterious stranger who breathes the spirit of Christmas into his empty restaurant — and his equally empty life.

This delightful production, which appears to be the oldest television *Carol* variation of which a recording still exists, is very well produced and acted, and while it has the overall look and feel of early live television, it also utilizes some very fluid and mobile camera movement. It is also worth noting that the production, as well as the original story on which it is based, has a decidedly "New Yorkish" flavor about it which is enhanced by the use of filmed establishing shots of mid-town Manhattan; this use of filmed inserts was also employed in the 1945 version. It also expands on a minor point suggested in the original story by populating the restaurant with an assortment of perennially unemployed actors and writers in the days before Christmas. This device enables the viewer to overhear several "show biz" conversations filled with inside comments about various NBC personalities.

The punchline comes when the mysterious stranger turns out to be none other than Charles Dickens himself. As Dickens, Melvyn Douglas turns in an engaging performance as he gently yet forcefully insists that Stubbs put up some Christmas decorations, light a fire, prepare a proper bowl of Christmas punch, and serve a proper Christmas dinner (they wind up having goose instead of pig's feet). Douglas's Dickens is also an omniscient deus ex machina who knows the intimate details of everyone's lives and sets in motion a number of positive changes. He also quotes Scripture, as well as the *Carol* and *Pickwick*, in conveying the true spirit and meaning of Christmas. All in all a memorable holiday diversion; one can only wonder why no one has produced a modern remake.

NOTE: In a somewhat similar vein, see also Ray Bradbury's short story entitled *Any Friend of Nicholas Nickleby Is a Friend of Mine*, which has been made into an excellent "featurette" starring Fred Gwynne.

DICKENS' CHRISTMAS CAROL

KTTV-TV   1949   USA   15m   b/w

Local broadcast. *The Los Angeles Times* (December 24, 1949/Part 2, p. 5) indicates that "Dickens' 'Christmas Carol' from the Children's Theater" was broadcast on Christmas Eve of 1949 from 6:15 P.M to 6:30 P.M.

CHARLES DICKENS' THE CHRISTMAS CAROL

Stokey and Ebert   1949   USA   25m   b/w

Producer: Mike Stokey; Bernard Ebert. Produced at: Jerry Fairbanks, Inc. for Teletec Company. Director and Adaptation: Arthur Pierson. Carols: The Mitchell Choirboys. Supervisor for Jerry Fairbanks, Inc.: Arnold Wester. Director of Photography: Meredith Nicholson. Production Manager: Glenn Miller. Film Editor: Art Seid. Sound: Lawrence Aicholtz. Art Director: Oscar Yerg. Musical Direction: Edward Paul.

CAST: Vincent Price (Narrator); Taylor Holmes (Ebeneezer [sic] Scrooge); Pat White (Bob Cratchit); Robert Clarke (Fred); Earl Lee (Ghost of Marley); Nelson Leigh (Ghost of Christmas Past); Joe Battista (Boy Scrooge); George James (Ghost of Christmas Present); Queenie Leonard (Mrs. Cratchit); Mike Miller (Peter Cratchit); Karen Kester (Belinda Cratchit); Jill Oppenheim (Missie Cratchit); Bobby Hyatt (Tiny Tim); Connie Cavendish (Martha); Jack Nestle (Ghost of Christmas to Come); Paul Maxey (Fat Gentleman); Leonard Carey (Thin Gentleman); Ann Howard (Caroline); and The Mitchell Choirboys [the choir is heard but not seen].

Syndicated television version. Because syndicated programs are shown at different times in different cities, it can be difficult, if not impossible, to determine precisely when the "official" premiere of this type of program took place. The earliest records that I have found indicate that this program was shown on Christmas Day of 1949 in New York, Chicago and Los Angeles. It was undoubtedly shown in other cities as well, however, no listings earlier than 1949 have appeared.

This short *Carol*, which appears to be the oldest extant straight adaptation of the story, misspells Scrooge's name in the opening credits and doesn't get much better after that. Veteran stage and film actor Taylor Holmes, who focused on television work in his later years, is a passable but far from great Scrooge. The only saving grace in this low-budget affair is the presence of Vincent Price, who introduces the story and at various times reads from Dickens's text. In fact, his mellifluous voice and sophisticated charm make one wish that the camera would stay with his reading instead of cutting to the other actors.

NOTE: Queenie Leonard would reprise her role as Mrs. Cratchit in the 1954 television musical version discussed in Chapter 7.

Excerpts from this version are included in the 1997 *History Channel* production entitled *Christmas Unwrapped.*

A CHRISTMAS CAROL

BBC-TV   1950   Great Britain   120m   b/w

Producer: Eric Fawcett. Assistant Producer: T. Leslie Jackson. Adaptation: Eric Fawcett, from the play by Dominic Roche. Set Designer: James Bould. Stage Managers: Josephine Hunter; Archie Angus. Incidental Music Composed and Arranged by: Max Saunders. Sextet Conducted by: Eric Robinson. Rehearsal Pianists: Sybilla Marshal; Hathleen O'Hagen.

CAST: MacDonald Hobley (Narrator); Bransby Williams (Ebenezer Scrooge); John Ruddock (Bob Cratchit); Robert Cawdron (Mr Fred); Julian D'Albie (Portly Gentleman); Leonard Sharp (Crossing Sweeper); John Bentley (Night Watchman); W. E. Holloway (Marley's Ghost); Arthur Hambling (Spirit of Christmas Past); Sean Lynch (Boy Scrooge); Patricia Fryer (Fanny); Barbara Murray (Fiancée); John Bentley (Young Scrooge); Julian D'Albie (Ghost of Christmas Present); Adrian Evans (Boy Cratchit); Shirley Hose (Belinda Cratchit); John Young (Peter Cratchit); Thomas Moore (Tiny Tim); Kathleen Saintsbury (Mrs Cratchit); Pamela Cameron (Martha Cratchit); Michael Edmunds (Boy Waif); Gillian Stirrup (Girl Waif); W. E. Holloway (Spirit of Christmas to Come); Arthur Hambling, Howard Douglas, Stanley Vines (Gentlemen of the Stock Exchange); Dorothy Summers (Mrs Dilber); Leonard Sharp (Joe); Tony Lyons (Boy with goose); Ann Wrigg (Mrs Fred); Michael Edmunds, Tony Lyons, Adrian Evans, Sean Lynch (Carol Singers); Ewart Wheeler (Scrooge's double). Dancers were from the Cecil Sharp Folk Dance Society, arranged by John Armstrong.

Televised production broadcast (live) on the BBC on December 25 and 27, 1950.

"We are proud to claim the first presentation of a full length Dickens dramatic adaptation on television as the work of a Vice-President of the Fellowship. Mr. Bransby Williams appeared as Ebenezer in a two-hour adaptation of *A Christmas Carol* on Christmas Day, followed by another performance for the children on 27th December. Mr. Williams put everything we have learnt to expect of him into his presentation of Scrooge. Besides being a fine piece of characterization, it was a great feat of endurance, under the hot and tiring studio lights for one who has attained the grand age of 80, culminating with his appearance with Tiny Tim on his shoulder. It is true there were transpositions for dramatic purposes, and some minor examples of miscasting. Nevertheless, it was a very interesting production. We were sorry to learn that during the second performance Mr. Williams was taken ill, but as would be expected from such an artiste he betrayed no sign of it. It is with great pleasure that we hear that he has made a good recovery."— Leslie C. Staples in *The Dickensian* (March 1951): 63

DANGER

CBS-TV 1951 USA 30m b/w
Producer: Charles W. Russell. Director: Sidney Lumet. From an original mystery by Harold Taub, adapted by Norman Rosten. Music by: Tony Mottola (guitarist). Host/Narrator: Richard Stark.

CAST: Joseph Anthony; Rita Gam.

Dramatic anthology series. Episode title: "Marley's Ghost." Broadcast live from New York on June 26, 1951.

In spite of its tantalizing title, this episode of *Danger* is not a *Carol* variation. While it does not seem to have been reviewed, a CBS press release at the time indicated that it was the "story of a writer's fight to establish his identity after ten years of ghost-writing for a famous novelist." (Quoted from press release on file at CBS television in New York.) This appears to be a very early example of television borrowing an idea or image — or in this case, apparently, just a name — from the instantly recognizable *Carol*. From the above quote, we can probably infer that the famous novelist in question is named Marley.

SCROOGE* (released in USA as A CHRISTMAS CAROL)

Renown Pictures Corporation/George Minter
1951 Great Britain 86m b/w
Producer: Brian Desmond-Hurst. Director: Brian Desmond-Hurst. Adaptation & Screenplay: Noel Langley. Musical Score: Richard Addinsell. Conductor: Muir Mathieson. Director of Photography: C. Pennington-Richards. Production Manager: Stanley Couzins. Art Director: Ralph Brinton. Camera Operator: C. Cooney. First Assistant: Denis O'Dell. Makeup Artist: Eric Carter. Film Editor: Clive Donner. Sound Recordist: W. H. Lindop. Hair Stylist: Betty Lee. Casting Director: Maude Spector. Costume Designer: Doris Lee. Costumes for Mr. Sim, Mr. Hordern and Miss Edwardes designed by: Constance Da Pinna. Mechanical Victorian Dolls loaned by: Mr. M. Steiner. Mechanical Toys loaned by: Bracher and Partner.

CAST: Alastair Sim (Ebenezer Scrooge); Kathleen Harrison (Mrs Dilber); Jack Warner (Mr Jorkins); Mervyn Johns (Bob Cratchit); Hermione Baddeley (Mrs Cratchit); Clifford Mollison (Mr Wilkins); Michael Hordern (Jacob Marley); George Cole (Scrooge as a young man); Patrick MacNee (Marley as a young man); Rona Anderson (Alice); John Charlesworth (Peter Cratchit); Glyn Dearman (Tiny Tim); Francis de Wolff (Ghost of Christmas Present); Carol Marsh (Fan); Brian Worth (Fred); Miles Malleson (Old Joe); Ernest Thesiger (Undertaker); Michael Dolan (Ghost of Christmas Past); Roddy Hughes (Mr Fezziwig); Olga Edwardes; Hattie Jacques; Peter Bull; Hugh Dempster; Eleanor Summerfield; Louise Hampton; C. Konarski; Eliot Makeham; Douglas Muir; Noel Howlett; Fred Johnson; Henry Hewitt; David Hannaford; Maire O'Neill; Richard Pearson.

NOTE: Highlights from Richard Addinsell's impressive score can be found in "A Christmas Carol (Suite)" which is included on the compact disc entitled "Sundance Film Music Series, Volume 1" (Telarc CD-88801).

*See discussion in Chapter 6.

A CHRISTMAS CAROL

NBC-TV 1951 USA 30m b/w
Producer: Fred Coe. Director: Gordon Duff. Television Play: David Swift. Technical Direction: O. Tamburri. Lighting: Leo Tarrenkopf. Makeup: Dick Smith. Costumes: Rose Bogdanoff. Production Supervision: Leonard Kole. Settings: Otis Riggs. Musical Direction and Composition: Harry Sosnik. Announcer: Nelson Case.

CAST: Sir Ralph Richardson (Ebenezer Scrooge); Arthur Treacher (Christmas Past); Melville Cooper (Christmas Present); Margaret Phillips (Mrs Cratchit); Malcom Keen (Marley's Ghost); Alan Napier (Charles Dickens); Norman Barrs (Bob Cratchit); Robin Craven (Mr. Fezziwig); Robert Hay Smith (Tiny Tim); Judson Rees (Johnny); Roderick Walker (Fred); Bobby White (boy singer); Richard Wigginton (Peter Cratchit); Mary Lee Dearring (Belinda Cratchit); Ronald Long (Solicitor); Pat Malone (Christmas Future); Betty Sinclair. [Note: Vincent Terrace's *Television Specials: 3,201 Entertainment Spectaculars, 1939–1993* (Jefferson NC: McFarland, 1995) indicates that the part of Mrs. Fezziwig was played by Charles Dickens's great-granddaughter, Gypsy Raine; however, she is not listed in the on-screen credits. (Scrooge notes the presence of Fezziwig's wife and daughter at the party in the Christmas Past sequence, but the viewer really cannot tell who they are among the various people shown dancing.) *The Billboard's* review

(January 5, 1952, p. 8) also notes that Raine was in the cast.]

"Fireside Theatre" telecast (on film) on December 25, 1951.

The most surprising aspect of this adaptation is that it includes an "appearance" by Charles Dickens. Portrayed by veteran character actor Alan Napier, an older, full-bearded Dickens provides a brief but charming introduction and epilogue that frame the story proper. However, it is the presence of Ralph Richardson in the central role of Scrooge that is this version's major claim to fame. Unfortunately, it is also its weakest link.

While he was a brilliant actor who distinguished himself in a wide range of roles, Richardson was simply not the "Scrooge type." He was, for example, excellent in roles that called for a certain type of low-key villainy, as in his portrayal of Dr. Austin Sloper in *The Heiress*. And he was also without peer in playing — and usually with a great deal of deliciously broad humor — a certain type of befuddled, blustery, or slightly daffy English eccentric. Along this latter line, when the reformed Scrooge calls on his nephew on Christmas morning and is greeted at the door by a young female servant, Richardson looks slyly into the camera, adjusts his tie, and with his uniquely twinkling eye and oddly nasal delivery, says "What a pretty girl." Classic Ralph Richardson, but not really what Dickens had in mind.

In short, the role of Scrooge calls for a strength and solidity that one does not normally associate with Ralph Richardson. While this version is not fatally flawed because of Richardson's presence — on the contrary, it is very interesting because of it — one is conscious of it being a bit "off key" nonetheless. (*The Billboard* had an interesting assessment, finding Richardson's Scrooge to be "softer and more rounded than the usual American deliniation of the miser.") Please also note that very similar reservations apply to Michael Hordern's 1977 turn as Scrooge; see entry below.

Richardson is not helped by a rather superficial script which races through the story (as all half-hour versions must) at breakneck speed. A couple of unique touches are in evidence, however, in terms of how the film handles some necessary transitions. For example, while Scrooge is witnessing the festivities at old Fezziwig's with the Ghost of Christmas Past, the Ghost of Christmas Present turns up as one of the dancers; Scrooge is then whisked off to witness new visions of Christmas in the present. And while holding the hand of the Ghost of Christmas Present at his nephew's Christmas party, Scrooge suddenly realizes that he is holding the hand of the Ghost of Christmas Future. Such variations

add a little spice to the mix, but in the final analysis, this is an interesting but far from classic *Carol*.

THE GEORGE BURNS AND GRACIE ALLEN SHOW

CBS-TV   1951   USA   30m   b/w

Producer: Ralph Levy. Director: Ralph Levy. Written by: Paul Henning; Sid Dorfman; Harvey Helm; Willy Burns. Music Direction: Lud Gluskin. Scenic Design: Chris Choate; Harry R. Kemm. Gracie Allen's Gowns by: Howard Greer.

CAST: George Burns (Himself); Gracie Allen (Herself); Harry Von Zell (Himself); Bea Benadaret (Blanche); Fred Clark (Harry); Sarah Selby (Mamie); Gerry James (Gerry); Melinda Plowman (Linda); Jill Oppenheim (Jill); Kathleen O'Malley (Julie).

Situation comedy. First broadcast on December 30, 1951.

George and Gracie have guests for the Christmas holiday and Gracie relates her own version of the *Carol* as a children's bedtime story; her version, however, is a mixture of Dickens, Goldilocks and the Three Bears, and Cinderella. Gracie's *Carol* is brief and comes near the end of the program. While clever, it is nowhere near as funny or fully developed as many of her other routines. Very minor stuff as *Carol* spoofing goes, but it's always a delight to visit the near surreal world of the Burns residence.

A CHRISTMAS CAROL

NBC-TV   1952   USA   60m   b/w

Teleplay: Robert Howard Lindsay. Makeup: Dick Smith.

CAST: Malcolm Keen (Ebenezer Scrooge); Harry Townes (Bob Cratchit); Valerie Cossart (Mrs. Cratchit); Glenn Walken (Tiny Tim); Veronica Dangel (Edith); Buzzy Martin (Peter); Norma Jean Marlowe (Belinda); Noel Leslie (Ghost of Christmas Past); Melville Cooper (Ghost of Christmas Present); George Spelvin (Ghost of Christmas Future); Richard Purdy (Jacob Marley); Richard Newton; Naomi Riordon; Eric Sinclair; Biff McGuire; Ken Walken; Geoffrey Lumb; Geoffrey Lumb, Jr.; Douglas Wood; Rex O'Malley; Eric Berry; Eva Condon; Philip Brady. Christmas Carols [as background music] sung by The Saint Ignatius Boy's Choir under the direction of Dr. Reginald Silby.

Telecast live on December 24, 1952, as part of the *Kraft Television Theatre* dramatic anthology series.

"Productionwise it was a slick entry, with good sets. The script by Robert Howard Lindsay was fine, except in one lapse. That was the incident of Scrooge's seeing himself dead while two citizens steal the deceased's possessions. While the pilfering was called for by Dickens, the original did not make the characters repulsive. Business of the man pulling a knife on the cleaning woman wasn't in keeping with the overall theme.

"Basically the fault lay in uninspired direction and pedestrian thesping. Scrooge, played by Malcolm Keen, didn't convince until his final transformation, and many other characters missed the Dickens charm." — *Variety*, December 31, 1952, p. 26

NOTE: An NBC press release dated December 15, 1952, indicates that this production was adapted from Dickens's reading version of the *Carol*, and that it included a very large London street scene set as well as a replica of a nineteenth-century church.

BRANSBY WILLIAMS
BBC-TV   1953   Great Britain   25m   b/w
Producer: Kenneth Milne-Buckley.
CAST: Bransby Williams; Kathleen Saintsbury.

Production (not seen) appears to have been partially devoted to a recreation of Williams's legendary one-man version of the *Carol*. Shot on film and broadcast on December 21, 1953.

"The Dickens touch to the Christmas programmes will be added by that superb veteran Bransby Williams. His portrait of Ebenezer Scrooge has been filmed and will be presented on Monday. It will begin with scenes shot in Bransby Williams' study at his home in London. Among his many souvenirs there is one — which viewers will see — of his self portrait in the role of Scrooge." — *Radio Times*, December 18, 1953, p. 16

NOTE: Bransby Williams appeared often on British television throughout the fifties, including some programs that were devoted to his reminiscences about his long career. It is likely that the subject of Dickens in general, and the *Carol* in particular, was raised in some of these appearances.

A CHRISTMAS CAROL
ABC-TV   1953   USA   60m   b/w
CAST: Noel Leslie (Ebenezer Scrooge); Harry Townes (Bob Cratchit); Valerie Cossart (Mrs. Cratchit); Melville Cooper [It seems likely that Cooper, who was both physically and temperamentally suited for the part, reprised his role as the Ghost of Christmas Present from the earlier 1951 and 1952 productions, but this could not be confirmed. In any event, he *did not* play Scrooge as various sources have erroneously reported]; Denis Greene; Geoffrey Lumb; Jack Raine; Naomi Riordan; The Trinity Boys Choir of New York.

Telecast live on December 24, 1953, as part of the *Kraft Television Theatre* dramatic anthology series.

NOTE: *The Kraft Television Theatre* was a long-running (late forties through late fifties) series on NBC. However, for a short time in the mid-fifties, a second broadcast also ran simultaneously on ABC. Because of this anomaly and because of similarities in cast lists, some confusion exists regarding this program and the Kraft version of the previous year (see 1952 entry above). Unfortunately, this production does not seem to have been reviewed anywhere.

TOPPER
CBS-TV   1953   USA   30m   b/w
A John W. Loveton/Bernard L. Schubert Production. Producer: John W. Loveton. Director: Paul Landres. Supervising Story Editor: Philip Rapp. Written by: George Oppenheimer. Based on the Characters Originally Created by: Thorne Smith. Production Manager: Herbert E. Stewart.
CAST: Leo G. Carroll (Cosmo Topper); Anne Jeffreys (Marion Kerby); Robert Sterling (George Kerby); Buck (Neil); Lee Patrick (Henrietta Topper); Kathleen Freeman (Katie); Mary Field (Thelma Gibney); Frank Ferguson (Dr. Lang).

Situation comedy. Episode title: "Christmas Carol." First broadcast on: December 25, 1953.

Cosmo Topper attempts to continue his holiday tradition of reading selections from the *Carol*. He tires of his wife's interruptions and asks her to read instead. While listening, he falls asleep and dreams the story with himself in the role of Scrooge. ("Do we have to go out again?" a weary Topper asks a Ghost of Christmas Present who is dressed, quite literally, as a Christmas present. "Don't blame me, blame Dickens" is his reply.) This poor man's version of the delightful trio of late thirties and early forties *Topper* films is always mildly amusing; this particular episode appears to qualify as the first in an endless line of television sitcom spoofs in which the *Carol* is transposed to a familiar setting and group of characters.

NOTE: CBS does not have an official episode title on file for this production. However, *TV Guide* (December 25–31, 1953 [New York Metro Ed.], p. A-12) lists the episode title as "Christmas Carol."

A CHRISTMAS CAROL*
CBS-TV   1954   USA   60m   color
Producer/Director: Ralph Levy. Adaptation and Lyrics: Maxwell Anderson. Music Composed and Conducted by: Bernard Herrmann. Director of Photography: George E. Diskant. Associate Producer: Richard Fisher. Vocal Supervisor:

Roger Wagner. Associate Conductor: Victor Bay. Choreographer: Donald Sadler. Production Manager: Lloyd Richards. Art Directors: Albert M. Pyke, Ralph Berger. Costumer: Kate Drain Lawson. Set Decorator: Edward Boyle. Makeup Man: Karl Herlinger. Assistant director: Jack R. Bern. Host [of *Shower of Stars*]: William Lundigan.

CAST: Fredric March (Ebenezer Scrooge); Basil Rathbone (Jacob Marley); Ray Middleton (Fred and the Ghost of Christmas Present); Bob Sweeney (Bob Cratchit); Christopher Cook (Tiny Tim); Sally Fraser (Belle and the Ghost of Christmas Past); Craig Hill (young Scrooge); Queenie Leonard (Mrs Cratchit); Rex Evans (Solicitor); Tony Pennington ([Solicitor's] Companion); William Griffiths (The Book Buyer); Peter Miles (Peter Cratchit); Janine Perreau (Belinda Cratchit); Bonnie & Judy Franklin (Susan & Martha Cratchit); June Ellis ([Scrooge's] Housekeeper); The Roger Wagner Chorale (Singers); John Murphy (Lamplighter); Jimmy Baird (Boy); Dick Elliott (Fezziwig); Ezelle Poule (Woman); John Meek (Goose Boy).

Filmed in color and telecast on December 23, 1954, on the musical variety program *Shower of Stars*, which appeared about every four weeks in place of the weekly anthology series *Climax!* It was rebroadcast in 1955 and 1956. The rebroadcast of December 15, 1955, is currently available on videotape and includes commercials and framing scenes with host Bill Lundigan.

*See discussion in Chapter 7.

DEAR PHOEBE
NBC-TV 1954 USA 30m b/w

Created and Produced by: Alex Gottlieb. Director: Don Weis. Writer: Alex Gottlieb; Barbara Hammer. Director of Photography: Joseph Biroc. Editorial Supervisor: Jason H. Bernie. Art Director: C. Daniel Hall. Film Editor: Edward Mann; Mike Pozen. Assistant Director: Paul Wurtzel. Music Supervisor: Raoul Kraushaar. Photographic Effects: Jack Rabin; Louis DeWitt. Assistant to Producer: Margaret Jennings. Production by Conne-Stephens, Inc. Filmed at American National Studios/Hollywood, CA. Sponsored by Campbell Soup Company.

CAST: Peter Lawford (Bill Hastings/Miss Phoebe Goodheart); Marcia Henderson (Mickey Riley); Charles Lane (Mr. G. R. Fosdick); Joe Corey (Humphrey Humpsteader); George Winslow (Joey Kragon); Jesse White (Murray Kragon); Ruth Perrott (Mrs. Kragon); Grady Sutton (store manager).

Situation comedy. First broadcast on December 24, 1954. Episode title: "Scrooge Fosdick."

This short-lived series starred Peter Lawford as a former teacher who writes a lonelyhearts newspaper column under the pseudonym Phoebe Goodheart. The main storyline in this episode concerns Phoebe's efforts to reunite a troubled young boy with his father at Christmas. It is not a *Carol* variation. However, a mild *Carol* angle is present in a subplot involving Phoebe's boss, editor G. R. Fosdick, who is behaving like "an old Scrooge" by refusing to provide an office Christmas party. (As Fosdick, veteran character actor Charles Lane makes a perfect modern day Scrooge!) Needless to say, all is well as the story fades out: Father and son are reunited, and Fosdick is singing Christmas carols and promising a New Year's bonus for one and all. Nothing special here, but an interesting early example of television's propensity for drawing from the bottomless well of Dickensian characterization and imagery.

THE MERRY CHRISTMAS
Associated Rediffusion 1955 Great Britain 45m b/w

Producer: Douglas Hurn. Writer: Donald Cotton. Music: Brian Burke. Musical Director: Steve Race.

CAST: Hugh Griffith (Ebenezer Scrooge); John Gower (Night watchman); Michael O'Halloran (Topper); Norman Tyrell (Bob Cratchit); Peter Reeves (Fred); Edmund Willard (Marley's Ghost); Martin Lawrence (Ghost of Christmas Past); George Murcell (Fezziwig); Peter Reeves (Young Scrooge); Eira Heath (Belle); Irene Byatt (Mrs. Cratchit); Barry Huband (Tiny Tim); Madi Head (Mrs. Fred).

Musical *Carol* adaptation broadcast on December 21, 1955. Also produced in 1958 with different cast; see entry below.

STORY OF THE CHRISTMAS CAROL
WNBQ/WMAQ 1955 USA 30m b/w

Director: David Barnhizer. Music: Joseph Gallicchio and the NBC orchestra with the Illinois Bell Choir. Announcer: Mike Kirby.

CAST: Ken Nordine (off-screen narrator); Norman Gottschalk (Ebenezer Scrooge); Eugene Troobnick (Bob Cratchit); Gertrude Breen (Mrs Cratchit); Morton Friedman (Tiny Tim); Kurt Kupfer (Fezziwig); George Greer (young Scrooge).

Simulcast by Chicago NBC stations WNBQ and WMAQ on December 22, 1955.

"Bulk of the half-hour was a smooth adaptation of Dickens' classic, cleverly unspooled through a cluster of realistic sets. Truncated version of Scrooge & Co. was expertly narrated off-screen by Ken Nordine as the local AFTRANs went through their pantomime paces before the cameras. Venerable yarn was graphically told, thanks to imaginative camerawork and some skillful silent thesping."—*Variety*, December 28, 1955, p. 31

IGOR CASSINI SHOW

DuMont-TV   1955   USA   30m   b/w

Variety and talk program hosted by New York society columnist Igor Cassini, brother of designer Oleg Cassini. This episode was broadcast on December 23, 1955.

"We see the original copy of Dickens' 'A Christmas Carol.' STANY, an organization of Wall Street investment brokers, sings Christmas carols. Ski, skating fashions."—*TV Guide* [New York Metro Ed.], December 17-23, 1955, p. A-78

NOTE: This program often used filmed inserts and segments. It seems likely that this technique was employed to bring viewers into New York's Pierpont Morgan Library, where the original *Carol* manuscript is preserved.

OUR MISS BROOKS

CBS-TV   1955   USA   30m   b/w

CAST: Eve Arden (Connie Brooks); Gale Gordon (Osgood Conklin); Bob Sweeney (Oliver Munsey); Ricky Vera (Benny Romero); Jane Morgan (Margaret Davis); Isabel Randolph (Mrs. Nestor); Jesslyn Fax (Angela).

Situation comedy. Episode title: "Music Review." First broadcast on December 23, 1955.

This episode of *Our Miss Brooks*, starring the wonderful Eve Arden as wisecracking teacher Connie Brooks, provided the forum for the first of many televised "plays within plays" involving the *Carol*. Here Mrs. Nestor's Elementary School is the setting for a production featuring principal Conklin as Scrooge, vice-principal Munsey as Marley's Ghost, and student Benny as an angel. In another storyline, Miss Brooks buys a music box that will play "Jingle Bells"—but only for those who have the true Spirit of Christmas.

A CHRISTMAS CAROL

WCBS-TV   1955   USA   30m   b/w

Producer: Bill Leonard. Teleplay: Bill Leonard. Host: Bill Leonard.

CAST: Jonathan Harris ("Ebenezer Scrooge"); Biff McGuire ("Bob Cratchit"); Howard Wierum (voice of "Jacob Marley").

Local telecast on the "Eye on New York" program on December 25, 1955. This appears to be the first formal updating of the *Carol* into a twentieth-century setting. The use of a television to show the familiar visions—the *Variety* review quoted below also notes that "Marley's" voice is heard over an intercom—predates by many years

such later efforts as *Skinflint*, *Scrooged* and *Ebbie* in which various modern electronic media are employed in converting their respective Scrooge surrogates.

"A middle-20th century version of Charles Dickens's 'Christmas Carol.' The clever conversion preserved the spirit of the original but in the milieu of lower Park Ave. and big industry.

"Ebenezer Scrooge became the president of the fictitious Metropolitan Plastics Corp.; Bob Cratchit switched from the bookkeeper to elevator operator in Scrooge's building; and the late and unlamented biz partner, Jacob Marley, combined the parts of Xmases Past, Present, and Future, using a TV receiver as an up-to-date medium for the unearthly visions."—*Variety*, December 28, 1955, p. 40

THE ADVENTURES OF OZZIE AND HARRIET

ABC-TV   1956   USA   30m   b/w

Producer: Ozzie Nelson. Director: Ozzie Nelson.

CAST: Ozzie Nelson, Harriet Nelson, David Nelson, Rick Nelson (Themselves); Lyle Talbot (Joe Randolph); Frank Cady (Doc Williams); Isabel Randolph (Mrs. Brewster); Louanna Gardner (Lady in Orphanage); Phil Arnold (Tailor).

Situation comedy. Episode title: "The Busy Christmas." First broadcast on: December 19, 1956.

The longest-running sitcom in television history, *The Adventures of Ozzie and Harriet* was preceded by a long-running radio show of the same name; there was also a 1950 feature film entitled *Here Come the Nelsons*. This episode revolves around Ozzie's attempts to cope with an onslaught of chores and obligations in the days leading up to Christmas—one of which is to play Scrooge in a local production on Christmas Eve. As with Burns and Allen's earlier effort, this one is very minor stuff as *Carol* spoofing goes: the "play within a play" is just one of several threads in the storyline, and it is glimpsed only briefly toward the end of the episode. (One would actually like to have been shown more of Ozzie's turn as Scrooge, as the production in which he appears may well be the most appallingly bad *Carol* adaptation in history!) Perhaps the most interesting aspect of this episode is the fact that it does not opt for the predictable approach of having a Scrooge-like Ozzie reformed by his appearance in the play. He is more than a bit harried by his Christmas duties, but he basically stumbles through the episode as his familiar, cheerful self, and at no time is he presented as "an old Scrooge."

NOTE: A 1964 rebroadcast of this program is

available on home video, complete with commercials for the New York World's Fair.

THE STINGIEST MAN IN TOWN*

NBC-TV 1956 USA 90m color

A Theatrical Enterprises Production. Producer: Joel Spector. Director: Daniel Petrie. Book and Lyrics: Janice Torre. Music: Fred Spielman. Orchestra Conductor: Camarata. Assistant to Producer: Kathleen Greene. Unit Manager: Hank Shensky. Choreographer: John Heawood. Scenic Designer: Kim Swados. Costumes: Motley. Makeup: Bob O'Bradovich. Technical Director: O. Tamburri. Lighting Director: Bill Raker. Audio: Don Frey. Video: Tony Nelle. Stage Managers: Bill Post; Dean Grant. Graphic Artist: Robert A. Jones. Announcer: Brook Taylor.

CAST: Basil Rathbone (Ebenezer Scrooge); The Four Lads (Chorus/Narrators; Beggars); Johnny Desmond (Fred); Robert Weede (Ghost of Jacob Marley); Vic Damone (Young Scrooge); Patrice Munsel (Belle); Martyn Green (Bob Cratchit); Betty Madigan (Martha); John McIver (First Charitable Gentleman); Robert Wright (Christmas Present); Alice Frost (Mrs. Cratchit); Philippe Bevans (Mrs. Dilber); John McGovern (Second Charitable Gentleman); Ian Martin (Christmas Past); Dennis Kohler (Tiny Tim); Bryan Herbert (Mr. Fezziwig); Richard Morse (Peter); Karyl Ann Traum (Belinda); Carson Woods (Billie); Karen Wolfe (Annie); John Heawood (The Rag Picker); Olive Dunbar (Betty); Stephen Meininger (An Urchin); Keith Herrington (Christmas Yet to Come); The Jerry Packer Chorus.

SONGS: "A Christmas Carol"; "An Old-Fashioned Christmas"; "Humbug"; "The Stingiest Man in Town"; "I Wear a Chain"; "Golden Dreams"; "It Might Have Been"; "The Christmas Spirit"; "Yes, There Is a Santa Claus"; "One Little Boy"; "The Birthday Party of the King"; "Concerto Inferno"; "Mankind Should Be My Business."

Musical version broadcast live by NBC on *The Alcoa Hour*, December 23, 1956.

To follow up on comments made in Chapter 7, the physical status of this version, briefly stated, is as follows: The Library of Congress has a complete soundtrack and the final third of the picture portion (in black-and-white); both consist of 16mm elements. At present, it is unclear as to whether the first two-thirds of the picture were ever deposited with the Library of Congress; if so, they are currently missing. NBC is believed to possess more complete materials, and one can only hope that this particular *Carol* will someday find its way back into circulation. (For the record, years of searching the collector's marketplace, where sooner or later just about anything can be found for the right price, have turned up nothing on this title.)

A viewing of the final third of *The Stingiest Man in Town* reveals a very interesting and impressive production and suggests that it was a major *Carol* indeed. In its complete version, the ninety minute broadcast was divided into three acts of roughly twenty to twenty-five minutes each; various previews, promotions and messages accounted for the rest of the time. Part Three opens with the Four Lads, who serve as a kind of Greek chorus, providing a singing narration that is clearly designed to welcome viewers back from a commercial. It then cuts to a deserted street where we find the Ghost of Christmas Present saying farewell to Scrooge. While we don't see the familiar urchins Ignorance and Want, an effective variation of Dickens's words and message is achieved as the ghost remarks: "I, the spirit of the present Christmas Day, will die at midnight. The world, touched for a brief moment with the Christmas feeling of goodwill toward men, will soon revert to its philosophy of tooth and claw and dog eat dog. Where during Christmas angels sat enthroned, now devils lurk and menace men with evil." And the highlight of the Christmas Future sequence is a macabre dance in which Scrooge winds up chained to his tombstone; the intent is to suggest that he has seen a vision of Hell. It is highly theatrical and expressionistic in style and tone, and the overall effect is quite chilling. Needless to say, however, the mood is much lighter when the reformed Scrooge wakes up on Christmas morning. Rathbone sings (very well!) and dances with great energy and style, and, after an extended visit at the Cratchits, the story fades out on a very pleasant note. (Later, the entire cast is briefly shown singing "An Old-Fashioned Christmas" as the broadcast winds down.

From a visual standpoint, *The Stingiest Man in Town* appears to have been a fairly lavish affair with excellent production values in evidence everywhere. It has the look and "feel" of live television, although one also notes some very fluid camera work in a couple of spots. It should also be noted that the musical numbers appear to have been carefully integrated into the storyline; they are, in effect, part of the script. (One could argue, however, that in an overall sense the songs lack the subtlety found in the 1970 *Scrooge* with Albert Finney.) In this regard, the recording that was released to coincide with the broadcast provides something of the flavor of the complete production; see Columbia CL 950. The same songs can also be heard in the 1978 Rankin/Bass animated remake which is also called *The Stingiest Man in Town*; see entry below.

In the final analysis, it is, of course, impossible to offer any definitive conclusions about this *Carol* based on incomplete evidence. Thus a number of questions must linger in the air until this one surfaces (one hopes) in the future. Unfortunately, contemporary reviews cannot always be relied upon to settle any questions:

"Any resemblance that 'The Stingiest Man in Town' has to Charles Dickens' 'A Christmas Carol' is purely coincidental. The characters and the setting were there but the flavor of Dickens' perennial Yule story was missing in the musical transition." — *Variety*, December 26, 1956, p. 27

"The Dickens story lost none of its spirit or flavor in the musical translation and the production was as lavish as any on the spec time." — *Daily Variety*, December 26, 1956, p. 10

"A lavish, well-acted, handsomely mounted distortion of Dickens fell flat on its aspirations last week. Everyone knows only Oscar Hamerstein II can get away with making song lyrics out of moral values. By the time Scrooge got to a patter song called 'Mankind Should Be My Business,' all was lost." — *The Billboard*, January 5, 1957, p. 9

NOTE: A photograph from this production can be found in Daniel Blum, *Pictorial History of Television* (Philadelphia & New York: Chilton Company — Book Division, 1959), p. 230. For a color photo see *TV Guide* [New York Metro ed.], December 22–28, 1956, p.4.

*See discussion in Chapter 7.

SCROOGE LOOSE

A Clokey Production   1957   8m   USA   Color

Producer: Art Clockey

The character of Gumby, a clay figure animated by a stop-motion filming process, was introduced on NBC's *Howdy Doody* show in 1956, and then spun off into his own series entitled *The Gumby Show*, also on NBC, in 1957.

Yes, Virginia, there is a Gumby version of *A Christmas Carol*. Well, almost. In that strange but delightful world where surrealism and children's television join forces, we find Gumby gazing upward through his telescope at a book entitled "Dicken's [sic] Christmas Carol." He is just in time to see Scrooge escaping from the book, and he and his horse Pokey, in the guise of Sherlock Holmes and Dr. Watson, set off in hot pursuit. While constantly muttering "humbug," Scrooge first commandeers a bulldozer and begins pushing children's toys over the edge of a table. He then sees a book entitled "Stories of Santa Claus" and, since Santa is the cause of all this Christmas humbug, he enters the book. Gumby and Pokey follow and observe Scrooge opening one

of Santa's bags of toys and replacing children's presents with rocks. Gumby comes to the rescue by lassoing Scrooge and wraping him up in a bag. Santa mistakenly loads the bag on his sleigh, and the film ends with Gumby and Pokey watching Santa (with the "bagged" Scrooge) begin his Christmas Eve rounds. Any attempt at serious criticism here is obviously pointless. However, it is certainly worth noting that a film like this underscores the unique role that the *Carol* plays in our popular culture, as demonstrated by the extent to which the name Scrooge — or even the very *idea* of Scrooge — has become a universally recognized synonym for meanness as well as miserliness.

THE TRAIL TO CHRISTMAS

CBS-TV   1957   USA   30m   b/w

Producer: William Frye. Director: James Stewart. Teleplay : Frank Burt and Valentine Davies, from a story by Frank Burt. Camera: William H. Daniels. Editor: Michael McAdam. Art Director : John Meehan.

CAST: Ronald Reagan (Host); James Stewart (Bart); Richard Eyer (Johnny Carterville); John McIntire (Ebenezer Scrooge); Sam Edwards (Bob Cratchit); Will Wright (Jake Marley); Kevin Hagen (Ghost); Sally Frazier (Belle); Mary Lawrence (Mrs. Cratchit); Dennis Holmes (Tiny Tim); Russell Simpson; Tom Pittman; Tony Hilder; Ted Mapes; Gregg Barton; Hope Summers.

A Western variation telecast (on film) on December 15, 1957, on *The General Electric Theatre*.

"'A Christmas Carol' takes on a new perspective in this oater version, and the trail it rides is one that's true to the spirit of the original Dickens work. James Stewart stars and for the first time takes over the directorial chores. As an actor he's charming, but it was his direction that took precedence here, and it turned out to be masterful.

"[The story] brings Richard Eyer, one of the brightest moppethesps [child performers] around, to the desert, where he meets cowboy Stewart. He explains he's run away from home and that he's got very little faith in anything connected with Christmas. So Stewart retells the story of Ebenezer Scrooge, and the yarn takes shape with the miserly gentleman playing a ranch owner and Bob Cratchit his ranch hand." — *Daily Variety*, December 17, 1957, p. 23

NOTE: A photograph from this production can be found in Daniel Blum, *Pictorial History of Television* (Philadelphia & New York: Chilton Company — Book Division, 1959), p. 202.

CAPTAIN KANGAROO

CBS-TV   1957   USA   45m   b/w

CAST: Bob Keeshan (Captain Kangaroo); Hugh Brannum (Mr. Green Jeans).

Children's program; this episode broadcast on December 17, 1957.

"Everyone sings 'It's Beginning to Look a Lot Like Christmas.' Mr. Green Jeans, Bunny Rabbit and the Captain tell the story of 'Ebenezer Scrooge' based on Charles Dickens' 'Christmas Carol.'"—*TV Guide* [New York Metro Ed.], December 14–20, 1957, p. A-45

CAPTAIN KANGAROO

CBS-TV   1958   USA   45m   b/w

CAST: Bob Keeshan (Captain Kangaroo); Hugh Brannum (Mr. Green Jeans).

Children's program; this episode broadcast on December 16, 1958.

"Mr. Green Jeans dresses up as Scrooge."—*TV Guide* [New York Metro Ed.], December 13–19, 1958, p. A-43

CIMARRON CITY

NBC-TV   1958   USA   60m   b/w

A Mont Production. Producer: Richard H. Bartlett; Norman Jolley. Director: Richard H. Bartlett. Writer: Norman Jolley. Director of Photography: William A. Sickner. Art Director: George Patrick. Editorial Supervisor: Richard G. Wray. Film Editor: Marston Fay. Music Supervisor: Frederick Herbert. Set Decorator: John McCarthy. Sound: Earl Crain, Jr. Assistant Director: Charles S. Gould. Costume Supervisor: Vincent Dee. Makeup: Jack Barron. Hair Stylist: Florence Bush.

CAST: George Montgomery (Matthew Rockford); Audrey Totter (Beth Purcell); John Smith (Lane Temple); Ken Mayer; Linda Leighton; Dan Blocker (Tiny Budinger); George Dunn (Jesse Williams); Pete Dunn (Dody Hamer); Tom Fadden (Silas Perry); Claire Carleton (Alice Purdy); Harry Harvey, Sr. Guest Star: Tim Hovey.

Western series. Episode title: "Cimarron Holiday." First broadcast on December 20, 1958.

This episode of the short-lived western series is not a *Carol* variation per se, but it is one of several television programs to use the *Carol* as a play within a play. In this one, the locals decide to stage a dramatic production of the *Carol*. (Curiously, we are told that the celebration is taking place in July as part of their Founders Day celebration, and not in December as part of their Christmas festivities. It is explained that the character of Beth Purcell has a script of the play from a school production that she once participated in and that there is not time to choose another title.)

As far as the play within a play is concerned, this one takes the familiar route of having a group of well-meaning amateurs stumble their way through a hopelessly inept production of the *Carol*. Its most interesting aspect is a brief appearance by a pre–*Bonanza* Dan Blocker as an appropriately cast Ghost of Christmas Present. However, another *Carol* angle does show up in a subplot involving the conversion of shiftless Pru Wickham, and his obnoxious son Avery, who plays Tiny Tim in the play.

NOTE: Various sources indicate that Dinah Shore, who was married to series star George Montgomery at the time, appeared as a guest star in this episode. However, she is not mentioned in any way in the credits, nor is she visible in any copies of this episode that proved available. (It is possible that Shore had a brief cameo that was deleted from the copies.)

THE MERRY CHRISTMAS

Associated Rediffusion   1958   Great Britain   45m   b/w

Director: Ronald Marriott. Book and Lyrics: Donald Cotton. Television Adaptation: Tom Twigge. Music Composed by: Brian Burke. Orchestrations: Phil Cardew. Musical Director: Steve Race. Settings: Frank Nerine.

CAST: Stephen Murray (Ebenezer Scrooge); Forbes Robinson (Night watchman); Hugh Latimer (Topper); John Glyn-Jones (Bob Cratchit); Peter Gilmore (Fred); Percy Cartwright (Marley's Ghost); Julian Orchard (Ghost of Christmas Past); Cameron Hall (Fezziwig); Peter Gilmore (Young Scrooge); Frances Youles (Belle); Colin Cunningham (Ghost of Christmas Present); Beryl Ede (Mrs. Cratchit); Dennis Mallard (Tiny Tim); Howard Williams (Ghost of Christmas Future); Peter Soule (Peter Cratchit); Judy Robinson (Martha Cratchit); Anthony Wilson (Boy); Paddy Turner (Mrs. Fred); Joan Brown (Cousin Arabella); Howard Williams (Fred's Guest); The Barney Gilbraith Singers; The Singing Boys of the Saint Mary of the Angels Song School.

Musical *Carol* adaptation broadcast on December 24, 1958. Also produced in 1955 with different cast; see entry above.

A CHRISTMAS CAROL

Harry Alan Towers   1959   Great Britain   25m   b/w

Produced by Desmond Davis, with the cooperation of the Dickens Society of London.

CAST: Fredric March (Host); Basil Rathbone (Ebenezer Scrooge); Kaplam Kaye (Scrooge as a boy); Howard Williams (Scrooge as a young man); Toke Townley (Bob Cratchit); Mary Jones

(Mrs. Cratchit); Michael Lewis (Peter Cratchit); Monica Marlow (Martha Cratchit); Mark Milcham (Tiny Tim); Laura Henderson (Fan); Brian McDermott (Fred); Patricia Cree (Mrs. Fred); Roberta Wooley, Stella Riley (sisters); Wilfred Fletcher (Jacob Marley); Walter Hudd (Ghost of Christmas Past); Alexander Gauge (Ghost of Christmas Present); Michael McCarthy (Ghost of Christmas Future); Mary Webster (Belle); Gabriel Toyne (Fezziwig); Rita Webb (charwoman); Sydney Arnold (Old Joe); Joey White (urchin boy); Keith Smith, Michael Logan (thin and fat businessmen).

This short *Carol* was part of independent producer Harry Alan Towers's *Tales from Dickens* series, first televised in England in 1959. Fifteen of a projected thirty-nine episodes were filmed, all of which were hosted by Fredric March.

Given the participation of such venerable talents as March and Rathbone, one would like to think that this version had the potential to become a minor classic. However, the truth is that these great actors were not given much to work with, and the end result is just another bare bones adaptation that races through the familiar story at breakneck speed. The "essence" of the story survives, as indeed it always does, but there is little to recommend this version beyond its obvious interest to hardcore *Carol* completists. On the plus side, its treatment of the Christmas Past, Present, and Future sequences is noteworthy from a stylistic standpoint in that it opts for a highly theatrical, and decidedly expressionist, approach which jettisons all realistic details. Instead we see freestanding windows and doorways set against blank backgrounds with the characters and minimal props enshrouded in a heavy mist. The decision to take this approach may have had more to do with economics than art; the skillful deployment of fog and darkness can do much to stretch a low budget by hiding a cheap or nonexistent set. Nevertheless, it adds an interesting touch to an otherwise shoddy treatment of the *Carol*.

A CHRISTMAS CAROL

Alpha (Anglo Amalgamated Film Distributors Ltd.) 1960 Great Britain 28m b/w

Presented by: Nat Cohen & Stuart Levy. Producer and Director: Robert Hartford-Davis.

CAST: John Hayter (Scrooge); Stewart Brown (Bob Cratchit); Gordon Mulholland (Nephew); Jimmy Mentis (Portly Gentleman); Bruce Anderson (Marley's Ghost).

Theatrically released short subject (or "featurette").

It is surprising that a short, low-budget *Carol* was produced for theatrical exhibition in 1960.

By this time television was pretty much the standard marketplace for this type of production. Nevertheless, the review quoted below, which was aimed at exhibitors, suggests that the *Carol* still had some drawing power at the box office well into the television age. Despite its relatively recent vintage, this *Carol* is unavailable for viewing, but a publicity release describes a couple of minor but interesting embellishments: Bob Cratchit, for example, asks for an extra day's holiday on Boxing Day (presumably in addition to Christmas Day); and later, Bob is the only mourner present as Scrooge's dead body lies wrapped on a bed.

"[Robert Hartford-Davis] relates the familiar story as economically as possible, managing to retain the spirit without dwelling in detail on the background. Performances are adequate and with some suitable music backing Tiny Tim's final Christmas wish the showman could add some presentation touches to satisfy family audiences." — *The Daily Cinema*, November 21, 1960, p. 8

THE ANDY GRIFFITH SHOW

CBS-TV 1960 USA 30m b/w

A Mayberry Enterprises Production. Executive Producer: Sheldon Leonard in association with Danny Thomas. Producer: Aaron Ruben. Director: Bob Sweeney. Writer: David Adler. Music: Earle Hagen. Director of Photography: Sid Hickox. Associate Producer: Richard O. Linke. Story Consultant: Aaron Ruben. Art Director: Ralph Berger; Kenneth A. Reid. Set Decorator: Bob Priestley.

CAST: Andy Griffith (Andy Taylor); Don Knotts (Barney Fife); Ronny Howard (Opie Taylor); Frances Bavier (Aunt Bee); Elinor Donahue (Ellie Walker); Will Wright (Ben Weaver); Sam Edwards (Sam Muggins); Margaret Kerry (Bess Muggins); Joy Ellison (Effie Muggins).

Situation comedy. Episode title: "Christmas Story." First broadcast on December 19, 1960.

This is not a formal *Carol* variation per se. There are no ghostly visitors, and the Scrooge surrogate is ultimately revealed to be an old softie underneath a gruff exterior. Nevertheless, it is a classic case — perhaps *the* classic case — of how just a little *Carol* iconography can be skillfully used to inform, motivate, and dominate an entire production.

The story takes place on Christmas Eve in the legendary television town of Mayberry, North Carolina, and centers on Ben Weaver, who is a prosperous businessman — but also a nasty, grumpy, greedy, old goat. He is, in short, "an old Scrooge." After Ben causes a family to be jailed for moonshining, Sheriff Taylor and the Mayberry regulars decide to have a Christmas party at the jail so that their holiday won't be ruined. However, to everyone's surprise, Ben keeps trying to get himself arrested — not out of spite, but because he is lonely and really wishes to join the party. He ultimately succeeds and, just like Scrooge, appears to be a new man as the story fades out.

The character of Ben Weaver would appear in only two more episodes of *The Andy Griffith Show*: "Andy Forecloses" (April 24, 1961) and "The Merchant of Mayberry" (March 5, 1962). In both of these we find him still behaving in a very Scrooge-like manner. Nevertheless, he is one of the most memorable on the long list of memorable characters that were created for this extraordinary television show, and the Dickensian inspiration is unmistakable.

MY SISTER EILEEN

CBS-TV 1960 USA 30m b/w

CAST: Elaine Stritch (Ruth Sherwood); Shirley Bonne (Eileen Sherwood); Leon Belasco (Mr. Appopolous); Paul Wexler (joyous devil); Betsy Hale (Pamela); Rose Marie (Bertha); Mary Grace Canfield (Doris); George Kennedy (Harry).

Short-lived situation comedy about two career-minded sisters who move to New York; started out as a book, which in turn spawned two feature film adaptations. Episode title: "Ebenezer Scrooge Appopolous." First broadcast on December 21, 1960.

"Piqued at not having been invited to the Yule party being arranged by tenants of his apartment building, Mr. Appopolous, the Sherwood sisters' landlord, clamps down on the Christmas festivities.... During the night before Christmas Appopolous is invited by a very happy devil who gleefully takes him on a tour, showing him the many miseries he has inflicted."— Press release on file at CBS television in New York

THE CHARLIE DRAKE SHOW

BBC-TV 1960 Great Britain 30m b/w

Producer: Ronald Marsh. Script: Charlie Drake; Richard Waring. Designer: Frederick Knapman. Music by Harry Rabinowitz and Orchestra.

CAST: Charlie Drake (Bob Cratchit); Philip Locke (Scrooge); Fred Stone (First Gentleman); Kenneth Thornett (Second Gentleman); Jennifer Browne (Nancy); Howard Lang (Bill Sikes); Kenneth Gouge (David Copperfield); Edwin Richfield (Mr. Murdstone); Lloyd Pearson (Mr. Pickwick); Marjory Hawtrey (Miss Havisham); Frazer Hines (Nicholas Nickleby); Austin Trevor (Mr. Micawber); Martin Benson (Fagin); Peter Delmar (The Artful Dodger); Hennie Scott

(Oliver Twist); William Lyon Brown (Ghost of Jacob Marley).

Carol variation broadcast on December 23, 1960. As the cast of characters indicates, this one might also be described as a Dickensian pastiche.

"Charlie Drake's version of *A Christmas Carol* is bound to be — we can't resist saying — a Dickens of a good story. Charlie, of course, falls naturally into the role of the meek, long-suffering Bob Cratchit, employed by Scrooge to collect money from his debtors. Some of Dickens's most famous characters are on his list, and when we tell you that one of them is the crafty Fagin, you will realize that the little man is going to have to earn his Christmas dinner the hard way!"— *Radio Times*, December 15, 1960, p. 53

MISTER MAGOO'S CHRISTMAS CAROL*

UPA [United Productions of America]/ A Henry G. Saperstein Production 1962 USA 52m color

Executive Producer: Henry G. Saperstein. Producer: Lee Orgel. Director: Abe Levitow. Adaptation: Barbara Chain. Music: Jule Styne. Lyrics: Bob Merrill. Music Scored and Conducted by: Walter Scharf. Sequence Directors: Steve Clark, Gerard Baldwin, Duane Crowther. Animation: John Walker, Hank Smith, Xenia, Casey Onatis, Ed Solomon, Tom McDonald. Production Design: Lee Mishkin, Robert Singer, Richard Ung, Corny Cole, Shirley Silvey, Tony Rivera, Marty Murphy, Sam Weiss. Color Stylists: Phill Norman, Gloria Wood, Robert Inman, Jack Heiter, Dave Weidman. Film Editing: Sam Horta, Earl Bennett, George Probert, Wayne Hughes. Production Manager: Earl Jonas. Mr. Magoo created under the supervision of Stephen Bosustow [one of the founders of UPA].

VOICES: Jim Backus (Mr. Magoo/Ebenezer Scrooge); Morey Amsterdam (Brandy/James); Jack Cassidy (Bob Cratchit); Royal Dano (Marley's Ghost); Paul Frees (Old Fezziwig/undertaker); Joan Gardner (Tiny Tim/Ghost of Christmas Past); Jane Kean (Belle Fezziwig); Marie Matthews (Young Scrooge); Laura Olsher (Mrs. Cratchit); Les Tremayne (Ghost of Christmas Present); John Hart.

SONGS: "Alone in the World"; "It's Great to Be Back on Broadway"; "The Lord's Bright Blessing"; "Ringle, Ringle"; "We're Despicable"; "Winter Was Warm."

Produced by UPA (United Productions of America), this animated film premiered on NBC-TV on December 18, 1962. In 1970 it was paired with "Mr. Magoo's Snow White" and released theatrically as "Mr. Magoo's Holiday Festival."

*See discussion in Chapter 7.

A CHRISTMAS CAROL

BBC-TV 1962 Great Britain 60m b/w
Produced and Designed by: Hal Burton.
Music: Edwin Coleman. Libretto: Margaret
Burns Harris. The Pro Arte Orchestra: Max
Salpeter, Leader; William Reid, Conductor;
Alan Boustead, Associate Conductor.

CAST: Stephen Manton (Ebenezer Scrooge);
Derick Davies (Bob Cratchit); David Hillman
(Scrooge's nephew); Marion Lowe (Woman can-
vasser; Charwoman); Trevor Anthony (Ghost of
Jacob Marley; Ghost of Christmas Present);
Edmund Donlevy (Ghost of Christmas Past;
Shopkeeper); Andrew Clark (Scrooge as a boy);
Sheelagh Mulholland (Scrooge's sister); Brenda
Marshall (Scrooge's fiancée); Rhys McConnochie
(Scrooge as a young man); Catherine Wilson
(Mrs. Cratchit); Sylvia Eaves, Janette Lynn, Lynn
Williams (Bob Cratchit's daughters); Forrester
Pyke (Tiny Tim); Gerwyn Morgan (Nephew's
friend); Carole Rosen (Nephew's visitor; laun-
dress); Elizabeth Boyd (Nephew's wife); Giles
Havergal (Ghost of Christmas Future); Francis
Egerton (Business man); Norman Lumsden
(Undertaker's man); David Pinto (Errand boy);
Christopher Brett; Edward Morgan.

The first performance of an opera version of
the *Carol*. First broadcast in England on December 24, 1962, it was later shown on American
public television. American composer Edwin
Coleman, who was studying in England, is
reported to have approached the BBC with an
idea to produce his then unfinished opera and was
rewarded with a commission to complete it.

"The tale of the skinflint who was reformed
into benevolence is so familiar that it's become
common knowledge. For operatic treatment, it
needs the uplift of melody to concentrate its
pathos and moral. This was what Coleman's arid
and spikey note-spinning failed to provide. He
tended to use musical motifs to illustrate character, but these were so unmemorable that they
would have only registered with the cognoscenti.
And a TV opera must appeal more widely than
to those who can tell a minim from a semi-
breve."—*Variety*, January 16, 1963, p. 32

MR. SCROOGE

CBC-TV 1964 Canada 60m b/w
Producer: Bob Jarvis. Director: Bob Jarvis.
Lyrics: Richard Morris, Dolores Claman, Ted
Wood. Music: Dolores Claman. Book: Richard
Morris, Ted Wood. Orchestration and Musical
Director: Howard Cable. Musical Numbers
Staged by: Robert Tucker. Dialect Director:
Andrew Allan. Audio Consultant: Roy Smith.
Settings Designed by: Trevor Williams. Cos-
tumes: Stuart McKay. Properties: Fred Brown.

Graphic Design: Anton van Dalen. MakeUp:
Margaret Epp. Special Effects: George Clark.
Technical Producer: Joe Parkinson. Lighting
Direction: John Grozelle. Audio: Ed Rickwood.
Sound Effects: Fredrick Tudor, William McClin-
tock.

CAST: Cyril Ritchard (Ebenezer Scrooge);
Tessie O'Shea (Mrs Cratchit); Alfie Bass (Bob
Cratchit); Eric Christmas (Jacob Marley); Gillie
Fenwick (Ghost of Christmas Past); Elizabeth
Cole; Neil Culleton; Norman Welsh; Eric
Clavering; Loro Farrell; John Madison; Michael
Dodds; Barbara Gryfe; Billy Van; Don Francks.

Musical version, based on an earlier Canadian
stage production, telecast (on tape) by The Canadian Broadcasting Corporation on December 21,
1964.

Mr. Scrooge appears to be the earliest in a relatively small group of *Carol* adaptations that have
been produced over the years in Canada. Its most
interesting aspect undoubtedly lies in the casting
of Cyril Ritchard, who is best known to American audiences for his legendary Broadway and
television performances as Captain Hook in *Peter
Pan*, and to film buffs for a relatively rare film
appearance in Alfred Hitchcock's *Blackmail*
(1929). Ritchard was born in Australia, but it
would be fair to say that he usually projected the
kind of charm and urbane sophistication that one
generally associates with an upper-class English
gentleman. Hence his performance contains qualities that one does not usually associate with the
character of Ebenezer Scrooge. This is not to
suggest that his Scrooge is in any way flawed or
deficient — on the contrary it is most interesting
and quite unique — but simply to note that his
performance is delivered in a different key. (Please
also note that similar reservations apply to Ralph
Richardson's 1951 turn as Scrooge, as well as to
Michael Hordern's 1977 performance; see entries
above and below respectively.)

Mr. Scrooge is well cast and acted in all supporting roles, with the wonderful Tessie O'Shea
turning in a particularly fine and energetic performance as Mrs. Cratchit. And it is also noteworthy for presenting three of the most unique
ghostly visitors on record. The Ghost of Christmas Past, for example, arrives on an old-fashioned penny-farthing bicycle via which he whisks
Scrooge off to the past; the Ghost of Christmas
Present is a rather daffy (and drunken!) English
soldier; and the Ghost of Christmas Future is a
decapitated phantom who carries his talking head
under his arm.

However, it must also be noted that the story
comes across as rather sparse and heavily truncated. It is, in fact, a shortened version of the
original stage production. Scrooge's nephew and

the charity solicitors do not appear, and in the Christmas Past, Present and Future sequences, Scrooge visits just one location with each respective spirit — a technique that is clearly designed to set the stage for an extended musical number but which eliminates much necessary motivation and detail. One is conscious of a script that does not quite come together, a situation that is compounded by songs that are pleasant but unmemorable. This description, in fact, might be applied to this production overall. It is a good, but not great, musical *Carol*.

CAROL FOR ANOTHER CHRISTMAS

ABC-TV 1964 USA 84m b/w

A Telsun Foundation, Inc. Production. Producer: Joseph L. Mankiewicz. Director: Joseph L. Mankiewicz. Written by: Rod Serling. Music: Henry Mancini. Song: "Don't Sit Under the Apple Tree" recreated by The Andrews Sisters. Director of Photography: Arthur J. Ornitz. Production Design: Gene Callahan. Costumes: Anna Hill Johnstone. Supervising Film Editor: Robert Lawrence. Production Manager: Jim Digangi. Assistant Director: Dan Eriksen. Assistant to the Producer: Eleanor Wolquitt. Script Supervisor: Marguerite James. Make Up: Irving Buchman. Sound: James Shields. Re-recording: Richard Vorisek. Film Editor: Nathan Greene. Music Editor: Richard Carruth. Sound Effects Editor: Jerry Greenberg. Choral Supervision: Thomas Pyle; Alice Parker. Assistant Art Director: Lee Aronsohn. Property Master: Thomas Wright. Set Decorator: Jack Wright, Jr. Titles: Film Dimensions, Inc. Filmed at the Michael Myerberg Studios, New York. For the Telsun Foundation: Associate Producer: C. O. Erickson. Executive Producer: Edgar Rosenberg.

CAST: Sterling Hayden (Daniel Grudge); Percy Rodriguez (Charles); Ben Gazzara (Fred); Barbara Ann Teer (Ruby); Steve Lawrence (Ghost of Christmas Past); Eva Marie Saint (Wave [Lt. Gibson]); James Shigeta (Doctor); Pat Hingle (Ghost of Christmas Present); Robert Shaw (Ghost of Christmas Future); Peter Sellers (Imperial Me); Britt Eklund (Woman).

Carol variation airing December 22, 1964.

Carol for Another Christmas is a difficult *Carol* to come to terms with — and to judge fairly. Because of its tantalizing scenario and heavyweight credits, as well as its general unavailability for over thirty years, it has achieved a kind of legendary status among *Carol* aficionados, the general assumption being that it is a lost masterpiece. The reality is a bit different and, as such, it does not quite qualify as a major *Carol*.

The story is a very explicit propaganda piece which was concerned with promoting the cause of world peace in general and the United Nations in particular. It concerns one Daniel Grudge, a man of considerable wealth and power, whose mourning over his son Marley's death in a foreign war has led him to adopt a strongly isolationist point of view. Anti-isolationism is in fact the specific issue on which the story pivots; just as Dickens explicitly called for "charity, mercy, forbearance, and benevolence," this *Carol* explicitly and repeatedly calls for engagement and talking with one's fellow man as a means of avoiding war. As the Ghost of Christmas Past (a streetwise soldier who died in World War One, very well played by singer Steve Lawrence) tells Grudge: "Isolation? I got news. It went out with gas light and fifty-cent steaks. It's for the dinosaurs." In the Christmas Future sequence, Grudge is shown a world devastated by nuclear war, a war which happened because people stopped talking and started fighting. This nightmarish future is populated by anarchic and savage bands of survivors; the group that Grudge encounters is headed by a crazed character known as the Imperial Me (Peter Sellers) who continues to call for isolation and a new form of supreme selfishness. Among this group Grudge sees his butler Charles, who speaks of reason and compassion to the mob. Charles is subsequently charged with "the treason of involvement" and shot by a little boy who pulls a gun from a box labeled "Just Like Daddy's." (As this last incident might suggest, subtlety is not one of this *Carol's* strengths.)

Since the desire for world peace and positive engagement is a subject that people of all political stripes can presumably agree upon, there is indeed an important universal message present in this *Carol* that is not at all inconsistent with what Dickens had in mind. A more specifically political subtext is present, however, which does not work in the film's favor. While we are told very little of the specifics of Grudge's life, he is clearly painted as an evil Right-Winger. (While the character of Grudge does not indulge in any form of overtly irrational histrionics, it seems plausible to suppose that Sterling Hayden's presence in the role is intended to at least subliminally recall his brilliant characterization of General Jack D. Ripper in *Dr. Strangelove* which had come out earlier in 1964.) And listening to the exchange between Grudge and his nephew Fred on Christmas Eve, it is indeed clear that Grudge is wrong about certain things. It is, however, equally clear that Fred has come, not to spread a little holiday cheer, but to make a sanctimonious speech. And there will be more heavily didactic speeches before this *Carol* is through. The early 1960s were heady days for those who wanted to be provocative and profound on television, but this production is thrown off balance by a chic and self-satisfied Hollywood Left sensibility that frequently threatens to drown out what should be a non-partisan message, and which reaches its denouement on Christmas morning when the reformed Grudge decides to have breakfast in the kitchen with his black servants.

It is far more successful when focusing its message on Grudge as an individual human being, rather than branching off into larger politically charged issues. The Christmas Present sequence is in fact quite powerful as the spirit (Pat Hingle as a rather uncouth spirit who reflects both the good and bad in man) shows Grudge a vision of a displaced persons camp filled with hungry people huddling in the cold while he sits feasting at a table filled with food. When Grudge chides the spirit for eating in front of these people, the spirit replies: "Shall I tell you how many times you've stuffed yourself while two-thirds of the world starved in a cage?" "Yeah," he tells Grudge while offering him a drumstick, "throw 'em a bone." (A powerful point is made here, and while it is true that, in 1964, a significant portion of the world's population was indeed in a cage, one cannot help noticing that the spirit fails to mention who the jailer was...) And a bit later, after hearing a sobering litany of statistics on the reality of world hunger, Grudge turns away, saying, "No more now," to which the spirit replies in words that could have been written by Dickens himself: "No more now? No more this moment? When, Mr. Grudge? Tomorrow? Thursday? A week from today will you think about them? A month from today will you involve yourself?" As noted elsewhere, Dickens's vision had little to do with mere politics, but much to do with such questions of morality and responsibility. (In this context, it is interesting to note that this version does not include a Bob Cratchit surrogate with whom Grudge can interact, and whom he can ultimately rescue, in a direct and personal way.)

In the final analysis, *Carol for Another Christmas* is very much a product of its times. On a purely aesthetic or artistic level, it is a very impressive production. Although it came along a few years after the formal end of television's much heralded "Golden Age," it exhibits all of the qualities associated with television drama from that period: The look is stark black-and-white, the feel is undeniably theatrical and yet intensely realistic, the acting uniformly excellent, and the writing, as one would expect from Rod Serling, is sharp, literate and intelligent. And from a thematic standpoint, it very much reflects its postwar, cold war times. In this context, it scores points for sounding a very Dickensian call for individual responsibility and involvement, as well

as what might be termed collective sanity, but is far less successful in its attempts to relate its message to the then current geo-political scene; clever speeches and well-intentioned platitudes do not an automatic classic make. It is a noble, but ultimately flawed, *Carol* variation.

A CHRISTMAS CAROL
WNDT-TV   1964   USA   45m   b/w

Music: Angelo Badalamenti. Lyrics/Narration: John Clifford.

CAST: Roger Glickman (Narrator); John Monestero (Scrooge); Theresa Ursino (Fan); Connie DiGiovanni (Scrooge's sweetheart); Leonard Johnson (Tiny Tim); Phillip Petrone (Nephew); Phillip Strumolo (Third Spirit).

Local broadcast on December 24, 1964, on New York public television, of a musical *Carol* staged by students from the High School of Performing Arts and Junior High School 201 from Brooklyn. Composer Angelo Badalamenti, who had formerly taught at Junior High School 201, would later create the memorable score for David Lynch's *Twin Peaks*.

"[The fact that this is a non-professional production] is precisely the charm of the 45 minutes. It is what we see so seldom on TV—truly amateur work. It's refreshing, even the fluffs and stumbles....

"Roger Glickman narrates ... with skill and an accurate ear for accents. Teresa Ursino, as Scrooge's sister Fan, sings touchingly of a shepherd who tended his flock the first Christmas Day. The voice of Connie DiGiovanni, who appears as Scrooge's sweetheart, adds beauty to a nice song, 'My World Without You.' And Leonard Johnson, as Tiny Tim, stops the show with a rousingly cheerful 'Some Day.'"—*New York Herald Tribune*, December 24, 1964, p. 13

JACKIE GLEASON AND HIS AMERICAN SCENE MAGAZINE
CBS-TV   1964   USA   60m   b/w

Comedy/Variety series. Broadcast on December 26, 1964.

"The ingredients of this session had, as [one of] its major items, Frank Fontaine's version of Dickens' 'Christmas Carol.' He also did a Christmas medley."—*Variety*, December 30, 1964, p. 26

NOTE: Fontaine's version of the *Carol* was presumably told by his character of Crazy Guggenheim, who appeared in regular sketches with Jackie Gleason's character of Joe the Bartender.

MY FAVORITE MARTIAN
CBS-TV   1965   USA   30m   b/w

A Production of Jack Chertok Television, Inc. Created by: John L. Greene. Producer: Jack

Chertok. Director: Oscar Rudolph. Writer: Al Martin; Bill Kelsay. Music Composed and Conducted by: George Greeley. Production Executive: Harry H. Poppe. Script Consultant: Marty Roth. Director of Photography: Frank Carson. Art Director: James Hulsey. Film Editor: Thomas Neff. Assistant Director: Nate Levinson. Set Decorations: Ross Dowd. Sound Engineer: James S. Thomson. Makeup: Kiva Hoffman. Hair Stylist: Jean Udko. Sound: Glen Glenn Sound Co. Photographic Effects: Howard Anderson Co. Special Effects: Herman Townsley. Costumer: Marjorie Henderson. Casting: Lynn Stalmaster. Automobile Furnished by: Chrysler Corporation. Wardrobe for Ray Walston & Bill Bixby: Andrew Pallack. Fashions for Barbara Britton: Peggy Hunt, "California Designs."

CAST: Ray Walston (The Martian/"Uncle Martin"); Bill Bixby (Tim O'Hara); Pamela Britton (Mrs. Lorelei Brown); Harry Lauter (Detective Smithers); Len Lesser (Hank); Paul Sorensen (1st Policeman); Ray Kellogg (2nd Policeman); Gloria S. Marshall (Police Dispatcher).

Situation comedy. Episode title: "Humbug, Mrs. Brown." First broadcast on February 21, 1965.

This episode of the popular series about a Martian living incognito in southern California is not a *Carol* variation, nor does it have anything to do with Christmas; in fact, its only connection with Dickens's tale is that it is yet one more example of how a story can be constructed, and an instant connection made with an audience, simply by invoking the name "Scrooge," or the word "humbug." The story here concerns Martin and Tim's realization that their landlord, Mrs. Brown, is incapable of handling her financial affairs because of her overly generous and rather gullible nature. By using his special Martian powers, Martin convinces her to change her ways; unfortunately, she overcompensates and becomes what Martin calls "an absolute and unmitigated Scrooge." Needless to say, Mrs. Brown is back to normal at the end of this particularly idiotic episode but, as Dickens himself might put it, chalk up one more for the "vagabonds."

THE ROGUES

NBC-TV 1965 USA 60m b/w

Executive Producer: Thomas J. McDermott. Producer: Collier Young. Director: Don Taylor. Writer: Warren Duff. Created by Ivan Goff and Ben Roberts, in association with Four Star. Associate Producer: Bruce Fowler, Jr. Production Supervisor: Norman S. Powell. Editorial Supervisor: Bernard Burton. Supervising Art Director: Bill Ross. Director of Photography: Robert Tobey. Theme Music Composed by: Nelson Riddle. Music: Joseph Mullendore. Music Supervision: Alfred Perry. Art Director: Gibson A. Hollby. Production Manager: Don Torpin. Assistant Director: Pat Casey. Story Editor: Bud Kay. Editor: Richard Heermance. Set Decorator: Pierre Ludlam. Sound Effects: Kay Rose. Music Editor: Aubrey Lind. Casting: Robert Walker. Makeup: Carlie Taylor. Sound: Don Rush. Wardrobe: Robert B. Harris.

CAST: Charles Boyer (Marcel St. Clair); Robert Coote (Timmy); Gladys Cooper (Aunt Margaret). GUESTS: John McGiver (Horatio T. White); Jill Haworth (Timothea); Larry Hagman (Mark Fleming); Hedley Mattingly (Hutchins); Michael St. Clair (Inspector); John Trayne (Man); Doris Lloyd (Mrs. Hackett); Trevor Cuming (Sergeant); William Beckley (Young Man).

Drama/Comedy series. Episode title: "Mr. White's Christmas." First broadcast on April 4, 1965.

The Rogues was a short-lived series that revolved around the adventures of a family of fun-loving, good-deed-doing con artists who were particularly fond of swindling those who genuinely deserved to be swindled. It was neither the first, nor the last, television series to cover this ground, but a strong case can be made that it was the best. Charles Boyer, David Niven and Gig Young appeared in rotating feature roles, with regular support from Robert Coote and Gladys Cooper.

This episode concerns a very Scrooge-like London tycoon named Horatio T. White, played with great relish by the wonderful John McGiver, who is eventually brought to his senses via the utilization of various ideas borrowed from the *Carol*. This production is actually quite original in that it does not opt for the tired and lazy approach of having its Scrooge surrogate fall asleep and dream of ghostly visitors, etc. Instead, Boyer and company, aided by a young Larry Hagman who plays a visiting relative, con him into thinking that he is being haunted by his deceased partner (whose name was Farley). It also goes a step further in terms of originality in that its Scrooge does not miraculously wake up a new man on Christmas morning; instead, he has simply been "softened up" by the invocation of the familiar *Carol* machinery, and it is a stranger's act of kindness on Christmas Day that actually brings about his conversion. All things considered, *Carol* enthusiasts will find this one a pleasantly surprising oasis in that vast desert of televised atrocities that have been perpetrated upon Dickens's "Ghostly little book."

A CHRISTMAS CAROL [READ BY DR. FRANK BAXTER]

KCET-TV 1965 USA 60m b/w
Director: Tom Mossman. Art Director: David Rose. Graphics: Sherman Labby. Lighting Director: Malcolm Waring. Technical Director: Gordon Baird. Video: Harold Baert. Audio: Dan Bergman. Sponsor: Western Federal Savings and Loan Association.

CAST: Dr. Frank Baxter, Professor Emeritus English, Reader in Residence, University of Southern California.

Taped *Carol* reading, produced by Los Angeles public television station KCET. First broadcast on December 21, 1965.

Frank C. Baxter was a professor of English who did much to popularize the study of both Shakespeare and science on television. He began in the early fifties and received several Emmys and a Peabody Award for his efforts. His *Shakespeare on TV* series and the *Bell Science Series* are especially well remembered; the latter, in which he explains a variety of scientific subjects for children, is still used in many classrooms and is available on home video.

In this program he is seen standing at a podium while reading his own condensed version of the *Carol*, and while his reading cannot be compared to that of a professional actor in terms of overall impact, it is, nevertheless, an interesting and amiable interpretation. Dr. Baxter seems to be improvising at times, and he occasionally addresses an explanatory aside to the audience, all of which contributes to a warm and congenial hour of seasonal television. Note: Dr. Baxter also did a program of "Christmas Readings" in the mid-fifties (see, for example, *The Los Angeles Times* December 24, 1953, Part 1, p. 18). It seems reasonable to assume that at least part of the program dealt with the *Carol*.

LEYENDA DE NAVIDAD*

Televisión Española 1966 Spain 103m b/w
Director: Alberto Gonzáles Vergel. Writer: Manuel Tamayo.

CAST: Luis Prendes (Scrooge); Nuria Carresí (Mary); Joaquin Pamplona (Marley); José Luis Coll (Ghost of Christmas Past); José Martín (Miguel); Manuel Soriano (grandfather); Mario Moreno (Tackleton); Isabel María Peréz (girl); Agustín Bescós (caretaker); José María Escuder (gentleman #1); Ascunción Villamil (Elizabeth); Carlos Galván (gentleman #2); José Segura (Bob Cratchit); Maria Luisa Moneró (Señora Hilte); Antonio Acebal (bank employee); Antonio Roca (Jack); Mary Gonzáles (Mrs. Cratchit); Alberto Calvo (Tiny Tim).

Carol adaptation that was broadcast in five parts on the *Novela* program from December 19 through December 23, 1966.

*See references in chapters 6 and 7.

SCROOGE McDUCK AND MONEY

Walt Disney 1967 USA 17m color
Director: Hamilton Luske. Art Director: McLaren Stewart. Layout: Joe Hale. Background: Elmer Plummer. Animation: Ward Kimball; Julius Svendsen; Art Stevens; Charlie Downs; Jack Boyd. Story: Bill Berg. Music and Lyrics: Mel Leven. Scored and Conducted by: Franklyn Marks. Special Effects: Eustace Lycett.

VOICES: Bill Thompson; The Mellomen.

A theatrically released educational short in which Scrooge McDuck teaches his nephews about the history and value of money. On the Disney family tree, Scrooge McDuck is Donald Duck's miserly uncle. The character was created by Disney veteran Carl Barks and first appeared in the 1947 comic book story entitled *Christmas on Bear Mountain*; he then went on to star in his own successful comic book series.

Scrooge McDuck and Money has nothing to do with the *Carol*, but is noteworthy in that it marks the first appearance on film or television of the Scrooge McDuck character. Most importantly, however, we see yet another example of how the name Scrooge itself—in this case working in tandem with the familiar stereotype of the penny-pinching Scotsman—can be called upon to create a universally recognizable image of someone who is, at the very least, obsessed with money. Scrooge McDuck would later star in the *Ducktales* television series, as well as the film *Ducktales: The Movie, Treasure of the Lost Lamp*, but for present purposes is best remembered as the star of *Mickey's Christmas Carol*.

BEWITCHED

ABC-TV 1967 USA 30m color
Executive Producer: Harry Ackerman. Producer: William Asher. Director: William Asher. Written by: Lila Garrett; Bernie Kahn. Created by: Sol Saks. Music: Warren Barker. Associate Producer: Richard Michaels. Director of Photography: Robert Tobey. Art Director: Ross Bellah; Robert Purcell. Film Editor: Aaron Nibley.

CAST: Elizabeth Montgomery (Samantha Stephens); Dick York (Darrin Stephens); David White (Larry Tate); Erin Murphy (Tabitha); Don Beddoe (Santa Claus); Martin Ashe (Hawkins); Rosalyn Burbage (Margaret); Charles Lane (Mr. Mortimer).

Situation comedy. Episode title: "Humbug Not to Be Spoken Here." First broadcast on December 21, 1967.

When a Scrooge-like client (played by the very

Scrooge-like Charles Lane) tries to make her husband work on Christmas Eve, lovable witch Samantha, calling herself the "Spirit of Christmas," takes him on a nocturnal journey that includes a glimpse of his Cratchit-like employee enjoying the holiday — as well as a visit with Santa Claus at the North Pole! Needless to say, he wakes up a new man on Christmas morning. Yet another perfunctory television variation. Montgomery is as charming and attractive as ever, but this one is nothing to get excited about.

THE SMOTHERS BROTHERS COMEDY HOUR

CBS-TV 1967 USA 60m color

Comedic Productions, Inc. in association with Ilson/Chambers Productions. Producer: Saul Ilson; Ernest Chambers. Director: Sam Gary. Writers: Al Gordon; Hal Goldman; Sam Bobrick; Mason Williams; Allan Blye; Ron Clark; Gene Farmer; Ted Bergman; Jerry Music; Saul Ilson; Ernest Chambers. Associate Producer: George A. Sunga. Production Coordinators: Ken Kragen; Ken Fritz. Musical Director: Nelson Riddle. Art Director: Romain Johnston. Costume Designer: Sal Anthony.

CAST: Tom Smothers; Dick Smothers; Pat Paulsen. Guests: Jack Benny; Nanette Fabray.

Variety series. This episode first broadcast on December 24, 1967.

At the center of this hour of Christmas-themed music and comedy is a parodic *Carol* sketch which runs about eighteen minutes in length. In a bit of surprise casting, Tommy Smothers is Ebenezer Scrooge III, and Jack Benny is Bob Cratchit; at one point Benny turns to the audience and says: "I bet you thought I was gonna play Scrooge." The central idea here offers a novel twist on the old story: In this version Bob Cratchit actually wants to work on Christmas Eve and Christmas Day so that he can collect the overtime pay that he says is needed to buy presents for his family. However, the payoff comes on Christmas morning when Scrooge learns that by saving his pennies and investing wisely, Bob actually leads a life of wealth and luxury. Despite Benny's presence, this is basically just another typical television sketch that strains for laughs and goes on too long, although it does contain one genuinely funny moment when Scrooge breaks a window in his office with a rifle and shoots at a group of caroling children. Nanette Fabray appears as Mrs. Cratchit, and Pat Paulsen as the Ghost of Christmas and Bob's butler Jeeves.

CARRY ON CHRISTMAS

Thames TV 1969 Great Britain 55m

Producer: Peter Eton. Director: Ronnie Baxter. Writer: Talbot Rothwell.

CAST: Sid James (Scrooge); Charles Hawtrey (Spirit of Christmas Past).

One of several British television entries entitled *Carry On Christmas*, all starring the legendarily ribald and raucous *Carry On* gang. This one, which was first broadcast on Christmas Eve in 1969, finds Scrooge joined by Elizabeth Barrett, Robert Browning, Frankenstein, Dracula and Cinderella!

THE GHOST & MRS. MUIR

ABC-TV 1969 USA 30m color

Executive Producer: David Gerber. Producer: Howard Leeds. Director: Jay Sandrich. Writer: Jean Holloway. Developed for television by: Jean Holloway. Based on a novel by: R. A. Dick. Associate Producer: Robert Mintz. Script Consultants: Arthur Alsberg; Don Nelson. Production Supervisor: Jack Sonntag. Unit Production Manager: Wes McAfee. Assistant Director: Eli Dunn. Director of Photography: Richard A. Kelley. Art Director: Jack Martin Smith; Leroy Deane. Music: George Greeley. Music Supervision: Lionel Newman. Film Editor: Bill Lewis. Post Production Supervisor: Samuel E. Beetley. Set Decorators: Walter M. Scott; Bert F. Allen. Wardrobe for Hope Lange: Evan-Picone. Theme: Dave Grusin.

CAST: Hope Lange (Carolyn Muir); Edward Mulhare (Captain Daniel Gregg); Reta Shaw (Martha Grant); Charles Nelson Reilly (Claymore Gregg); Harlen Carraher (Jonathan Muir); Kellie Flanagan (Candice Muir); Scruffy.

Situation comedy. Episode title: "The Ghost of Christmas Past." First broadcast on December 25, 1969.

This short-lived series was inspired by the classic 1947 film starring Gene Tierney and Rex Harrison. This particular episode is not a *Carol* variation, but it does contain what might charitably be called a brief *Carol homage*: On a particular Christmas Eve, Captain Gregg causes all the regulars to share a dream in which their characters are transposed to the nineteenth century. Among the story lines contained in the dream is a "bit" in which Claymore is depicted as a miserly Scrooge-like character; several lines of dialogue are in fact taken directly from the *Carol*. However, instead of the familiar succession of ghostly visitors, "Claymore Scrooge" is haunted by the voice of "the ghost of the conscience [he] used to have." The payoff comes on Christmas morning when the modern day Claymore, who had indeed been behaving like "an old Scrooge" the day before, wakes up a changed man. Once again, even by sitcom standards, this is not a full-fledged

Carol variation; it would be far more accurate to say that among its various plotlines, one will find a few minutes of always reliable *Carol shtick*. This show shares a certain affinity with the 1967 *Bewitched* episode cited above in that neither the presence of Dickens, nor the presence of one of the most charming and attractive heroines in television history, can prevent the proceedings from becoming mired in the usual sitcom idiocy.

A CHRISTMAS CAROL
Air Programs International 1969 Australia 46m color

Producer: Walter J. Hucker. Director: Zoran Janjic. Adaptation: Michael Robinson. Music: Richard Bowden. Editing: Richard Bowden. Animation: John Burge; Chris Cuddington; Peter Luschwitz; Don MacKinnon; Jean Tych. Layouts: Leif Gram. Backgrounds: Ann Williams. Camera: Graham Sharpe; Jenny Ochse. Studio Supervisor: Zora Bubica; Negative Cutting: M. Cardin. Sound Mixing: Harry Medak.

VOICES: Ron Haddrick; C. Duncan; John Llewellyn; T. Mangan; Bruce Montague; Brenda Senders. SINGERS: T. Kaff; C. Bowden.

Animated "featurette" first telecast on American television by CBS-TV on December 13, 1970, on the Famous Classic Tales program.

This *Carol*, which was a perennial television favorite throughout the seventies and early eighties, set the standard for most of the animated versions that have followed: tedious, lifeless affairs that are not helped at all by modern limited animation techniques. This one is particularly lifeless; however, it utilizes a rather dark color scheme which, in tandem with its quasi-abstract backgrounds, does achieve a certain eeriness in terms of overall tone and visual style.

SCROOGE*
Waterbury Films Limited/Cinema Center Films (20th Century Fox) 1970 Great Britain 118m color Panavision

Producer: Robert H. Solo. Director: Ronald Neame. Executive Producer, Screenplay, Music and Lyrics: Leslie Bricusse. Screen Titles: Ronald Searle. Associate Producer: David W. Orton. Musical Director: Ian Fraser. Production Manager: Ed Harper. Director of Photography: Oswald Morris. Production Designer: Terry Marsh. Editor: Peter Weatherley. Costume Designer: Margaret Furse. Assistant Director: Ted Sturgis. Choreographer: Paddy Stone. Camera Operator: Jim Turrell. Sound Mixer: Jock May. Continuity: Elaine Schreyeck. Makeup: George Frost. Hairdresser: Bobbie Smith. Wardrobe Supervisor: Ivy Baker. Special Effects: Wally Veevers. Unit Publicist: Geoff Freeman. Stills Photographer: Norman Gryspeerdt.

CAST: Albert Finney (Ebenezer Scrooge); Alec Guinness (Jacob Marley); Edith Evans (Ghost of Christmas Past); Kenneth More (Ghost of Christmas Present); Michael Medwin (Nephew); Laurence Naismith (Mr. Fezziwig); David Collings (Bob Cratchit); Anton Rodgers (Tom Jenkins); Suzanne Neve (Isabel); Kay Walsh (Mrs. Fezziwig); Richard Beaumont (Tiny Tim); Frances Cuka (Mrs. Cratchit); Karen Scargill (Kathy); Derek Francis (1st Gentleman of Charity); Roy Kinnear (Second Gentleman of Charity); Mary Peach (Nephew's Wife); Paddy Stone (Ghost of Christmas Yet To Come); Gordon Jackson (Nephew's Friend); Geoffrey Bayldon (Toyshop Owner); Molly Weir (1st Woman Debtor); Helena Gloag (2nd Woman Debtor); Reg Lever (Punch and Judy Man); Keith March (Well-wisher); Marianne Stone (Party Guest).

SONGS: "A Christmas Carol"; "Christmas Children"; "I Hate People"; "Father Christmas"; "See the Phantoms"; "December the Twenty-Fifth"; "Happiness"; "The Beautiful Day"; "You...You"; "I Like Life"; "Thank You Very Much"; "I'll Begin Again"; "Father Christmas" (Reprise).

Theatrically released musical version.

*See discussion in Chapter 6.

THE ODD COUPLE
ABC-TV 1970 USA 30m color

Paramount Television. Executive Producer: Garry Marshall; Jerry Belson. Producer: Jerry Davis. Director: George Tyne. Writer: Ronald I. Friedman. Developed for television by: Garry Marshall; Jerry Belson. Executive Vice-President in charge of production: Douglas S. Cramer. Script Consultants: Alan Mandel; Charles Shyer. Associate Producer: Charles Shyer; Tony Marshall. Music: Neil Hefti. Music Supervisor: Kenyon Hopkins. Director of Photography: Lester Shorr. Art Director: John M. Elliott. Film Editor: Bob Moore.

CAST: Jack Klugman (Oscar Madison); Tony Randall (Felix Unger); Larry Gelman (Vinnie); Ryan MacDonald (Roy); Al Molinaro (Murray); Garry Walberg (Speed); Ogden Talbot (Messenger Boy).

Situation comedy. Episode title: "Scrooge Gets an Oscar." First broadcast on December 17, 1970.

Felix is directing an amateur production of *A Christmas Carol* for charity and naturally wants Oscar to play Scrooge; unfortunately, Oscar is even grouchier than usual this particular Christmas and refuses. After a meal of spicy food (and with the *Carol* playing on his television) Oscar falls asleep and, guess what, dreams that he is Scrooge. Needless to say, he wakes up a new man in the morning. Despite the generally high quality of this series, this is a very lame and uninspired *Carol* variation.

A CHRISTMAS CAROL

Anglia Television   1970   Great Britain
58m   color

Produced, Adapted and Narrated by: Paul Honeyman. Director: John Salway. Illustrator: John Worsley. Theme Music: Peter Fenn, sung by the Norwich Cathedral Choir.

Animated *Carol* adaptation. First broadcast on Anglia Television in England on December 25, 1970.

An interesting variation in style comprised of watercolor paintings by John Worsley. There is no motion per se; instead, still images are linked together by cuts, dissolves, zooms and pans. Intelligently adapted by Paul Honeyman, who also narrates. One particularly unique touch: We see the reformed Scrooge beaming and shaking hands with the vicar after church services on Christmas morning.

A CHRISTMAS CAROL*

Richard Williams Productions, Ltd.   1971
Great Britain   26m   color

Executive Producer: Chuck Jones. Producer and Director: Richard Williams. Music and Special Sounds: Tristram Cary. Master Animator: Ken Harris. Animators: Bill Hajee; Sergio Simonetti; Roy Naisbitt; Janet Chapman; Anwar Rassam. Design Supervision: Richard Purdom. Associate Artists: Hal Ambro; George Nicholas. Guest Artist: Abe Levitow. Production Supervisor: Roy Naisbitt. Production Consultant: Omar Ali-Shah. Camera: Roy W. Watford.

VOICES: Sir Michael Redgrave (Narrator); Alastair Sim (Ebenezer Scrooge); Michael Hordern (Jacob Marley); Melvin Hayes (Bob Cratchit); Jean Sims (Mrs Cratchit); Paul Whitsun-Jones (Ragpicker, Mr Fezziwig); David Tate (Scrooge's Nephew, Charity Man); Diana Quick (Ghost of Christmas Past); Felix Felton (Ghost of Christmas Present); Annie West (Ghost of Christmas Future); Mary Ellen Ray (Mrs Dilber); Alexander Williams (Tiny Tim).

Animated short made for American television. Premiered December 21, 1971, on ABC-TV.

*See discussion in Chapter 7.

MARCEL MARCEAU PRESENTS A CHRISTMAS CAROL

BBC-TV 1973 Great Britain 40m color

Executive Producer: Mike Wooller. Producer: Tristram Powell. Film Editor: Jesse Palmer. Film Cameraman: John Hooper. Music: John Dalby.

CAST: Marcel Marceau. Narrator: Michael Hordern.

Mime version of the *Carol* produced (on film) for the *Omnibus* program. First broadcast was scheduled for December 23, 1973; however, transmission was delayed until December 27, 1973. On page 28 of the issue cited below, *Radio Times* indicates that this version's "setting is a deserted Victorian music hall in the East End of London where Marceau himself brings all the characters to life."

"Of *A Christmas Carol*, he [Marcel Marceau] says firmly, 'I know what I want to do. Scrooge looks nice, not too nasty, for he was once a good-looking young man, whose life went wrong. He's a man with a past, and there's a part of him in all of us, when we get bitter and selfish.'"—From an interview with Marcel Marceau by Jenny Rees in *Radio Times*, December 20/27, 1973, p. 9. Marceau also indicates that Dickens was a major influence on his life and art, and that his famous white-faced character of Bip was named after Pip in *Great Expectations*.

THE CHARLES DICKENS SHOW

Seabourne Enterprises/Educational Foundation for Visual Aids 1974 Great Britain 27m
color

Producer: John Seabourne. Director: Piers Jessop. Photography: Mike Davis. Editor: Ken Holt. Sound: Pat Jeffery.

CAST: Victor Spinetti; Roy McArthur; Paula Jacobs.

Educational film which presents Dickens's life via the kind of nineteenth century magic lantern show discussed in Chapter 4. Includes dramatized excerpts from the *Carol*, as well as *Oliver Twist*, *Martin Chuzzlewit*, and *David Copperfield*. From *Great Authors* series, this appears to be a companion piece to *Charles Dickens* below.

CHARLES DICKENS

Seabourne Enterprises/Educational Foundation for Visual Aids 1974 Great Britain 26m
color

Director: Hermann Schlenker.

CAST: Victor Spinetti; Roy McArthur; Paula Jacobs.

Educational film which includes dramatized excerpts from the *Carol*, as well as *Oliver Twist*, *Martin Chuzzlewit*, and *David Copperfield*. This appears to be a companion piece to *The Charles Dickens Show* above.

LITTLE HOUSE ON THE PRAIRIE

NBC-TV 1975 USA 60m color

An NBC Production in association with Ed Friendly. Executive Producer: Michael Landon.

Producer: John Hawkins. Director: Victor French. Writer: Hindi Brooks. Based on the "Little House" books by Laura Ingalls Wilder. Developed for television by: Blanche Hanalis. Music: David Rose. Co-producer: B. W. Sandefur. Associate Producer: Kent McCray. Director of Photography: Ted Voightlander.

CAST: Michael Landon (Charles Ingalls); Karen Grassle (Caroline Ingalls); Melissa Gilbert (Laura); Melissa Sue Anderson (Mary); Lindsay and Sidney Greenbush (Carrie); Richard Bull (Mr. Oleson); Katherine MacGregor (Mrs. Oleson); Charlotte Stewart (Miss Beadle); Karl Swenson (Mr. Hanson); Ted Gehring (Ebenezer Sprague); Janice Carroll (Mrs. Kennedy); Alison Arngrim (Nellie Oleson); Ed Crick (Mr. Taylor); Ruth Foster (Mrs. Foster); Jonathan Gilbert (Willie Oleson); James Kilmond (Johnny); Lloyd "Sunshine" Parker (Freight Man); Tracie Savage (Christy Kennedy); Donna Anderson (Woman).

Dramatic series. Episode title: "Ebenezer Sprague."

Banker Ebenezer Sprague sets up a new bank in the town of Walnut Grove, Minnesota, and quickly develops a reputation as the meanest, nastiest, stingiest man in town. In the end, however, he is "converted" by the friendship of young Laura Ingalls. This is not a *Carol* variation; it is not set at Christmas time, and there are no ghostly visitors. However, it is a classic example of how just a little *Carol* iconography, in this case a mean individual who is connected by profession with money, can be used as the foundation and framework for a story; the implicit assumption that audiences will make the connection with Scrooge is all that is necessary for a story like this to work. (Of course this one takes no chances and gives the character in question a name that is virtually identical to that of Ebenezer Scrooge.)

THE PASSIONS OF CAROL

Ambar 1975 USA 76m color

Director: Amanda Barton. Screenplay: Amanda Barton. Camera: David Measles. Editor: Amanda Barton. Sound: Ravla Graguts. Lighting: Jackson Rider; Pietro Nevardi. Costumes: Helene. Assistant Director: Brenda Morganstern. Production Design: Graig Esposito.

CAST: Mary Stuart (Carol Screwge); Marc Stevens (Marley); Jamie Gillis (Mr. Hatchet); Kim Pope (Mrs. Hatchet); Arturo Millhouse, Kevin Andre, Helmuth Richler (Spirits); Rose Cranston; Daniela Di Orici; Angela Dermer; Sonny Landham; Alan Barow; Stuart Dickerson; Alan Grodin.

Theatrically released hardcore pornographic variation. *Variety* gets the last word on this one:

"Except for generally inventive execution of the Dickensonian [sic] plot recreation, 'The Passions of Carol' is just another N.Y.–originated hardcore entry, with overly familiar faces in the Gotham porno stable performing assigned chores …with a modicum of athletics and a disquieting lack of passion."—*Variety*, March 19, 1975, p. 36

THE ENERGY CAROL

National Film Board of Canada 1975 Canada 11m color

Story & Direction: Les Drew. Backgrounds: Timothy Elliott.

Animation: Pino Vanlamsweerde; John W. Weldon; Robert Browning; Robert Douchet; Blake James.

VOICES: Grant Munro; George Geertsen; Gerald Budner; Don Arioli; Les Drew.

Animated educational short produced by the National Film Board of Canada and the Office of Energy Conservation department of Energy Mines and Resources.

Ebenezer Stooge, president of Zeus Energy, Inc., learns to conserve energy when his wasteful past comes back to haunt him on Christmas Eve. An amusing little *Carol* with many clever touches; Jacob Moorlite, for example, visits Stooge in the form of a pig chained to a giant toaster! All in all the kind of film that one expects from the National Film Board of Canada: intelligent, sophisticated, and more than a little bit unusual.

SANFORD AND SON

NBC-TV 1975 USA 30m color

A Bud Yorkin Norman Lear Tandem Production. Executive Producer: Bud Yorkin. Director: James Sheldon. Produced and Written by: Saul Turtletaub; Bernie Orenstein. Story Supervisor: Ted Bergman. Based on the British television series "Steptoe and Son." Associate Producer: Normand C. Hopps. Music: Quincy Jones. Art Director: Edward Stephenson. Technical Director: O. Tamburri.

CAST: Redd Foxx (Fred Sanford); Demond Wilson (Lamont Sanford); LaWanda Page (Aunt Esther); Nathaniel Taylor (Rollo); Don Bexly (Bubba); Eric Laneuville (Ron); Adrian Ricard (Mrs. Small); Marc Copage (Fredsie); Jay Merreman (Mr. Small); Kathryn Jackson (Mother); Herb Ellis (Landlord); Lynn Hamilton (Donna).

Situation comedy. Episode title: "Ebenezer Sanford."

First broadcast on December 12, 1975.

The Scrooge surrogate here is cantankerous junk dealer Fred Sanford, who learns the true meaning of Christmas when the familiar succession of spirits appears to him in a dream. Son

Lamont, in different guises, appears as all four spirits. In terms of its storyline, this one is pretty standard stuff; however, Foxx's broad and frequently outrageous humor provides a dose of energy and genuine laughter that is sadly missing in most sitcom variations.

THE FIRST PICTURE SHOW

BBC2-TV   1976   Great Britain   color
Produced by: Mike Dibb. Introduced and hosted by Gavin Millar. "Scrooge" sequence Directed and Written by: Norman Stone.
CAST [of "Scrooge" sequence]: Ron Moody (Ebenezer Scrooge); Graham Stark (Bob Cratchit).
Variety program first broadcast on February 28, 1976.
This episode of *The First Picture Show* contained a *Carol* variation entitled *Scrooge* in which the story is updated to modern times and the title character changed into a heartless television executive. *Scrooge* runs about ten minutes in length and appears to have been a pilot for a longer, but unrealized, project.
NOTE: For more on this *Carol*, see Michael Pointer's *Charles Dickens on the Screen* (Lanham MD: Scarecrow, 1996).

THE ALL STAR RECORD BREAKERS

BBC-TV   1976   Great Britain   50m   color
Producer: Alan Russell. Designer: Ken Starkey. Studio Sound: Adrian Stocks. Studio Lighting: Geoff Shaw. Choreographer: Sally Gilpin. Musical Director: Johnny Pearson. Musical Arrangements: Larry Ashmore; Johnny Coleman; Johnny Pearson; Derek Warne.
CAST: Roy Castle (Ebenezer Scrooge); Toni Arthur; Keith Chegwin; John Craven; Bernard Cribbins; Maggie Henderson; Jan Hunt; Lesley Judd; Pat Keysell; Susan King; Johnny Morris; John Noakes; Peter Purves; Julie Stevens; David Wood; Norris McWhirter.
Musical version of the *Carol* entitled *Scrooge*. Broadcast on December 24, 1976. Several selections from the score of the 1970 film *Scrooge* are included.

JACKIE GLEASON PRESENTS THE HONEYMOONERS

ABC-TV   1977   USA   60m   color
Peekskill Enterprises, Inc. Executive Producer: Jack Philbin. Producer: Ed Waglin. Director: Jackie Gleason. Writer: Walter Stone; Robert Hilliard. Music composed and conducted by: Jackie Gleason. Music arranged by: George Williams. Associate Producer: Phil Cuoco. Scenic Designer: James Reilly. Production Supervisor: Dutch Hardie. Associate Director: Gary Bowen. Technical Supervisor: Spears Mallis. Assistant to the Producer: Geraldine Smith. Lighting Director: Bob Raley. Set Director: Len Simons. Audio: A. J. Gulino. Makeup: Ruth Regina. Stage Managers: Len Grahm; Fred Wardell. Production Assistant: Patricia Raymond. Program Staff: Sydell Spear; Betty Schafer; Penny Olson. Video Tape Editor: Terry Greene. Taped at Gusman Hall in Miami.
CAST: Jackie Gleason (Ralph Kramden); Art Carney (Ed Norton); Audrey Meadows (Alice Kramden); Jane Kean (Trixie Norton); Gale Gordon (Mr. Marshall); Johnny Olson (Town Crier); Budd Truland (Pop Parker); Templeton Fox (Mrs. Marshall); Suntones (Quartet).
Carol variation which first aired on ABC-TV on November 28, 1977.
Jackie Gleason revived his classic *Honeymooners* cast of characters for a group of specials in the late 1970s. In this one, in an effort to curry favor with his boss, Mr. Marshall, Ralph volunteers to direct a performance of *A Christmas Carol* for the benefit of Mrs. Marshall's favorite charity (needy cats). The bulk of this program actually focuses on Ralph's efforts to get the production off the ground, with the *Carol* variation, such as it is, appearing as a brief play within a play toward the end of the hour.
In his version of the story, Ralph is Daddy Cratchit and Alice is his wife, Mother Cratchit; Trixie Norton plays their thirteen year old daughter, and husband Ed plays both Scrooge and Tiny Tim. All of the familiar *Carol* machinery is jettisoned, however, as Ralph rewrites Scrooge into a Simon Legree type villain who shows up to evict the Cratchits from their home on Christmas morning. The result really has nothing to do with the *Carol*, but is more a parody of a bad performance of a bad play that recalls W. C. Fields's production of *The Drunkard* in *The Old-Fashioned Way*.
In the final analysis, as every fan of the legendary series knows, the various later incarnations of *The Honeymooners* never matched the overall brilliance of its 1950s heyday, and Gleason and company are clearly working with second-rate material here. Nevertheless, a visit from the Kramdens and the Nortons was still (and always will be) most welcome.

BING CROSBY'S MERRIE OLDE CHRISTMAS

CBS-TV   1977   USA   60m   color
Executive Producer: Frank Konigsberg. Producer: Gary Smith; Dwight Hemion. Director: Dwight Hemion. Writer: Buzz Kohan.
CAST: Bing Crosby; Kathryn Crosby; Mary Frances Crosby; Harry Crosby; Nathaniel

Crosby; David Bowie; Twiggy; Ron Moody; Stanley Baxter; Trinity Boys Choir.

Variety special which first aired on November 30, 1977. One segment of this musical/comedy special relates to Dickens and the *Carol*. *Variety* noted:

"Everyone in the show appeared to be having a good time. Ron Moody was all over the place in his quicksilver impressions of the fictive "Sir Percival Crosby" and as a crusty Charles Dickens. This latter role led into a charming musical segment in which Moody and Twiggy joined in song and dance portrayals of Scrooge & Tiny Tim, Fagin & the Artful Dodger and Quilp and Little Nell, all Dickens creations. It was a stunning sequence set handsomely among the narrow streets of an old English village."—*Variety*, December 7, 1977, pp. 44 & 64

THE FAT ALBERT CHRISTMAS SPECIAL

CBS-TV 1977 USA 30m color

A Filmation Presentation in association with Bill Cosby Productions. Executive Producer: William H. Cosby, Jr. Producer: Lou Scheimer; Norm Prescott. Director: Hal Sutherland. Writer: Bill Danch; Jim Ryan. Music: Yvette Blais; Jeff Michael.

VOICES: Bill Cosby; Jan Crawford; Gerald Edwards; Eric Suter; Erika Carroll; Eric Greene; Kim Hamilton; Julius Harris; Ty Henderson.

Animated special first broadcast on December 18, 1977. Later distributed to television and home video under the title "A Christmas Story [with Fat Albert and the Cosby Kids]."

Bill Cosby's characters of Fat Albert and friends were inspired by his real life boyhood pals, and this Christmas special was one of several televised efforts that led to a regular animated series for children—*Fat Albert and the Cosby Kids*; later called *The New Fat Albert Show*—that combined fun with positive and educational messages. This is not a *Carol* variation, but it does include a central character, named Tightwad Tyrone, who was clearly inspired by one Ebenezer Scrooge. (Tyrone is a prosperous local merchant and businessman—in effect, an animated version of Ben Weaver from *The Andy Griffith Show*; see entry above.)

The main storyline is an effective Christmas allegory which finds Fat Albert and friends helping a homeless family—a family that just happens to include an expectant mother. In a subplot, our "old Scrooge," who has become embittered over the years by the death of his wife, is convinced by a fellow old-timer that he should stop being a "taker" and start being a "giver." Needless to say, he sees the light. Once again, this one is not a *Carol* variation; it is, however, an interesting example of *Carol* iconography at work—this time in the somewhat unlikely arena of children's television.

A CHRISTMAS CAROL

BBC-TV 1977 Great Britain 58m color

Producer: Jonathan Powell. Director: Moira Armstrong. Dramatized by: Elaine Morgan. Designer: Barry Newberry. Script Editor: Betty Willingale. Sound: Colin Dixon. Lighting: Sam Barclay. Makeup Artist: Ann Ailes. Costume Designer: Barbara Kidd. Music Composed and Conducted by: Herbert Chappell. Production Unit Manager: Denis Curran. Production Assistant: Carol Wiseman.

CAST: Michael Hordern (Scrooge); John Le Mesurier (Marley's Ghost); Bernard Lee (Ghost of Christmas Present); Patricia Quinn (Ghost of Christmas Past); Paul Copley (Fred); Clive Merrison (Bob Cratchit); Carol Macready (Mrs. Cratchit); Maev Alexander (Fred's Wife); Zoe Wanamaker (Belle); Stephen Churchett (John); Will Stampe (Fezziwig); Christopher Biggins (Topper); Tricia George (Little Blonde); John Salthouse (Scrooge as a young man); Veronica Doran (Caroline); John Grillo (Caroline's Husband); June Brown (Mrs. Dilber); David Hatton (Undertaker's Man); John Ringham (Charity Gentleman); Brian Hayes, Roy Desmond (Businessmen); Michael Mulcaster (Ghost of Christmas Future); Nicholas John (Dick Wilkins); Dorian Healy (Scrooge as a schoolboy); Tracey Childs (Fan); Zelah Clarke (Martha Cratchit); David Ronder (Peter Cratchit); Claire McLellan (Belinda Cratchit); Timothy Chasin (Tiny Tim); David Corti (Carol-singer).

Television dramatization first shown in England on December 24, 1977.

A surprisingly disappointing version—not because there is anything terribly wrong with it, but because it is clearly not the classic that one might expect. The primary point of attraction for most *Carol* fans would be the presence of Michael Hordern; given his association with the role of Marley in two earlier classics (he also narrated the 1973 BBC version with Marcel Marceau), the thought of him as Scrooge would seem most promising. In terms of his film and television career, Hordern, later Sir Michael Hordern, was one of the finest British character and supporting actors of the last half century; general audiences in America may remember him best as the voice of Paddington the Bear.

Unfortunately, the role of Scrooge requires a certain strength and a capacity for meanness. Hordern is particularly adept at *other* types of roles—a befuddled country clergyman, a spineless bureaucrat, an eccentric inventor — but not at this type. In short, there is a certain softness about Hordern's screen persona, while the role of Scrooge demands a certain hardness much of the time. None of this is meant to suggest that this *Carol* is fatally flawed because of Hordern's casting as Scrooge — he is in fact, as always, quite good — but one cannot help noticing that it is somehow just a bit "off key" nonetheless. (Note: Very similar reservations apply to Ralph Richardson's 1951 turn as Scrooge; see entry above.)

Apart from the issue of casting, there is actually much to recommend this version. To begin with, it is always interesting to see the results of any attempt to tell the tale in less than ninety minutes (the minimal running time of most modern feature-length films). In this regard, the pace of the production is very brisk, and a great deal of trimming is done in all the usual places. However, as is usually the case with *Carol* abridgments, there are some interesting surprises in terms of what *is* included: The Ghost of Christmas Past, for example, carries the seldom seen bonnet described in Dickens's original text, and in the Christmas Future sequence, we see the young couple to whom news of Scrooge's death means nothing more than a postponement of their debt. Most surprisingly, however, in the sequence with Marley's Ghost, we notice that the phantom is in a great deal of discomfort. As Dickens puts it, Marley's Ghost was "provided with an infernal atmosphere of its own" and "though the Ghost sat perfectly motionless, its hair, and skirts, and tassels, were still agitated as by the hot vapour from an oven." Clearly, wherever Marley's spirit is forced to wander, it enjoys no relief from the physical tortures of Hell. To the best of this author's recollection at the time of this writing, this is the only *Carol* adaptation to include this truly frightening bit of detail.

From a purely visual standpoint, this version is interesting in that it uses a number of painted backgrounds in exterior scenes, while interior scenes rely on small, confined sets and heavy pools of darkness and shadow. To some extent this approach may have been dictated by a limited budget, but the overall effect — let's call it a highly stylized theatricality — is quite successful. (Apart from some very effective superimpositions and freeze-frames, as well as that curiously "flat" look common to all productions that are shot on tape rather than film, this one does, in fact, have a more theatrical look to it than many of the filmed plays considered elsewhere in this text.) All things considered, this is a minor *Carol*, but it is still worth a look nevertheless.

SCROOGE

ITV-TV 1978 Canada 70m color

Producer: Joan Krisch. Director: John Blanchard. Writer: Warren Graves. Artistic Director: Keith Digby. Associate Producer: Claire Verret. Technical Coordinator: Dan MacLean. Art Director: Scott Dobbie. Costume & Prop Design: John Madill. Lighting Director: Des Spence. Audio: Harvey Popowich. Studio Director: Don Zacharuk. Video Tape Editor: Malcolm Knox. Sound Effects: Paul Moulton. Switcher: Norm Vallee. Cameramen: Norm Michaelis; Wayne Mock; Randy Tomiuk. Maintenance: Dave Proc. Stage Manager: Marian Brant. Makeup: Chris McRae. Property Master: Jack Boschman. Lighting: Terry Sims; Cody Emslie. Boom Operators: Glen Corness; Kim Elaschuk. Production Assistants: Brian Lemisko; Bob Blair. Staging: Bill Herron; Bill Rayment; Mike Hawryluk. Titles: Dan Hardie. Thanks to Goodwood's Antiques; The Citadel. Originally staged by Theatre 3.

CAST: Warren Graves (Ebenezer Scrooge); Drew Borland (Marley); Ray Hunt (Bob Cratchit/Dick Wilkins); Crystal Fleuty (Belinda Cratchit/Belle); Colin Graves (Tim Cratchit/ Young Scrooge); Peter Messaline (Mr. Monty/ Mr. Fezziwig); Nicole Evans (Mrs. Monty/Mrs. Fezziwig).

Televised production of Warren Graves's original adaptation of the *Carol* that was first staged at Theatre Three in Edmonton, Alberta, in December of 1978. First broadcast locally in Edmonton on December 22, 1978; later shown on Canadian and American cable television.

This Canadian production was one of the earliest modern stage adaptations of the *Carol* to be transferred to television — and it qualifies as one of the best. On the surface, it might appear to pale in comparison with the other televised plays discussed in this filmography in that it is a comparatively modest production originally conceived and written for a small theatrical company in a small theater. On closer examination, however, one realizes that its modest scope and production values are anything but a weakness. Many modern stage adaptations of the *Carol* rely heavily on costumes, sets and music, as well as increasingly elaborate special effects; in fact, several *Carol* spectaculars staged in the nineties have as much in common with a night at the circus as they do a night at the theater. This version allows the audience to remain focused on the fact that the *Carol* is a marvelously entertaining tale filled with wonderful characters and important ideas.

From a visual standpoint, this *Scrooge* is highly theatrical in conception and design in that it utilizes well-designed flats set against black backgrounds. The result is an almost dreamlike look that is quite effective but never becomes overpowering by taking the plunge into full-blown expressionism.

In terms of story construction, considerable streamlining is in evidence as Marley's Ghost handles all of the ghostly chores, thus eliminating the need for the familiar Ghosts of Christmas Past, Present and Future; the Cratchit family is also reduced in size to Bob, Tim and daughter Belinda. However, in spite of this compression, some interesting and original touches have been added: The new characters of Mr. and Mrs. Monty, for example, are an effective composite of various characters, primarily Scrooge's nephew and the charity solicitors, who keep the story moving forward at a brisk pace. And in a charming opening scene, we find Tiny Tim selling matches in the street so that he can earn enough money to buy his father a present. (Tim is revealed to be an excellent man of business; nevertheless, Scrooge still manages to walk away with a box of matches that he hasn't paid for!) It should also be noted that the production is very well acted by a uniformly excellent ensemble cast headed by playwright Warren Graves in the title role. The performance of Graves's young son Colin is also particularly noteworthy in that he adds a subtly roguish quality to his portrayal of Tiny Tim, thus avoiding the cloying sweetness that has plagued many another interpretation of this small but important role.

As a final recommendation, let the record also note that this *Carol* can take its place among those adaptations that offer significant insight into the background and motivation of its central character. Indeed, the Christmas Past sequence is probably its strongest and, as suggested in Chapter 7, it offers considerable insight into the "cold, dark place" that is Scrooge's heart.

THE STINGIEST MAN IN TOWN

Rankin/Bass Productions, Inc.   1978   USA 49m   color

Produced and Directed by: Arthur Rankin, Jr.; Jules Bass. Written by: Romeo Muller. Book and Lyrics: Janice Torre. Music: Fred Spielman. Design: Paul Coker, Jr. Animation Coordinator: Toru Hara. Animation Supervisor: Tsuguyuki Kubo. Animation Director: Katsuhisa Yamada. Background Design: Minoru Nishida. Backgrounds: Kazusuke Yoshihara; Kazuko Ito. Layouts: Kazuyuki Kobayashi; Tadakatsu Yoshida; Hidemi Kubo. Animation: Yoshiko Sasaki; Masahiro Yoshida. Sound Recording: John Curcio; Dave Iveland; John Richards; Robert Elder. Sound Effects: Tom Clack. Vocal Arrangements: Jerry Graff. Music Supervision: Maury Laws.

Music Arranged and Conducted by: Bernard Hoffer. Associate Producer: Masaki Tizuka.

CAST: Walter Matthau (Ebenezer Scrooge); Tom Bosley (Narrator: The London Humbug, B.A.H. Humbug, Esq.); Theodore Bikel (Jacob Marley); Robert Morse (Young Scrooge); Dennis Day (Nephew Fred); Paul Frees (Ghost of Christmas Past); Sonny Melendrez; Debbie Clinger (Martha); Robert Rolofson (Tiny Tim); Steffani Calli (Belinda); Eric Hines (Peter); Dee Stratton; Darlene Conley (Mrs. Cratchit); Shelby Flint; Diana Lee; and Charles Matthau (as the boy).

SONGS: "A Christmas Carol"; "The Stingiest Man in Town"; "An Old-Fashioned Christmas"; "Humbug"; "I Wear a Chain"; "Golden Dreams"; "It Might Have Been"; "The Christmas Spirit"; "Yes, There Is a Santa Claus"; "Birthday Party of the King"; "One Little Boy"; "Mankind Should Be My Business." [Note: Songs are mostly abbreviated versions of those used in the 1956 production discussed above.]

Animated musical version of the *Carol* that was first broadcast on NBC-TV on December 23, 1978.

The prolific team of Arthur Rankin, Jr., and Jules Bass has been responsible for an almost countless number of children's specials since the mid-sixties, including many that feature a Christmas theme, such as the classic *Rudolph, the Red-Nosed Reindeer* (1964), made with their stop-motion puppet animation process known as Animagic, and the charming animated cartoon *Frosty the Snowman* (1969). And, as noted elsewhere, they had previously drawn upon the reliable combination of Dickens and Christmas with their adaptations of *The Cricket on the Hearth* (1967) and *A Christmas Tree* (1972).

The Stingiest Man in Town is an interesting if unspectacular version of the *Carol*. It is particularly noteworthy as a shortened remake of the 1956 live-action production of the same name that premiered on NBC-TV on December 23, 1956; as noted above, it even uses the same songs. As with all Rankin/Bass productions, the quality level is high here, and if this *Carol* does not attain the classic status of Mr. Magoo and Richard Williams's earlier efforts, it is still one of the better animated versions to date. There are no complaints to speak of, although one can be distracted by the fact that Scrooge is drawn to look just like Walter Matthau, who provides the character's voice.

As for the story itself, one can note a couple of intriguing surprises. For example, in the Ghost of Christmas Present sequence, we see the green-garbed ghost briefly transform himself into a traditional Santa Claus as the song "Yes, There Is a

Santa Claus" is heard; a likening of the Ghost of Christmas Present to Santa Claus is perhaps a natural step for modern audiences, but the implicit connection is rarely explored by film or television. And in the joyous celebration at nephew Fred's home, the ghost shows Scrooge a manger underneath the Christmas Tree and, as the song "The Birthday Party of the King" is heard, the manger dissolves into a montage of stained glass–style images depicting various scenes from the Nativity story. One can argue that the *Carol's* religious underpinnings are implicitly present in all adaptations, but they are rarely confronted this directly. And it is surely worth noting that such a direct confrontation was somewhat surprising, coming as it did in a late seventies production that was made for commercial television.

NOTE: *TV Guide*, December 23–29, 1978, contains a brief illustrated discussion of the production of *The Stingiest Man in Town.*

RICH LITTLE'S CHRISTMAS CAROL

Canadian Broadcasting Corporation (CBC) in association with Tel-Pro Entertainments Inc. and Dudley Enterprises Inc. 1978 Canada 50m color

Produced by: Norman Sedawie; Gayle Gibson Sedawie. Directed by: Trevor Evans. Written by: Rich Little. Special Musical Material by: Saul Ilson. Choreographed and Staged by: Kevin Carlisle. Additional Choreography: James Hibbard. Music Arranged and Conducted by: Jerry Toth. Art Director: Douglas Higgins. Assistant Designer: Stephen Geaghan. Lighting Director: Les Erskine. Costume Designer: Philip Clarkson. Makeup: Jackie Wilkinson. Set Decorators: Garry Olson; Sean Kirby. Special Effects: John Sleep. Staging Crewleader: Dave Sutherland. Graphic Designer: Jeff Pritchard. Technical Producer: Bill Kyashko. Video: Jerry Williamson. Sound Effects: Eric Batut. Cameras: Gene Baedak; Hugh Henderson; Ray Waines. Audio: Bob Paley; Jim Rogers. VTR Editor: Brad Baldwin. Casting: Lee Livingston. Production Assistants: Lara Fox; Gordon Gill; Susan Weir. Unit Manager: Neil Simpson.

CAST: Rich Little appears as the following celebrities portraying the familiar Dickens characters: W. C. Fields (Ebenezer Scrooge); Paul Lynde (Bob Cratchit); Johnny Carson (Nephew Freddie); Stan Laurel & Oliver Hardy (Charity Solicitors); Richard Nixon (Jacob Marley); Humphrey Bogart (Ghost of Christmas Past); Groucho Marx (Fezziwig); James Stewart (Dick Wilkins); Peter Falk as Lieutenant Columbo (Ghost of Christmas Present); Jean Stapleton as Edith Bunker (Mrs. Cratchit); Truman Capote

(Tiny Tim); Peter Sellers as Inspector Clouseau (Ghost of Christmas Future); James Mason, George Burns and John Wayne (Businessmen who discuss Scrooge's death in Christmas Future sequence); Jack Benny (young boy who fetches turkey on Christmas morning). Assorted uncredited extras also appear.

Carol variation first broadcast by CBC television in Canada on December 24, 1978.

Famed impressionist Rich Little's take on the *Carol* can be traced back to his 1963 recording entitled *Scrooge and the Stars.* Unfortunately, this television version is considerably less successful. The basic premise, that of telling the story through celebrity impersonations, is certainly a good idea; however, good ideas are the proverbial dime a dozen unless properly executed. The main problem is a weak and very episodic script that simply goes nowhere while straining for laughs. At best, one is painfully aware of watching a television skit that is running about thirty minutes longer than it should. Compounding this problem is the ubiquitous shot-on-tape look that has been noted elsewhere, an extremely annoying laugh-track, and a preponderance of over-the-shoulder shots that are apparently intended to convince us that characters played by the same performer can appear in the same scene and actually talk to each other. A few clever touches are in evidence here and there — a cantankerous W. C. Fields as Scrooge is certainly an inspired bit of casting, and those old enough to pick up on the 1970s context of some of the humor will certainly be rewarded with a few scattered chuckles — but, all things considered, this is one of the poorest *Carol* variations to date.

NOTE: A recording based on this production, also entitled *Rich Little's Christmas Carol*, was released in 1979. Also, a video record of Little performing a condensed version of his *Carol* on The Ed Sullivan Show in the late sixties is available on *A Classic Christmas from the Ed Sullivan Show* which is distributed by Buena Vista Home Video. In this version, "George Burns" narrates, "Jack Benny" is Scrooge, and "Ed Sullivan" is a phantom.

A CHRISTMAS CAROL

Harlech Television 1978 Great Britain 55m color

Producer: Michael Hayes. Director: Michael Hayes. Libretto: John Morgan. Music: Norman Kay. Designer: Doug James. The Philharmonia Orchestra conducted by David Lloyd Jones.

CAST: Sir Geraint Evans (Ebenezer Scrooge); Ryland Davies (Bob Cratchit); Elizabeth Gale (Mrs. Cratchit); Gwynne Howell.

An original opera version of the *Carol* created

for the Welsh HTV television channel. First
broadcast on December 25, 1978.

BUGS BUNNY'S LOONEY CHRISTMAS
TALES

Produced by DePatie-Freleng Enterprises,
Inc. and Chuck Jones Enterprises in association
with Warner Bros., Inc.   1979   USA   25m
color

"Bugs Bunny" sequences produced/directed by
Friz Freleng.

"Road-Runner" sequences produced/directed
by Chuck Jones.

Executive Producer: Hal Geer. Written by:
Friz Freleng; Chuck Jones; John Dunn; Tony
Benedict. Music: Doug Goodwin. Animators:
Irv Anderson; John McGuire; Warren Batch-
elder; Phil Monroe; Bob Bransford; Tom Ray;
Malcolm Draper; Virgil Ross; Mark Kausler;
Benny Washam; Ruth Kissane; Don Williams.

VOICES: Mel Blanc; additional voices by June
Foray.

Animated special that originally aired on
CBS-TV on November 27, 1979. This *Carol*
comprises the first third of what is actually a three
cartoon "package" hosted by Bugs Bunny. The
final two-thirds are, respectively, Road Runner
and Tasmanian Devil cartoons.

The always grouchy Yosemite Sam makes an
appropriate Scrooge in this very abbreviated and
rather uninspired *Carol*. Bugs Bunny and company are always a treat, but there is nothing special happening here.

AN AMERICAN CHRISTMAS CAROL

ABC-TV 1979 USA color 98m

An Edgar J. Scherick/Stanley Chase/Jon Slan
Production in association with Smith-Hemion
Productions. Executive Producer: Gary Smith;
Edgar J. Scherick. Producer: Jon Slan; Stanley
Chase. Director: Eric Till. Written by: Jerome
Coopersmith. Director of Photography: Richard
Ciupka. Editor: Ron Wisman. Music: Hagood
Hardy. Special Makeup Consultant: Rick Baker.
Mr. Winkler's Makeup created by: Greg Can-
non. Production Designer: Jack McAdam. Pro-
duction Manager: Gerry Arbeid. First Assistant
Director: David Robertson. Continuity: Diane
Parsons. Production Secretary: Angela Heald.
Location Recording: Douglas Ganton. Re-
Recording: Gary Bourgeois; Tony van den Akker.
Sound Editors: Bruce Nyznik; Terry Burke;
Robin Leigh. Key Grip: Norman Smith. Gaffer:
John Berrie. Props Master: Jaques Bradette. Set
Dresser: Dan Conley. Special Effects: Martin
Malivoire. Costume Designer: Julie Ganton.
Hair Design: James Brown. Makeup: Valli.

CAST: Henry Winkler (Benedict Slade);
David Wayne (Mr. Merrivale/Ghost of Christ-
mas Past); Chris Wiggins (Mr. Brewster); R. H.
Thomson (Thatcher); Kenneth Pogue (Jack
Latham); Gerard Parkes (Jessup/Ghost of
Christmas Present); Susan Hogan (Helen Brew-
ster); Dorian Harewood (Matt Reeves/Ghost of
Christmas Future); Tammy Bourne (Sarah
Thatcher); Chris Crabb (Jonathan Thatcher);
James B. Douglas (Sam Perkins); Arlene Duncan
(Mrs. Reeves); Linda Goranson (Mrs. Thatcher);
Derrick Jones (Harry Barnes); Cec Linder (Auc-
tioneer); Sylvia Llewellyn (Latham's Secretary);
Jefferson Mappin (Joe); Mary Pirie (Mrs. Brew-
ster); Sammy Snyders (Young Slade); Ruth
Springford (Mrs. Tydings); Justine Till (Young
Helen); Michael Wincott (Choir Leader);
William Ballantyne (Minister); Frank Gibbs
(Fire Chief).

Carol variation first broadcast on December 16, 1979.

An American Christmas Carol is set in Con-
cord, New Hampshire, in 1933; however, anyone
looking for cozy glimpses of an old-fashioned
New England Christmas will be greatly disappointed. The prevailing color of exterior scenes
is gray: a cold, bleak, depressing gray. You can
feel an unhealthy dampness in the air and sky; the
bracing, exhilarating winter cold that Dickens
describes so memorably in *Pickwick* will not be
found here. And most interior scenes are equally
cheerless, all muted colors and stale air.

In this same vein, this production is very
effective at striking a note of wistful melancholy
that reverberates throughout much of the story,
as in the Ghost of Christmas Present's response
to Scrooge's lament that he could have had a child
with his former sweetheart "if only things were
different." The spirit replies: "If. That word can
be found on dry river beds and on trails long over-
grown by weeds. What's more important are the
paths we follow now." Good advice, but the pain
still lingers. Add the fact that the story is played
out against the backdrop of the Great Depres-
sion and you have the most downbeat (and occasionally downright depressing) variation to date.
None of this should be taken as negative criticism, however, for this *Carol* functions beautifully as a very effective and at times rather disquieting mood piece — a mood which, in effect,
seems to mirror the state of its Scrooge's soul.

The Scrooge in question here is Benedict
Slade (played by Henry Winkler), a merchant and
manufacturer whose hardhearted ways enable
him to prosper while everyone else in town is
barely surviving. In a revealing variation on the
standard storyline, we find him spending his
Christmas Eve repossessing various pieces of
merchandise from customers who can no longer

make their payments. (One of the confiscated items is a first edition of *A Christmas Carol* owned by an unfortunate bookseller.) On the plus side, Winkler turns in a fine performance as a truly nasty twentieth-century Scrooge. Unfortunately, the character of Slade is written as an old man, and Winkler appears in *very* heavy makeup and long white hair that is both unconvincing and distracting. It might have been wiser to take a more restrained approach here, as in Albert Finney's 1970 *Scrooge*, and present Slade as a man in his fifties. One hates to carp too much about a single point, but the credibility of a given production's Scrooge is no minor detail.

This *Carol* should be remembered as an interesting but flawed variation, one that earns solid marks for its decidedly low-key approach and for finding an original angle from which to approach a very familiar story.

SKINFLINT

NBC-TV 1979 USA 120m color

The Cates Brothers Company. Executive Producers: Joseph Cates; Gilbert Cates. Producers: Marc Daniels; Joseph Cates. Director: Marc Daniels. Book: Mel Mandel. Lyrics and Music: Mel Mandel; Norman Sachs; Aaron Schroeder. Choreographer: Scott Salmon. Musical Director: Bill Walker. Production Designer: Roy Christopher. Art Director: Mark Batterman. Costume Designer: Evelyn Thompson. Production Manager: Chuck Smith. Assistant Art Director: Jane Mancbach. Nashville Consultant: Chet Hagen. Casting: Pamela Parker. Technical Director: O. Tamburri. Assistant to the Producer: Carol Kahl. Associate Director: Herb Stein. Assistant Choreographer: Vera Mazzeo. Music Coordinator: D'Vaugn Pershing. Production Assistant: Virginia Schmidt. Show Assistants: Jeff Schwedock; Jim Gaston. Stage Managers: Ted Baker; Gordon Morris. Makeup: Harry Blake. Hairdresser: Mari Loshin. Lighting Director: John Freschi. Videotape Editors: Harvey W. Berger; Carol Phillips. Audio: Bill Cole. Audio Consultant: Scott Moore. Video: Ed Huston. Associate Producer: Al Lowenstein.

CAST: Hoyt Axton (Cyrus Flint [Ebenezer Scrooge]); Mel Tillis (Dennis Pritchett [Bob Cratchit]); Lynn Anderson (Laura Pritchett [Cratchit's wife]); Larry Gatlin (Roger [Scrooge's nephew]); Julie Gregg (Joan [nephew's wife]); Tom T. Hall (Ghost of Jacob Burley); Martha Raye (Ghost of Christmas Past); Danny Davis (Ghost of Christmas Present [Note: Davis's band, The Nashville Brass, also appears at the beginning and end of the Christmas Past sequence]); The Statler Brothers (The Flint City Four); Barbara Mandrell (Emmy [Scrooge's former

fiancée]); Dottie West (Annabelle Williams); Steven Lutz (T. J. [Tiny Tim]); Byron Webster (Mr. Abbey); Carol Swarbrick (Mrs. Abbey); Jean Howell (Sarah); Dave Madden (Stanley Gershen); Mickey McMeel (Announcer); Gordon Connell (The Pawnbroker); David Bond ([Ghost of] Christmas Yet to Come); Scott Craig; Pat Cranshaw; Marcus Ginnaty; Mark Harrison; Austin Hartman; Adam Hill; Ted Lehmann; Brian Miller; Claude Stroud; Penelope Sudrow; Susie Carr; Gayle Crofoot; Christine Cullen; Leeyman Granger; Mark Harryman; Spencer Henderson; John King; Karen Lorhan; Judy Pierce; Jimmy Roddy; Ted Sprague; Eddie Verso.

Country & western musical variation that originally aired, in a two-hour time slot, on December 18, 1979.

This *Carol* assembles an impressive collection of top shelf country & western musical talent in transposing the story to the American South. (An opening credit informs us that it takes place "somewhere in Tennessee"; we later learn that it is actually a small town called Flint City and that the locals are under the thumb of a Scrooge-like bank president named Cyrus Flint.) Unfortunately, *Skinflint* fails to live up to its interesting premise, and the result is one of the lamest live-action *Carol* variations to date. Its problems are many, but one immediately notices a low-budget sensibility that is particularly evident in its rather cramped and obviously artificial sets, the overall impact of which is exacerbated by that unmistakable shot-on-tape look that can undermine even the most opulent production values. However, the primary fault lies in a very poor script that lacks any semblance of subtlety or character development. The whole story seems rushed and more than a bit ragged, resulting in a *Carol* that more closely resembles a skit on *The Carol Burnett Show* (minus the energy and humor) rather than a full-fledged, feature-length adaptation.

Perhaps the most glaring example of this type of general ineptitude is the Ghost of Christmas Future sequence, which actually starts out interestingly enough with Flint viewing the familiar visions on a television set. Unfortunately, this particular Ghost of Christmas Future sports facial makeup that would be more appropriate at a children's Halloween party, and, in an apparent attempt to be "spooky," flits about the room while moaning, "You're dead" to an understandably horrified Flint. If an adaptation is going to break with tradition by having this particular phantom speak — this is one of a very few *Carols* to do so — then he ought to be given something meaningful and intelligent to say!

On the plus side, the country & western stars — who are, of course, primarily singers and musicians rather than actors — acquit themselves quite well in spite of a deadly combination of weak script and largely forgettable songs. Hoyt Axton is particularly good, lending a roguish charm to his role that can help us overlook the fact that this Southern Scrooge is written as a stereotypically (almost cartoonish) one-dimensional miser; and Martha Raye, who comes from a different musical tradition than the rest of the cast, adds a much needed infusion of spunk and energy as a Ghost of Christmas Past who summarizes Flint's situation by telling him (in song) that he's "a dummy." All things considered, this one stands as a mildly interesting curio that should have been much better than it is.

A CHRISTMAS CAROL AT FORD'S THEATRE

WETA-TV 1979 USA color 87m

Producer: Christopher Sarson. Director: Rae Allen; Kirk Browning. Stage Adaptation by: Rae Allen; Timothy Near. Produced for the Stage at Ford's Theatre by: Frankie Hewitt. Associate Producer: Jackson Frost. Associate Director: David Deutsch. Production Manager: Sonja Dollison. Production Assistant: Cynthia Mitchell. Production Secretary: Lynne Harris. Engineers-In-Charge: Gerry Lob; William Maylett. Technical Director: Michael Mayes. TV Lighting Directors: Harry Bottorf; John Gisondi; William Knight; Dick Weiss. Audio: David Gillette; Jerry Butler. Video: Gregory King; Erv Brandt. Camera: Gary Allen; Joseph Camp; Julius Fauntleroy; Jerry Gallagher; Joan Leahy. Video Tape Editor: Ismael Jimenez. Video Tape: Susanne Risher. Utility: Jim Adams; Virginia Higgins; J. P. Whiteside. TV Stage Manager: Mark Potocki. Stage Direction: Ron Bishop. Settings and Costumes Designed by: Christina Weppner. Stage Lighting Designed by: John Gisondi. Musical Direction: Michael Howe. Associate Stage Director: Judy Jurgaitis. Production Stage Manager: John Vivian. Puppet Design and Creation: Ingrid Crepeau. Assistant Stage Manager: John Concannon. Entire Stage Production under the supervision of Rae Allen and Timothy Near. For Ford's Theatre: Executive Producer: Frankie Hewitt. Managing Director: Ted Parker. Technical Director: Tommy Berra. For WETA: Executive Producer: Gerry Slater.

CAST: Ron Bishop (Ebenezer Scrooge); Jennifer Borge; Thomas Dillon; Geoff Garland (Bob Cratchit); Mary Irey; Judy Jurgaitis; Josie Lawrence; David Long; Paul Milikin; John Morgal (Tiny Tim); Steve O'Connor; Chris Romilly; Eva Rose; Nancy Sellin; David Silber; Anita Sorel; Scott Sorrel; Gary Thomas, Jr.; Kathy Vivian; Steve Worth.

Theatrical adaptation first broadcast on PBS on December 22, 1979.

This *Carol*, which was taped in front of a live audience at historic Ford's Theatre in Washington, D.C., is the most theatrical, and the least successful, of all televised stage adaptations to date. Unlike some others, it does not utilize any special effects for the benefit of the television audience; consequently it is particularly adept at conveying something of the closeness and intimacy of a live performance, right down to its actors projecting to the live audience. Unfortunately, projecting comes across as yelling to a television audience, and the overall effect, if not necessarily fatal, can be very distracting.

Aesthetically, the production is quite impressive, with a beautiful multi-purpose set and colorful costumes being particular standouts. It also features the two largest and tallest ghosts (Christmas Present and Future) on record. There are, however, a few technical lapses in the areas of audio level and camera focus that one is frankly surprised to find in a prestigious, nationally broadcast program.

The adaptation itself is also something of a mixed bag. While there are a few interludes of music and song, it is in no sense a musical, but rather a fairly straightforward dramatic presentation that offers no new insights into the story. Its most significant innovation is that various characters, particularly Bob Cratchit, also serve as narrator at various points by directly addressing the audience in the voice of Dickens's omniscient narrator. This is an interesting technique which not only keeps the story moving, but also helps to remind the audience of the ultimate primacy of Dickens's original text. (If there is a downside to this approach, it is that it can be interpreted as lending yet another note of overt theatricality to the proceedings.) And in a less successful vein, its Scrooge (the most uncharacteristically rotund Scrooge to date) is played with an undercurrent of broad humor that doesn't quite work at all times. All things considered, this is an attractive, but rather uneven, adaptation.

THE DUKES OF HAZZARD

CBS-TV 1980 USA 60m color

A Lou Step Production. Supervising Producer: Rod Amateau. Producer: Myles Wilder; Ralph Riskin. Director: Denver Pyle. Writer: Martin Roth. Created by: Gy Waldron. Executive Producer: Paul R. Picard. Associate Producer: Skip Ward; Gilles A. de Turenne. Director of Photography: Jack Whitman. Art Director:

Bob Jillson. Title Song Composed and Sung by: Waylon Jennings. Music: Fred Werner.

CAST: Tom Wopat (Luke Duke); John Schneider (Bo Duke); Catherine Bach (Daisy Duke); Denver Pyle (Uncle Jesse); Rick Hurst (Cletus); Ben Jones (Cooter); James Best (Sheriff Rosco Coltrane); Sorrell Booke (Boss Hogg); Waylon Jennings (The Balladeer). GUEST CAST: Woody Strode (Willie); Brian Libby (Russ); Roy Jenson (Lacey); Dale Pullum (Little Boy); Roger Pancake (Hank).

Comedy/Adventure series. Episode title: "The Great Santa Claus Chase." First broadcast on December 19, 1980.

This episode of the amiable series about the fun-loving Duke clan is not directly concerned with the *Carol*, and is therefore not really a *Carol* variation. The story involves Bo and Luke's efforts to clear their name after the always Scrooge-like Boss Hogg frames them for the theft of a truckload of Christmas trees. However, Dickens's tale does briefly enter into the story twice. First, the cousins make an unsuccessful attempt to convince a sleeping Hogg that he is hearing the Ghost of Christmas Past (via a two-way radio) warning him to reform. And second, things wrap up on a Dickensian note when a lonely Hogg reads a copy of *A Christmas Carol* that he has received as a present. Needless to say he has a change of heart, and shows up at the Dukes' Christmas Eve party loaded with presents and holiday cheer.

The Dickensian subplot does not seem completely integrated into the storyline here, and one has to wonder if it was an afterthought or last-minute addition. On the other hand, the writer should probably be credited for not opting for the reliable and predictable (and usually quite tedious) formal *Carol* variation that so many television series feel obligated to offer. And there is, after all, something quite profound in the idea of someone being changed for the better simply by reading Dickens's "Ghostly little book." Interestingly, a formal *Carol* variation did appear on *The Dukes*, the animated version of *The Dukes of Hazzard*, in 1983; see entry below.

WKRP IN CINCINNATI

CBS-TV 1980 USA 30m color

Executive Producer: Hugh Wilson. Supervising Producer: Rod Daniel. Producer: Blake Hunter; Steven Kampmann; Peter Torokvei. Director: Rod Daniel. Writer: Lissa Levin. Story Editor: Lissa Levin. Story Consultants: Steve Marshall; Dan Guntzelman. Associate Producer: Max Tash. Art Director: Jacqueline Webber. Set Decorator: Catherine Arnold. Theme Music: Tom Wells. Director of Photography: George La Fountaine.

CAST: Gary Sandy (Andy Travis); Gordon Jump (Arthur Carlson); Loni Anderson (Jennifer Marlowe); Richard Sanders (Les Nessman); Frank Bonner (Herb Tarlek); Jan Smithers (Bailey Quarters); Howard Hesseman (Johnny Caravella/Dr. Johnny Fever); Tim Reid (Gordon Sims/Venus Flytrap); Parley Baer (Mr. Armor); Don Diamond (Don Bassett); Merle Earle (Mrs. Butterworth).

Situation comedy. Episode title: "Bah, Humbug." First broadcast on December 20, 1980.

The Scrooge surrogate here is Arthur Carlson, manager of radio station WKRP, who alienates his staff by refusing to give out Christmas bonuses. However, after visits by the Ghosts of Christmas Past (Jennifer), Present (Venus) and Future (Fever), he sees the light and reaches for his check book. The twist here is that Arthur's visions are triggered by the "secret ingredient" in Johnny Fever's brownies. The usual sitcom stuff, although quite well done.

A CHRISTMAS CAROL*

ABC Video Enterprises in cooperation with the American Conservatory Theatre 1981 USA 110m color

Produced by the American Conservatory Theatre/William Ball, General Director. Director: Laird Williamson. Adapted for Television by: Joshua White. Original Stage Adaptation: Dennis Powers; Laird Williamson. Executive Producers: David M. Sacks; James B. McKenzie. Produced for Television by: Benjamin Moore. Associate Producer: Judith Patterson. Art Director: Robert Blackman. Editor: Bob Sweeney. Costume Designer: Robert Morgan. Music: Lee Hoiby. Associate Director: James Haire. Assistant to the Director: Eugene Barcone. Production Manager: John A. Woods. Technical Director: John Brown. Stage Managers: Elizabeth Huddle; David Hyslop. Assistant Art Director: Michael Becker. Lead Scenic Designer: Dale Haugo. Assistant Costume Designer: Warren Caton. Scenic Artist: Charley Campbell. Assistant Scenic Artist: Eric Norton. Zellerbach Auditorium Staff: Master Carpenter: Phillip Heron. Master Electrician: Dan Niles. Properties Master: Larry Hunt. Special Effects Supervisor: Thayne Morris. Lighting Director: Richard Tidwell. Cameramen: Walt Bjerke; Matt Elmore; Joe Peterson; Richard Reizner. Video Control: Larry Bentley. Video Tape: Robert Frey, Jr. Audio Supervisor: Carl Olson. Audio: John Hicks; Japji Singh Khaisa.

CAST: Casey Peterson (The Caroler); William Paterson (Ebenezer Scrooge); Lawrence Hecht (Narrator); Mark Murphey (Bob Cratchit); Bruce Williams (1st Charitable Gentleman); Isiah

Whitlock (2nd Charitable Gentleman); Nicholas Kaledin (Fred); Raye Birk (Marley's Ghost); Thomas Oglesby (Ghost of Christmas Past); Jennifer Rogers (Little Fan); Casey Peterson (The Boy Scrooge); Peter Belden, Toby Brenner, Jared Brown, Patrick O'Brien, Joral Schmale (School Boys); Janice Hutchins (Belle); Thomas Harrison (Young Scrooge); Randall Richard (Dick Wilkins); Sydney Walker (Fezziwig); Marrian Walters (Mrs. Fezziwig); Lawrence Hecht (Ghost of Christmas Present); Jennifer Rogers (Toy Clown); Rebecca Garrett (Toy Ballerina); Delores Mitchell (Mrs. Cratchit); Toshi Harrison (Belinda Cratchit); Corina Benjet (Sally Cratchit); Joral Schmale (Peter Cratchit); Patrick O'Brien (Ned Cratchit); Rebecca Patterson (Martha Cratchit); Tyson Thomas (Tiny Tim); Julia Fletcher (Mary, Fred's Wife); Mimi Carr, Julia Fletcher, Lydia Hannibal, Toshi Harrison, Randall Richard, Frank Ottiwell, Isiah Whitlock, Bruce Williams (Party Guests); Mimi Carr (Mrs. Dilber); Marrian Walters (Mrs. Filcher); Frank Ottiwell (Old Joe); Randall Richard (The Undertaker's Boy); Nicholas Kaledin (Ghost of Christmas Future).

Televised production of the American Conservatory Theatre's stage adaptation. First broadcast on December 21, 1981, on the ARTS cable network.

Quite possibly the best overall televised stage adaptation of the *Carol*. It is well done in terms of all technical and aesthetic considerations, but what gives it an edge over similar productions is the subtlety and restraint with which the familiar tale is told — an approach which, nevertheless, still allows the script to present the *Carol's* serious side in a very direct manner. If one must generalize, it is probably safe to say that most theatrical adaptations of the *Carol* tend to emphasize its lighter side. This seems particularly true in recent decades when stagings of the *Carol* have become an annual holiday tradition in big cities and small towns alike, a tradition which usually stresses its appeal for the entire family. Unfortunately, as we have also seen with numerous film and television versions, this kind of "packaging" can sometimes cause the *Carol's* more serious dimensions to fade a bit too far into the background. Needless to say, a world of difference lies between *A Christmas Carol* and, say, *Long Day's Journey into Night*, but the ideal adaptation does not allow the strains of Sir Roger de Coverley to drown out the cries of suffering children. This one achieves a delicate and very stimulating sense of balance.

Once again, a restrained approach, including a very low-key Scrooge, dominates this particular production; and yet this is also one of the most emotionally gripping *Carols* yet seen. As noted in Chapter 7, in the Christmas Past sequence we gain tremendous insight into old Scrooge's character through the revelations of his father's psychological and physical cruelty toward his younger self. And one can point to other similarly innovative set pieces in which the *Carol's* message of moral and social consciousness is powerfully underscored; for example, at the end of the Christmas Present sequence, the Ghost embellishes his famous closing speech by adding an adaptation of Dickens's own words from *The Haunted Man*: "Mark me. From every seed of evil in that boy [Ignorance] a field of ruin shall grow that shall be gathered in and garnered up and sown again in many places till all the earth is overrun with bitter strife. Open and unpunished murder in the city streets will be less guilty in its daily toleration than one such spectacle as this. They [the children, Ignorance and Want] are the growth of man's indifference." Played out in complete darkness, and against an eerie sound effects track, the scene is chilling, pure and simple.

And in the Christmas Future sequence, this *Carol* finds a new way of showing Scrooge the consequences of his actions (or rather his inaction) by expanding on a fragment of the scene where Scrooge visits the Cratchits' home after Tiny Tim has died. In that scene in the book, Scrooge hears the words (read by Peter), "And He took a child, and set him in the midst of them." This adaptation takes the unique step of showing us Tiny Tim's funeral while two of the other Cratchit children, in a slight modification of the text from Dickens's *The Life of Our Lord*, declaim: "He called the little child to Him and took him in His arms and stood among them and said: 'A child like this is the greatest in the kingdom of Heaven. I say to you that none but those who are as humble as little children shall enter into Heaven. Whosoever shall receive one such little child in my name receiveth me, but whosoever hurts one of them, it were better for him that he had a millstone tied around his neck and were drowned in the depths of the sea. The angels are all children.' Our Savior loved the child, and loved all children. Yes, and all the world. No one loved all people so truly, and so well, as He did." (See Matthew 18:2–6.) This brief scene is shattering in its intensity, and yet so simple. And it may well be the purest distillation of Dickens's "*Carol* philosophy" ever committed to film or tape. (See also the entry for *The Gospel According to Scrooge*, 1983.)

*See discussion in Chapter 7.

ALICE
CBS-TV   1981   USA   30m   color

Executive Producer: Madelyn Davis; Bob Carroll, Jr. Producer: Linda Morris; Vic Rauseo. Co-producer: Jerry Madden. Director: Marc Daniels. Writer: Vic Rauseo; Linda Morris. Based on the feature film "Alice Doesn't Live Here Any More." Created by: Robert Getchell. Story Editor: Gail Honigberg. Art Director: Tho E. Azzari; Lynn Griffin. Associate Director: Christine Ballard. Director of Photography: V. Dale Palmer. Music: David Shire.

CAST: Linda Lavin (Alice Hyatt); Vic Tayback (Mel Sharples); Beth Howland (Vera Gorman); Philip McKeon (Tommy Hyatt); Celia Weston (Jolene Hunnicutt); Marvin Kaplan (Henry Bessmyer); Jack Gilford (Jake Farley).

Situation comedy. Episode title: "Mel's Christmas Carol." First broadcast on December 20, 1981.

The usually grumpy Mel, owner of Mel's Diner, becomes our Scrooge when he fires his waitresses for refusing to work until midnight on Christmas Eve. Needless to say, events transpire that will make a new man out of him. In this case, his sole ghostly visitor is his former partner Jake Farley. (Mel and Jake once ran a diner together in Brooklyn and, in a clever touch, this modern day Marley appears chained to a set of stainless steel kitchen utensils.) The usual sitcom stuff; enough said.

A CHRISTMAS CAROL

Burbank Films 1982 Australia 72m color

Producer: Eddy Graham. Executive Producers: Tom Stacey; George Stephenson. Director of Animation: Jean Tych. Editor: Peter Siegl. Script: Alex Buzo. Music: Neil Thurgate. Conductor: Billy Burton. Camera: Tom Epperson; Carole Laird. Character Design: Jean Tych. Storyboard: Steve Lumley. Production Manager: Roz Phillips. Animators: Warwick Gilbert (Supervisor); Maria Szemenyei; Gairden Cooke; Astrid Nordheim; Jacques Muller; Alain Costa; Kaye Watts; Janey Dunn; Pam Lofts; Lucie Quinn; Brenda McKie; Don MacKinnon; John Burge. Animation Layouts: Yosh Barry; Kevin Roper; Jane le Rossingol. Extra Sequences: Kevin Roper. Background Layouts: David Skinner. Backgrounds: John King; Sheila Christofides; Peter Connell; Carol Lumsden; Paul Pattie. Painting Supervisor: Jenny Schowe. Animation Checkers: Kim Craste; Liz Lane.

VOICES: Ron Haddrick; Phillip Hinton; Sean Hinton; Barbara Frawley; Robin Stewart; Liz Horne; Bill Conn; Derani Scarr; Anne Hardy.

Animated feature first syndicated on American television in the fall of 1984.

Part of an ambitious plan to bring all of Dickens's major works to worldwide television and home video audiences via a new series of animated features. While one has to applaud anything that exposes young viewers to Dickens, particularly in a feature-length format, this *Carol*, as well as other titles in the series, can only be described as dull. On the plus side, however, it does feature beautifully drawn and colored backgrounds, as well as a few surprises in terms of content: For example, in the Christmas Past sequence, we see the visit of Ali Baba to young Scrooge's lonely schoolhouse, as well as the poignant look at the happiness that Scrooge's former fiancée has found with another man. In the Christmas Present sequence, Scrooge receives a lesson in how Christmas is kept at an isolated lighthouse, as well as a very effective vision of Ignorance and Want.

In addition to the *Carol*, the following titles are also available on tape: *Oliver Twist*, *Great Expectations*, *David Copperfield*, *A Tale of Two Cities*, *The Old Curiosity Shop*, *Nicholas Nickleby*, and *The Pickwick Papers*. This version of the *Carol* is also available with a Spanish soundtrack, under the title *Posada Navidena*.

A CHRISTMAS CAROL

The Guthrie Theater in association with Elm Video Theater and the Entertainment Channel 1982 USA 87m color

Executive Producer: Donald Schoenbaum. Coordinating Producer: Lou Moore. Producer: Bill Siegler. Director for Television: Paul Miller. Director for the Stage: Jon Cranney. Adaptation: Barbara Field. Music Composed by: Hiram Titus. Associate Producer: Wendy Cornell. Lighting Director: Greg Brunton. Musical Director: Dick Whitbeck. Scenic Designer: Jack Barkla. Costume Designer: Jack Edwards. Production Manager: Michael Facius. Camera: John Clouse; John Feher; Jay Millard; Jake Ostroff. Makeup: Gary Boham. Original Stage Production Conceived by: Stephen Kanee. Executive Producer for The Entertainment Channel: Sarah Frank.

CAST: Marshall Borden (Charles Dickens); Catherine Burns (Mrs. Dickens, Mrs. Fezziwig); Oliver Cliff (John Dickens, Marley's Ghost); Stephen D'Ambrose (Young Scrooge, Ghost of Christmas Yet-to-Come); Jonathan Fuller (Ghost of Christmas Past, Topper); Sara Hennessy (Mamie, Martha Cratchit, Thin Sister); Richard Hilger (Ebenezer Scrooge); Paul Laasko (Dick Wilkins, Poulterer); Chuck Bailey (Tapster, Undertaker); John Lewin (Round Gentleman, Man-with-Newspaper); J. Patrick Martin (Bob Cratchit); Robert Nadir (Fred); Peggy O'Connell (A Miss Fezziwig); Laurence Overmire (Albert Hall); Suzanne Petri (Carol Mistress, Another

Miss Fezziwig, Plump Sister); Martin Ruben (Mr. Fezziwig, Man-with-Snuff Box); Peggy Shoditsch (Mrs. Cratchit); Mim Solberg (Cook); Peter Thoemke (Ghost of Christmas Present); Keliher Walsh (Belle, Mrs. Fred); Alan Woodward (Deaf Gentleman, Man-with-Pound Notes); Kathleen Bock, John Cunningham, Bridget Foreman, Larissa Kokernot, Gregory Leifeld, Peter Passi, Paul Reighard, Debra Spencer, Jaime Warhol (Children); Roxanne Patton Haine, Nancy Moyer, Michael Stayton, Michael Walker, Mary Walker, Sally Ann Wright (Guests and Street People).

Television production of the Guthrie Theater's stage adaptation.

The prestigious Minneapolis-based Guthrie Theater has been staging Barbara Field's excellent adaptation of the *Carol* since 1975. This version of the stage production was produced for television and first aired on the Entertainment Channel in December of 1982; it was subsequently released on home video. Featuring fine performances all around, as well as impressive costumes, set design, and lighting effects, this is a very handsome *Carol*. While it is essentially a faithful transposition of the stage play, cuts, dissolves, and a number of prerecorded transitional segments help it to avoid the "canned theatre" look that can sometimes plague this type of production.

Some interesting touches have been added: For example, in the opening sequence, Scrooge throws a paperweight at his troublesome nephew, who jokingly accepts it as a Christmas present. Later, the reformed Scrooge calls on the nephew under the pretense of recovering the missing paperweight. In the Christmas Past sequence, the paperweight is revealed to have been a gift from Scrooge's young sister; it is, in effect, a concrete connection to what may well be the only warm corner of his heart. And while all versions deal with the young Scrooge's ill-fated romance, this one shows us his initial meeting with Belle, on the night before he begins work at Fezziwig's. The story then flashes forward two years where their breakup occurs at Fezziwig's famous Christmas Eve party — the young Scrooge even bolts from the room shouting, "Humbug!"

However, the most significant departure from tradition is that this version opens in the home of Charles Dickens himself, where we find the author desperately trying to finish writing the *Carol* amidst the distractions of a noisy family Christmas party. After dispersing the revelers, chief among them his troublesome father John, Dickens then serves as a very effective on and off screen narrator. Interestingly, Dickens and

family were dropped when the play was revised for the 1996 season. It underwent further revision in 1997 when the prerecorded voice of Sir John Gielgud was added to provide narration. One certainly hopes that this version will find its way to television or home video.

NOTE: This production also appeared on the Arts & Entertainment Network's *Stage*, in 1984, with an introduction and recurring commentary about Dickens and the *Carol* by actor Len Cariou. Unfortunately, the segments with Cariou are poorly written (or, more to the point, poorly researched) and the distinct impression given is that Dickens's sole motivation in writing the *Carol* was to make money.

A CHRISTMAS CAROL

BBC-TV 1982 Great Britain 60m (4 x 15m) color

Producer: Angela Beeching. Director: Christine Secombe. Script: Janie Grace.

Serial adaptation of the *Carol*, broadcast in four fifteen minute episodes, on December 21-22-23-24, 1982. Narrated by Michael Bryant; illustrations by Paul Birbeck.

A CHRISTMAS CAROL

Granada TV 1982 Great Britain 109m color

Presented by the Royal Opera House, Covent Garden, in association with Virginia Opera Association. Executive Producer: Steve Morrison. Producer: Steve Hawes. Directed for Television by: Dave Heather. Libretto and Music: Thea Musgrave. Producer: David Farrar. Associate Producer: Michael Rennison. Set Designer: Miguel Romero. Costume Designer: Alex Reid. Lighting: Robert Bryan. Choreography: Romayne Grigorova. Conductor: Peter Mark. Leader, The London Sinfonietta: Nona Liddell. **For Television:** Production Manager: Keith Thompson. Production Assistant: Joan Lally. Floor Managers: Josh Dynevor; Ken Mair. Lighting Director: Stuart Wilson. Senior Cameraman: Roger England. Sound Mixer: Mike Dunn. Dubbing Mixer: Alex Dobos. Technical Supervisor: Phil Carr. Musical Associate: Jonathan Burton. Vision Mixer: Anne Birtwell. Videotape Editors: D. L. Heyes; Ron Swain. Makeup: Lois Richardson. Graphics: Carole Ricketts. Research: Helen McMurray. Casting Director: Doreen Jones.

CAST: Frederick Burchinal (Ebenezer Scrooge); Murray Melvin (Spirit of Christmas); Sandra Dugdale (Fan, Belinda Cratchit, Liza Fezziwig, Lucy); Elaine Mary Hall (Caroller, Starving Woman); Eiddwen Harrhy (Belle Fezziwig, Rosie); Vivien Townley (Martha

Cratchit, Laundress); Elizabeth Bainbridge (Mrs. Fezziwig, Charwoman, Aunt Louise); Phyllis Cannan (Caroller, Mrs. Cratchit); Robin Leggate (Bob Cratchit); Terry Jenkins (Mr. Dorrit, Man with snuff box); Philip Gelling (Ben); William Shimell (Fred, Man with red face); Forbes Robinson (Mr. Fezziwig, Fat man); Eric Garrett (Portly Gentleman, Topper); Philip Locke (Marley's Ghost, Great Aunt Ermintrude, Joe); Howard Bell (Mr. Grubb); Ivo Martinez (Tiny Tim); Children Carol Singers from: London Oratory School, St. John the Evangelist School, St. Thomas of Canterbury School, Cardinal Vaughan Memorial School, Ellen Wilkinson School for Girls, St. Clement Dane's School, London Boys Choir; Jean Povey (Children's Coach).

Opera version that was first staged in America, in 1979, by the Virginia Opera Association. This production was first broadcast on Granada TV in England on December 24, 1982.

No attempt will be made here to criticize this production *as an opera*, the opera being a very specialized branch of the arts that this writer has no expertise in. That said, from the standpoint of a general audience, one does not have to be an opera aficionado to appreciate this very impressive, and very accessible, production.

As with most stage adaptations, the action takes place against the backdrop of a strikingly designed set that is highly stylized and yet thoroughly convincing. Add beautiful costumes and lighting effects, and the variety of visual perspectives made possible by multiple cameras, and you have a very good looking *Carol* indeed. What's more, while this performance took place in front of a live audience, the camera's ability to bring us in close to the action (as opposed to the fixed viewpoint of someone sitting in the audience) leaves no doubt that this opera is very well acted as well as very well sung.

In terms of its approach to the original source material, it draws on both the "light" and the "dark" sides of the *Carol*, which is, of course, as it should be. It does, for example, present an appropriately festive party at old Fezziwig's; and the Christmas dinner at nephew Fred's home, which is very effectively moved up to the end of the production *after* the reformed Scrooge awakens on Christmas morning, is a genuinely joyous affair. (The latter sequence then segues into a series of curtain calls during which carol-singing children march through the audience.) But in spite of an overall approach that is quite balanced, this *Carol* nevertheless contains an edge of social criticism that is, at times, quite sharp. Its Scrooge, for example, is capable of incredible callousness, as when he tells the charity solicitor that "when people are

poor, it's because they're stupid and lazy." And, in the Christmas Past sequence, the young Scrooge is equally callous when he justifies his approach to life by telling his unhappy fiancée Belle, "This is not coldness. It is wisdom." Later, in the Christmas Present sequence, Mrs. Cratchit is almost violent in her refusal to drink to Scrooge's health, calling him "a murderer and a thief" and "the one who destroys the Spirit of Christmas."

While experienced operagoers will obviously be able to appreciate this production on a more sophisticated level, for present purposes it is enough to say that *Carol* enthusiasts looking for a fresh treatment of an old standard will not be disappointed. Unfortunately, this version is not available on home video. However, an excellent original cast recording from its initial American run was released in 1980 (Moss Musical Group 3-MMG-302).

THE DUKES

CBS-TV 1983 USA 30m color

A Hanna-Barbera Production. Executive Producer: Joseph Barbera; William Hanna. Producer: Kay Wright. Associate Producer: Doug Paterson. Writer: David R. Toddman. Story Editor: Ray Parker. Supervising Director: Ray Patterson. Executives in Charge of Production: Jayne Barbera; Jean MacCurdy. Supervising Executive: Margaret Loesch.

VOICES: Catherine Bach (Daisy Duke); John Schneider (Bo Duke); Tom Wopat (Luke Duke); James Best (Sheriff Rosco Coltrane); Sorrell Booke (Boss Hogg); Denver Pyle (Uncle Jesse).

Animated series for children (a spinoff from the live-action series *The Dukes of Hazzard*). Episode title: "A Dickens of a Christmas."

This short-lived cartoon series involved an automobile race around the world between the Duke cousins and Boss Hogg. Each episode found them having a new adventure, in a new location. In this episode, which actually qualifies as a formal *Carol* variation, they find themselves in England on Christmas Eve where the scheming and very Scrooge-like Hogg is shown the error of his ways in the traditional Dickensian manner. From a technical standpoint, *The Dukes* represents typical low-grade television animation. However, this episode must certainly be credited for injecting a brief taste of great literature into that wasteland that is Saturday morning children's television. Stars from the live-action series provide voices for their animated counterparts; see *The Dukes of Hazzard* entry, 1980.

MICKEY'S CHRISTMAS CAROL

Walt Disney Productions 1983 USA 25m color

Producer and Director: Burny Mattinson. Story Adapted by: Burny Mattinson; Tony L. Marino; Ed Gombert; Don Griffith; Alan Young; Alan Dinehart. Animators: Glen Keane; Mark Henn; Ed Gombert; Dale Baer; David Block; Randy Cartwright. Effects Animators: Ted Kierscey; Jeff Howard; Mark Dindal; Jack Boyd. Animation Consultant: Eric Larson. Art Direction: Don Griffith. Layout: Michael Peraza, Jr.; Sylvia Roemer; Gary M. Eggleston. Background: Jim Coleman; Brian Sebern; Kathleen Swain; Tia W. Kratter; Donald A. Towns. Production Manager: Edward Hansen. Editors: James Melton; Armetta Jackson. Music Editors: Jack Wadsworth; Dennis Ricotta. Assistant Director: Timothy O'Donnell. Production Assistant: Don Hahn. Song: "Oh, What a Merry Christmas Day"/Words and Music by: Fredrick Searles; Irwin Kostal. Music Composed and Conducted by: Irwin Kostal.

VOICES: Alan Young (Scrooge); Wayne Allwine; Hal Smith; Will Ryan; Eddy Carroll; Patricia Parris; Dick Billingsley; Clarence Nash.

Mickey's Christmas Carol originated as a record album in 1974 and was transferred to the big screen in this "featurette" which marked the long awaited return to a theatrically released film of many favorite Disney characters. (Disney's interest in the *Carol* can actually be traced back a bit further to a charming 1957 illustrated short story, featuring one Cedric Mouse, entitled *Walt Disney's Christmas Carol*; see *McCall's*, December 1957: 29–36.) Not surprisingly, the animation is superb; in fact, if we assume that the Mr. Magoo and Richard Williams versions are highly stylized and therefore very "different looking," then this one unquestionably stands as the best of all "normal looking" animated *Carols*.

However, good looks alone do not a classic make. The script is too heavily truncated, and one is constantly aware of the feeling of being rushed through the familiar story. It is of course fun to see Disney favorites adopting Dickens's familiar roles — Mickey Mouse as Bob Cratchit, Donald Duck as nephew Fred, Goofy as Jacob Marley, and, of course, Scrooge McDuck as Scrooge — but there is simply nothing special about this version. The only thing that distinguishes it from other animated fare in which a familiar stable of cartoon characters (the Flintstones, the Jetsons, et al.) take their turn with Dickens is the prestige, and the undeniably high quality animation, that is implicit in the Disney name. In their televised film review program, both Gene Siskel and Roger Ebert expressed grave disappointment in the film for similar reasons. Ebert, in fact, brilliantly summed up this *Carol* (as well as many others) when he called it

"absolutely a forced march through the same old story."

On the plus side, as with the later Disney/Jim Henson production of *The Muppet Christmas Carol*, this one will undoubtedly introduce many youngsters to both Dickens and the *Carol*, and for that we should indeed be truly grateful.

NOTE: A twenty-five minute promotional short entitled *The Making of Mickey's Christmas Carol* is also available on some home video releases of *Mickey's Christmas Carol*.

THE GOSPEL ACCORDING TO SCROOGE

Hope Productions Int'l   1983   USA   120m color

Executive Producer: Dennis E. Worre. Director: Mark S. Vegh. Adapted and Written by: James P. Schumacher. Music Written by: Thomas Elie; John Worre. Television Producer: John Worre. Stage Producer: Tom Elie. Associate Director: Robert Buchanan. Stage Manager: Michael Kraft. Art/Scenic Designer: Truman Kelly. Director of Choreography: Robert Whitesel. Choreographer: Marilyn Slentz. Orchestra Arranged and Conducted by: Don Hart. Prop Master: Greg Irmiter. Costume Design: Kathy Barnes; Lynnette Uzzell. Secretary: Kathy Worre. Adapted for Television by: Mark S. Vegh. Lighting Directors: John Burch; Denny Carlson. Audio Director: John Parotti. Audio Engineers: Matt Warhol; Cliff Hall. Recording Engineers: Scott Rivard; Craig Hartman. Video Switcher: Alan Harrer. Video Engineer: Larry Eckblad. Video Tape: Randy Berglund. Cameras: Dale Paulson; Steve Fleegel; Mark Meyer; Mike Miller; Michelle Becker; Mark Lundeen. Crane and Crab Operators: Mark Lundeen; Tom Countryman. Key Grip: Dan Jurek. Unit Manager: John Erickson. Production Assistant: Susan Peterson. Editing Engineer: Paula Ribaudo.

CAST: Robert Buchanan (Ebenezer Scrooge); Robert Whitesel (Bob Cratchit); Melanie Burve (Tiny Tim); Kathy Worre (Caroline Cratchit); Eric Worre (Young Adult Scrooge); Debbie Anderson (Young Adult Belle); Charlie Hubbell (Child Scrooge); Larissa Uzzell (Child Belle); Sara Renner (1st Angel); Jim Shumacher (2nd Angel); Joe Vincent (3rd Angel); Buddy VanLoon (Mr. Fezziwig); Linda VanLoon (Mrs. Fezziwig); Donna Bittner (School Teacher); Alida Bradley (Woman Solicitor); Chris Vincent (Man Solicitor); Ken Salaman (Pawn Broker); Kathi Winger (Charwoman); Karin Merkouris (Laundress); Mary Hammarland (Chamber Maid); Stephen Roufs (Uncle Fred); Greg Irmiter, George Hausier, Dave Hanson, Dan Schaffer (Gentlemen); Dave Mulmberg (Voice of "I AM").

Carol variation first broadcast on the Christian Broadcasting Network in December of 1983.

The Gospel According to Scrooge is a musical play that was taped in front of a live (and audible) audience at the Jesus People Church in Minneapolis, Minnesota, and it stands as one of the most original, provocative — and ultimately most important — variations to date. Where it parts company with virtually all others, both the "straight" adaptations as well as the variations, is that it directly confronts the religious precepts which lie at the heart of Dickens's "*Carol* philosophy." Its Scrooge is not motivated by greed or miserliness; nor is he one of the pre–Freudian walking wounded, some lost soul playing out the consequences of an unresolved conflict with his mother, father or lover. Instead, we are presented with a Scrooge whose problems can be traced directly to the fact that he has allowed himself to become separated from God.

In terms of its basic structure, this *Carol* proceeds along more or less traditional lines, although a few exceptions are worth noting. First, actor Dean Jones, serving as host and dressed in casual twentieth-century attire, enters the story at various points and comments on the action. Second, this production takes the unique step of combining Bob Cratchit and Scrooge's nephew into one character — i.e., Scrooge is both Bob Cratchit's employer and his uncle. This interesting change may have been motivated purely by a desire to streamline the story, but it also seems to up the ante a bit for Scrooge by effectively doubling his obligation to the familiar character of Bob Cratchit.

In an early exchange between Scrooge and Cratchit, this *Carol's* tone is set and its conflict defined as Scrooge declares that "[Jesus] has given me no gifts, Cratchit. I've worked for everything I have." A bit later he is perplexed by the fact that his nephew is happy in spite of a lack of money. He consoles himself, however: "My money has made me happy enough. I can spend it alone. I don't need any people. And that God of his, I don't need Him either." But shortly after this speech, it is the voice of God, and not the ghost of Jacob Marley, that warns Scrooge that his soul is in peril, and tells him that he will be visited by three angels.

The cause of this Scrooge's estrangement from God is explored in the Christmas Past sequence, where we learn that young Ebenezer actually came from a happy home but that, at Christmas time, his father was sent to debtor's prison and his mother and sister to the workhouse, leaving the young man feeling deserted and betrayed. Much is revealed as he sings: "But if God is real, loving and strong, then He made a mistake when

He let all this happen. So who can I trust anymore?" The pattern of his life is set when he continues: "I think I'll do it by myself from now on. I won't ask any kind of help from now on."

As a play and as an audiovisual production, this *Carol* earns solid marks all around, although it would be fair to say that it lacks some of the polish that can be found in certain other televised plays from this period. But what distinguishes it, once again, is the fresh angle from which it approaches the source material, and the fact that while it is indeed quite explicit about the message that it seeks to convey, it stops short of being preachy or overly didactic. A certain evangelical fervor is unquestionably in evidence, and while that is something that Dickens might wish to discuss with the playwright, there is nothing in this adaptation that he would not approve of. On the contrary, we have seen that Dickens called for solutions that were moral, and not political or economic, in nature; evidence of this will be found in his books, and in his letters, and in the practical good works that he tried to accomplish in his lifetime. And it is well worth noting, as many Dickens scholars have over the years, that Dickens's faith was very much New Testament oriented; he even created a special adaptation of the Gospels for his children which was originally titled *The Children's New Testament* and posthumously published as *The Life of Our Lord*. Here too, Dickens and the playwright are very much on the same page, so much so that this *Carol* might just as easily have been called *The Gospel According to Dickens*. (See also the entry for the American Conservatory Theatre's 1983 version of the *Carol*.)

FAMILY TIES

NBC-TV 1983 USA 30m color

Ubu Productions. Created by: Gary David Goldberg. Executive Producer: Gary David Goldberg; LLoyd Garver. Producer: Michael J. Weithorn. Director: Will MacKenzie. Teleplay: Rich Reinhart. Story: Robert Caplain. Executive Script Consultant: Alan Uger; Ruth Benett. Associate Producer: June Galas. Director of Photography: Mikel Neiers. Art Director: James F. Claytor. Editor: Gary Anderson. Set Decorator: Chuck Rutherford. Music: Tom Scott.

CAST: Meredith Baxter Birney (Elyse Keaton); Michael Gross (Steven Keaton); Michael J. Fox (Alex Keaton); Justine Bateman (Mallory Keaton); Tina Yothers (Jennifer Keaton); Kaleena Kiff (Young Mallory); Chris Hebert (Young Alex).

Situation comedy. Episode title: "A Keaton Christmas Carol." First broadcast on December 14, 1983.

Family Ties was one of the most popular sit-coms of the 1980s. Although eventually down-played, one of its running gags was the idea that a pair of 1960s flower children had at least two children of their own who were moving in very different directions, eldest daughter Mallory being a materialistic airhead, and eldest son Alex being a staunch conservative. And since Reagan bashing was virtually mandatory on network tele-vision in this period, it naturally follows that Alex, played by Michael J. Fox, is our Scrooge surrogate.

In terms of its basic structure, this one fol-lows the familiar line of most sitcom variations: Alex goes to bed and is visited by younger sister Jennifer as the Ghost of Christmas Past and by sister Mallory as the Ghost of Christmas Future. There is no Marley figure, nor is there a Ghost of Christmas Present. However, the tone is quite different from most sitcom variations: Alex is very mean and inconsiderate toward his family, and he is particularly nasty and disrespectful in declar-ing his dislike of Christmas. And by the time we get to the Christmas Future sequence, the whole affair has descended into farce, with Alex's par-ents and siblings living in a very unfunny carica-ture of abject poverty — Jennifer sells dirt for a living and Mallory, in Alex's words, is "barefoot and pregnant again" — while he leads a life of wealth and splendor in New York. (Alex has arrived by helicopter on Christmas morning and is shown to have become a grotesquely fat, bald-ing, cigar-chomping stereotype of a fatcat capi-talist pig — i.e., an evil Republican.)

Needless to say, Alex wakes up a new man on Christmas morning. However, even this "morn-ing after" sequence contains the flavor of farce as Alex, who has gone shopping at a convenience store, gives his father a cup of coffee, his mother a copy of *TV Guide*, and sister Mallory some beef jerky for presents. While the episode fades out, in true sitcom fashion, on an appropriately syrupy note, it leaves a curiously sour taste behind.

ALVIN'S CHRISTMAS CAROL
DIC/Bagdasarian Productions   1983   USA   23m   color
Creators and Executive Story Editors: Ross Bagdasarian; Janice Karman. Written by: Dianne Dixon. Supervising Producer: Don Spencer. Associate Producers: Brian Miller; Thomas Watkins; Stephen Worth. Production Coordina-tor: Robert Winthrop. Assistant Story Editor: Denice Ferguson. Original Songs and Music: Chase/Rucker Productions, Inc. Executive Art Director: Andy Gaskill. Art Director: Lou Police. Storyboard Supervisor: Mike Sosnowski. Character Design: Andy Gaskill; Sandra. Story-

board Artists: Andy Gaskill; Chris Schouten; Doug McCarthy; Dan Fausett; Scott Jorgenson; Phil Robinson; Dave Feiss; Liz Rathke; Kathy Carr. Animation Timing: Bill Reed; Greg Hill. Lip Assignment: Mike Stribbling; Bill Reed.
CAST: Ross Bagdasarian (Alvin; Simon; David Seville); Janice Karman (Theodore); Thom Watkins; Dody Goodman.
Animated *Carol* variation first broadcast on NBC-TV.

Alvin, Simon and Theodore, who started out as recording stars in 1958 and moved on to tele-vision in 1961, took their turn with the *Carol* dur-ing a 1980s resurgence of chipmunk fever. In this version we find a Scrooge-like Alvin acting in a *very* selfish and inconsiderate manner as Christ-mas draws near. He is shown the error of his ways in the usual manner after falling asleep while writing an essay for school on the true meaning of Christmas.

This is one of the least ambitious animated *Carols* to date; nevertheless, the chipmunks are charming, and Dickens's message is presented in a way that young children can both understand and enjoy.

THE QUALITY CAROL
Philip Crosby Associates, Inc.   1984   USA   36m   color
Written by: Philip B. Crosby. Producer/ Director: Tim A. Tchinski. Project Manager: Wayne A. Fogel. Project Coordinator: Diane Morgan. Assistant Producer/ Director: Michael A. Gorenflo. Art Director/Set Designer: John Krohne. Production Coordinator: Deidre A. Rector. Music: Bob Goldberg. Camera: Carol Cummings; Michael Mijon; Jerry Johus. Steadi-cam: Jim "Smokey" Knudsen. Lighting Director: John Haritan. Floor Director: John Cummings.
CAST: Efrem Zimbalist, Jr. (Emery Spell-man); Pamela Roberts (Rebecca Thompson); Tony Dreyspool (Jacob Masters); Howard Baily (Prof. Barrington).
Educational and motivational short aimed pri-marily at the corporate community.

The message here is that all employees, in-cluding top management, must care about qual-ity now or face unhappy customers and a loss of business in the future. Efrem Zimbalist, Jr., is the Scrooge surrogate in this interesting *Carol* variation which transposes Dickens's basic mes-sage — i.e., caring — to the world of business. A major highlight comes when we learn that the modern Jacob Marley is condemned to an eter-nity of fixing faulty washing machines and toasters that he knowingly allowed to leave his factory. This *Carol* is also available on tape with a Spanish and Japanese soundtrack. It originally appeared as a short story in Philip B. Crosby's *Quality Without Tears* (New York: McGraw-Hill, 1984).

SCROOGE'S ROCK N' ROLL CHRISTMAS

SYNDICATED-TV 1984 USA 44m color
Executive Producer: Rex Sparger. Producer: Bob Franchini. Director: Lou Tedesco. Written by: Rex Sparger. Director of Photography: Tom Harvey. Editor: Kelly Sandefur. Production Designer: Russell Pyle. Associate Producer: Faye Oshimal. Coordinating Producer: Dan Dusek. Associate Director: Bob Graner. Production Assistants: Judie Franchini, Vivica Tedesco. Location Auditor: Pam Caughell. Set Decorators: Carrol Sonntag, Robert Bovill. Costumer: Lid Kellas. Makeup: Roberta Meir, Michele Ross. Cameras: Dan Webb, Chuck Cohen, John Laughridge.

CAST: Jack Elam (Scrooge); Lee Benton ("The Girl"). The following musical performers appear as themselves: The Association; Bobby Goldsboro; Mike Love (of The Beach Boys); Mary MacGregor; Paul Revere & the Raiders; Merrilee Rush; Three Dog Night; Dean Torrence (of Jan & Dean); and introducing Bridget.

SONGS: "Rocking Around the Christmas Tree" (Three Dog Night); "White Christmas" (Merrilee Rush); "Jingle Bells" and "The Christmas Song" (Paul Revere & the Raiders); "Some Children See Him" (Bridget); "Do You Hear What I Hear" (Mary MacGregor and Mike Love); "Jingle Bell Rock" (Mike Love and Dean Torrence); "Sleigh Ride" and "Home for the Holidays" (The Association); "Winter Wonderland" (Bobby Goldsboro); "Have Yourself a Merry Little Christmas" (Mike Love).

Syndicated television special that first aired in December of 1984.

In what has to be the most inane *Carol* variation to date, a young woman who has mistaken Scrooge's office for a record store helps the old grouch (grouchily played by legendary character actor Jack Elam) find some Christmas spirit by showing him visions of various performers singing Christmas songs. The visions appear as they both gaze into a snow globe. (As presented, the young woman and the various performers are obviously of the twentieth century, and Scrooge and his office are obviously of the nineteenth. The story does not explain this conflict, although there is a vague implication that someone has either gone forward or backward in time.) An obviously low-budget affair that must be seen to be believed. The lip-synched musical segments can only be described as embarrassing.

A CHRISTMAS CAROL*

Entertainment Partners (Enterprise) 1984 Great Britain 101m color
Executive Producer: Robert E. Fuisz. Producer: William F. Storke; Alfred R. Kelman. Director: Clive Donner. Teleplay: Roger O. Hirson. Director of Photography: Tony Imi. Editor: Peter Tanner. Production Designer: Roger Murray-Leach. Costume Designer: Evangeline Harrison. Music: Nick Bicat (composer), Tony Britten (conductor). Song "God Bless Us Every One": Tony Bicat (lyrics), Nick Bicat (music). Production Supervisor: Norman Foster. Casting Director: Noel Davis. Assistant Director: Roger Simons. Art Director: Peter Childs; Harry Cordwell.

CAST: George C. Scott (Ebenezer Scrooge); Frank Finlay (Jacob Marley); Angela Pleasence (Ghost of Christmas Past); Edward Woodward (Ghost of Christmas Present); Michael Carter (Ghost of Christmas Yet to Come); David Warner (Bob Cratchit); Susannah York (Mrs. Cratchit); Anthony Walters (Tiny Tim); Roger Rees (Fred Holywell); Caroline Langrishe (Janet Holywell); Lucy Gutteridge (Belle); Nigel Davenport (Silas Scrooge); Young Scrooge (Mark Strickson); Joanne Whalley (Fan); Timothy Bateson (Mr. Fezziwig); Michael Gough (Mr. Poole); John Quarmby (Mr. Hacking); Peter Woodthorpe (Old Joe); Liz Smith (Mrs. Dilber); Brian Pettifer (Ben); Catherine Hall (Meg); John Sharp; Derek Francis.

First broadcast on CBS television on December 17, 1984.

*See discussion in Chapter 7.

A CHRISTMAS CAROL

WNEO-TV 1984 USA 90m color
CAST: Ron Spangler (Ebenezer Scrooge); Jim Bob Stephenson (Narrator); Jeff Richmond (Jacob Marley); Ryan Scarlett (Tiny Tim); Tina Callari (Mrs. Cratchit); Mark Hare (Spirit of Christmas Present); Troy O'Neal, Joseph Cowperthwaite, Peter McAllister, Robert Stephenson (Businessmen); Megan Kerr; Lauren Spies; Matt Haines; Misty Sommers.

Taped stage performance of original musical adaptation. First broadcast on December 22, 1984, on Ohio Public Television.

This adaptation was written by Kent State University graduate William Curtis and was first staged at Kent State's Stump Theatre in 1982. Its 1984 theatrical run began on November 30 and concluded on December 8, and it is presumably one of these performances that was taped for broadcast. The review of the stage production quoted below suggests that it was an interesting and admirable production. [Note: Credits listed above are from the 1984 stage production; they are presumably the same for the broadcast, although this assumption could not be confirmed.]

"The third annual presentation of 'A Christmas Carol' by the Kent State University Theater is alive with color, music and the holiday spirit.

"This light-hearted version of the story of Ebenezer Scrooge is told through music and dancing. The musical starts out on a lively note with the cast appearing from all sides of the theater.

"Scrooge is seen as more than a money miser in this version. In an impressive performance by Ron Spangler, Scrooge is also seen as a very humorous person."—*Daily Kent Stater*, December 4, 1984, p. 7

CHRISTMAS CAROL*

TF1-TV 1984 France 90m color

TF1 Films Production. Director: Pierre Boutron. Adaptation & Script: Pierre Boutron. Director of Photography: Francis Junek. Costumes: Pierre Cadot; Francoise Poillot.

CAST: Michel Bouquet (Ebenezer Scrooge); Pierre Clementi (Spirit of Christmas Past); Georges Wilson (Spirit of Christmas Present); Lisette Malidor (Spirit of Christmas Future); Pierre Olaf (Bob Cratchit); Manuel Bonnet (Young Scrooge); Bernard Bauguil; Philippe Brizard; Serge Cacic; Bernard Cazassus; Philippe Cousin; Pierre Devilder; Arnoud-Didier Fuchs; David Gabison; Jeanne Herviale; Franck Lapersonne; Luc Lavandier; Maiwenn Le Besco; Florent Leriche; Christophe Leroux; Jacques Marchand; Nadine Marcovici; Jean Martin; Laurence Masliah; Andre Mortamais; Jean Mossat; Patrick Poivey; Herve Rigollet; Marie-Christine Rousseau; Frederique Ruchand; Claude Tissot; Valerie-Pascale; Lionel Vitrant.

First broadcast on French television on December 25, 1984.

*See discussion in Chapter 7.

A CHRISTMAS CAROL AND OLIVER TWIST

The Congress Video Group 1985 USA 30m color

Executive Producer: Frederick W. Ramsdell; Nicholas Patruno. Producer: David Oliphant. Director: David Oliphant. Associate Director: Deborah A. Kalman. Technical Supervision: Lester Becker, Custom Films/Video, Inc.

From the Congress Classics Series. This animated home video release contains a fifteen minute condensation of the *Carol* that is followed by a similar treatment of *Oliver Twist*. Utilizing comic book style artwork, this version is essentially a series of still images that are linked with cuts and pans. The soundtrack contains music and narration. A dull and tedious affair. See also the Pendulum's Video Classics version (ca. 1995) below, which uses the same artwork.

FAME

SYNDICATED-TV 1985 USA 60m color

Executive Producer: Patricia Jones; Donald Reiker. Consulting Producer: David de Silva. Created by: Christopher Gore. Director: Nicholas Sgarro. Writer: Robert Caplain. Executive Script Consultant: Ira Steven Behr. Creative Consultant: Carol Gary. Executive Story Editor: Michael McGreevey. Story Editor: Frank South. Associate Producers: Frank Merwald; Randall Torno. Choreography: Jaime Rogers. Assistant Choreographer: Tony B. White. Director of Photography: William W. Spencer. Art Director: Ira Diamond. Editor: Jim McElroy. Unit Production Manager: Denny Salvaryn. First Assistant Director: Win Phelps. Second Assistant Director: Tony Mason. Set Decorator: Sam Gross. Producer's Coordinator: Robert Caplain. Property Master: John Klima. Costumer: Nanrose Buchman. Script Supervisor: Bob Gary. Makeup: Jack Wilson. Hair Stylist: Gloria Montemayor. Music Producer: Gary Scott. Music Supervisor: Harry V. Lojewski. Music Coordinator: Maureen Crowe. Score by: John Debney. "Fame" Theme by: Michael Gore. Lyrics by: Dean Pitchford.

CAST: Debbie Allen (Lydia); Jesse Borrego (Jesse); Loretta Chandler (Dusty); Cynthia Gibb (Holly); Albert Hague (Shorofsky); Billy Hufsey (Christopher); Carlo Imperato (Danny); Carol Mayo Jenkins (Sherwood); Ann Nelson (Mrs. Berg); Nia Peeples (Nicole); Gene Anthony Ray (Leroy); Ken Swofford (Morloch); Isabelle Walker (Francine); David Greenlee (Dwight Mendenhall).

Dramatic series; originally broadcast on network television (NBC), later switched to first-run syndication. Episode title: "Ebenezer Morloch." First broadcast on: Syndicated.

Based on the 1980 theatrical film of the same name, *Fame* followed the ups and downs of students preparing for a career in show business at New York's High School for the Performing Arts. The Scrooge in this episode is Quentin Morloch, the school's overbearing principal, who is acting in a very Scrooge-like manner on Christmas Eve.

Unfortunately, there is little to recommend in this *Carol* variation as it is yet another tired, predictable and perfunctory rehash of the television formula: Designate a recurring character as the Scrooge du jour, have him fall asleep and be visited by other recurring characters in the guise of

Dickens's familiar spirits and then — surprise, surprise — have him wake up a new man on Christmas morning. This version is particularly disappointing in that the one-hour dramatic format, by definition, provides a forum with which something meaningful (or at least reasonably original) can be done with the *Carol*. Sadly, this one more closely resembles the results found in most of the half-hour sitcom variations discussed elsewhere in this filmography: trite, uninspired — and ultimately unnecessary.

BUCKANEEZER SCROOGE

CFCN-TV 1985 Canada 26m color
Executive Producer: Hugh Dunne. Producer: Stephanie Morgan-Black. Director: Stephanie Morgan-Black. Writer: Ron Barge; Jim Lewis. Audio: Joe Dylke. Lighting Director: Sid Bailey. Camera: Dennis Southgate. Production Assistant: Carla Bridgewater. Editor: Mike Morey; Carla Bridgewater. Makeup: John Cox. Puppet Costumer: Lynn McNeil. Set Construction: Wilf Kalina; Oskar Radke. Stage Design: Charles Heine. Production Secretary: Sandra Jonsson.

CAST: Ron Barge (Buckaneezer Scrooge); Jim Lewis (Character Voices); Jennifer Lipka (Boy at Window); Sue Kenyon (Mother); Neil Kenyon (Father); Nicola Kenyon (Teenage Girl); Dana Kvisle (Little Girl); Dennis Collier, Pat Winkler (Couple).

SONGS: "Money Means the Most to Me"; "When the Spirit Moves Me." Words and lyrics by Jim Lewis.

Carol variation for children; produced by CFCN Television in Calgary. First broadcast in December of 1985.

This *Carol*, which is subtitled, "With apologies to Chuck Dickens," and which was produced several years before *The Muppet Christmas Carol*, finds the real life character of Buckaneezer Scrooge mingling with a variety of puppet characters in a very entertaining and essentially faithful adaptation for children. Scrooge is played by Ron Barge, whose character of Buck Shot, in tandem with his puppet pal Benny the Bear, was a popular fixture on Calgary television for thirty years. Produced on a modest budget, with local businesses and volunteers contributing to its making in various ways, *Buckaneezer Scrooge* is a classic example of high-quality, community-based programming at its best. And in this day and age — in any day and age — an opportunity to introduce children to Dickens and his "Ghostly little book" is most welcome indeed.

A JETSON CHRISTMAS CAROL

Hanna-Barbera Productions, Inc.   1985
USA   22m   color

Executive Producer: William Hanna; Joseph Barbera. Story by: Marc Paykuss; Barbara Levy. Producer: Bob Hathcock. Associate Producer: Jeff Hall; Alex Lovy. Creative Supervisor: Joe Taritero. Story Editors: Arthur Alsberg; Tony Benedict; Don Nelson; Art Scott. Supervising Director: Ray Patterson.

VOICES: George O'Hanlon (George Jetson); Penny Singleton (Jane Jetson); Janet Waldo (Judy Jetson); Daws Butler (Elroy Jetson); Don Messick (Astro); Mel Blanc (Cosmo Spacely).

Syndicated animation special broadcast, in a thirty-minute time slot, during December 1985.

This *Carol* appeared during a 1980s revival of *The Jetsons*, Hanna-Barbera's popular Space Age companion to their even more popular Stone Age *Flintstones*. In this one, a Cratchit-like George Jetson is forced to work on Christmas Eve by his very Scrooge-like boss, Mr. Spacely. The latter falls asleep while counting his money and is visited by his former partner (named Marsley) who warns him to expect the usual three visitors. Enjoyable enough, but certainly nothing special. The most interesting moment comes, perhaps, when Jane Jetson and children head off to a crowded mall for some last minute shopping. The more things change…

GEORGE BURNS COMEDY WEEK

CBS-TV 1985 USA 30m color
40 Share Productions, Inc. in association with Universal City Studios, Inc. Executive Producer: Steve Martin; Carl Gottlieb. Producer: George E. Crosby; Paul Perlove. Director: Carl Gottlieb. Written by: Carl Gottlieb; David Axelrod. Creative Consultant: Earl Pomerantz. Executive Story Editor: Pamela Pettler; David Axelrod. Associate Producer: Deborah Hwang; William Cairncross. Theme: Claude Debussy. Conductor: Charles Fox. Music: David Frank. Director of Photography: Ronald W. Browne. Art Director: Francis J. Pezza. Editor: Janice Hampton. Unit Production Manager: Mitchell L. Gamson. First Assistant Director: Barbara Bass. Second Assistant Director: Warren R. Turner. Casting: Don Pemrick. Set Decorator: Michele Guiol. Sound: Thomas E. Allen, Sr. Sound Editor: Phil Haberman. Music Editor: Mary Morlas. Costume Supervisors: Charles DeMuth; Dorothy Baca. Production Executive: Marcia Zwilling.

CAST: George Burns (host); James Whitmore (Ebenezer Scrooge); Samantha Eggar (Mrs. Cratchit); Roddy McDowall (Bob Cratchit); Ed Begley, Jr. (Tiny Tim as an Adult); James Widdoes; Conrad Janis; Carolyn Seymour; Paul Benedict; Severn Darden; Larry Hankin (Mr. Sneavil); Shawn Southwick (Spirit One); Dean Dittman (Portly Man); Bernard Kuby (Publican);

Stuart Rogers (Urchin); Jerry Supiran (Tiny Tim, Jr.); Hy Pyke (Cabbie); Martin Clark (Spirit Three); Signy Coleman (Carol/Alice).

Comedy anthology series. Episode title: "Christmas Carol II: The Sequel." First broadcast on December 11, 1985.

This short-lived series was hosted by George Burns who, on this occasion, informs us that he was seventeen years old when the *Carol* was first published. The premise of this variation is both interesting and funny as, one year after his famous Christmas conversion, Scrooge is visited by the same succession of spirits who inform him that he now has a different kind of problem on his hands. As Burns tells us: "In one short year Ebenezer Scrooge had become honest, openhanded, decent, charitable, cheerful, considerate, and generous. A pushover." And indeed he is taken advantage of by nearly everyone he meets, including Mr. and Mrs. Cratchit, who have become a pair of scheming weasels, and Tiny Tim, who turns out to be an obnoxious brat. In the end he undergoes a second "reformation" but does not return to his former life of greed and avarice as one might expect. Instead, he simply resolves to be "hard but fair" (on this Christmas morning, he sends the Cratchits a turkey that is "small enough for the average family of six").

This *Carol* features solid production values and fine acting, and its premise, once again, is a good one. Unfortunately, its script is virtually nonexistent; at best, one is aware of an amusing central idea, but genuine laughs are few and far between. In the end, what could have been a brilliant farce plays like just another limp television sketch.

NOTE: For a *Carol* sequel that is brilliant in every sense, see Andrew Angus Dalrymple's *God Bless Us Every One!* (New York: St. Martin's Press, 1985). This is a very funny book which, if faithfully filmed or televised, would produce the first screwball comedy *Carol*!

CHRISTMAS PRESENT

Telekation International   1985   Great Britain   75m   color

Producer: Barry Hanson. Director: Tony Bicat. Screenplay: Tony Bicat. Cinematography: Gabriel Beristain. Editor: Bill Shapter. Production Design: Nigel Phelps. Designer: Jocelyn James. Music: Nick Bicat. Costumes: Andrea Galer. Sound: Terry Hardy.

CAST: Peter Chelsom (Nigel Playfayre); Bill Fraser (Sir Percy); Lesley Manville (Judy Tall); Karen Meagher (Anne); Hetty Baynes (Pamela); Richard Ireson (Ned); Badi Uzaman (Mr. Mehrban); Jamila Massey (Mrs. Mehrban);

Danny Wooder (Viv); Clive Parker (Gos); Mark Harvey (Sticky); Sohan Maharaj.

An original story (shot on 16mm film) which was shown at the 1985 London Film Festival. While not a formal variation per se, it was clearly inspired by the *Carol*. First broadcast on England's Channel 4 on December 19, 1985.

"The odds against the occurrence of a modern Christmas fable which is both charming and anti-sentimental are overwhelming; *Christmas Present* (Channel 4), a film by Tony Bicat, beat them triumphantly.

"It was a scenario with more ingredients than a plum pudding. The central story concerned an obnoxious, overprivileged City whizz-kid bound by a potty tradition of his bank to award a turkey and some money to a selected specimen of the deserving poor — failure to comply would end his career. It was a delightful performance by Peter Chelsom, who appeared reptilian but capable of redemption as he lost the address of the appointed paupers and began a desperate struggle to meet his deadline.

"The film was spiced with Dickensian allusions, and enlivened by fantasy sequences as the characters dreamed their private visions of happiness. The figures of Mary and Joseph, in biblical dress, also wandered through the London landscape but were less effective in probing the spirit of the season."—*The* [London] *Times*, December 20, 1985, p. 13

"Although we are about to be drenched and drowned in a swelling ocean of Christmas TV programmes, we may be fairly certain that few of them will have any real connection with the meaning and spirit of the holiday.

"A special welcome, then, to last night's enterprising *Christmas Present* (Channel 4). Written and directed by Tony Bicat, this was an intelligently considered seasonal drama deeply rooted in the myths and messages of Christmas."—*Daily Mail*, December 20, 1985, p. 19

JOHN GRIN'S CHRISTMAS

ABC-TV   1986   Canada   60m   color

Guillaume/Margo Productions. Executive Producers: Phil Margo; Robert Guillaume. Producer: Mark Brull. Director: Robert Guillaume. Written by: Charles Eric Johnson. Director of Photography: Anthony Richmond. Editor: Harvey E. Stambler. Art Director: David Jaquest. Production Manager: Gerry Arbeid. Assistant Director: Karen Pike. 2nd Assistant Director: Gordon Yang. Music: Mitch Margo; Dennis Dreith. Song: "You Forgot About Love"/Written and Performed by Kevin Guillaume. Casting: Eleanor Ross/Los Angeles; Karen Hazzard/Toronto. Assistant Art Director: Anne Richardson. Set Dresser: Alexa Anthony. Props: Alex Kutschera. Camera Operator: Paul Mitchnick. Special Effects: Ted Ross.

CAST: Robert Guillaume (John Grin); Roscoe Lee Browne (Christmas Past); Ted Lange (Christmas Present); Geoffrey Holder (Christmas Future); Alfonso Ribeiro (Timothy "Rocky" Williams); Candy Ann Brown (Mrs. Oliver); Kevin Guillaume (Sam Oliver); H. B. Barnum (Preacher); Philip Akin (Union Representative); Jo-Ann Brooks; Tony Craig (John Grin — age 21); Phyllis Marshall; Richard Mills; Charlene Richards (Maria); Djanet Sears (Mrs. Williams); Bobbi Sherron (Mrs. Clark); Jackie Richardson (Mrs. Alcott); Robert O'Ree (Tramp); Lloyd White (Kramer); Melissa Hill-Guillaume (Mary); Kyler Richie (Billy).

Made-for-television variation that originally aired on December 6, 1986.

This heavily truncated updating was the first attempt by film or television to present the *Carol* with a black cast. (A short-lived musical entitled *Comin' Uptown* [also known as *Christmas Is Comin' Uptown*] with a black cast featuring Gregory Hines premiered on Broadway on December 20, 1979.) This version features black performers in all of the central and supporting roles. However, it is very important to note that this production does not appear to have been an attempt to create a "black *Carol*" per se; indeed, an understanding of the universality of Dickens's message is clearly in evidence here. John Grin is a human being who just happens to be black, and, like all human beings, he is capable of losing his way in life — and of finding it again.

Apart from the issue (or non-issue) of race, *John Grin's Christmas* should be remembered as an interesting but somewhat disappointing production — disappointing in the sense that its central idea cries out for a feature-length treatment. Unfortunately, the decision to tell the tale in less than one hour requires a breakneck pace that leaves little room for details and character development. This *Carol* eliminates the famous Christmas Eve visit from Grin's former partner and jumps right to the appearance of the character identified as Christmas Past; it also jettisons the Tiny Tim character.

And yet, in spite of this streamlining, we do get some interesting insight into what makes this Scrooge tick when we are told that, as a boy, he lost his family in a fire at Christmastime and that he subsequently took refuge in the pursuit of wealth. As he says in the Christmas Past sequence, "You're nothing without money ... Money [not love] makes life worth living." And finally, Robert Guillaume's performance is worth noting here because, in spite of the lack of time

for character development, there are strong suggestions that his Scrooge is a very complex and deeply troubled individual. Guillaume is an interesting actor who, like George C. Scott, is capable of conveying a unique combination of brooding intelligence and smirking arrogance that adds a curious and somewhat disturbing undercurrent to this modern *Carol*.

NOTE: 1997's *Ms. Scrooge* with Cicely Tyson presents a more integrated view of Scrooge's circle of family and business associates. See the entry for *Ms. Scrooge* below. See also Davis pp. 229–232.

MOONLIGHTING

ABC-TV   1986   USA   60m   color

Executive Producer: Glenn Gordon Caron. Co-Executive Producer: Jay Daniel. Director: Ed Sherin. Written by: Debra Frank; Carl Sautter. Music: Alf Clausen. Director of Photography: Gerald Perry Finnerman. Production Design: James J. Agazzi. Costumes: Robert Turturice. Film Editor: Roger Bondelli.

CAST: Cybill Shepherd (Maddie Hayes); Bruce Willis (David Addison); Allyce Beasley (Agnes Dipesto); Richard Libertini (Albert, Maddie's guardian angel); Lucy Lee Flippen (Secretary); Lionel Stander (Max); Charles Rocket (Richard Addison); Scanlon Gail; William Hubbard Knight; Eric Poppick; Tim Ryan; James F. Kelly; Eric Love.

Comedy/Drama series. Episode title: "It's a Wonderful Job." First broadcast on December 16, 1986.

This is not a variation of the *Carol*, even though it has acquired that reputation over the years. It is a variation of Frank Capra's classic 1946 film *It's a Wonderful Life* and, notwithstanding the extent to which the former has unquestionably influenced the latter, they are indeed two separate animals. In this version, Maddie Hayes is feeling overwhelmed by the pressures of running her detective agency and wishes that she had never gotten into the business. Needless to say she gets her wish when her guardian angel appears and whisks her two and a half years into the future to witness the results of that wish come true.

If one must look for *Carol* connections here, the only real similarity is that fact that Maddie and her angel are invisible to those that they encounter in the future, whereas in *It's a Wonderful Life*, George and Clarence can be seen. And there is the fact that the setting is Christmas time and Maddie is acting more than a bit grumpy about the office; hence, one automatically thinks of Scrooge. However, she is not normally a Scrooge-like character. Instead, in this episode, she is the victim of an unfortunate chain of circumstances — just like George Bailey, who is also not normally a Scrooge-like character. And there is also one throwaway reference to Tiny Tim. But these are all minor points, and this is, once again, not a *Carol* variation.

SEE HEAR!

BBC-TV 1987 Great Britain color

CAST: Doug Alker; Dorothy Miles; Craig Flynn; John Lee; Maureen Denmark; Clive Mason. Also featuring children from the Heathlands School: Craig Russell; Billy Harris; Shazia Nasreen; Kate Pepper.

A special adaptation of the *Carol* for deaf and hearing-impaired viewers in which the story is told via sign language. First broadcast by the BBC and BBC2 on December 22, 1987.

SCROOGED

Paramount 1988 USA 101m color

Producer: Richard Donner & Art Linson, in association with Mirage Productions. Director: Richard Donner. Written by: Mitch Glazer; Michael O'Donoghue. Director of Photography: Michael Chapman. Production Designer: J. Michael Riva. Editing: Fredric Steinkamp; William Steinkamp. Co-Producer: Ray Hartwick. Associate Producer: Jennie Lew-Tugend. Costume Designer: Wayne Finkleman. Music Score: Danny Elfman. Casting: David Rubin. Production Associate: Peter Frankfurt. Set Decorator: Linda DeScenna. Art Director: Virginia L. Randolph. Camera Operator: Michael A. Genne. Special Makeup Effects: Thomas R. Burman; Bari Dreiband-Burman. Special Effects Coordinator: Allen L. Hall. Special Visual Effects: Dream Quest Images. Visual Effects Supervisor: Eric Brevic.

CAST: Bill Murray (Frank Cross); Karen Allen (Claire Phillips); John Forsythe (Lew Hayward); John Glover (Brice Cummings); Bobcat Goldthwait (Eliot Laudermilk); David Johansen (Ghost of Christmas Past); Carol Kane (Ghost of Christmas Present); Robert Mitchum (Preston Rhinelander); Nicholas Phillips (Calvin Cooley); Michael J. Pollard (Herman); Alfre Woodard (Grace Cooley); Mabel King (Gramma); John Murray (James Cross); Jamie Farr (Jacob Marley [TV]); Robert Goulet (Himself); Buddy Hackett (Scrooge [TV]); John Houseman (Himself); Lee Majors (Himself); Pat McCormick (Ghost of Christmas Present [TV]); Brian Doyle Murray (Earl Cross); Mary Lou Retton (Herself); Al "Red Dog" Weber (Santa Claus); Jean Speegle Howard (Mrs. Claus); June Chandler (June Cleaver); Michael Eidam (Wally Cleaver); Mary Ellen Trainor (Ted); Bruce Jarchow (Wayne);

Sanford Jensen, Jeffrey Joseph, Dick Blasucci (Executives); Peter Bromilow (Archbishop); Bill Marcus, Cal Gibson (IBC Guards); Damon Hines (Steven Cooley); Tamika McCollum (Shasta Cooley); Koren McCollum (Randee Cooley); Reina King (Lenzil Cooley); Paul Tuerpe (Stage Manager); Lester Wilson (Choreographer); Ronald Strang (Art Director); Kate McGregor-Stewart (Lady Censor); Jack McGee, Bill Hart (Carpenters); Kathy Kinney (IBC Nurse); Ralph Gervais (Mouse Wrangler).

One wants to be fair to this theatrically released updating of the *Carol*, but it ain't easy. *Scrooged* does contain some very funny bits of business, as well as a genuinely funny idea or two, but the end result is a very coarse, cold, and off-putting film that will leave even the most charitable viewers among us with a bad taste in our mouths.

On the plus side, there *is* something wickedly brilliant about presenting us with a modern Scrooge, played by Bill Murray, in the guise of a slimy network television executive. The story revolves around his efforts to stage a live international broadcast of *A Christmas Carol*; this establishes the context for a devastatingly funny, over-the-top assault on television (and television culture) that recalls some of the wilder moments of films like *Network* and *A Face in the Crowd*. For example, one has to love even the very idea of a *Carol* adaptation that casts Mary Lou Retton as a somersaulting Tiny Tim, and Buddy Hackett as Scrooge! The film is at its best when it draws on this goofy, absurd, and subtly cynical brand of humor.

Unfortunately the film simply does not ring true when, after a ninety minute barrage of forced hipness and Murray's patented blend of smartass shtick and mock sincerity, not to mention a visit from a Ghost of Christmas Future that appears to have escaped from one of the *Alien* films, we are suddenly expected to believe that it wants us to take Dickens's message seriously. As noted elsewhere, Dickens's message is rooted in some rather old-fashioned religious precepts and this, like it or not, has never been the stock-in-trade of the *Saturday Night Live* school of humor that spawned this film.

TAKUGINAI

Inuit Broadcasting Corporation 1988 Canada 30m color

Producer: Leetia Inneak.

Inukitut language children's program. First broadcast in December of 1988.

The Inuit Broadcasting Corporation has been bringing television programming, in the Inukitut language, to Canada's remote Arctic regions since 1982. Like radio broadcasting before it, television has proved to be an important tool in helping the Inuit people to explore and celebrate their rich cultural heritage. It also makes it possible to communicate in an area where travel is difficult and very often impossible; as an IBC promotional brochure puts it: "The only roads connecting communities are electronic."

In the tradition of programs like *Sesame Street*, *Takuginai*, which translates as *Look Here*, is a program that offers a pleasant combination of entertainment and education for young children. This particular episode includes a brief segment (just over three minutes in length) in which the story of the *Carol* is told via a series of colorful drawings with accompanying narration. As with several similar productions listed elsewhere in this filmography, there is no motion per se; instead, cuts and a panning and zooming camera advance a sequence of still images. The results are most satisfying as children are given an entertaining introduction to the *Carol* and older viewers are reminded of the universality of its message.

BLACKADDER'S CHRISTMAS CAROL

BBC-TV 1988 Great Britain 43m color
Producer: John Lloyd. Director: Richard Boden. Written by: Richard Curtis; Ben Elton. Designer: Antony Thorpe. Music: Howard Goodall.

CAST: Rowan Atkinson (Blackadder); Tony Robinson (Baldricks); Miranda Richardson (Queens Elizabeth I/Asphyxia XIX); Stephen Fry (Lords Melchett/Frondo); Hugh Laurie (Princes Regent/Pigmot); Robbie Coltrane (Spirit of Christmas); Miriam Margolyes (Queen Victoria); Jim Broadbent (Prince Albert); Patsy Byrne (Nursie/Bernard); Denis Lill (Beadle); Pauline Melville (Mrs. Scratchit); Philip Pope (Lord Nelson); Nicola Bryant (Millicent); Ramsay Gilderdale (Ralph); David Barber/Erkan Mustafa/David Nunn (Enormous Orphans).

Episode in the popular *Blackadder* television series. First broadcast on December 23, 1988.

This production starts out in Victorian London where we meet Ebenezer Blackadder, described as "the kindest and loveliest man in London." (Our hero is played by Rowan Atkinson, best known to American audiences as *Mr. Bean*.) He is shown visions of his nefarious relatives in the past (Elizabethan and Regency periods) and in a distant science-fiction tinged future. The result is more a *Carol* inversion than parody as this Scrooge wakes up on Christmas morning and decides that it is better to be mean and greedy than kind and generous. As with all extended television skits, a certain straining to keep the gag

going can be detected here and there. However, this one makes the most of an inspired comic conception, and a spirit of broad, irreverent farce prevails — and it does not resort to the nastiness and deliberate lack of respect for the *Carol* found in some other recent variations.

CONTO DE NATAL

1988 Portugal
Director: Lauro António. Cinematography: Manuel Costa e Silva. Sound: Carlos Alberto Lopes. Editor: Teresa Tainha.

CAST: Raul Solnado; Adelaide João.

Short film made for Portuguese television.

THE FAMOUS TEDDY Z

CBS-TV 1989 USA 30m color
CAST: John Cryer (Teddy Z); Alex Rocco (Al Floss). GUEST: Bill Macy.

Situation comedy. Episode title: "Season's Greetings from Al Floss." First broadcast on December 11, 1989.

This short-lived series followed the exploits of Teddy Zakalokis, a very unlikely (and untalented) Hollywood talent agent. The Scrooge surrogate here is Teddy's overbearing fellow-agent, Al Floss, who gets the usual Dickens treatment on Christmas Eve. Serious analysis of this type of sitcom *Carol* is ultimately pointless. However, it is interesting, and perhaps a bit revealing, to note how even a series that no one watches or cares about will jump on the *Carol* bandwagon when searching for a reliable if unoriginal way to fill thirty minutes.

MATLOCK

NBC-TV 1989 USA 60m color
CAST: Andy Griffith (Ben Matlock); Don Knotts (Les); Nancy Stafford (Michelle); Peter Michael Goetz (Steven Abbot); Bill Kalmenson (Stewart Lister); Ron Hale (Eldon Williams); Brooke Bundy (Sherry Lister); Mary Cadorette (Donna); Thomas Ryan (Carl Lister); T. J. Evans (Matthew); Timothy Eyster (Street Kid No. 1).

Dramatic Series. First Broadcast on December 19, 1989.

In this episode, crafty but charming lawyer Ben Matlock defends the Scrooge-like owner of a toy store who has been accused of murder.

A DIFFERENT WORLD

NBC-TV 1989 USA 30m color
Producer: Debbie Allen. Director: Debbie Allen. Written by: Cheryl Gard. Producer: Joanne Curley Kerner. Supervising Producer: Susan Fales. Co-Executive Producers: Margie Peters; Thad Mumford. Created by: William H. Cosby, Jr., Ed.D.

CAST: Jasmine Guy (Whitley Gilbert); Kadeem Hardison (Dwayne Wayne); Sinbad (Walter Oakes); Charnele Brown (Kim Reese); Cree Summer (Freddie Brooks); Glynn Turman (Colonel Clayton Taylor); Dawnn Lewis (Jaleesa Vinson); Lou Myers (Vernon Gaines); Diahann Carroll (Marion, Whitley's mother); Brandi Royale Petway (Young Whitley); Kenneth Washington.

Situation comedy. First broadcast on December 21, 1989.

Self-centered Whitley, who is in a nasty mood at Christmastime, is shown the error of her ways via the usual succession of ghostly visitors. This one is typical of many recent sitcom *Carols* in which the familiar Dickensian framework is trotted out but no one knows what to do with it.

THE SPIRITS OF CHRISTMAS
Todd Rogers 1990 USA
Amateur production shot on video by Connecticut high school student Todd Rogers. This version transforms Dickens's London into an urban housing project and Scrooge into an unscrupulous drug dealer.

A CHRISTMAS CAROL
Fuji Television/Saban International Services 1991 USA/Japan 28m color
Executive Producer: Jerald E. Bergh. Producer: Eric S. Rollman. Supervising Producer: Winston Richard. Voice Director: Doug Parker. Writer: Mark Ryan-Martin. Story Editor: Tony Oliver. Music: Shuki Levy. Casting: Josanne B. Lovick Productions.
VOICES: Richard Newman (Narrator, Scrooge); Doug Parker (Bob); Mike Donovan (Marley); Lisa Bunting (Mrs Cratchet, Nun); Al Jordan (Mr Blister); Llainia Lindberg (Molly, Street Urchin, Sally); Kevin Hayes (Uncle Bill); Andrew Seebaran (Zach, Boy Scrooge); Julie E. Fay (Ghost #1, Ghost #2); Katie Murray (Ghost #3); Tony Ail (Tiny Tim); Phil Hayes (Pharmacist); Doug Parker (Butcher); Britain Durham (Kitten).
Animated quasi-parody that is clearly "inspired" by the *Simpsons* and *Beavis and Butt-head* brand of animation and humor. Vulgar, offensive, and thoroughly unnecessary. This was released on home video in 1991, but there appears to be no record of television broadcasts.

SISTERS
NBC-TV 1991 USA 60m color
A Cowlip Production in association with Lorimar Television.
Dramatic series. Episode title: "Egg Nog." First broadcast on December 21, 1991.

CAST: Swoosie Kurtz (Alex); Sela Ward (Teddy); Patricia Kalember (Georgie); Julianne Phillips (Frankie); Ed Marinaro (Mitch); Tony Jay (Charles Dickens); David Gianopoulus (Victor); Riff Regan (Young George); Jill Novick (Teenage Teddy); Tasia Schutt (Little Frankie).

This rather pretentious soap-opera was set in the quiet town of Winnetka, Illinois, and centered around the lives and loves of the four Reed sisters. In this episode, a general lack of Christmas spirit, as well as an outbreak of salmonella, make for a less than joyous holiday. However, a Scrooge-like Teddy manages to salvage her Christmas in a meaningful way by spending a quiet evening with "Charles Dickens."

THE MUPPET CHRISTMAS CAROL
Jim Henson Productions/Walt Disney Pictures 1992 USA color 89m
Executive Producer: Frank Oz. Producer: Brian Henson; Martin G. Baker. Director: Brian Henson. Screenplay: Jerry Juhl. Co-Producer: Jerry Juhl. Director of Photography: John Fenner. Film Editor: Michael Jablow. Production Designer: Val Strazovec. Line Producer: David Barron. Original Score: Miles Goodman. Songs: Paul Williams.
MAJOR ON-SCREEN CAST: Michael Caine (Ebenezer Scrooge); Kermit the Frog (Bob Cratchit); Miss Piggy (Emily Cratchit); The Great Gonzo (Charles Dickens); Rizzo the Rat (Himself); Fozzie Bear (Fozziwig). MUPPET PERFORMERS AND OTHER CAST MEMBERS: Dave Goelz (The Great Gonzo/Robert Marley/Bunsen Honeydew/Betina Cratchit); Steve Whitmire (Rizzo the Rat/Bean Bunny/Kermit the Frog/Beaker/Bellinda Cratchit); Jerry Nelson (Tiny Tim Cratchit/Jacob Marley/Ma Bear); Frank Oz (Miss Piggy/Fozzie Bear/Sam Eagle/Animal); David Rudman (Peter Cratchit/Old Joe/Swedish Chef); Donald Austen, Jerry Nelson (Ghost of Christmas Present); Donald Austen, Rob Tygner (Ghost of Christmas Yet to Come); Karen Prell, Rob Tygner, William Todd Jones, Jessica Fox (Ghost of Christmas Past); Steven Mackintosh (Fred); Meredith Braun (Belle); Robin Weaver (Clara); Raymond Coulthard, Russell Martin, Theo Sanders, Kristopher Milnes, Edward Sanders (Young Scrooge); Anthony Hamblin (Boy #1); Fergus Brazier (Boy #2); David Shaw Parker (Voice of Old Joe); Mr. Caine's Double (Reginald Turner).
SONGS: "Overture"; "Scrooge"; "Room in Your Heart"; "Good King Wenceslas"; "One More Sleep 'Til Christmas"; "Marley and Marley"; "Christmas Past"; "Chairman of the Board"; "Fozziwig's Party"; "When Love Is Gone"; "It Feels Like Christmas"; "Christmas Scat"; "Bless

Us All"; "Christmas Future"; "Christmas Morning"; "Thankful Heart"; "Finale — When Love Is Found/It Feels Like Christmas."

Theatrically released *Carol* variation.

You say you're looking for a Christmas classic that both children and adults can really cherish? Something special, maybe with some Muppets in it? If so, you are referred to the 1978 Emmy Award winning special entitled *Christmas Eve on Sesame Street* which is still shown on television and is available on home video. This is not to suggest that there is anything terribly wrong with *The Muppet Christmas Carol*; it's just that it is clearly not the instant classic that its marketers would have us believe it to be.

At the heart of the film is Michael Caine who at first glance does not seem entirely comfortable in his role as the screen's first cockney Scrooge. However, Caine is a fine and uniquely charming actor, and on closer examination one notices that he turns in a very understated performance that ultimately upstages his more colorful co-stars. And it is interesting to note that in this predominantly upbeat *Carol*, there are strong suggestions that this Scrooge is genuinely tortured by his past, as in the scene in which, after witnessing himself as a schoolboy left all alone for the holidays, he tells us that "They [his childhood Christmasses] were all very much the same. Nothing ever changed."

As for the story itself, it *is* fun to see Muppets and humans interacting in a beautifully realized recreation of Victorian London, and a few interesting twists have been added as well: For example, Charles Dickens himself, played by the Great Gonzo, appears on screen and narrates the tale, and the pair of heckling old men from *The Muppet Show* turn up as Jacob *and Robert* Marley on Christmas Eve. But apart from Caine's interesting performance, nothing of any significance is added to, or drawn from, the *Carol* itself, and the feeling that one is actually watching a feature-length commercial is never very far off. It is likely, though, that this film will introduce many young children to both Dickens and the *Carol*, and, given the rampant illiteracy and electronic barbarism that children are inundated with these days, that is no small accomplishment.

BRER RABBIT'S CHRISTMAS CAROL

Magic Shadows, Inc. (Video Treasures) 1992 USA color 60m

Written, Produced and Directed by: Al Guest; Jean Mathieson. Executive Producers: Irv Holender; Michael R. Ricci. Associate Producers: Michael S. Smith; Fellcimo Reyes. Music: Joey Viera; David Seibels. Animation: Neil Breen; Paul Rosevear; Ciso Santiago; Boy Cibulo; Carol

Kearns; Dani Milla; Aldan Walsh; Ray Sherlock; Egay Francisco; Damien Farrell; Vic Santiago; Danny Dela Cruz. Assistant Animators: Stella Kearns; Aaron Corr; Salve Abo; Boyet Amaranto; Mon Flores; Marie Bonis; John Flanagan; Zeldy Partosa; Al Soltura; Cecillio Legaspi. Layout: Bay Cabangbang; Dioni Roquqe; Angel Martinez; Ruben Yandoc. Backgrounds: Gerry Glynn; Marilyn Magsaysay; Mark Redulla; David Nolan; John Robbins; Bob Lopez; Cris Merang; Ngo Dong Sahn.

VOICES: Ginny Tyler; Christopher Smith; Tom Hill; David Knell. Additional Dialogue: William Mathieson.

Syndicated animated *Carol* variation.

Certainly no classic, but this may be the most unique animated *Carol* to date as Joel Chandler Harris's *Uncle Remus* stories merge with Dickens. Brer Fox is the Scrooge surrogate who is shown the error of his ways when the animals stage the *Carol* at their local theatre. In this one, the reformed Scrooge orders smoked turkey, yams and berry pie for the entire town on Christmas morning!

A CHRISTMAS CAROL

A BBC/Arts & Entertainment Network/ RPTA Primetime Co-production 1993 Great Britain color 86m

Production: Christopher Gable. Director: Kriss Rusmanis. Choreography: Massimo Moricone. Music: Carl Davis. Set and Costume Design: Lez Brotherston. Original Scenario by Carl Davis developed with Christopher Gable. BBC Philharmonic: Tom Bangbala (Leader); John Pryce-Jones (Conductor). Lighting Design: Paul Pyant. **Northern Ballet Theatre:** Artistic Director: Christopher Gable. Administrator: Stephen Revell. Technical Director: Steve Hodgkinson. Assistants to the Artistic Director: Elaine McDonald; Graham Fletcher. Company Manager: Mark Skipper. Chief Electrician: Stuart Lister. Wardrobe Mistress: Kim Brassley. BBC: Graphic Design: Linda Sherwood-Page. Makeup Design: Joyce Dean. OB Stage Manager: Craig MacGregor. Vision Supervisor: Hedley Parker. Cameras: Dave Taylor; Steve Coleman; Steve Porritt; Ivars Galdins. Vision Mixer: Sue Thorne. Production Co-ordinator: Anne Murray. Engineering Manager: Dave Parker. Videotape Editors: John Pearce; Mike Curd; Spencer Hill. Sound Supervisor: Don Hartridge. Television Lighting: Steve Whittaker. Executive Producer: Bob Lockyer. Recorded at the Victoria Theatre (Halifax).

CAST: Jeremy Kerridge (Scrooge); William Walker (Bob Cratchit); Polly Benge (Mrs. Cratchit); Katherine Fletcher, Claire Rowland

(Daughters); Christopher Akril (Son); Ryan Ward (Tiny Tim); Matthew Madsen (Ghost of Marley); Lorena Vidal (Ghost of Christmas Past); Royce Neagle (Ghost of Christmas Present); Steven Wheeler (Ghost of Christmas Future); Graham Fletcher (Mr. Fezziwig); Victoria Westall (Mrs. Fezziwig); Fergus Logan (Young Scrooge); Jayne Regan (His Fiancée); Peter Parker (Scrooge's Nephew); Graciela Kaplan (His Wife); with Artists of the Northern Ballet Theatre.

Ballet version first broadcast on December 25, 1993.

A beautiful production that is surprisingly accessible and thoroughly enjoyable. The story is told almost entirely through dance and pantomimic action on an impressive and highly mobile set with Carl Davis's sumptuous score complementing and propelling the action. While watching, it is interesting to note how one's knowledge of the *Carol* silently kicks in and provides a kind of subliminal framework that makes this virtually wordless production very easy to follow; one suspects, however, that it would be rather tough going for anyone unfamiliar with the story. From a thematic standpoint, it is also worth noting that it is quite faithful to the spirit of Dickens's original text; in this regard, one particularly interesting touch is that Scrooge's isolation from the world around him is underscored by the fact that he does not dance until he wakes up, a new man, on Christmas morning. A variety of camera angles and shots, as well as some basic but well-executed optical effects, keep things flowing briskly and smoothly. The overall effect is anything but static or stagebound. All things considered, this is one of the most unique and diverting *Carol* variations to date.

NORTHERN EXPOSURE

CBS-TV 1994 USA 60m color

Created by: Joshua Brand; John Falsey. Consulting Producer: Sam Egan. Supervising Producers: Cheryl Bloch; Michael Fresco. Co-Executive Producers: Michael Vittes; Robin Green; Jeff Melvoin. Director: James Hayman. Writer: Jeff Melvoin. Executive Producers: David Chase; Diane Frolov; Andrew Schneider. Co-Producer: Martin Bruestle. Executive Story Editor: Mitchell Burgess. Associate Producers: Joe Lazarov; John Vreeke. Post Production Supervisor: Steve Turner. Director of Photography: Gordon C. Lonsdale. Production Designer: Woody Crocker. Film Editor: David Strohmaier. Music: David Schwartz. Unit Production Manager: Charles S. Carrol. First Assistant Director: Patrick McKee. Second Assistant Director: Brian Faul. Costume Designer: Katharine Bentley.

Casting: Megan Branman. Seattle Casting: Heidi L. Walker. Chief Lighting Technician: Jack Todd. Key Grip: Bob Blair. Camera Operator: Paul Pollard. Art Director: Kenneth J. Berg. Property Master: Paul Byers.

CAST: Rob Morrow (Dr. Joel Fleischman); Barry Corbin (Maurice Minnifield); Janine Turner (Maggie O'Connell); John Cullum (Holling Vincouer); Darren E. Burrows (Ed Chigliak); John Corbett (Chris Stevens); Cynthia Geary (Shelly Tambo); Elaine Miles (Marilyn Whirlwind); Peg Phillips (Ruth-Anne Miller); Jerry Adler (Rabbi); Jill Gascoine; Moultrie Patten (Wolf); Earl Quewezance (Eugene); Mitchell Thrush (Pilot); Bob Morrisey (Guy Le Fleur); Lori Larsen (Helen Le Fleur); James L. Dunn (Hayden Keyes); Al Denbeste (Patient).

Comedy-Drama series. Episode title: "Shofar, So Good." First broadcast on October 3, 1994.

This refreshingly different (although at times rather pretentious) series about the quirky residents of the tiny town of Cicely, Alaska, provided the backdrop for one of the most original *Carol* variations to date. (Unfortunately, the *Carol* is just one of several plotlines woven throughout this episode; as such, this is one of the few television variations that actually leaves the viewer wanting more.) The idea is that Dr. Joel Fleischman, the town's reluctant doctor who would much prefer to be in New York, is in a particularly grumpy mood as the Jewish feast of Yom Kippur approaches. However, he is shown the error of his ways when his rabbi from back home appears to him as the Spirits of Yom Kippur Past, Present and Future.

In terms of its handling of Dickens's basic *Carol* machinery, there are no major deviations from the norm; however, some effective variations and updates are present nonetheless. For example, the Spirit of Yom Kippur Past uses Joel's VCR and television to show him some of his past transgressions. The idea of video as a Dickensian teaching tool had been used before; nevertheless it is always effective in any modern updating of the *Carol*. More significant, however, is the sequence with the Spirit of Yom Kippur Present which ends, as it should, with a vision of two children. However, instead of the familiar Ignorance and Want, the spirit reveals two very modern children of the late twentieth century: a boy named Arrogance, and a girl named Self-Absorption. The former seems obsessed with a handheld video game, while the latter listens to music through headphones. Both look, among other things, surly, sullen and bored and, as the spirit notes, "They choose not to hear anything." These children are glimpsed just briefly, but a genuinely disturbing image lingers.

In the final analysis, however, it is most important to note that Dr. Fleischman is not the town's resident "old Scrooge"—i.e., he does not normally bluster about acting nasty and greedy or selfish. As such, this *Carol* easily avoids the conventional (and predictable) territory that is usually staked out by television variations. Instead, a much more sophisticated point is made when he realizes how often he has been unconsciously arrogant, inconsiderate and unkind in his daily dealings with people—and when he realizes that he, like all of us who are not necessarily "old Scrooges" in any overt way, has much to atone for. While an undercurrent of humor is unquestionably present, the result here is a serious and effective transposition of the *Carol* from one religious tradition to another—and a very important reminder that its message is indeed universal.

ANIMANIACS

Warner Bros.   1994   USA   color   12m

Executive Producer: Steven Spielberg. Senior Producer: Tom Ruegger. Producers: Rich Arons; Sherri Stoner. Director: Rusty Mills. Written by: Randy Rogel; Paul Rugg. Music: Richard Stone; Steve Bernstein; Carl Johnson. Orchestration: Julie Bernstein. Casting and Voice Direction: Andrea Romano.

VOICES: Rob Paulsen (Yakko); Jess Harnell (Wakko); Tress MacNeille (Dot); Frank Welker (The C. E. O., Thaddeus Plotz); Sherri Stoner (Slappy Squirrel).

Cartoon short entitled "A Christmas Plotz" from the *Animaniacs* television series.

The Animaniacs brand of smartass shtick wears very thin after just a minute or two, and, in the end, this series is a rather trashy attempt to continue (or merely cash in on?) the great tradition of Warner Bros. cartoons. The Scrooge surrogate here is Thaddeus Plotz, head of the Warner Bros. film studio, who is brought to his senses by three familiar spirits played by Yakko, Wakko, and Dot. One interesting touch: The Ghost of Christmas Past sets up a projector and screen and shows Plotz his past in the form of home movies.

A CHRISTMAS CAROL

Jetlag Productions (Goodtimes Entertainment) 1994 USA color 48m

Executive Producers: Cayre Brothers. Producer: Mark Taylor. Director: Toshiyuki Hiruma; Takashi. Writer: Jack Olesker. Music Production: Andrew Dimitroff. Associate Producer for Goodtimes Home Video: Gayle Franco. Associate Producer: Jennifer Blohm. Animation Production: KKC & D Asia. Overseas Production Directors: Masanori Miura; Shigeo Koshi. Animation Producer: Takahiko Tsuchiya. Animation Produc-

tion Coordinators: Seiichi Kikawada; Hirofumi Otsuki; Yasue Oki; Hidetaka Shimizu. Animation by: Amisong Production; Animal House; Samil Animation Co., Ltd.; Sung Production; Yong Woo Production. Voice Direction: Michael Donovan.

VOICES: Tony Ail; Nathan Aswell; Cheralynn Bailey; Kathleen Barr; Gary Chalk; Lilliam Carlson; Ian Corlett; Michael Donovan; Kent Gallie; Phil Hayes; Roger Kelly; Ellen Kennedy; Terry Klassen; Joanne Lee; Andrean Libman; Tom McBeath; Lois McLean; Scott McNeill; Jesse Moss; Doug Newell; Richard Newman; Crystaleen O'Bray; Doug Parker; Gerard Plunkett; Susan Sciff; Raouel Shane; Scott Swanson; Venus Terzo; Louise Vallance; Wanda Wilkinson; Dale Wilson.

Yet another lifeless, limited animation borefest. It does contain one interesting touch: When Scrooge opens the door to meet the Ghost of Christmas Present, he walks into a lush, idyllic outdoor setting which seems to suggest the Garden of Eden.

This one was released direct to the home video market with its tape packaging proudly proclaiming it to be "THE VERSION CHILDREN LOVE!" Since no one could have seen this version before unwrapping the tape, one wonders how it was determined that children love it. Nevertheless, this advertisement seems to suggest that the *Carol* is still perceived as a hot commercial property and that there is considerable competition among the various *Carols* in the Christmas marketplace.

A FLINTSTONES CHRISTMAS CAROL

Hanna-Barbera Cartoons, Inc.   1994   USA color   90m

Executive Producers: William Hanna; Joseph Barbera; Buzz Potamkin.

Producer & Director: Joanna Romersa. Written by: Glenn Leopold. Supervising Producer: Gordon Kent. Music: Steve Bernstein. Story Editor: Gordon Kent. Storyboard Artists: John Dorman; William Edwards; Jan Falkenstein; Kirk Hanson; Robert Nesler; Floyd Norman; David Reed; Scott Shaw. Animation Directors: Frank Andrina; William Edwards; Robert Nesler; Carl Urbano; Allen Wilzbach. Character Designers: James Stenstrum; Michael Takamoto; Jan Falkenstein; Pete Alvarado; Kirk Hanson; Lewis Ott; Tony Sgroi. Design Assistants: Donna Zeller; Dana Jo Granger.

VOICES: Fred Flintstone (Henry Corden); Wilma Flintstone (Jean Vander Pyl); Barney Rubble & Dino (Frank Welker); Betty Rubble (BJ Ward); Pebbles Flintstone (Russi Taylor); Bamm Bamm Rubble & Joe Rockhead (Don

Messick); Mr. Slate (John Stephenson); Maggie & Miss Feldspar (Marsha Clark); Ned (Will Ryan); Ghost of Christmas Present (Brian Cummings); Philo Quartz (Rene Levant); Charles Brickens (John Rhys Davies). ADDITIONAL VOICES: Joanie Gerber; Maurice LaMarchie; Howard Morris; Jan Rabson.

Animated *Carol* variation first syndicated in 1994.

An entertaining *Carol* variation in which the citizens of Bedrock stage a production of *A Christmas Carol* with Fred Flintstone in the role of Scrooge. Complications ensue when Fred takes his role as star of the show a bit too seriously and becomes, in effect, a prehistoric Scrooge. The "play within a play" motif recalls *Mister Magoo's Christmas Carol*, but that is where any similarity to the earlier classic ends. It is possible, though, that the producers hoped this one would register with baby boomers who remember both *The Flintstones* and *Mister Magoo's Christmas Carol* from childhood.

BAH! HUMBUG!

PBS-TV 1994 USA color 60m

MacNeil/Lehrer Productions in Association with WNET/Thirteen. Producer: Richard Somerset-Ward. Director: Derek Bailey. Coordinating Producer: Susan Malin. Executive Producer: Al Vecchione. Lighting Designer: Alan Adelman. Technical Director: Frank O'Connell. Audio: Gary Palamara. Video: Sue Noll. Videotape Operator: James Mac Privette. Cameras: Miguel Armstrong; Bill Finley; Rob Liberman; Ron Washburn. Associate Director: Karen Scott. Music: John Adams. Stage Manager: Janet Friedman. Makeup: Debra Phillips.

CAST: Robert MacNeil; Martin Sheen; James Earl Jones.

An entertaining and informative program broadcast on American public television on Christmas night in 1994, one year after the 150th anniversary of the publication of the *Carol*. Shot before a live audience at New York's Pierpont Morgan Library which houses Dickens's original manuscript of the *Carol*, the program is hosted by Robert MacNeil and presents a dramatic reading of the *Carol* with Martin Sheen handling the narration and James Earl Jones speaking as Scrooge. The performance is interrupted at various points for prerecorded segments that provide background information on Dickens and the writing of the *Carol*.

EBBIE

Lifetime Cable Network 1995 Canada color 100m

Crescent Entertainment Ltd. Producer: Harold Tichenor. Co-Producer: Jayme Pfahl. Executive Producers: Jean Abounader; Frederick DeMann. Director: George Kaczender. Writers: Paul Redford; Ed Redlich. Photography: Thomas Burstyn. Production Designer: Jill Scott. Music: Lawrence Shragge. Editing: Roger Mattiussi.

CAST: Susan Lucci (Elizabeth "Ebbie" Scrooge); Wendy Crewson; Ron Lea; Molly Parker; Lorena Gale; Jennifer Clement; Nicole Parker; Susan Hogan; Kevin McNulty; Taran Noah Smith (Tiny Tim); Jeffrey DeMunn (Jake Marley); Adrienne Carter (Little Ebbie); Bill Croft (Luther); Elan Ross Gibson (Homeless Woman); Laura Harris (Martha); Sarah Hayward (Nurse #2); Maria Herrera (Nurse #1); Gary Jones (Floor Manager); Tamsin Kelsey (Mrs. Taylor); Karin Konoval (Ebbie's Mother); David Lougren (Michael); Tom McBeath (Van Munsen); Hrothgar Matthews (Ralph); Larry Musser (Ebbie's Father); Malcolm Stewart (Patterson).

Made-for-Television variation that premiered in the United States on December 4, 1995.

In the first of two recent *Carols* to present us with a female Scrooge, Susan Lucci is very effective as Ebbie Scrooge, a career-driven businesswoman who runs a major department store the way Captain Bligh ran the *Bounty*. It also presents us with a *Carol* that is firmly rooted in the modern world, particularly the modern world of business. This environment comes across with chilling clarity in the portion of the film that corresponds to Stave One of Dickens's original text: After picking up a frozen microwave dinner for her solitary Christmas Eve feast, Ebbie sees her former partner, Jake Marley, appear on her television screen. He tells her, "You and me have got to conference," and he uses a remote control to "zap" her to a meeting in which she is told to "change the agenda, Ebbie. Reverse the priorities." The scene winds down as Marley, who, figuratively speaking, is chained to his cellular phone, informs her that she must "take these meetings. Three appointments, at 12:01, 1:11, and 2:15. This A.M." And, needless to say, the ghost is not amused when she asks if she can take them all at once via a conference call.

It is important to note here, however, that the effect of this infusion of late twentieth-century business lingo is anything but comic. The sequence works beautifully because it is still Dickens's voice — contemporary, conversational, angry, direct — doing the talking. It is also interesting to note that, in spite of its very modern edge, the film recalls the "Alastair Sim version" in a touching deathbed scene with Ebbie's sister, and in the scene where Jake and Ebbie gain control of the department store via some rather questionable tactics. *Ebbie* is no classic, but it does deserve high marks for being an inventive, and yet warm and faithful, updating of the familiar story. See also the entry for *Ms. Scrooge*, 1997.

A CHRISTMAS CAROL

Pendulum's Video Classics   ca. 1995   USA   color   50m

Producer/Director: Marc Sheib.

An excruciatingly bad adaptation that uses comic book style artwork to tell the story of the *Carol*. As in the 1970 version from Britain's Anglia Television, there is no actual motion; instead, we see a progression of still images linked by cuts and dissolves. Speech balloons provide dialogue, as does an incredibly monotonous soundtrack. It is possible, of course, that a production like this could be of some value to a child who is learning to read, or to a hearing impaired person. Nevertheless, this is one of the worst audiovisual *Carols* to date. And yet, as noted earlier, even the most dreadful adaptations often contain interesting surprises. In this one we are shown that very brief and usually neglected moment in Dickens's text, just before the end of Stave Four, when the Ghost of Christmas Yet to Come shows Scrooge a vision of his office — an office with new furniture that is occupied by someone other than Ebenezer Scrooge. (See also *A Christmas Carol and Oliver Twist*, 1985 [Congress Classics]; this version includes the same shot of Scrooge seeing someone else at his desk in the Christmas future sequence.)

BEAVIS AND BUTT-HEAD

MTV-TV   1995   USA   color   13m

Producer: John Andrews. Director: Mike Judge. Writer: Kristofer Brown; David Felton; David Giffels; Mike Judge; Joe Stillman; Guy Maxtone-Graham. Created by: Mike Judge. Co-Producer: Kristofer Brown; Nick Litwinko; Susie Lewis Lynn; John Lynn. Animation Director: Tony Kluck; Brian Mulroney; Mike de Seve.

VOICES: Mike Judge.

Animated *Carol* parody. Episode title: "Huh-Huh-Humbug."

In this charming holiday treat† for the nineties, Beavis falls asleep at work and becomes our Scrooge surrogate in a dream. The familiar ghostly visitors pop out of his television set as he attempts to spend his Christmas Eve watching a porno film entitled "Ebenezer Screw."

MARTIN

FOX-TV   1996   USA   color   30m

CAST: Martin Lawrence (Martin Payne); Tisha Campbell (Gina); Tichina Arnold (Pam).

Situation comedy. First broadcast on December 19, 1996.

The usually obnoxious character of Martin Payne is the modern day Scrooge who is taught a lesson in the Dickensian manner. The usual sitcom stuff.

A CHRISTMAS CAROL

DIC Productions & Twentieth Century Fox   1997   USA/Canada   color   72m

Executive Producers: Andy Heyward; Robby London; Mike Maliani. Supervising Producer: Janice Sonski. Producer and Director: Stan Phillips. Adapted by: Jymn Magon. Musical Director: Karyn Ulman. Music: Megan Cavallari; John Campbell. Songs: Megan Cavallari; David Goldsmith. Production Supervisor: Emily Wensel. Casting/Voice Direction: Marsha Goodman. Animation Direction: Glenn Wright. Character Design: Luisito Escauriaga; Mauro Casalese; Tina Akland; Meliza Espinoza; Greg Reeve. Background Design: Dean Sherritt; Colleen Holub; Trevor Bentley; Ian Bartolo; Olaf Miller. Storyboard Supervisor: Brad Neave. Storyboards: Eduardo Soriano; Tony Lovett; Santos Gan; Colleen Holub; Laz Baarde; Glen Lovett; Renato Otacan; Lil Reichmann.

VOICES: Tim Curry (Scrooge); Whoopi Goldberg; Michael York (Bob Cratchit); Ed Asner; Frank Welker; Kath Soucie; Jodi Benson; John Garry; Amick Byram; Ian Whitcomb; Joe Lala; David Wagner; Bettina Bush; Jerry Houser; Sam Saletta; Alan Shearman; Jarrad Kritzstein; Cathy Riso; Sidney Miller; Kelly Lester; Anna Mathias; Judy Ovitz.

This most recent animated *Carol* earns an honorable mention for being one of the best looking animated versions ever. Aided by modern computer technology, this *Carol* utilizes a wide range of camera angles and fluid camera movements, as well as richly drawn and colored characters and backgrounds, all of which contribute to a polished and highly cinematic visual style. It also incorporates a number of minor but interesting touches. Scrooge has a pet bulldog (named Debit) that follows him everywhere; the Ghost of Christmas Past appears as a young male cockney costermonger, and the Ghost of Christmas Present as a bubbly woman; and in the Christmas Present sequence, Scrooge's childhood memories are rekindled when he sees Tiny Tim reading *Robinson Crusoe* by the fireside. As for social conciousness, the Ghost of Christmas Present

---

†Author's Note: *Those who do not appreciate sarcasm can replace "charming holiday treat" with the description of their choice. May I suggest "loathsome trash"?*

departs without showing us those famous children named Ignorance and Want; however, in the sequence with Marley's Ghost, we do see his fellow phantoms vainly attempting to help a woman and child huddling together in the cold.

In the end, however, the script is an all too familiar rehash that contributes nothing new to our appreciation of the *Carol*. And also on the downside, it is worth noting that the musical numbers possess that instantly recognizable Broadway Wannabe quality that has become an annoying trend in so many recent animated features.

MS. SCROOGE
USA Cable Network   1997   USA/Canada color

Wilshire Court Productions. Producer: Julian Marks. Director: John Korty. Teleplay: John McGreevey. Photography: Eleme'r Raga'lyi. Production Designer: Gerald Holmes. Editing: Louise A. Innes. Music Composer/Conductor: David Shire.

CAST: Cicely Tyson (Ebenita Scrooge); Michael Beach; John Bourgeois; Raeven Larrymore-Kelly; Karen Glave; Ken James; Arsinee Khanjian; Katherine Helmond (Maude Marley); William Greenblatt (Tim Cratchit); Michael J. Reynolds (Spirit Past); Shaun Austin-Olsen (Spirit Present); Julian Richings (Spirit Future); Ashley Brown (Chris).

Made-for-Television variation that premiered on December 9, 1997.

As the most recent female Scrooge variation, this *Carol* obviously has much in common with the earlier 1995 *Ebbie*. However, it should be noted that neither contains any sort of female or feminist angle per se. Instead, each recognizes the universality of the human condition, and of Dickens's message. These female Scrooges are capable of both damnation and redemption, just like their male counterparts. And we can add that this universal message is taken one step further in *Ms. Scrooge* in that the film contains no racial angle or message of any kind, despite the fact that its Scrooge is black. As with the earlier *John Grin's Christmas*, a certain cultural subtext is of course present, particularly as we see flashes of this Scrooge's past life, just as it would be if the character was Italian, Irish, Polish or whatever. However, Ebenita Scrooge just happens to be a black woman and race is simply a non-issue. (See the entry for *John Grin's Christmas*, 1986.)

On the downside, however, this *Carol* does contain a few slightly bizarre touches that strain its credibility a bit in places. The Ghost of Christmas Past, for example, looks like he crawled out of a Mickey Spillane novel. And the Ghost of Christmas Present is a somewhat morose fellow who actually identifies himself as a tortured soul like Marley; instead of being the familiar essence of bubbly good cheer, he has "been given this job"—a job for which he has had to do "some boning up." More significantly, however, Cicely Tyson's Scrooge comes dangerously close at times to being a caricature of a sour old miser as she mumbles and purses her lips and sharply declaims "garbage" instead of "humbug." In the film she is the owner of what appears to be a small private bank, something akin to the Bailey Building and Loan Association from *It's a Wonderful Life*; this provides an opportunity for us to see her lovingly salting away her cash in a private vault. Later we even see her at home ironing her paper money! These oddities can be forgiven, however, because the film is ultimately quite faithful to Dickens, as in the scene where Ms. Scrooge's nephew (a minister) tells her in no uncertain terms that she has "climbed to the top of [her] pile of gold on the backs of [Bob] Cratchit and [her other employees]," or in the understated climax in which she attends his church on Christmas morning. Like *Ebbie*, *Ms. Scrooge* is no classic, but it is another warm and engaging variation for the nineties. And perhaps it is fitting that the last truly serious *Carol* in our filmography presents us with a black Scrooge in a film in which race does not matter. Perhaps some of Dickens's message is being heard after all…

DISNEY'S 101 DALMATIANS
ABC-TV   1997   USA   22m   color

Walt Disney Television Animation in Association With Jumbo Pictures. Executive Producers: Jim Jinkins; David Campbell; Tony Craig; Roberts Gannaway. Produced and Directed by: Victor Cook. Written by: Ken Koonce; Michael Merton. Storyboard: Denise Koyama; Yi-Chih Chen. Based on the novel *The 101 Dalmatians* by Dodie Smith. Producer: Martha Ripp. Co-Producers/Supervising Story Editors: Cydne Clark; Steve Granat. Consulting Producer/Executive Story Editor: Carin Greenberg Baker. Music: Mark Watters; Dan Sawyer. Main Title Theme: Randy Petersen; Kevin Quinn; Tim Heintz. Voice Casting: Jamie Thomason. Dialogue Director: Kelly Ward. Animation Director: Colin Baker. Timing Director: Bob Zamboni. Character Design: Dana Landsberg. Key Layout Design: Andrew Ice; Alexander McCrae. Prop Design: Brian Brookshier. Key Background Stylists: Tom Cain; Andrea Coleman; Richard Evans.

VOICES: Jeff Bennett; Tara Charendoff; David

Lander; Michael McKean; Charlotte Rae; Kath Soucie; Frank Welker; April Winchell.

Animated series. Episode title: "A Christmas Cruella." First broadcast on December 20, 1997.

Quite similar in tone to the *Animaniacs* version cited above (1994), this one follows a recent trend that says that today's children need noisy cartoons filled with pseudo-sophisticated wisecracks and pop culture references. The result is a rather unpleasant *Carol* which features an extremely dislikable Scrooge surrogate in Cruella de Vil.

AN ALL DOGS CHRISTMAS CAROL

Metro-Goldwyn-Mayer Animation, Inc. 1998 USA color 73m

Producer: Paul Sabella; Jonathan Dern. Director: Paul Sabella. Writer: Jymn Magon. Based upon Goldcrest's original motion picture "All Dogs Go to Heaven." Score: Mark Watters. Songs: Lorraine Feather; Mark Watters. Voice Direction: Maria Estrada. Associate Producer: Cary Silver. Co-Producer: Jymn Magon. Art Director: Sean Platter. Production Supervisor: Debbie Nodella. Supervising Editor: Michael Bradley. Music Supervisor: Richard Kaufman. Co-Director: Gary Selvaggio. Casting Director: Maria Estrada. Looping: The L. A. Mad Dogs. Post Production Supervisor: Helene Blitz.

VOICES: Ernest Borgnine (Carface); Dom DeLuise (Itchy/Ghost of Christmas Past); Sheena Easton (Sasha/Ghost of Christmas Present); Taylor Emerson (Timmy); Bebe Neuwirth (Anabelle/Belladonna); Charles Nelson Reilly (Killer); Steven Weber (Charlie Barkin/Ghost of Christmas Future); Carlos Alazraqui; Beth Anderson; Dee Bradley Baker; Edie Lehmann Boddicker; Billie Bodine; Susan Boyd; Amick Byram; Alvin Chea; Randy Crenshaw; Jamie Cronin; Aria Noelle Curzon; Lorraine Feather; Myles Jeffrey; Jon Joyce; Megan Malanga; Chris Marquette; Gail Mathius; Laurie Schillinger; Ashley Michelle Tisdale; Carmen Twillie; Vanessa Vandergriff.

SONGS: "When I Hear a Christmas Carol"; "Puppyhood"; "I Always Get Emotional at Christmas Time"; "Clean Up Your Act."

Direct-to-video animated feature released in the fall of 1998. Made its television premiere on Fox Family Channel on December 6, 1998.

One of several sequels inspired by *All Dogs Go to Heaven* (1989), a remarkably unappealing animated feature. This one is an idiotic and yet rather complex story of the evil Belladonna's plot to ruin Christmas for the people of San Francisco; needless to say, Itchy and Charlie, with the help of some heavenly intervention from Annabelle, come to the rescue. (Someday someone will undoubtedly compile a book about the curious sub-genre of Christmas films that has been flourishing in recent years, that being films which, in one way or another, are concerned with the need to "save Christmas.") The "*Carol* angle" here involves the conversion of a nasty and very Scrooge-like bulldog named Carface who is in Belladonna's employ. There is also a puppy with a bad leg named Timmy.

EBENEZER

Nomadic Pictures 1998 USA/Canada color 94m

Executive Producer: Chad Oakes; Cindy Lamb; Barbara Ligeti. Producer: Michael Frislev; Douglas Berquist. Director: Ken Jubenvill. Created by the NOMADS: C. Oakes; M. Frislev; D. Berquist. Screenplay: Donald Martin. Story Editor: Michael Frislev. Director of Photography: Henry Lebo. Editor: Paul Mortimer. Production Design: Rick Roberts. Costume Design: Joanne Hansen. Visual Effects Supervisors: Barry Morrissette; Jillian Backus. Music Composed by: Bruce Leitl. Co-Producer: Chad Oakes. Second Unit Director: Douglas Berquist. First Assistant Director: Jack Hardy. Art Director: Tracey Baryski. Senior Visual Effects/Animator: Mike Tomiuk. Visual Effects Editor: Marino DiNapoli.

CAST: Jack Palance (Ebenezer Scrooge); Jack Palance (Future Scrooge); Rick Schroder (Sam Benson); Amy Locane (Erica); Albert Schultz (Cratchitt); Daryl Shuttleworth (Fred); Richard Comar (Ghost of Christmas Present); Michelle Thrush (Ghost of Christmas Past); Richard Halliday (Jacob Marlowe); Susan Coyne (Clara Cratchitt); Joshua Silberg (Tiny Tim); Zoe Rose Hesse (Cratchitt Daughter); Jeffrey Derwent (Cratchitt Son); Darcy Dunlop (Martha); Jocelyn Loewen (Rebecca Gordon); J. C. Roberts (Benjamin Gordon); Kyle Collins (Ebenezer age 8, 12); Aaron Pearl (Ebenezer age 17, 18, 25); James Dugan (Fezziwig); Linden Banks (Simon Scrooge); Heather Lea MacCallum (Mary Scrooge); Morris Chapdelaine (Cloaked Phantom); Billy Morton (Cowboy); Brenda Shuttleworth (Bess); Hal Kerbes (Minister); Daniel Libman (Mr. Hoffman); Thomas F. Legg (Shopkeeper); John R. Nelson (Easterner); Des Jardine (Beggar); Karina Frislev (Eliza Scrooge); Jim Shield (Poker Player #1); Marcel Henry (Poker Player #2); James Baker (Poker Player #3); Danny Glasswick (Boy #1); Anthony Dalla Lana (Boy #2); Alex Kulchycki (Conductor); Lara Huget (Caroler #1); Christine Huget (Caroler #2); Jari Huget (Caroler #3); Marlowe Huget (Caroler #4); Celeste Huget (Caroler #5).

Made-for-television western variation. Premiered on the TNT network on November 25, 1998.

By definition, all *Carol* variations are unusual, and this is particularly true of the handful that have transferred the tale to a western setting replete with cowboys, horses and six-shooters. However, *Ebenezer* is particularly unusual in that the bulk of its action takes place — sometime, we can infer, in the latter part of the last century — in western Canada. It is also unusual in that it does not attempt to slavishly include every major detail and incident found in the original story. It does add numerous details and plot twists of its own to Scrooge's résumé, giving a certain freshness or element of surprise to its treatment of a very familiar story.

For example, its Scrooge, played with great relish by Jack Palance, is a genuine villain who cheats at cards and, apparently, at everything else. In a particularly revealing and innovative Christmas Past sequence we learn that he came from a comfortable home in Philadelphia and actually had a very happy childhood up until the point when his father withdrew him from the school that he loved. Though the young Scrooge did not know it at the time, his father's action was not motivated by meanness, but was instead made necessary by financial troubles. Nevertheless, this was a turning point in Scrooge's life and he soon set out on a path of greed and selfishness that would eventually put his soul in peril. We see him as he steals money from his employer (here called Fessiwig) and heads west in search of gold. He marries the daughter of a local cattle rancher, and after being put in charge of the ranch he sells it in an unscrupulous business deal, an act which hastens his father-in-law's death. He then heads north to Canada where his wife, tired of his greedy ways, leaves him for another man.

Without question, then, *Ebenezer* contributes many fresh ideas to the collected sum of *Carol* folklore, and for this it deserves much credit. However, its script also contains what might charitably be called a lack of seriousness that frequently pushes this production dangerously close to the realm of unintentional parody. Scrooge, for example, frequently comes out with jargon that is clearly of the late twentieth, rather than the late nineteenth, century: "Don't screw it up"; "Gimme your best shot"; "Put that in your peacepipe and smoke it"; "I've been there, done that"; "I'm really on a roll." And there are other details that quietly chip away at its credibility. The Ghost of Christmas Past, for example, is played by a very attractive young Indian woman, an interesting approach, given the western setting,

which could have been used to inject a subtle layer of social consciousness and relevance. Instead she wears an outfit that recalls Cleavon Little's Gucci cowboy garb in *Blazing Saddles*, and her demeanor is very modern; she even spouts soothing pop psychology and quasi–New Age platitudes: "There's always a door, Ebenezer, if you choose to open it"; "Don't let fear rule your life. Open your eyes, Ebenezer. Who knows what you'll find?" And finally, one can point to the film's grand finale in which, while appearing as Father Christmas in the town's Christmas pageant, the reformed Scrooge belts out a Christmas song that positively reeks of contemporary songwriting sappiness.

All things considered, this *Carol* is very much a mixed bag. It looks good, and is well acted all around, and at its heart lies a lively and original concept. What it needs is a more serious and substantive script. In other words, it joins that long list of interesting but far from classic *Carol* variations that we nevertheless look forward to every December.

Phantom Carols

As a footnote to the filmography just concluded, let us note for the record that research has confirmed the existence of all of the films and television programs listed above. In contrast, a small handful of *Carols* listed in other published sources have proved to be either erroneous or unverifiable. After an extensive attempt to trace and verify each of the following, this author declares that until proven otherwise, the following should be treated as "Phantom *Carols*":

• A 1911 or 1912 short *Carol* directed by Charles Kent. Kent was indeed an active director in this period, primarily for Vitagraph, but no record of a *Carol* directed by him has been found. It is possible that his name has somehow been linked to the 1910 Edison version regarding which the directorial credit is still very much in doubt.

• *Spalicek*. A portion of famed puppet animator Jiří Trnka's 1947 Czech feature entitled *Spalicek* has been reported to deal with the *Carol. Spalicek* is a six-part film dealing with various aspects of traditional Czech culture: *Shrovetide, Spring, Legend about St. Prokup, The Fair, The Feast* and *Bethlehem*. However, archival sources, as well as the film's distributor, in the Czech

Republic confirm that none of the six segments are related to the *Carol*.

• A 1957 *CBS Television Workshop* production entitled *The Stingiest Man in Town* starring Gerald Floyd, reported to have been a remake of the 1956 NBC production of the same name. Every conceivable attempt to confirm this one's existence has come up empty. For the record: *CBS Television Workshop* was not on the air in 1957, and CBS itself has no record of such a production in any year. The name Gerald Floyd has also proved impossible to trace. Misinformation on this one is also due in part to its being confused with the 1978 Rankin/Bass animated production entitled *The Stingiest Man in Town*.

• It is worth mentioning here that a 1965 episode of *The Avengers* television series entitled "Too Many Christmas Trees" is often assumed to be some sort of *Carol* variation because Steed and Mrs. Peel attend a Christmastime gathering at which those in attendance dress as characters from Dickens's works. One key character appears as Marley's Ghost; this, however, is the only significant *Carol* reference, and this program is definitely not a *Carol* variation in any sense of the word.

Notes

Author's Note: For the convenience of the general reader for whom this book is primarily intended, I have cited both The Oxford Illustrated Dickens and the Penguin Classics editions whenever possible when quoting Dickens.

Introduction

1. See Anthony Slide and Edward Wagenknecht, *Fifty Great American Silent Films, 1912–1920: A Pictorial Survey* (New York: Dover, 1980), p. 77.

Prologue

1. How I wish that I had written these words, for I cannot imagine a better thumbnail sketch or "explanation" of Charles Dickens. However, they were written by R. J. Cruikshank in his *Charles Dickens and Early Victorian England* (London: Sir Isaac Pitman, 1949), pp. 10–11. This book is hereafter referred to as Cruikshank.

1. Literary Roots

Epigraph: Jeff Smith, *The Frugal Gourmet Celebrates Christmas* (New York: William Morrow, 1991), p. 187.

1. Theodore Watts-Dunton, "Dickens and 'Father Christmas': A Yule-Tide Appeal for the Babes of Famine Street," in *The Nineteenth Century and After* (December 1907): 1016. This essay also includes the text of Watts-Dunton's poem "Dickens Returns on Christmas Day."

2. Paul Davis, *The Lives and Times of Ebenezer Scrooge* (New Haven: Yale University Press, 1990), p. 3. Hereafter referred to as Davis.

3. Dickens's January 2, 1849, letter to the Earl of Carlisle is quoted in S. A. Muresianu, *The History of the Victorian Christmas Book* (New York: Garland, 1987), p. 16. Hereafter referred to as Muresianu. The complete letter is reprinted in *The Letters of Charles Dickens, Volume Five 1847–1849*, ed. by Graham Storey and K. J. Fielding (Oxford: Clarendon, 1981), p. 466.

4. This passage originally appeared in *The Spectator* (No. 269, Tuesday, January 8, 1712). I quote from *The Spectator Volume II*, ed. By Donald F. Bond (Oxford: Oxford University Press, 1965), p. 550. For the complete text, converted into modern English, see Edward Wagenknecht, ed., *The Fireside Book of Christmas Stories* (Indianapolis: Bobbs-Merrill, 1945), pp. 279–282.

5. Sir Walter Scott, "Marmion, Introduction to Canto VI," in *The Poems and Ballads of Sir Walter Scott, Volume II* (Boston: Dana Estes, 1900), pp. 242–244.

6. Washington Irving, "Christmas," from *The Sketch Book of Geoffrey Crayon, Gent.*, in *History, Tales and Sketches* (New York: Library of America, 1983), p. 913.

7. As countless scholars in this area have pointed out, Irving, using the pseudonym Diedrich Knickerbocker, makes several references to Saint Nicholas in his 1809 *A History of New York*.

For the most recent and enlightening scholarship on the history of Christmas in America see Stephen Nissenbaum's meticulously researched *The Battle for Christmas* (New York: Alfred A. Knopf, 1996).

8. Quoted with permission from George F. Will's December 23, 1993, syndicated column.

9. Davis, p. 19.

10. In the "Plough Monday" chapter of his 1835 publication *Abbotsford and Newstead Abbey*, which comprises one-third of *The Crayon Miscellany*, Irving responds to those who felt that the old holiday traditions had died out completely. His fictional narrator, Geoffrey Crayon, speaks:

> During my recent Christmas sojourn at Barlboro' Hall, on the skirts of Derbyshire and Yorkshire [where Irving visited in late 1831 and early 1832], I had witnessed many of the rustic festivities peculiar to that joyous season, which have rashly been pronounced obsolete, by those who draw their experience merely from city life. I had seen the great Yule clog put on the fire on Christmas Eve, and the wassail bowl sent round, brimming with its spicy beverage. I had heard carols beneath my window by the choristers of the neighboring village, who went their rounds about the ancient Hall at midnight according to immemorial custom. We had mummers and mimers too with the story of St. George and the dragon and other ballads and traditional dialogues, together with the famous old interlude of the Hobby Horse, all represented in the antechamber and servants' hall by rustics, who inherited the custom and the poetry from preceding generations.

See Washington Irving, "Plough Monday," from *Newstead Abbey*, in *The Crayon Miscellany* (Boston: Twayne, 1979), p. 187.

11. See Davies Gilbert, *Some Ancient Christmas Carols* (London: John Nichols, 1822), and William Sandys, *Christmas Carols, Ancient and Modern* (London: R. Beckley, 1833).

12. Thomas Kibble Hervey, *The Book of Christmas* (London: William Spooner, 1836).

13. See William Sandys, *Christmastide: Its History, Festivities, and Carols* (London: John Russel Smith, 1852).

14. In his excellent survey of Christmas history and traditions entitled *A Book of Christmas*, William Sansom underscores Irving's point in Note 10. He also cautions against assuming that the classic "Dickens Christmas" was immediately and universally accepted as the law of the land:

> Returning [from a discussion of American Christmas traditions] to Dickens, and to a

Victorian England less disturbed, we still find that tradition has not set in firmly anywhere. Pip's Christmas dinner (pickled pork and greens, and a pair of roast stuffed fowls) was eaten at half-past one on Christmas Day. That is about 1860. Scrooge (1843) purchased his prize turkey on Christmas morning for Cratchit's mid-day dinner. These and many other sources tell us only one thing — that habits change only slowly with the times, and one must wait for many years for any tradition to set solid; these also were days of much slower communication, so that country habits even near London hung a half-century and more back behind those of the capital, just as a village in the west of Ireland hangs decades behind Dublin today, or a Castilian village behind Madrid.

See William Sansom, *A Book of Christmas* (New York: McGraw-Hill, 1968), pp. 18–19.

15. See Preface to the 1867 Charles Dickens Edition in Charles Dickens, *The Pickwick Papers* (Oxford: Oxford University Press, 1948), p. x. Hereafter referred to as Oxford *Pickwick*. See p. 50 in the Penguin Classics edition edited by Robert L. Patten; hereafter referred to as Penguin Classics *Pickwick*.

16. Charles Dickens, "A Christmas Dinner," in *Sketches by Boz* (Oxford: Oxford University Press, 1957), p. 220. Hereafter referred to as Oxford *Sketches by Boz*.

17. *Ibid.*, p. 220.

18. See Introduction by Frederick Busch in *A Christmas Carol and Other Christmas Stories* by Charles Dickens (New York: Signet Classic, 1984), pp. 26–27. This introduction, which is actually a substantial essay, focuses on the important role that the past — and our memory of it — plays in Dickens's Christmas fiction. It is fascinating and essential reading.

19. "What Christmas Is as We Grow Older" in Charles Dickens, *Christmas Stories* (Oxford: Oxford University Press, 1956), pp. 24–25. Hereafter referred to as Oxford *Christmas Stories*.

20. Rachel Trickett quoted in Norman Page, *A Dickens Companion* (New York: Schocken, 1984), p. 74.

21. Dylan Thomas, *A Child's Christmas in Wales* (New York: New Directions, 1995), p. 27.

22. While *A Christmas Carol* is certainly the most famous example of what has become its own literary subgenre, Dickens did not invent the practice of telling ghost stories at Christmas. See W. F. Dawson, *Christmas: Its Origins and Associations* (London: Elliot Stock, 1902). Reprinted by Gale Research, Detroit, 1968.

23. Oxford *Pickwick*, p. 402. Penguin Classics

Pickwick, p. 487. (The story of Gabriel Grub is also reprinted in the Penguin Classics edition of Dickens's *Selected Short Fiction* edited by Deborah A. Thomas; hereafter referred to as Penguin *Selected Short Fiction*.)

24. Much has been written on the relationship between the conversion of Gabriel Grub and that of Ebenezer Scrooge. See John Butt, "A Christmas Carol: Its Origin and Design," in *The Dickensian* (December 1954): 15–18.

25. Oxford *Pickwick*, pp. 374–375. Penguin Classics *Pickwick*, p. 458.

26. Oxford *Pickwick*, p. 393; Penguin Classics *Pickwick*, p. 476.

27. Charles Dickens, *Master Humphrey's Clock and A Child's History of England* (Oxford: Oxford University Press, 1958), p. 34.

28. *Ibid.*, pp. 34–35.

29. Peter Ackroyd, *Dickens* (New York: HarperCollins, 1990), p. 34. Hereafter referred to as Ackroyd.

30. Chaplin's parents separated when he was very young and, after his father's death and his mother's severe breakdown, he and half-brother Sydney (who would also become an accomplished comedian) knew poverty and hunger on the streets of London as well as in an orphanage. These experiences account for the frequently bittersweet tone of his films. Like Dickens, he was haunted by his past and yet determined to overcome it; his character of the "little tramp" is very much an exercise in autobiography.

31. Oxford *Pickwick*, p. 382. Penguin Classics *Pickwick*, p. 466.

32. Fields (like Chaplin) had a "Dickensian childhood" and, in what may be the most perfectly cast role in Hollywood history, gives one of his greatest performances in this film. He is also known to have liked and respected Dickens's work; as such, in this film he kept his legendary ad-libbing and outrageous humor in check.

33. Muresianu, p. 19.

34. Washington Irving, "Christmas," from *The Sketch Book of Geoffrey Crayon, Gent.*, in *History, Tales and Sketches* (New York: The Library of America, 1983), p. 915.

35. Washington Irving, "The Stage Coach" from *The Sketch Book of Geoffrey Crayon, Gent.* in *History, Tales and Sketches* (New York: Library of America, 1983), pp. 922–923.

36. *Ibid.*, p. 922.

2. Political-Economic Roots

Epigraph: George Orwell, "Charles Dickens," in *Dickens, Dali and Others* (New York: Harcourt, Brace & World, 1946), p. 71. Hereafter referred to as Orwell. This important essay, written in 1939, originally appeared in Orwell's *Inside the Whale*; it is also available today in an unabridged audio cassette from Recorded Books, Inc.

1. For information on this branch of Dickens scholarship see Cedric Dickens [Great-Grandson of Charles Dickens], *Drinking with Dickens* (New York: New Amsterdam, 1988). This work was first published in England in 1980. See also Edward Hewett and W. F. Axton, *Convivial Dickens: The Drinks of Dickens and His Times* (Athens: Ohio University Press, 1983). I hasten to add, however, that scholars have pointed out that Dickens himself was a very moderate drinker and that he did not approve of, or encourage, any form of excess in this area. Nevertheless, the consumption of various forms of spirits does contribute much to the atmosphere of certain of his works. In this context, one might, for example, wish to compare *The Pickwick Papers* with the *Thin Man* films.

2. Cruikshank, p. 38.

3. See the chapter entitled "The Dream of Free Trade" in Cruikshank, pp. 42–48.

4. Many specialized studies are available on the subject of Dickens's politics and radicalism. A superb summary and analysis of these complex issues will be found in Ackroyd. Also, George Orwell's stimulating discussion of this subject, in "Charles Dickens" cited above, should not be missed.

5. Steven Marcus, *Dickens: From Pickwick to Dombey* (London: Chatto & Windus, 1965), p. 242.

6. Madeline House, Graham Storey, and Kathleen Tillotson, eds., *The Letters of Charles Dickens, Volume Three 1842–1843* (Oxford: Clarendon Press, 1974), p. 156.

7. For a definitive account of Dickens's two visits to America see Michael Slater, ed., *Dickens on America & the Americans* (Austin & London: University of Texas Press, 1978).

8. For an excellent overview of Dickens's religious/moral beliefs, see Ackroyd, pp. 504–508. The discussion here includes Dickens's *The Life of Our Lord* which was written for his children and not published until 1934; a beautiful edition is available from The Westminster Press of Philadelphia. And, again, George Orwell's analysis on this subject should not be missed. See also "The Man and His Soul" in Edward Wagenknecht, *The Man Charles Dickens*, rev. ed. (Norman: University of Oklahoma Press, 1966), pp. 212–248.

9. Fred Kaplan, *Dickens: A Biography* (New York: William Morrow, 1988), p. 142.

10. Quoted in Ackroyd, p. 379.

11. *Ibid.*

12. *The Letters of Charles Dickens, Volume Three 1842–1843*, ed. by Madeline House, Graham Storey, and Kathleen Tillotson (Oxford: Clarendon, 1974), p. 459.

13. *Ibid.*, p. 461.

14. Elizabeth Barrett Browning, "The Cry of the Children," in Harriet Waters Preston, ed., *The Complete Poetical Works of Mrs. Browning* (Boston: Houghton Mifflin, 1900), pp. 156–158.

15. Thomas Hood, "The Song of the Shirt," in *The Poetical Works of Thomas Hood*, enlarged and rev. ed. (New York: Thomas Y. Crowell), pp. 123–125.

16. Cruikshank, pp. 60–61. As Cruikshank points out, Disraeli's 1845 novel *Sybil* provides powerful reading in this context.

17. Charles Dickens, "A Sleep to Startle Us," on page 328 in the Penguin Classics edition of *Selected Journalism* 1850–1870, ed. by David Pascoe (hereafter, Penguin Classics *Selected Journalism*). Originally appeared in Household Words (March 13, 1852).

3. This Ghostly Little Book

Epigraph: G. K. Chesterton, *Appreciations and Criticisms of the Works of Charles Dickens* (New York: Haskell House, 1966), p. 103. Reprint edition; originally published in 1911.

1. John Forster, *The Life of Charles Dickens*, edited and annotated by J. W. T. Ley (London: Cecil Palmer, 1928), p. 299.

2. *The Letters of Charles Dickens, Volume Four 1844–1846*, ed. by Kathleen Tillotson (Oxford: Oxford University Press, 1977), pp. 2–3.

3. William Makepeace Thackeray, "A Box of Novels," in *Fraser's Magazine* (February 1844): 169.

4. As Paul Davis observes: "Probably the most famous statement of this point of view was [John] Ruskin's comment to a friend that Dickens' Christmas was nothing more than 'mistletoe and pudding—neither resurrection from the dead, nor rising of new stars, nor teaching of wise men, nor shepherds.'" See Davis, p. 59.

5. Charles Dickens, "A Christmas Carol," in *Christmas Books* (Oxford: Oxford University Press, 1954), p. 20. Hereafter referred to as Oxford *Christmas Books*. See p. 62 in Volume One of the Penguin Classics edition edited by Michael Slater; hereafter referred to as Penguin Classics *Christmas Books* (*Volume 1* or *Volume 2*).

6. Oxford *Christmas Books*, p. 47; Penguin Classics *Christmas Books, Volume 1*, p. 97.

7. Orwell, p. 6.

8. *Ibid.*, p. 23.

9. For an interesting perspective on the commercialism of our modern Christmas see Aldous Huxley's 1931 essay "New-Fashioned Christmas," which is reprinted in Jack Newcombe, ed., *A New Christmas Treasury*, rev. ed. (New York: Viking, 1991), pp. 225–227.

10. Oxford *Christmas Books*, p. 10. Penguin Classics *Christmas Books, Volume 1*, p. 49.

11. See C. S. Lewis's 1957 essay "What Christmas Means to Me" in *God in the Dock*, Walter Hooper, ed. (Grand Rapids MI: William B. Eerdmans, 1970), p. 304.

12. Oxford *Christmas Books*, p. 24. Penguin Classics *Christmas Books, Volume 1*, pp. 67–68.

4. Pre-Cinema

Epigraph: Anna Laura Zambrano, *Dickens and Film* (New York: Gordon, 1977), p. 383.

1. *The Letters of Charles Dickens, Volume Four 1844–1846*, ed. by Kathleen Tillotson (Oxford: Clarendon, 1977), p. 651.

2. For an overview of the piracy case see Michael Patrick Hearn's *The Annotated Christmas Carol* (New York: Clarkson N. Potter, 1976), pp. 23–26. Hereafter referred to as *The Annotated Christmas Carol*.

3. Penguin Classics *Pickwick*, p. 19.

4. *The Letters of Charles Dickens, Volume Four 1844–1846*, ed. by Kathleen Tillotson (Oxford: Clarendon Press, 1977), p. 50.

5. Discussions of theatrical adaptations are indebted to Malcolm Morley's "Curtain Up on *A Christmas Carol*" in *The Dickensian* (June 1951): 159–164; and to H. Philip Bolton's *Dickens Dramatized*. See also Chapter 9, *n*4.

6. H. Philip Bolton, *Dickens Dramatized* (Boston: G. K. Hall, 1987), p. 3.

7. See Charles Dickens, *Charles Dickens: The Public Readings*, ed. by Philip Collins (Oxford: Clarendon, 1975); and Charles Dickens, *A Christmas Carol: The Public Reading Version* with Introduction and Notes by Philip Collins (New York: The New York Public Library, 1971).

8. See Davis, p. 87.

9. *Charles Dickens: The Public Readings*, ed. by Philip Collins (Oxford: Clarendon, 1975), p. 4.

10. "Mr. Seymour Hicks and 'A Christmas Carol,'" in *The Dickensian* (March 1909): 76. See also Davis, p. 92.

11. Exactly how and why the *Carol* began to spread its popular wings is a complex question requiring a cultural-historical survey that is beyond the scope of this volume. Paul Davis offers a valuable discussion of this topic in his illuminating chapter entitled "The Children's

Hour"; see Davis, pp. 89–130. This issue will also be touched on in Chapter 9.

12. From a thematic standpoint, the play is actually quite simplistic in its approach; its real importance lies in the role that it played in popularizing the *Carol* in the first quarter of this century. I have so far been unable to determine exactly when it was written, although it appears to have been sometime in 1901. An item on page 12 of the September 7, 1901, issue of *The Era* refers to the forthcoming "new version" of the *Carol*. This item also refers to earlier dramatizations (in 1844 and 1860) and concludes by noting that "The piece was very popular at one time." This last bit of commentary would seem to confirm a popular perception that considerable time had passed since the *Carol* was a "force" on the London stage, and that its reappearance was worth taking note of. For what appears to be the earliest published edition of the play see *Scrooge* (New York: Samuel French, 1927).

13. *The Illustrated London News* (October 12, 1901): 520.

14. *The Era* (October 5, 1901): 15.

15. "The Birthday Dinner in London," in *The Dickensian* (June 1955): 113.

16. *The Era* (December 28, 1901): 19.

17. *Ibid.* (January 4, 1902): 21.

18. Bransby Williams, *My Sketches from Dickens* (London: Chapman & Hall, 1913), p. 3.

19. Dickens's September 24, 1858, letter to his friend and close associate W. H. Wills is reprinted in *The Letters of Charles Dickens, Volume Eight 1856–1858*, ed. by Graham Storey and Kathleen Tillotson (Oxford: Clarendon, 1995), pp. 668–669.

20. Angus Wilson, *The World of Charles Dickens* (New York: Viking, 1970), p. 33; see also illustration on p. 34.

21. The appearance of the magic lantern at this party is cited, and other portions of this December 31, 1842, letter are quoted, in Edgar Johnson, *Charles Dickens: His Tragedy and Triumph, Volume One* (New York: Simon and Schuster, 1952), p. 449. The complete letter is reprinted in *The Letters of Charles Dickens, Volume Three 1842–1843*, ed. by Madeline House, Graham Storey, and Kathleen Tillotson (Oxford: Clarendon, 1974), p. 416.

22. Erik Barnouw, *The Magician and the Cinema* (Oxford: Oxford University Press, 1981).

23. The classic text on the pre-history of the cinema is C. W. Ceram's *Archaeology of the Cinema* (New York: Harcourt, Brace & World, 1965). Also indispensable is Brian Coe's beautifully illustrated *The History of Movie Photography* (Westfield NJ: Eastview, 1981). For an authoritative and meticulously researched study reflecting the most recent scholarship on the subject see Charles Musser's *The Emergence of Cinema: The American Screen to 1907* (New York: Charles Scribner's Sons, 1990), hereafter referred to as Musser.

24. Quoted with permission from Terry Borton's forthcoming book on the relationship between the magic lantern and the movies, tentatively titled "Cinema Before Film."

25. For the Lionel Barrymore version, see *Life* (December 25, 1944): 51–57. This is a twelve-shot spread of black-and-white photographs with Barrymore and other actors depicting various scenes from the story; the accompanying text constitutes a heavily condensed version of the *Carol* itself. An introductory section briefly discusses Barrymore's radio appearances as Scrooge, and notes that this *Carol* was staged at the Metro-Goldwyn-Mayer studio in Hollywood and photographed by *Life's* Ralph Crane. It also lists the following as the cast of this most unusual *Carol* adaptation: Lionel Barrymore (Ebenezer Scrooge); Robert O'Connor (Bob Cratchit); Bruce Kellogg (Scrooge's Nephew); Mitchell Lewis (Solicitor); Francis Stevens (Marley's Ghost); June Lockhart (Christmas Past); Jeff York (Christmas Present); Francis Stevens (Christmas Future); Billy Chiles (Little Boy); Dickie Hall (Tiny Tim).

For the Trevor Howard version, see *The Saturday Evening Post* (December 19–26, 1964): 24–31, a ten-shot spread of color photographs with Howard and other actors depicting various scenes from the story. The boy portraying Tiny Tim also appears on the cover of this issue of the *Post*. As with the Barrymore version, the photographs are accompanied by a heavily condensed *Carol* text. Unfortunately, the *Post* does not list cast members other than Howard, although it notes that the photographs were shot in England by Mark Kauffman. (I have been unable to trace whether this version was produced exclusively for the *Post*, or whether it appeared originally or simultaneously in an English publication.)

26. Musser, p. 15.

5. Silent Film

Epigraph: This evocative tribute to the silent film begins American artist and avant-garde filmmaker Joseph Cornell's elegant tribute to actress Hedy Lamarr entitled "'Enchanted Wanderer': Excerpt from a Journey Album for Hedy Lamarr" in *View* (December 1941–January 1942): 3.

1. The following is a short list of a few of the most essential sources of information on the silent era: A definitive, single-volume history will

be found in William K. Everson's *American Silent Film* (Oxford: Oxford University Press, 1978). Kevin Brownlow's *The Parade's Gone By...* (New York: Alfred A. Knopf 1968) is an invaluable survey of the period; it is currently available in paperback from the University of California Press. Edward Wagenknecht's equally invaluable *The Movies in the Age of Innocence* (Norman: University of Oklahoma Press, 1962) offers a firsthand account of what the movies were like, as well as commentary on various personalities from this period; it is currently available in paperback from Limelight Editions. Walter Kerr's *The Silent Clowns* (New York: Alfred A. Knopf, 1980) is the definitive book on silent comedy; it is currently available in paperback from Da Capo Press.

2. See Michael Pointer, *Charles Dickens on the Screen* (Lanham MD: Scarecrow, 1996), pp. 8–13. The synopsis originally appeared in the November 30, 1901, issue of *The Era*.

3. *Ibid.*, p. 9.

4. See Chapter 18 in F. A. Talbot, *Moving Pictures: How They Are Made and Worked* (Philadelphia: J. B. Lippincott, 1912), pp. 197–206. Published in London by William Heinemann.

5. Denis Gifford, *The British Film Catalogue 1895–1970* (New York: McGraw-Hill, 1973), catalogue number 00110.

6. *The Moving Picture World* (December 5, 1908): 458–459.

7. *The Bioscope* (December 1, 1910): 29.

8. *The Edison Kinetogram* (December 15, 1910): 8.

9. *The Moving Picture World* (January 7, 1911): 32.

10. *The Bioscope* (November 16, 1911): 483.

11. *The Dickensian* (December 1911): 312.

12. See *The American Film Institute Catalog: Film Beginnings, 1893–1910*, compiled by Elias Savada (Metuchen NJ: Scarecrow, 1995), p. 282 in volume labeled "Indexes A."

13. The definitive study of the social problem film in the silent era is Kevin Brownlow's *Behind the Mask of Innocence* (New York: Alfred A. Knopf, 1990). See also Kay Sloan, *The Loud Silents, Origins of the Social Problem Film* (Urbana: University of Illinois Press, 1988).

14. *The Bioscope* (September 18, 1913): 955.

15. *Ibid.*

16. *The Bioscope* (November 5, 1914): 508.

17. *The Moving Picture World* (December 30, 1916): 1974.

18. *The New York Dramatic Mirror* (December 23, 1916): 26.

19. *Exhibitors Herald* (January 13, 1917): 26.

20. For a brief introduction to British silent film see Fred Guida, "British Silent Films [:An American Perspective]" in *Films in Review* (June 1992): 162–165. Also, George Perry's history of British film *The Great British Picture Show* (London: Hart Davis/MacGibbon, 1974) contains an excellent overview of this period.

21. *The Bioscope* (January 26, 1922): 59.

22. *The Kinematograph Weekly* (January 26, 1922): 48–49.

23. *Ibid.*

24. *Ibid.* (May 10, 1923): 66.

25. *Ibid.*

26. *Ibid.*

6. The Talkies

Epigraph: Quoted from the legendary 1950 film directed by Billy Wilder. (Screenplay by Wilder, Charles Brackett, and D. M. Marshman, Jr.)

1. Edward Wagenknecht, *The Movies in the Age of Innocence* (Norman: University of Oklahoma Press, 1962), p. 244.

2. William K. Everson, "An Analysis of the British Cinema," in *Janus Films: The British Collection*. This important essay is contained in an impressive Janus Films 16mm film rental catalogue ca. 1975.

3. Oxford *Christmas Books*, p. 13; Penguin Classics *Christmas Books, Volume 1*, p. 52. See also Davis, pp. 147–150.

4. See Edward Wagenknecht, *The Movies in the Age of Innocence* (Norman: University of Oklahoma Press, 1962), p. 93.

5. A few points on radio and recorded versions are worth mentioning here: With the exception of 1936 and 1938, Barrymore's radio adaptations of the *Carol* ran from 1934 through 1953 inclusive. However, contrary to popular legend, it is important to note that there was not one "official" broadcast each year, nor was there an "official" time and place for the broadcast—i.e., Barrymore's radio *Carols* were not a sharply defined Christmas Eve or Christmas Day tradition. They took place on different days around the holiday, and often as part of different "packages" for different sponsors on different networks; there was also no standard length for his *Carols*, although the half-hour format seems to have been the most popular or practical. Also, in any given year, his version was not necessarily the only version to be heard. For example, WABC in New York broadcast a version of the *Carol* with Barrymore on December 22, 1943; however, on Christmas Day of that same year, it broadcast another version with Basil Rathbone.

Barrymore's most famous appearance in the thirties came in Orson Welles's 1939 production on *The Campbell Playhouse*. In the forties, many of his *Carols* were staged in the fictional town of Springdale on his *Mayor of the Town* series. In 1948, his *Carol* was just one of the "acts" on a two-hour Christmas Day variety program called *Christmas Festival*. In 1948 he also released a 78 rpm recording of the *Carol* (MGM 16A) that has been reissued in various formats over the years. And in the fifties we find his *Carol* being used to extol the virtues of A. O. Smith's water heaters and Hallmark's greeting cards. A number of his radio *Carols* have survived and are available through various commercial sources such as Radio Yesteryear (Box C, Sandy Hook CT 06482-0847).

In the final analysis, and notwithstanding the various qualifications just cited, there is no denying the extent to which audiences associated the role of Scrooge with Lionel Barrymore. As Margot Peters notes in her definitive book on the three Barrymores entitled *The House of Barrymore* (New York: Alfred A. Knopf, 1991), p. 470, his Scrooge seems to have been particularly well-received in the forties: "During these war years, Lionel as Dr. Gillespie on film [in the *Dr. Kildare* series] and Scrooge on radio functioned as a symbol of courage and survival; it is not too much to say that to the American public he was a powerful symbol of traditional values." So much so, in fact, that *Life* magazine ran the "photographic essay" version of Barrymore's *Carol* discussed in Chapter 4.

6. Oxford *Christmas Books*, p. 47; Penguin Classics *Christmas Books, Volume 1*, p. 97.

7. See the article (not a review) entitled "Shades of Marley's Ghost" in *The New York Times* (December 18, 1938, Section 9): 7.

8. *The Commonweal* (December 21, 1951): 278.

9. Oxford *Christmas Books*, p. xi; Penguin Classics *Christmas Books, Volume 1*, p. xxix.

10. Oxford *Christmas Books*, p. 39; Penguin Classics *Christmas Books, Volume 1*, p. 86.

11. Oxford *Christmas Books*, p. 28; Penguin Classics *Christmas Books, Volume 1*, p. 73.

12. Oxford *Christmas Books*, p. 29; Penguin Classics *Christmas Books, Volume 1*, pp. 73–74.

13. See Robert L. Carringer, *The Magnificent Ambersons: A Reconstruction* (Berkeley: University of California Press, 1993), p. 147.

14. *The Speeches of Charles Dickens*, ed. by K. J. Fielding (Oxford: Clarendon, 1960), p. 61.

15. *Variety* (November 14, 1951): 16.

16. *Ibid.*

17. *The New York Times* (November 29, 1951): 41.

18. *The Christian Century* (December 19, 1951): 1495.

19. *Harrison's Reports* (November 3, 1951): 174.

20. See the widescreen *Scrooge* on Fox Video laserdisc #7126-85.

21. I stand by my contention that, in an overall sense, this *Scrooge* has never received the kind of credit and respect that it deserves, and that it is an extremely underrated film. Nevertheless, it did receive some very good reviews at the time of its initial release. See, for example, *Variety* (November 4, 1970): 16; *Saturday Review* (December 5, 1970): 44; *The New York Times* (November 20, 1970): 29; *Commonweal* (December 25, 1970): 327. But even here the praise is often qualified or limited: Of these four very positive reviews, only *Variety* liked the music and lyrics; the others, in one way or another, all pointed to this area as a weakness or serious flaw.

22. See (and hear) *Scrooge The Musical*, distributed by JAY Productions, Ltd., on compact disc # CDJAY 1272.

7. Television

Epigraph: E. B. White, "One Man's Meat," in *Harper's Magazine* (October 1938): 553.

1. For a truly encouraging sign that this situation may be beginning to change, see film director Michael Ritchie's *Please Stand By: A Prehistory of Television* (Woodstock NY: Overlook, 1994). This scholarly, yet thoroughly engaging and accessible book is a perfect introductory text for general readers.

2. Albert Abramson, *The History of Television, 1880 to 1941* (Jefferson NC: McFarland, 1987), p. 3. This meticulously researched and documented book is essential reading for anyone interested in sorting out the complex story of television's technical roots and history.

3. See William Hawes, *American Television Drama: The Experimental Years* (University: The University of Alabama Press, 1986). Hereafter referred to as Hawes. Author's Note: Many of my impressions of what early television was like were formed during my tenure as researcher on the initial fourteen volumes of Garland Publishing's collection of *Variety* and *Daily Variety* television reviews: Howard H. Prouty, ed., *Variety Television Reviews 1923–1988* (New York: Garland, 1989–90). However, I owe an enormous debt to Professor Hawes's unique book for providing a wealth of information and detail not easily available elsewhere.

4. A fascinating impression of what these early years were like can be had by browsing through the opening pages of Volume Three (1923–1950) of the Garland series cited above.

5. See the chapter entitled "The Race for Perfect Television" in Joseph H. Udelson, *The Great Television Race: A History of the American Television Industry 1925–1941* (University: The University of Alabama Press, 1982), pp. 119–131. Hereafter referred to as Udelson. This indispensable account of early television is available in paperback from the University of Alabama Press.

6. See Udelson, pp. 130–131.

7. For an invaluable account of this period see Frank Sturcken, *Live Television: The Golden Age of 1946–1958 in New York* (Jefferson NC: McFarland, 1990). Max Wilk's *The Golden Age of Television: Notes from the Survivors* (New York: Delacorte, 1976) is also must reading.

8. *Radio and Television Weekly* (December 22, 1943): 22.

9. *The Billboard* (January 1, 1944): 11. See also Hawes, p. 114.

10. *The Billboard* (January 1, 1944): 11.

11. See Hawes pp. 108–124.

12. *The Billboard* (December 30, 1944): 7–8.

13. *Ibid.*

14. Once again, this *Carol* does not seem to have been previewed or reviewed anywhere. Interestingly, however, a photograph from the production was printed in *The New York Times* on December 24, 1944. See also Hawes, p. 116.

15. *Daily Variety* (December 24, 1954): 25.

16. *The Billboard* (January 1, 1955): 7.

17. Robert C. Roman, "Dickens' 'A Christmas Carol'" in *Films in Review* (December 1958): 574.

18. Don Nardo, *Animation: Drawings Spring to Life* (San Diego CA: Lucent, 1992), p. 48. Part of an excellent series entitled "The Encyclopedia of Discovery and Invention," this volume is aimed at younger readers, but it offers an ideal introduction to anyone interested in animation.

19. See Fred Guida, "Gerard Hoffnung on Radio, Film and Television: Reflections and Speculations," in *Essays in Arts and Sciences* (October 1992): 53–59; and Fred Guida, "A Hoffnung Filmography," in *Essays in Arts and Sciences* (October 1992): 28–32.

20. For some interesting "behind-the-scenes" photos of the making of this *Carol*, see "The Spirit of Christmas Past" in *TV Guide* (December 18, 1971): 19–22.

21. Oxford *Christmas Books*, p.48; Penguin Classics *Christmas Books, Volume 1*, p. 99.

22. *Télérama* (December 19, 1984): 91. Review by Sophie Cachon; translation by Michele Snitkin.

23. Warren Graves, *Scrooge* (Toronto: Playwrights Canada, 1979), p. 28.

24. Davis, p. 234.

8. Dickens's "Other" Christmases

Epigraph: Katherine Carolan, "Dickens' Last Christmases," in *The Dalhousie Review* (Autumn 1972): 373. This article is hereafter referred to as *Carolan*.

1. See Penguin Classics *Christmas Books*. Along with its extensive annotation, this edition features a substantial general introduction which considers the *Christmas Books* in relation to Dickens's entire career, as well as a shorter introduction to each individual story. See also *The Annotated Christmas Carol*.

2. Along with the Penguin Classics *Christmas Books*, see "Dickens's Tract for the Times" in Michael Slater, ed., *Dickens 1970* (London: Chapman & Hall, 1970), pp. 99–123. See also "Dickens at Work: *The Chimes*" in Edward Wagenknecht, *Dickens and the Scandalmongers* (Norman: University of Oklahoma Press, 1965), pp. 50–70.

3. See Malcolm Morley, "Ring Up the Chimes" in *The Dickensian* (September 1951): 202–206. See also the *Chimes* chapter in Bolton, pp. 268–272.

4. See Malcolm Morley, "The Cricket on the Stage," in *The Dickensian* (December 1951): 17–24. See also the *Cricket* chapter in Bolton, pp. 273–295.

5. See the *Battle* chapter in Bolton, pp. 296–301.

6. *Ibid.*

7. See the general introduction in Penguin Classics *Christmas Books, Volume One*, viii.

8. See Malcolm Morley, "Pepper and the Haunted Man," in *The Dickensian* (September 1952): 185–190. See also the *Haunted Man* chapter in Bolton, pp. 302–305.

9. Oxford *Christmas Books*, p. 398; Penguin Classics *Christmas Books, Volume 2*, p. 353.

10. See Oxford *Christmas Stories*, pp. v–ix. (Several selections from the *Christmas Stories* will also be found in *Penguin Selected Short Fiction*.

11. See the *Pickwick* chapter in Bolton. For an account of the mammoth RSC production of *Nicholas Nickleby* see Leon Rubin, *The Nicholas Nickleby Story* (New York: Penguin, 1981).

12. See the *Clock* chapter in Bolton, pp. 187–188.

13. See Carolan, pp. 373–383.

14. Charles Dickens, *Great Expectations* (Oxford: Oxford University Press, 1953), p. 38.

Hereafter referred to as Oxford *Great Expectations*. See page 72 in the Penguin Classics edition edited by Angus Calder. This edition is hereafter referred to as Penguin Classics *Great Expectations*.

15. Charles Dickens, *The Mystery of Edwin Drood* (Oxford: Oxford University Press, 1956), p. 154. Hereafter referred to as Oxford *Edwin Drood*. See page 171 in the Penguin Classics edition edited by Arthur J. Cox, with an introduction by Angus Wilson. This edition is hereafter referred to as Penguin Classics *Edwin Drood*.

16. Oxford *Edwin Drood*, p. 154; Penguin Classics *Edwin Drood*, p. 171. For convenience — *Drood* is, I think, a book that the general reader is far less likely to have lying about than, say, the *Carol* or *David Copperfield* — the most relevant portion of this paragraph is reprinted here:

Seasonable tokens are about. Red berries shine here and there in the lattices of Minor Canon Corner; Mr. and Mrs. Tope [Mr. Tope is a verger — a kind of usher — at the Cloisterham Cathedral] are daintily sticking sprigs of holly into the carvings and sconces of the Cathedral stalls, as if they were sticking them into the coat-buttonholes of the Dean and Chapter. Lavish profusion is in the shops: particularly in the articles of currants, raisins, spices, candied peel, and moist sugar. An unusual air of gallantry and dissipation is abroad; evinced in an immense bunch of mistletoe hanging in the greengrocer's shop doorway, and a poor little Twelfth Cake, culminating in the figure of a Harlequin — such a very poor little Twelfth Cake, that one would rather call it a Twenty-fourth cake, or a Forty-eighth Cake — to be raffled for at the pastrycook's, terms one shilling per member. Public amusements are not wanting. The Wax-Work which made so deep an impression on the reflective mind of the Emperor of China is to be seen by particular desire during Christmas Week only, on the premises of the bankrupt livery-stable keeper up the lane; and a new grand comic Christmas pantomime is to be produced at the Theatre: the latter heralded by the portrait of Signor Jacksonini the clown, saying 'How do you do to-morrow?' quite as large as life, and almost as miserably. In short, Cloisterham is up and doing.

17. Carolan, p. 379.
18. Oxford *Christmas Books*, p. 349; Penguin Classics *Christmas Books, Volume 2*, pp. 288–289.
19. John Butt, "Dickens's Christmas Books,"

in *Pope, Dickens, and Others* (Edinburgh: Edinburgh University Press, 1969), p. 147.

20. Charles Dickens, "A December Vision," in *Miscellaneous Papers, Volume One* from the New National Edition of *The Works of Charles Dickens* (New York: Hearst's International Library), p. 245. Originally appeared in *Household Words* (December 14, 1850).

21. Carolan, p. 377.
22. Oxford *Great Expectations*, p. 36; Penguin Classics *Great Expectations*, p. 71.
23. Oxford *Great Expectations*, p. 457; Penguin Classics *Great Expectations*, p. 489.
24. Oxford *Great Expectations*, p. 391; Penguin Classics *Great Expectations*, pp. 424–425.
25. See the Introduction (p. 14) in Penguin Classics *Great Expectations* in which Angus Calder notes that the early part of the story takes place between approximately 1810 and 1830.
26. Oxford *Great Expectations*, p. 391. Penguin Classics *Great Expectations*, p. 425.
27. Dickens's original ending is reprinted in an appendix in both the Oxford and Penguin Classics editions. The latter includes useful annotation and commentary.
28. Oxford *Edwin Drood*, p. 154; Penguin Classics *Edwin Drood*, pp. 170–171.
29. Oxford *Sketches by Boz*, p. 220.
30. Oxford *Pickwick*, p. 375; Penguin Classics *Pickwick*, p. 458.
31. Oxford *Christmas Stories*, pp. 11–12; Penguin Classics *Selected Journalism*, p. 10.

9. Variations on a Theme by Dickens

Epigraph: William Makepeace Thackeray, "A Grumble about the Christmas-Books," in *Fraser's Magazine* (January 1847): 126. This important essay has been reprinted in John Charles Olmsted, ed., *A Victorian Art of Fiction: Essays on the Novel in British Periodicals 1830–1850* (New York: Garland, 1979), pp. 535–552.

1. "The Strange Christmas Dinner" first appeared in the December 1945 issue of *Good Housekeeping* magazine. Margaret Cousins wrote many excellent short Christmas stories, selections of which have been published as *Christmas Keepers: Eight Memorable Stories from The 40's and 50's* (San Antonio TX: Corona, 1996). Unfortunately, "The Strange Christmas Dinner" is not included in this collection.

2. As we have seen in the review of J. C. Buckstone's 1901 production of *Scrooge* quoted in Chapter 4, the *Carol* was a frequent point of

reference in contemporary discussions of *A Message from Mars*. *The Era's* review of a 1901 (that "*Carol* conscious" year again!) production of *Message* made the point very directly when it noted that "what Charles Dickens achieved with his 'Christmas Carol' Mr. Robert [sic] Ganthony has essayed and done in dramatic form." See *The Era* (December 7, 1901): 12.

Even more significantly, perhaps, one finds the same sentiments being expressed in reviews of the original 1899 stage production of *Message*. From *The Athenaeum*: "'A Message from Mars' is a curious hodge-podge, imitated from 'A Christmas Carol,' by Charles Dickens, but owing a good deal, it might be supposed, to 'El Diablo Cojuelo' of Luis Velez de Guevara, and something to the book of Job.... When he awakes [Horace Parker, after his sojourn with the Martian] he has undergone a transformation analogous to that of Ebenezer Scrooge." See *The Athenaeum* (November 25, 1899): 729. And from *The* [London] *Times*: "The central situation of his plot was doubtless suggested to him by the 'Christmas Carol'.... As Scrooge in the 'Christmas Carol' was led by his mysterious visitor through scenes calculated to cure him of his besetting vice, of niggardliness, so Mr. Ganthony's hero is taught by what he sees, and finally by hard personal experience, the meaning of sorrow and suffering." See *The* [London] *Times* (November 23, 1899): 6.

For the text of the play see *A Message from Mars* (New York: Samuel French, 1923; 1927 edition also available).

3. See Joseph McBride, *Frank Capra: The Catastrophe of Success* (New York: Simon & Schuster, 1992), pp. 331–332, p. 522 and p. 647. The definitive source of information on *It's a Wonderful Life* is Jeanine Basinger's *The It's a Wonderful Life Book* (New York: Alfred A. Knopf, 1990).

4. As noted in Chapter 4, the first three plays derived from the *Carol* all premiered simultaneously on February 5, 1844 — just over two weeks after the book was first published! However, these first plays did more than just start the endless stream of theatrical adaptation flowing. They also established the precedent of expanding, interpreting, modifying and otherwise tinkering with the *Carol* within the context of a dramatic adaptation. For example, Malcolm Morley's "Curtain Up on *A Christmas Carol*" reports that the Stirling version was, in essence, a musical, and that the Barnett version expanded upon the Carol's serious side via the introduction of at least two new and rather unsavory characters.

Interestingly, we are also told that a second production of the Webb play that was staged one week later incorporated a Diorama in its depiction of at least some of Scrooge's ghostly visions. The Diorama was a large translucent painting (or series of paintings) that could be viewed by an audience. It utilized elaborate lighting effects, sometimes including dissolves, to produce a spectacular experience. While this production does not qualify as an audiovisual adaptation of the Carol per se, it may well be the first occasion on which an audiovisual medium was employed in telling or adapting Dickens's story. See Chapter 4, n5.

5. See J. H. Ingraham, *Santa Claus, or the Merry King of Christmas: A Tale for the Holidays* (Boston: H. L. Williams, 1844). This story can also be found in Philip Reed Rulon's fascinating anthology of American Christmas writings entitled *Keeping Christmas: The Celebration of an American Holiday* (Hamden CT: Archon, 1990), pp. 23–52.

6. See W. M. Swepstone, *Christmas Shadows: A Tale of the Times* (London: T. C. Newby, 1850). Published in the United States as *Christmas Shadows: A Tale of the Poor Needle Women* (New York: Stringer & Townsend, 1850). See also Davis, pp. 46–47.

7. See Horatio Alger, "Job Warner's Christmas," in *Harper's New Monthly Magazine* (December 1863): 119–124. See also Davis, p. 252. In this story Job Warner is a very humble, Cratchit-like bookkeeper; however, I have probably been unfair, or a bit misleading, in characterizing his employer, John Bentley, as "Scrooge-like." While Bentley can indeed be viewed as this story's Scrooge surrogate, he is actually presented as a decent and honest man who has been temporarily blinded by success. As he puts it (p. 123): "Prosperity had begun to harden my heart. At any rate, it had made me thoughtless of the multitudes who are struggling with ills which my wealth could alleviate." This story is very sentimental, but as this quote suggests, it is also very much in touch with the aforementioned hardcore economics that did so much to shape and influence the *Carol*.

8. *The Haunted Man* first appeared in the December 30, 1865, issue of *The Californian*. It can be found in Bret Harte, *The Luck of Roaring Camp and Other Tales* (Boston: Houghton Mifflin, 1906), pp. 188–196.

9. See Louisa May Alcott, "A Christmas Dream, and How It Came True," in *Harper's Young People*, Part I (December 5, 1882): 65–67, and Part II (December 12, 1882): 82–84. This story can also be found in Edward Wagenknecht, ed., *A Fireside Book of Yuletide Tales* (Indianapolis: Bobbs-Merrill Company, 1948), pp. 157–171.

It was also reprinted in the December 23, 1950, issue of *Collier's* magazine.

10. Davis, pp. 93–94.

11. *Christmas Every Day* originally appeared in *St. Nicholas* (January 1886): 163–167. While there is no question that it has been granted a new lease on life thanks to its "appearance" in *The Christmas Box*, this is definitely not a case of discovery or even rediscovery since *Christmas Every Day* has appeared in many collections and anthologies over the years, including Edward Wagenknecht's aforementioned *A Fireside Book of Yuletide Tales*.

12. William Makepeace Thackeray, "A Grumble about the Christmas-Books," in *Fraser's Magazine* (January 1847): 116.

13. See Muresianu, p. 156.

14. Anthony Trollope, *An Autobiography* (Berkeley: University of California Press, 1947), pp. 296–297.

15. See the Introduction to Jack Newcombe, ed., *A New Christmas Treasury*, rev. and expanded ed. (New York: Viking, 1991). This extraordinary anthology contains excerpts from Hardy's *Under the Greenwood Tree* and Melville's *Moby-Dick*.

16. Lilly Golden, ed., *A Literary Christmas* (New York: Atlantic Monthly Press, 1992), p. 2.

17. There are, of course, many who would disagree. See, for example, the chapter entitled "The Tribe of Charles" in Tristram Potter Coffin, *The Book of Christmas Folklore* (New York: Seabury, 1973), pp. 154–181.

Epilogue

Epigraph: Richard Burton, *A Christmas Story* (New York: W. W. Norton, 1991), p. 3.

Bibliography

There have been many collected editions of Dickens's works over the years, some of which appeared during his lifetime. The more popular titles, like *A Christmas Carol* and *Oliver Twist*, frequently appear in "one shot" editions that can range from expensive, beautifully illustrated hardcover books to inexpensively produced paperbacks for the educational market. The standard scholarly edition of Dickens's works is *The Clarendon Dickens* published by Oxford University Press. However, since it is primarily of interest to professional literary scholars, it has not been utilized here. I have used the following two collected editions during the preparation of this book:

• *The Oxford Illustrated Dickens*, published by Oxford University Press, is the most complete uniform set of Dickens's works currently available. In addition to the fifteen novels, it includes the *Christmas Books, Christmas Stories, Sketches by Boz, Master Humphrey's Clock* and *A Child's History of England, American Notes and Pictures from Italy,* and *The Uncommercial Traveller and Reprinted Pieces.* Its handsome, hardcover volumes are available separately or in a twenty-one volume set.

• Penguin Classics (originally published by the Penguin English Library) has published paperback editions of the novels, as well as the *Christmas Books* (in two volumes), *American Notes for General Circulation, Sketches by Boz, Selected Short Fiction,* and *Selected Journalism 1850–1870.* Each volume includes an authoritative introduction and notes.

Please note, however, that the Oxford and Penguin editions utilized here are currently being superseded by *The Everyman Dickens*, published in paperback by J. M. Dent, under the general editorship of Michael Slater. The *Christmas Books* are scheduled to appear in the fall of 1999 and, when complete, *The Everyman Dickens* will be the most comprehensive and authoritative edition available.

Sources for other Dickens works, including letters, speeches, and public readings, will be found below.

On Dickens, History and/or Literature

Ackroyd, Peter. *Dickens.* London: Sinclair-Stevenson, 1990; New York: HarperCollins, 1992.

_____. *Introduction to Dickens.* London: Sinclair-Stevenson, 1991; New York: Ballantine, 1992.

Alcott, Louisa May. *Louisa's Wonder Book—An Unknown Alcott Juvenile.* With an introduction and bibliography by Madeleine B. Stern. Mt. Pleasant: Central Michigan University, 1975.

Altick, Richard D. *The Shows of London.* Cambridge MA: Harvard University Press, 1978.

Benet's Reader's Encyclopedia of American Literature. Edited by George Perkins, Barbara Perkins, and Phillip Leininger. New York: HarperCollins, 1991.

Bentley, Nicholas, Michael Slater, and Nina Burgis. *The Dickens Index.* Oxford: Oxford University Press, 1988.

Bolton, H. Philip. *Dickens Dramatized*. Boston: G. K. Hall, 1987.

Brenni, Vito J. *William Dean Howells: A Bibliography*. Metuchen NJ: Scarecrow, 1973.

Browning, Elizabeth Barrett. *The Complete Poetical Works of Mrs. Browning*. Edited by Harriet Waters Preston. Boston: Houghton Mifflin, 1900.

Busch, Frederick. "Introduction," in *A Christmas Carol and Other Christmas Stories* by Charles Dickens. New York: Signet, 1984.

Butt, John. *Pope, Dickens, and Others*. Edinburgh: Edinburgh University Press, 1969.

Chesterton, G. K. *Appreciations and Criticisms of the Works of Charles Dickens*. New York: Haskell House, 1966. Reprint of the 1911 edition.

Cruikshank, R. J. *Charles Dickens and Early Victorian England*. London: Sir Isaac Pitman, 1949.

Davis, Paul. *Charles Dickens A to Z: The Essential Reference to His Life and Work*. New York: Facts on File, 1998.

_____. *The Lives and Times of Ebenezer Scrooge*. New Haven: Yale University Press, 1990.

Dickens, Cedric. *Drinking with Dickens*. New York: New Amsterdam, 1988.

Dickens, Charles. *The Annotated Christmas Carol*. Edited by Michael Patrick Hearn. New York: Clarkson N. Potter, 1976.

_____. *Charles Dickens: The Public Readings*. Edited by Philip Collins. Oxford: Clarendon, 1975.

_____. *A Christmas Carol: A Facsimile Edition of the Autograph Manuscript from the Pierpont Morgan Library*. Introduction by John Mortimer. Essay on John Leech illustrations by David Tatham. New York: Pierpont Morgan Library; New Haven: Yale University Press, 1993.

_____. *A Christmas Carol: The Public Reading Version*. With introduction and notes by Philip Collins. New York: New York Public Library, 1971.

_____. *The Christmas Stories*. Edited by Ruth Glancy. London: J. M. Dent, 1996. Part of "The Everyman Dickens" edition.

_____. *The Letters of Charles Dickens, Volume Three 1842–1843*. Edited by Madeline House, Graham Storey, and Kathleen Tillotson. Oxford: Clarendon, 1974.

_____. *The Letters of Charles Dickens, Volume Four 1844–1846*. Edited by Kathleen Tillotson. Oxford: Clarendon, 1977.

_____. *The Letters of Charles Dickens, Volume Five 1847–1849*. Edited by Graham Storey and K. J. Fielding. Oxford: Clarendon, 1981.

_____. *The Letters of Charles Dickens, Volume Eight 1856–1858*. Edited by Graham Storey and Kathleen Tillotson. Oxford: Clarendon, 1995.

_____. *The Life of Our Lord*. Philadelphia: Westminster, 1981. Reprint of 1934 edition.

_____. *The Speeches of Charles Dickens*. Edited by K. J. Fielding. Oxford: Clarendon, 1960.

_____. *The Works of Charles Dickens: New National Edition*. New York: Hearst's International Library.

A Dictionary of British History. Edited by J. P. Kenyon. Ware, Hertfordshire: Wordsworth Editions, 1992.

Douglas, James. *Theodore Watts-Dunton: Poet, Novelist, Critic*. New York: John Lane.

Fawcett, F. Dubrez. *Dickens the Dramatist on Stage, Screen and Radio*. London: W. H. Allen, 1952.

Forster, John. *The Life of Charles Dickens*. Edited and annotated by J. W. T. Ley. London: Cecil Palmer, 1928.

Glancy, Ruth F. *Dickens's Christmas Books, Christmas Stories, and Other Short Fiction: An Annotated Bibliography*. New York: Garland, 1985.

Hake, Thomas, and Arthur Compton-Rickett. *The Life and Letters of Theodore Watts-Dunton*. 2 vols. London: T. C. & E. C. Jack, 1916.

Harte, Bret. *The Luck of Roaring Camp and Other Tales*. Boston: Houghton Mifflin, 1906.

Hewett, Edward, and W. F. Axton. *Convivial Dickens: The Drinks of Dickens and His Times*. Athens: Ohio University Press, 1983.

Hood, Thomas. *The Poetical Works of Thomas Hood*. Enlarged and rev. ed. New York: Thomas Y. Crowell.

Irving, Washington. *The Crayon Miscellany*. Boston: Twayne, 1979.

_____. *History, Tales and Sketches*. New York: Library of America, 1983.

Johnson, Edgar. *Charles Dickens: His Tragedy and Triumph*. 2 vols. New York: Simon and Schuster, 1952.

Kaplan, Fred. *Dickens: A Biography*. New York: William Morrow, 1988.

Marcus, Steven. *Dickens from Pickwick to Dombey*. London: Chatto & Windus, 1965; New York: W. W. Norton.

Merriam-Webster's Encyclopedia of Literature. Edited by Kathleen Kuiper. Springfield MA: Merriam-Webster, 1995.

Muresianu, S. A. *The History of the Victorian Christmas Book*. New York: Garland, 1987.

Newton, A. Edward. *The Greatest Book in the World and Other Papers*. Boston: Little, Brown, 1925.

Olmstead, John Charles. *A Victorian Art of*

Fiction: Essays on the Novel in British Periodicals, 1830–1850. New York: Garland, 1979.

Orwell, George. *Dickens, Dali and Others.* New York: Harcourt, Brace & World, 1946.

The Oxford Companion to English Literature. 5th ed. Edited by Margaret Drabble. New York: Oxford University Press, 1985.

Page, Norman. *A Dickens Chronology.* Boston: G. K. Hall, 1988.

_____. *A Dickens Companion.* New York: Schocken, 1984.

Pointer, Michael. *Charles Dickens on the Screen.* Lanham MD: Scarecrow, 1996.

Pool, Daniel. *What Jane Austen Ate and Charles Dickens Knew.* New York: Simon & Schuster, 1993.

Pope, Norris. *Dickens and Charity.* New York: Columbia University Press, 1978.

Schlicke, Paul. *Dickens and Popular Entertainment.* London: Allen and Unwin, 1985.

Scott, Sir Walter. *The Poems and Ballads of Sir Walter Scott, Volume II.* Boston: Dana Estes, 1900.

Slater, Michael, ed. *Dickens 1970.* London: Chapman & Hall, 1970.

_____. *Dickens on America and the Americans.* Austin: University of Texas Press, 1978.

The Spectator Volume II. Edited by Donald F. Bond. Oxford: Oxford University Press, 1965.

Stewart, George R., Jr. *A Bibliography of the Writings of Bret Harte in the Magazines and Newspapers of California 1857–1871.* Berkeley: University of California Press, 1933.

Trollope, Anthony. *An Autobiography.* Berkeley: University of California Press, 1947.

Wagenknecht, Edward. *Dickens and the Scandalmongers.* Norman: University of Oklahoma Press, 1965.

_____. *The Man Charles Dickens.* Rev. ed. Norman: University of Oklahoma Press, 1966.

Weintraub, Stanley. *Disraeli: A Biography.* New York: Truman Talley Books/Dutton, 1993.

Wilson, Angus. *The World of Charles Dickens.* New York: Viking, 1970.

Zambrano, Anna Laura. *Dickens and Film.* New York: Gordon, 1977.

On Christmas

Burton, Richard. *A Christmas Story.* New York: W. W. Norton, 1991.

Coffin, Tristram Potter. *The Book of Christmas Folklore.* New York: Seabury, 1973.

Dawson, W. F. *Christmas: Its Origins and Associations.* Detroit: Gale Research, 1968. Reprint of 1902 edition.

Gilbert, Davies. *Some Ancient Christmas Carols.* London: John Nichols, 1822.

_____. *Some Ancient Christmas Carols.* 2d ed. London: John Nichols, 1823.

Golden, Lilly, ed. *A Literary Christmas.* New York: Atlantic Monthly, 1992.

Hervey, Thomas Kibble. *The Book of Christmas.* London: William Spooner, 1836.

Ingraham, J. H. *Santa Claus, or the Merry King of Christmas: A Tale for the Holidays.* Boston: H. L. Williams, 1844.

Lewis, C. S. *God in the Dock.* Edited by Walter Hooper. Grand Rapids MI: William B. Eerdmans, 1970.

McInnes, Celia. *An English Christmas.* New York: Henry Holt, 1986. Originally published in Great Britain as *A Christmas Celebration.*

Newcombe, Jack, ed. *A New Christmas Treasury.* Rev. ed. New York: Viking, 1991.

Nissenbaum, Stephen. *The Battle for Christmas.* New York: Alfred A. Knopf, 1996.

Restad, Penne L. *Christmas in America: A History.* New York: Oxford University Press, 1995.

Rulon, Philip Reed. *Keeping Christmas: The Celebration of an American Holiday.* Hamden CT: Archon, 1990.

Sandys, William. *Christmas Carols, Ancient and Modern.* London: R. Beckley, 1833.

_____. *Christmastide, Its History, Festivities, and Carols.* London: John Russel Smith, 1852.

Sansom, William. *A Book of Christmas.* New York: McGraw-Hill, 1968.

Smith, Jeff. *The Frugal Gourmet Celebrates Christmas.* New York: William Morrow, 1991.

Studwell, William E. *Christmas Carols: A Reference Guide.* New York: Garland, 1985.

Swepstone, W. M. *Christmas Shadows: A Tale of the Times.* London: T. C. Newby, 1850. Published in the United States as *Christmas Shadows: A Tale of the Poor Needle Women.* New York: Stringer & Townsend, 1850.

Thomas, Dylan. *A Child's Christmas in Wales.* New York: New Directions, 1995.

Wagenknecht, Edward, ed. *The Fireside Book of Christmas Stories.* Indianapolis: Bobbs-Merrill, 1945.

_____. *A Fireside Book of Yuletide Tales.* Indianapolis: Bobbs-Merrill, 1948.

On Film, Television, Radio, Theatre and/or Recordings

Abramson, Albert. *The History of Television, 1880 to 1941.* Jefferson NC: McFarland, 1987.

The American Film Institute Catalog: Film Beginnings, 1893–1910. Metuchen NJ: Scarecrow, 1995.

The American Film Institute Catalog: Feature Films, 1911–1920. Berkeley: University of California Press, 1988.

The American Film Institute Catalog: Feature Films, 1921–1930. New York: R. R. Bowker, 1971.

The American Film Institute Catalog: Feature Films, 1931–1940. Berkeley: University of California Press, 1993.

The American Film Institute Catalog: Feature Films, 1961–1970. New York: R. R. Bowker, 1976.

Armes, Roy. *A Critical History of the British Cinema.* New York: Oxford University Press, 1978.

Barnouw, Erik. *The Magician and the Cinema.* Oxford: Oxford University Press, 1981.

_____. *Tube of Plenty: The Evolution of American Television.* 2d rev. ed. New York: Oxford University Press, 1990.

Basinger, Jeanine. *The It's a Wonderful Life Book.* New York: Alfred A. Knopf, 1990.

Bronner, Edwin. *The Encyclopedia of the American Theatre 1900–1975.* San Diego: A. S. Barnes, 1980.

Brooks, Tim, and Earle Marsh. *The Complete Directory to Prime Time Network and Cable TV Shows, 1946–Present.* 6th ed. New York: Ballantine, 1995.

Brownlow, Kevin. *Behind the Mask of Innocence.* New York: Alfred A. Knopf, 1990.

_____. *The Parade's Gone By....* New York: Alfred A. Knopf, 1968.

Buckstone, J. C. *Scrooge.* New York: Samuel French, 1927.

Callow, Simon. *Orson Welles: The Road to Xanadu.* New York: Viking, 1996.

Carringer, Robert L. *The Magnificent Ambersons: A Reconstruction.* Berkeley: University of California Press, 1993.

Ceram, C. W. *Archaeology of the Cinema.* New York: Harcourt, Brace & World, 1965.

Coe, Brian. *The History of Movie Photography.* Westfield NJ: Eastview, 1981.

D'Agostino, Annette M. *An Index to Short and Feature Film Reviews in the Moving Picture World: The Early Years, 1907–1915.* Westport CT: Greenwood, 1995.

Dunning, John. *On the Air: The Encyclopedia of Old-Time Radio.* New York: Oxford University Press, 1998.

Everson, William K. *American Silent Film.* New York: Oxford University Press, 1978.

Fisher, David E., and Marshall Jon Fisher. *Tube: The Invention of Television.* Washington DC: Counterpoint, 1996.

Ganthony, Richard. *A Message from Mars.* New York: Samuel French, 1923, 1927.

Gianakos, Larry James. *Television Drama Series Programming: A Comprehensive Chronicle, 1947–1959.* Metuchen NJ: Scarecrow, 1980.

_____. *Television Drama Series Programming: A Comprehensive Chronicle, 1959–1975.* Metuchen NJ: Scarecrow, 1978.

_____. *Television Drama Series Programming: A Comprehensive Chronicle, 1975–1980.* Metuchen NJ: Scarecrow, 1981.

_____. *Television Drama Series Programming: A Comprehensive Chronicle, 1980–1982.* Metuchen NJ: Scarecrow, 1983.

_____. *Television Drama Series Programming: A Comprehensive Chronicle, 1982–1984.* Metuchen NJ: Scarecrow, 1987.

_____. *Television Drama Series Programming: A Comprehensive Chronicle, 1984–1986.* Metuchen NJ: Scarecrow, 1992.

Gifford, Denis. *American Animated Films: The Silent Era, 1897–1929.* Jefferson NC: McFarland, 1990.

_____. *Books and Plays in Films, 1896–1915: Literary, Theatrical and Artistic Sources of the First Twenty Years of Motion Pictures.* London: Mansell, 1991; Jefferson NC: McFarland, 1991.

_____. *British Animated Films, 1895–1985: A Filmography.* Jefferson NC: McFarland, 1987.

_____. *The British Film Catalogue 1895–1970.* New York: McGraw-Hill, 1973.

Graves, Warren. *Scrooge.* Toronto: Playwrights Canada, 1979.

Hanhardt, John G., and Matthew Yokobosky. *Gregory J. Markopoulos: Mythic Themes, Portraiture, and Films of Place.* New York: Whitney Museum of American Art, 1996.

Hanson, Patricia King, and Stephen L. Hanson, eds. *Film Review Index, Volume 1: 1882–1949.* Phoenix AZ: Oryx, 1986.

_____. *Film Review Index, Volume 2: 1950–1985.* Phoenix AZ: Oryx, 1987.

Hawes, William. *American Television Drama: The Experimental Years.* University: University of Alabama Press, 1986.

Hess, Gary Newton. *An Historical Study of the DuMont Television Network.* New York: Arno, 1979.

Katz, Ephraim. *The Film Encyclopedia.* 2d ed. New York: HarperCollins, 1994.

Kerr, Walter. *The Silent Clowns.* New York: Alfred A. Knopf, 1980.

Lauritzen, Einar, and Gunnar Lundquist. *American Film-Index 1908–1915.* Stockholm: Film-Index, 1976.

_____. *American Film-Index 1916–1920.* Stockholm: Film-Index, 1984.

McBride, Joseph. *Frank Capra: The Catastrophe of Success.* New York: Simon & Schuster, 1992.

McNeil, Alex. *Total Television: The Comprehensive Guide to Programming from 1948 to the Present.* 4th ed. New York: Penguin, 1997.

Murray, R. Michael. *The Golden Age of Walt Disney Records, 1933–1988*. Dubuque IA: Antique Trader, 1997.

Musser, Charles. *The Emergence of Cinema: The American Screen to 1907*. New York: Charles Scribner's Sons, 1990.

Nardo, Don. *Animation: Drawings Spring to Life*. San Diego CA: Lucent, 1992.

Neely, Tim. *Goldmine Christmas Record Price Guide*. Iola WI: Krause, 1997.

Osborne, Jerry. *The Official Price Guide to Movie/TV Soundtracks and Original Cast Albums*. New York: House of Collectibles, 1991.

Perry, George. *The Great British Picture Show*. London: Hart Davis/MacGibbon, 1974.

Peters, Margot. *The House of Barrymore*. New York: Alfred A. Knopf, 1991.

Ritchie, Michael. *Please Stand By: A Prehistory of Television*. Woodstock NY: Overlook, 1994.

Robinson, Dale, and David Fernandes. *The Definitive Andy Griffith Show Reference*. Jefferson NC: McFarland, 1996.

Rubin, Leon. *The Nicholas Nickleby Story*. New York: Penguin, 1981.

Slide, Anthony. *Aspects of American Film History Prior to 1920*. Metuchen NJ: Scarecrow, 1978.

_____, and Edward Wagenknecht. *Fifty Great American Silent Films 1912–1920: A Pictorial Survey*. New York: Dover, 1980.

Sloan, Kay. *The Loud Silents: Origins of the Social Problem Film*. Urbana: University of Illinois Press, 1988.

Smith, Dave. *Disney A to Z: The Official Encyclopedia*. New York: Hyperion, 1996.

Sturcken, Frank. *Live Television: The Golden Age of 1946–1958 in New York*. Jefferson NC: McFarland, 1990.

Talbot, F. A. *Moving Pictures: How They Are Made and Worked*. Philadelphia: J. B. Lippincott, 1912.

Udelson, Joseph H. *The Great Television Race: A History of the American Television Industry 1925–1941*. University: University of Alabama Press, 1982.

Wagenknecht, Edward. *The Movies in the Age of Innocence*. Norman: University of Oklahoma Press, 1962.

_____. *Stars of the Silents*. Metuchen NJ: Scarecrow, 1987.

Wearing, J. P. *The London Stage 1890–1899: A Calendar of Plays and Players*. 2 vols. Metuchen NJ: Scarecrow, 1976.

_____. *The London Stage 1900–1909: A Calendar of Plays and Players*. 2 vols. Metuchen NJ: Scarecrow, 1981.

_____. *The London Stage 1910–1919: A Calendar of Plays and Players*. 2 vols. Metuchen NJ: Scarecrow, 1982.

Wilk, Max. *The Golden Age of Television: Notes from the Survivors*. New York: Delacorte, 1976.

Williams, Bransby. *My Sketches from Dickens*. London: Chapman & Hall, 1913.

Periodicals

The Athenaeum
The Billboard
The Bioscope
The Christian Century
Collier's
The Commonweal
Cue
Daily Kent Stater
Daily Mail
Daily Variety
The Dalhousie Review
Dickens Studies Newsletter
Dickens Quarterly
The Dickensian
The Edison Kinetogram
The Edmonton Sun
The Era
Exhibitors Herald

Films in Review
Fraser's Magazine
Good Housekeeping
Harper's Magazine
Harper's New Monthly Magazine
Harper's Young People
Harrison's Reports
The Hollywood Reporter
The Illustrated London News
The Kinematograph Weekly
Life
The Listener
McCall's
The Moving Picture World
The New Haven Journal-Courier
The New Haven Register
The New York Daily News
The New York Dramatic Mirror

The New York Herald Tribune
New York Post
The New York Times
The New Yorker
The Nineteenth Century and After
The Philadelphia Inquirer
Radio and Television Weekly
Radio Times
Ross Reports
St. Nicholas
The Sketch
The Talbot Tattler
Télérama
Televiser
Television
The [London] Times
Variety
View

Visit this book's website at www.dickensachristmascarol.com

Index

Note: The names of characters from A Christmas Carol *appear in* SMALL CAPITALS. *Page numbers in* **boldface** *indicate photographs.*